The Art of the King's Indian

Eduard Gufeld

B.T. Batsford Ltd, *London*

First published in 2000
© Eduard Gufeld 2000

ISBN 0 7134 8661 9

British Library Cataloguing-in-Publication Data.
A catalogue record for this book is
available from the British Library.

Printed in Great Britain by
Creative Print and Design (Wales), Ebbw Vale
for the publishers,
B.T. Batsford Ltd,
9 Blenheim Court,
Brewery Road,
London N7 9NT

A member of the Chrysalis Group plc

A BATSFORD CHESS BOOK

Contents

Acknowledgement

I wish to thank Oleg Stetsko who has been a valuable collaborator and contributor in the production of this work.

Eduard Gufeld

Symbols used in this book

+	check
+–	winning advantage for White
±	large advantage for White
⩲	slight advantage for White
–+	winning advantage for Black
∓	large advantage for Black
⩱	slight advantage for Black
=	level position
!	good move
!!	outstanding move
!?	interesting move
?!	dubious move
?	bad move
??	blunder
1-0	the game ends in a win for White
0-1	the game ends in a win for Black
½-½	the game ends in a draw
(ch)	championship
(m)	match
(izt)	interzonal tournament
(zt)	zonal tournament
(ol)	olympiad

Preface

Like it or not, the author of an opening book cannot be completely objective. This applies especially to systems and variations which he frequently plays himself (or plays against) in practice. The main idea of the King's Indian Defence (more exactly the King's Indian Attack!) —a fight against White's pawn centre by means of piece pressure supported by timely counterstrokes with the pawns—was expressed in an aphoristic way by that brilliant chess publicist Savielly Tartakower: "Not death in the centre, but death to the centre". Yet the fundamental problems of this highly complex and interesting opening are as yet unresolved.

The King's Indian Defence is an asymmetrical opening in which, at the core, Black's strategy is based on the 'wrecking' of his opponent's schemes. At the same time, at an early stage of the opening Black attempts to evolve his own plan of attack. For this reason the King's Indian can only be studied in operation, that is by examining the 'opening to middlegame' process. An accordingly large place in the present monograph is filled with games which allow us to trace the connection between opening and middlegame.

I have always yearned to comment on a chess game in such a way as to make it in effect a small chess manual, by weaving into the texture of a specific chess duel some general principles of struggle and illustrating this action with concrete examples.

However, understanding the futility of the desire to grasp the immensity of the whole, I will try to do it just for the early stage of the game. The easiest way for me to do this is with examples from the King's Indian Defence which is so dear to my heart. I'd like to warn the reader that the comments of the chess events appearing in this book will be given in an unusual form— they are based on my associated *feelings*.

Well, first a little introduction. Yes, chess is a struggle, or as the 11th World Champion R.Fischer said—"total war." But from another point of view this wonderful game, in my opinion, is a complete substitute for war. For a long time I have been thinking of offering the FIDE president a proposal to stage the World Championship between...top military men. And maybe then they would change their minds and stop the arms race?

In fact this is in accord with an ancient Indian legend about the origin of chess which relates how a fidgety rajah's wife, bored by never-ending wars, invented, with the aid of her retinue, such an exciting game that her husband forgot everything else, and lasting peace was established in those parts. That game was chess.

In my opinion chess strategy is absolutely related to the doctrine of war. But as we know, there are two doctrines of war: active, where open hostilities break out following preparations for a war, and passive, in which two sides maintain armaments only at a level sufficient for security, and eschew conflict. The latter, thank God, is more widespread in the world these days; but to everyone's regret it has also crept into chess, and many supporters of quick and colourless draws have emerged...

It seems to me that peace, which is so indispensable for humanity, is completely unacceptable in chess. If you sit down at the board, struggle is inevitable.

Let us agree, then, that chess strategy involves an active war doctrine. Just fancy that you are not a chess player but a general who has at his disposal a rather large army. Your responsibility is to plan a large-scale and absolutely inevitable battle. Your soldiers—representatives of different branches of the armed forces—are waiting for orders.

What is to be done then? First of all, you have to mobilize your army, deploy your forces in such a way that you are ready for open hostilities. A chess opening, on the whole, is preparation for the battle, mobilizing pieces towards the centre.

Precisely towards the centre, because from there you can properly observe the whole battlefield. And the one who is better prepared, better mobilized, has more chances for victory. It sometimes happens, of course, that the chess game is won in other ways, but we are talking

here about the scientific approach to chess.

Many things done in the opening strictly obey certain rules. In this sense chess is revealed as a science. But if this game were just a code of laws, it would have vanished long ago: everyone would have learned the laws, strictly abided by them, and that would have been the end of it. The point is that when abiding by the laws we achieve our objective in just 80 cases out of 100, and 20 per cent are exceptions—that is mysterious events, when the general rules 'suddenly' turn out to be invalid. On the other hand, if a chess player disregards the rules, the fundamental principles, I can guarantee that 80 per cent of the time he will be in error.

The conclusion is simple: one should know the rules very well in order to identify the exceptions! In this, and only in this, I see the scientific aspect of chess.

Let us try to formulate at least two laws. As was stated earlier, the first principle of the opening is to mobilize quickly the pieces towards the centre. The second one, closely related, is capturing the centre with pawns (naturally the opponent will resist this plan). The existence of the pawn centre (let us say on d4 and e4), on its own, does not promise any material benefits, and does not create any threats. But it interferes with the opponent's desire to carry out the first principle—to develop his pieces in the centre. The pawns hinder the opponent's forces, taking away from them comfortable centre squares.

Now let us have a look at how these principles come into play in a concrete opening—the King's Indian Defence.

1 d4 ♘f6 2 c4 g6 3 ♘c3 ♗g7 4 e4 d6

So what has happened in the first moves of the game? How were the first two principles realized in the opening? White has obviously succeeded in occupying the centre with pawns, but Black is ahead of his opponent in the development of forces. This is analogous to the law of connected vessels: as one vessel is being filled, the other is depleted by the same amount. You win in one way, but lose in another.

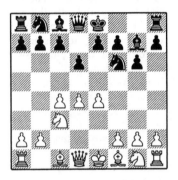

But what do the generals think about the position? This is absolutely clear: even as the Black general gives his rival the opportunity to occupy the centre with pawns, he plans to do his best in the future to destroy that centre. In his turn the White general will try to maintain his bridgehead and at the same time catch up with Black in development.

So White has to decide: to get down to piece development or to reinforce the pawn bridgehead. In order not to bore the reader I will confine myself to a consideration of the most high-profile decision: the White general decides to reinforce his e4 pawn.

5 f3

"I don't get it!" thinks the Black general. "Could it be that my rival does not know the laws of strategy?" And in fact the move f2-f3 seems to be against the rules: it is not aimed at the capture of the centre (compare it with f2-f4), and of course it is not a mobilization of forces. But one always has to have a high regard for one's rival, and the Black general is lost in thought. Gradually the White general's aggressive intentions become clear to him. It turns out that White is going to reinforce the centre and under its protection launch a swift flank attack on the enemy's king.

What are the grounds for this aggressive plan? The g6-pawn has moved and is a target. White can also see the clear intention of his rival to castle kingside. This is not difficult to guess, if we bear in mind the simple chess law: one usually has to develop the pieces on the flank where one is going to castle.

A few words about castling. The king becomes a real "king" only in the endgame. But at the start he is weak and unprotected like a child. Castling is an evacuation of the king to a safe place, to the rear, far away from strikes in the centre by enemy forces.

Having noticed this action by Black, the White general gets motivated: "What if I can organise an all-out assault on the kingside, weakened by the move ...g7-g6?—play f2-f3, then ♗c1-e3, ♕d1-d2, h2-h4-h5xg6, ♗e3-h6, ♘c3-d5, destroy all the defenders and capture the hostile king?"

Thus White prepares an attack, the object of which is the king. Let us formulate first what the attack is: it is an attempt to open up the lines in that part of the board where the object of your interest is situated, to exchange off or destroy pieces which are defending it.

Facing these threats, Black has to work out immediately a plan of counteraction. But castling comes first: if you say "A," you must also say "B."

5...0-0 6 ♗e3 ♘c6

We have just said that the best counterattack is a strike at the centre. But where does the knight come in? Does it assist Black in opening up a second front?

Let us gain an insight into the Black general's plan.

Just the plan, but not into any single move. I always tell my pupils, by the way: "It is better to play with a bad plan than no plan at all!" As for the move 6...♘c6 it is a kind of provocation: Black invites the pawn to attack the piece. But after 7 d5 ♘e5 he will play ...c7-c6! and will achieve his objective. First, he will open up lines for a counterattack, and second, he will open a "second front" and will force the opponent to divert his forces to the king's defence.

Of course, White is not going to yield to this provocation.

What is the Black general to do then? Let us monitor his thoughts: "White would hardly hide his king on the kingside, since in that case he would have to forget about the planned attack there. And he would not leave his king in the centre either—he might perish there from a strike by the opponent. So that means that he must evacuate his king to the queenside.

Therefore a "second front" should be opened in that part of the board! How to do it? That is very simple: ...♘b8-c6!, ...a7-a6, ...♖a8-b8, and afterwards, at an appropriate moment, ...b7-b5!" So the somewhat strange-looking move 6...♘c6 becomes absolutely clear. Black is not only following the principle of developing his pieces in the centre but he also foresees subsequent events and gets ready for the enemy king's arrival on the queenside. The Black general has figured out the intentions of his opponent and decided, for the time being, to postpone the counterblow in the centre for the sake of immediate counteraction on the flank. As for the centre, opening lines there will now be linked to the strike ...e7-e5. Let us point out White's blind spot, the d4 square.

Thus we have gradually reached the ideological point of the knight's development, ...♘b8-c6, with a concrete example. But this theme can be seen in broader terms. A book might be written where the theme of the development of the knight to c6 (in front of the c7 pawn) can be examined as a unique measure in other opening systems. In this book, however, I have concentrated on sharing with you my many years' experience of the King's Indian Defence which I believe offers the best solution to the problem of utilising the queenside knight, as indeed is evident in modern chess practice.

First Love Never Dies

Amazingly, my devotion to the King's Indian is associated with my first love, memories of whom I have cherished throughout my life.

All this happened a long time ago and I have my own system of counting time. It was 90lbs ago while I was playing for the Ukraine team in the Soviet Junior Team Championships. I was also...in love. Her name was Bella or, in the affectionate Russian diminutive, Bellochka. She was beautiful, had blonde hair, big blue eyes and she played chess—which made me love her all the more. Of course I had my rivals who offered her opening advice and adjournment analysis. I tried too. Incomprehensibly she ignored me and refused all my offers to help her in chess. But I still remember those five wonderful hours that I spent daily with her in the same hall.

I would share that time between playing my game and watching her beautiful eyes. Anybody, who has been in love at this age will understand me perfectly.

Then came the day when my team played against Uzbekistan and these memorable events for me took place against a background of the King's Indian Defence.

Game 1
Khasidovsky *White* **Gufeld** *Black*
Kharkov 1953

1 d4 ♘f6 2 c4 g6 3 ♘c3 ♗g7

If only Bellochka had understood what a faithful guy I am. After all this time, I am still true to my first love—the King's Indian Defence! And still, whenever I play this defence, I remember the sweetness of my love for Bellochka.

4 e4 d6 5 ♘f3 0-0 6 ♗e2 e5 7 0-0 ♘c6 8 d5 ♘e7 9 ♘e1 ♘d7 10 ♗e3 f5 11 f3

The reader might think that this opening is being played by modern chess players, but it dates from almost half a century ago!

11...f4 12 ♗f2 g5 13 ♘d3 ♖f6

The modern scheme of developing pieces is different ...♘d7-f6, ...♖f8-f7, ...♘e7-g6, ...♗g7-f8, but in those days the search for the right way in this system was still going on.

14 c5 ♖g6 15 h3 h5 16 ♘e1 g4 17 hxg4 hxg4 18 fxg4 ♘f6 19 g5 ♖xg5 20 cxd6 cxd6 21 ♘f3 ♖h5 22 ♘d2 ♖h7 23 ♖c1 ♘g6 24 ♕b3 ♗f8 25 ♘b5 ♗g4 26 ♕d3 f3! 27 ♗xf3 ♘f4! 28 ♕b3 ♕e8! 29 ♖c7

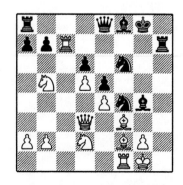

And here followed the stunning **29...♖h1+!! 30 ♔xh1 ♕h5+**. I had sacrificed a rook to gain a tempo and get this winning position. By now, many of the tournament participants had rushed to my table to see the combination. I was hoping to see Bellochka but she did not come. She remained in her seat playing for the Russian team. I ran over to her table and with my eyes and heart I said to her, "See my combination. This sacrifice that I have made—it's for you." Suddenly she looked up and pierced me with her beautiful big blue eyes. Surely she knew that I was not interested in her game. And I even thought that she had heard what my heart had said to her and maybe, just maybe, she understood my feelings. It was as if time stood still at that moment when we gazed into each other's eyes. Her eyes then turned away from me as she looked back at her game. She then quickly made her move and...blundered her queen! It was a tragedy and she immediately resigned her game.

A steady stream of tears began to flow from those beautiful blue eyes. I was stunned by her grief and blamed myself for what had befallen her. But I knew what had to be done—I had to share in her tragedy! I couldn't resign my game, as I was playing for my team. So I offered my opponent a draw, which he quickly accepted. The postmortem established that Black was winning. Here is the main variation: **31 ♗h4** (after 31 ♔g1 ♗xf3 Black wins) **31...♕xh4+ 32 ♔g1 ♗xf3 33 ♖xf3** (if 33 ♘xf3, then 33...♘e2 mate, and if 33 ♕xf3 then 33...♘g4 wins) **33...♘g4 34 ♖xf4 ♕h2+ 35 ♔f1 ♕h1+ 36 ♔e2 ♕xg2+ 37 ♔d3 exf4 38 ♘d4 ♘e5+ 39 ♔c2 f3 40 ♘4xf3 ♗h6! 41 ♔d1 ♘xf3 42 ♘xf3 ♖f8 43 ♖c3 ♖xf3 44 ♖xf3 ♕d2 mate!**

And what about Bellochka? She ran to her team trainer to complain that I was to blame for the loss of her game! The tournament officials reprimanded me for causing Bellochka to blunder away her queen and also forbade me from approaching the Russian Ladies' Team while they were playing games.

Since that time many years and countless tournaments have come and gone but I have not seen Bellochka again at chess events.

As for the King's Indian, I have been devoted to it all my life. Moreover, for nearly half a century I felt like I was chained to the King's Indian chariot. A classic case of voluntary slavery, as when one "begins to love his bondage" because I am sure that the advantages of this opening outweigh its drawbacks.

Sämisch System

Chess is a creative activity bordering on science, art and sport. I am sure that situations occurring on the chessboard depend not only on the will of the individual chess player, but also on extrapersonal factors that pertain to the life of a nation at a particular time. There are cultural trends in science and art that engulf an entire generation. Let us consider the Sämisch System, for instance, born in the 1920's: **1 d4 ♘f6 2 c4 g6 3 ♘c3 ♗g7 4 e4 d6 5 f3**

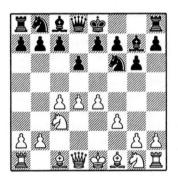

The set-up is a geometrically clear-cut line of white pawns on c4, d4, e4 and f3, backed up by a solid deployment of white pieces. There is a distinct plan for the capture of the centre and, proceeding from this, a kingside attack.

At the same time, White's set-up looks a bit bulky, undermining the

sense of harmony one should feel in an overall scheme of development. Isn't this set-up reminiscent of architectural ideas in the style of rationalism and constructivism which prevailed in those years? Sämisch, the chess Le Corbusier, also devised his own system against the Nimzo-Indian Defence—again with a powerful pawn structure in the centre: c3, c4, d4, e4.

Years have passed, constructivism is long gone, and the Sämisch System in the Nimzo-Indian has become less popular. I am also sure that the same will happen to his system in the King's Indian Defence. Our grandchildren will smile at the Sämisch System just as we are smiling now at the clumsy ferroconcrete monsters of the 1920's. I regard the Sämisch System as somewhat one-sided. And if you, my dear friends, disagree with me regarding 5 f3, which is the cornerstone of the Sämisch System, then you might want to ask the knight on g1 what he thinks about it.

Let us start to examine this system of development. The first moves of Fritz Sämisch's setup, **5...0-0 6 ♗e3**, constitute the main line even today (6 ♗g5 came later on). The author's original intention was to undermine the enemy defence, already weakened by the move ...g7-g6, with ♕d1-d2, 0-0-0, g2-g4, h2-h4-h5xg6, ♗e3-h6, ♘c3-d5. Later, when methods of counterplay were found for Black, other continuations became fashionable.

First, during the period of striving for classic methods of play, 6...e5 was considered the orthodox reply. Later on came other ideas in which Black prepared a ...c7-c5 attack on the centre by 6...♘bd7 and 6...b6. And 6...c6 and 6...a6 were also played, preparing ...b7-b5.

In my opinion the move 6...♘c6, which not only attacks the d4 square but helps with an attack on the c4-pawn after ...a7-a6 and b7-b5, takes centre stage in the King's Indian conception. This mode of development has become one of the most fashionable lines for struggling against the pawn centre.

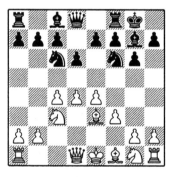

Let me say a few words of clarification. The move 6...♘c6 is a kind of provocation. After the obvious 7 d5 ♘e5 Black is ready to open up lines in the centre by ... e7-e6 or ...c7-c6 and opening this "second front" will force White to divert some of his forces from the operation on the kingside.

In fact, though I had to go through all the stages of Sämisch-System development, it turned out that 6...♘c6 was most dear to my character. I remained loyal to it for the whole of my chess life. Fate rewarded me for my devotion to the move 6...♘c6—as this was the variation where I managed to play my "Immortal Game".

My Immortal Game

Everyone is born to be a genius. But only a few people actually become geniuses. What about the rest? Some are lucky. With some people, their genius remains dormant all their lives. Louge de Lille wrote *Marseilleise* at the right time and became, in the words of Stefan Zweig, a "genius for one night."

I was also lucky. If I had some genius, it really was aroused on the night I played against Bagirov. Sad as it may be, I also turned out to be a "genius for one evening." This game was unique in my career. But I am grateful to my destiny for this particular evening.

Sometimes you hear that we are now more practical and rational chess players than in the 19th century. There is no doubt that the modern chess struggle proceeds along more positional and rational lines than in the last century. But sometimes it happens that sacrifices are quite necessary. In a critical situation I managed to carry out a counterattack with my opponent trailing just one tempo behind. And it was for this one tempo that I had sacrificed so many pieces...

Game 2
Bagirov *White* **Gufeld** *Black*
Kirovobad 1973

1 d4 g6 2 c4 ♗g7 3 ♘c3 d6 4 e4 ♘f6 5 f3 0-0 6 ♗e3 ♘c6 7 ♘ge2
The most flexible system of development. White reinforces the centre and in addition to the plan of queenside castling he has the plan of

transferring this knight to the queenside by ♘e2-c1-b3.

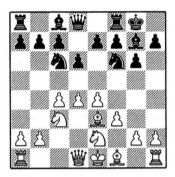

7...♖b8

Before embarking on operations in the centre (...e7-e5) it is advisable to capture, by means of ...b7-b5, some space on the queenside where White's king is going to hide.

This sequence of moves, where the rook first gets into position on b8, was introduced into tournament practice by Igor Zaitsev. The idea is that in the variation 8 ♘c1 e5 9 d5 ♘d4 10 ♘b3 c5 11 dxc6 bxc6 Black prepares to open the b-file in double-quick time.

However 7...a6 is now more often played, so that 8 ♕d2 can be met by 8...♖b8, setting up the counterblow ...b7-b5. In this game there was a transposition of moves, but after 8 a3 a6 9 b4, a8 is the best square for the rook, since after the possible ...b7-b5 the a-file will be opened.

8 ♕d2 a6 9 ♗h6

Bagirov chuckled to himself: "If I exchange the g7 bishop, Gufeld will be disarmed." Incidentally, there is a grain of truth in that.

But here I was in fact not so upset over losing my favourite bishop. White is wasting time and his kingside attack, though strategically justified, comes tactically too late since Black is allowed enough time to

create threats on the queenside. In those years theory gave 9 ♘c1— leading to the main variation of the system. My opinion of the position is a bit different. Besides, it is difficult to determine which variation is the main line. It is worth mentioning that two of the greatest experts on the King's Indian, E.Geller and T.Petrosian, filed this game for future reference.

9...b5

Later on I came to the conclusion that it is stronger to exchange the bishop by 9...♗xh6 10 ♕xh6, and then counterattack in the centre by 10...e5, taking advantage of the displacement of the queen.

10 h4 e5 11 ♗xg7 ♔xg7 12 h5

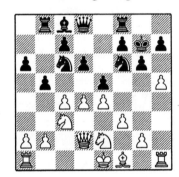

12...♔h8

Accepting the sacrifice by 12...♘xh5 13 g4 ♘f4 14 ♘xf4 exf4 15 cxb5 axb5 16 ♗xb5 ♘e7 17 ♕xf4 ♘g8 18 0-0-0 leads to a losing position for Black.

Geller thought the text was a bad move and suggested 12...bxc4 13 ♘d5 (useless is 13 hxg6 fxg6 14 ♕h6+ ♔g8 15 ♘f4 exf4 16 ♗xc4+ ♔h8 17 ♘d5 ♘h5 or 15 ♘d5 ♖f7 and Black has the advantage) 13...♘xd5 14 hxg6 (after 14 exd5 ♘b4 15 ♘g3 ♗f5! 16 ♗xc4 c6 and Black is better) 14...♘f4 (sharper is 14...♘f6 15 ♕h6+ ♔g8 16 g7 ♖e8

17 ♘g3 exd4? 18 ♘h5 ♘xh5 19 ♕xh5 ♔xg7, but not 19 ♖xh5? ♗f5! 20 ♖xf5 ♖e6 and Black maintains his material advantage) 15 ♘xf4 exf4 16 ♕xf4 hxg6 17 ♕h6+ ♔f6 18 ♕h4+ ♔g7 19 ♕h6+ ♔f6 with a draw.

These variations are very interesting. But I don't think that 12...♔h8 is so bad. The discrepancy in our assesssments was, according to Geller, due to the fact that later in the game White could have obtained an advantage. But I'll try to convince you that this is not the case.

To give you the full picture, note that 15 years later this position was studied by the 10th world champion Boris Spassky, who preferred 12...♘xd4. But even this active move has its drawbacks. And in spite of the fact that in the game Kerr-Spassky, Wellington 1988, after 13 ♘xd4 exd4 14 ♘d5 c5 15 hxg6 fxg6 16 ♕h6+ ♔f7 17 ♘xf6 ♕xf6 18 ♕xh7+ ♕g7 19 cxb5 axb5 20 a4 bxa4 21 ♖xa4? ♕xh7 22 ♖xh7+ ♔f6 Black managed to save the situation, White could have prolonged the king's agony by playing 21 ♗c4+! ♔f6 22 ♕h2.

13 ♘d5!

The right strategy. The threat is 14 ♘xf6 and 15 d5 after which the attack will develop all by itself. What is to be done?

Such moves as 13...♘e8 are too passive. And in such situations "he who hesitates is lost".

13...bxc4!

To justify the whole strategy, Black allows his opponent to attack him. But White still has to bring the rook on a1 into play and this is the idea of the queenside counterplay.

14 hxg6 fxg6 15 ♕h6

Now there is no hope of a quiet life. But who would not have gone

for such a menacing incursion? It seems improbable that this move will let go of the minimal advantage that White is supposed to have in the opening. Much quieter was 15 ♘xf6 ♕xf6 16 d5 with a complex positional struggle—but choosing this line meant abandoning, at least temporarily, the assault on the kingside which was so tempting and seemed to promise quick success.

15...♘h5!

The only, but sufficient, argument (bad is 15...♖f7? because of 16 ♕xg6 ♕g8 17 ♕xf6+!). But even now Black seems to be in danger.

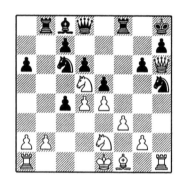

A few months later when the Soviet chess players were flying to the interzonal tournament in Brazil, I suggested, as a warming up exercise, that we analyze this position. The discussion was really top level, and not only because the plane was flying 35,000 feet above the Atlantic Ocean! At ground level I would never have managed to organize an analytical session in which such famous grandmasters as Smyslov, Keres, Bronstein, Vasiukov, Geller, Polugaevsky and Savon all took part. Almost all of them attacked Black's position. It was not until we had crossed a quarter of the earth's meridian that I succeeded in defending my opinion that the chances are equal.

16 g4

Geller recommended 16 0-0-0 ♘xd4 17 ♖xd4 exd4 18 ♘ef4! ♖xf4 (if 18...♖g8, then 19 g4 ♖g7 20 gxh5 g5 21 ♘g6+ ♔g8 22 ♗xc4 ♗e6 23 ♘ge7+ ♖xe7 24 ♘xe7+ winning) 19 ♘xf4 ♕g8 20 ♘xg6+ ♕xg6 21 ♕f8+ ♕g8 22 ♕xg8+ ♔xg8 23 ♗xc4+ ♔g7 24 ♖xh5 c6 25 ♖g5+ to White's advantage.

Having analysed all this, I suggested 16 0-0-0 ♖f7! 17 g4 ♘f6 18 ♕xg6 ♕g8! 19 ♕xg8+ ♘xg8 and the chances are about equal. For example, 20 ♖h3 a5! 21 ♘e3 ♗a6 22 d5 ♘b4 23 ♘c3 ♘d3+ 24 ♗xd3 cxd3 25 b3 ♘e7 26 ♔d2 ♘g6 27 ♘f5 ♘f4 etc.

Of course it is impossible to show all the variations, but later Geller agreed with me and in his book on the King's Indian he removed the question mark from 12...♔h8.

16...♖xb2!

Sacrifices are in the air. Of course this is just counterplay to distract White's attention.

17 gxh5 g5

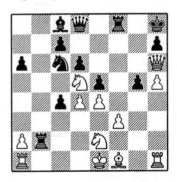

Chess is really an astonishing game. Just look at this position. The opponent has an extra piece and serious threats on the kingside. Nevertheless, Black manages to walk the tightrope. How can this be explained? It is the centre of the chessboard that matters most in this position and Black is striving to break it up, thereby nullifying his opponent's material advantage.

18 ♖g1 g4!

Now the battle is in full swing. White's king is also under fire. Bagirov takes the right decision.

19 0-0-0 ♖xa2

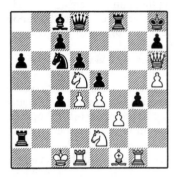

20 ♘ef4

Of course, if it had been possible to foresee the course of events, then a more effective continuation might have been chosen. For example, 20 dxe5 ♘xe5 21 ♘ef4 ♔g8! 22 ♘g6 hxg6 23 hxg6 ♕d7 24 ♖h1 ♖a1+ 25 ♔b2 ♕b5+ 26 ♔xa1 ♕a4+ 27 ♔b2 ♕b3+ 28 ♔c1 ♕a3+ 29 ♔c2 (29 ♔d2? ♕b2+) 29...♕b3+ 30 ♔c1 with a draw.

An even more fantastic draw would have occurred after the problem-like 20 ♗h3!! ♖xe2 21 ♗xg4 ♖f7! 22 ♗xc8 ♕xc8 23 ♘f6! ♕b8! 24 ♖g8+ ♕xg8 25 ♘xg8 ♘b4! 26 ♖d2 ♖e1+ 27 ♖d1 (not 27 ♔b2? ♖xf3! threatening 28...♖b3 mate) 27...♖e2.

20...exf4 21 ♘xf4?!!

Geller thought that White could now have punished Black for playing 12...♔h8, by continuing 21 ♗xc4, but in the analysis I

demonstrated that 21...♖a1+ 22
♔b2 ♖xd1 23 ♖xd1 ♖g8! 24 ♘f6
(if 24 ♘xf4 then 24...♕g5!)
24...♖g7 25 ♗g8! ♕e7 26 ♗xh7
♖xh7 27 ♘xh7 ♕xh7 28 ♕f8+ ♕g8
29 ♕h6+ is a draw.

So, why do I attach a question
mark and two exclamation marks to
21 ♘xf4? This is my gratitude—and
I hope everyone else feels this as
well—to Vladimir Bagirov for his
co-authorship in creating a chess
masterpiece. Now Black has enough
time to organize a powerful
counterattack.

21...♖xf4 22 ♕xf4

White has a material advantage,
but his immediate threats have been
repelled. To resume the attack,
White has to place his bishop on c4,
take with the pawn on g4 and move
the rook to f1. So Black has three
tempi in reserve but how can he exploit them? If 22... ♖a1+ 23 ♔d2
c3+ 24 ♔e1 ♖xd1+ 25 ♔xd1 ♘xd4
26 ♗c4! and White has the
initiative.

It is clear that all Black's forces
must support the rook.

22...c3!

Illustrating that good knowledge
of general principles and good technique makes the calculation of
variations easier.

While the rook cuts off the king
on the seventh rank, there is always
the possibility of coordination with
the pawn and the knight
(...♘c6-b4). Though this threat is
repelled, the c3-pawn remains a
kind of bayonet up against the
White king's throat.

23 ♗c4

23 ♕f7 ♘b4 24 ♗d3 ♖a1+ 25
♗b1 c2 26 ♔b2 cxd1=♕ 27 ♖xd1
looked very attractive but by playing 25...♗e6! 26 ♕xe6 ♕g5+ Black
could mate the king.

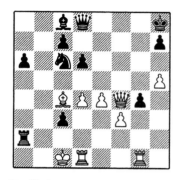

23...♖a3

The most difficult move in the
game and possibly in my whole life.
23...♖a4 looked very natural because in such situations you always
want to gain a tempo. But after the
quiet 24 ♗b3! Black's attack would
come to a standstill. For example,
24...♖a3 25 ♔c2 ♗e6 26 d5! ♘b4+
27 ♔xc3 and White wins. No better
was 23...♖a1+ 24 ♔c2 ♘xd4+ 25
♖xd4 ♖xg1 26 ♕e5+. The key to
the position, strange as it may seem,
is the f3-pawn.

The following continuation was
possible: 24 ♖g2 ♘b4 25 ♔b1 c2+
26 ♖xc2 ♖xf3 with Black gaining a
material advantage.

In the summer of 1987, when
speaking to Beliavsky, I again had
to defend my point of view. That
time my opponent tried to prove that
23...♖a4 led to an advantage for
Black. Our argument centred on the
position which arises after 24 ♗b3
♘xd4. I managed to prove that after
25 ♖xd4 ♖xd4 (25...♖a1+ 26 ♔c2
♖xg1 27 ♕e5+!) 26 fxg4 White's
threats along the opened file are
rather dangerous.

24 fxg4

Here 24 ♔b1 is met either by
24...♘b4? after which White wins
with 25 ♖df1 ♗e6 26 ♗xe6 ♘d3 27
♕f7 ♕b8+ 28 ♗b3 ♖xb3+ 29 ♔c2
♘b4+ 30 ♔d1!, or 24...♗e6! with

the decisive threat of 25...♕b8+. After 24 ♖df1, satisfactory is 24...♘xd4.

The value of this game is enhanced by the fact that White is not making "desperado" moves but is setting up, here and there, new obstacles for his opponent and is putting up a most stubborn resistance. By giving up the extra material Bagirov repels the immediate threats to the king and, just for a moment, Black's attacking pieces lose their coordination. Therefore Black has to make heroic efforts...

24...♘b4 25 ♔b1!

White has only one move to attack the king. That is why White hopes for 25...c2+ 26 ♔b2 cxd1=♕ 27 ♖xd1 and Black, although he is a piece up, is losing because there is no defence against 28 ♖f1! (with 28 ♔xa3 thrown in for good measure).

25...♗e6!!

Calculating the variations I suddenly felt that the pieces on the chessboard were jumping about as in a kaleidoscope. This image, vividly reflecting the law of coordination in chess, helped me with my following moves. One piece gives way to the other, then the third piece comes, and so on until the final picture. The chaos is only apparent; very rigid logic is in operation and

the pieces arrive at their destinations more punctually than trains...

26 ♗xe6 ♘d3!!

Black sacrifices piece after piece to open the b8-b1 highway for his queen. It seems that 26...♘d5 was also good, but after 27 exd5! the king had a narrow escape along the b1-f5 diagonal.

27 ♕f7

Setting new obstacles. 27 ♖xd3 would be met by a quick mate: 27...♕b8+ 28 ♔c2 ♕b2+ 29 ♔d1 ♖a1+.

27...♕b8+ 28 ♗b3 ♖xb3+ 29 ♔c2

This is the loss of coordination of the attacking forces Bagirov was striving for! White's king is surrounded but it has still not capitulated. Black's front line troops are not yet ready for the final assault. It is impossible to carry this out without heavy artillery. But how can this be done?

29...♘b4+!

The only and the decisive move.

30 ♔xb3

30 ♔c1 ♖b1+! 31 ♔xb1 ♘d5+ 32 ♔c2 ♕b2+ led to the same finale. Black has mate in eight. In bygone romantic times when opponents were held in high esteem, all combinations ended in mate. If this game had been played in the 19th century, Black could have announced "Checkmate in eight!" And White would have had to suffer until the bitter end. Now times have changed. Mate is not announced, but the execution is still on schedule until the opponent spoils the whole thing by simply resigning...

30...♘d5+! 31 ♔c2 ♕b2+ 32 ♔d3 ♕b5+!

And White resigned because of 33 ♔c2 ♕e2+ 34 ♔b3 ♕b2+ 35 ♔c4 ♕b5 mate! **0-1**

Every painter dreams of creating his own "Giaconda," every chess player wants to play his own "Immortal Game." No other game ever gave me so much satisfaction as this one. Even today I feel happy recalling it. Then I forget all my misfortunes and enjoy the dream that *did* come true.

Illustrative Games

Let us trace the development of playing 6...♘c6 against the Sämisch right up to the modern day. As in many other opening systems progress was made by trial and error.

Game 3
Gligorić *White* **Gufeld** *Black*
Belgrade 1974

1 d4 ♘f6 2 c4 g6 3 ♘c3 ♗g7 4 e4

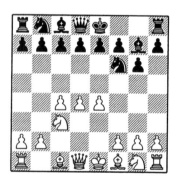

4...d6
I will allow myself a little digression from our theme by mentioning the possibility of 4...0-0. This innocent transposition of moves (castling before ...d7-d6, because 5 e5?! favours Black, but we will talk about this later) was the way of struggling against the Sämisch System in the 60s. The point is that after 5 f3 Black obtains

an extra resource in the form of an interesting pawn sacrifice 5...c5!? 6 dxc5 b6, which promises him sufficient counterplay.

I happened to try this recipe. A game Rabar-Gufeld, Baku 1964, continued: 7 ♗e3 bxc5 8 ♗xc5 ♘c6 9 ♕d2 ♖b8 10 ♖c1 ♖e8 11 b3 ♗b7 12 ♘h3 d6 13 ♗f2 e6 14 ♗e2 d5 15 exd5 exd5 16 cxd5 ♘b4 and Black obtained good counterplay for the pawn.

Soon afterwards, the game Bobotsov-Stefanov, Bulgaria (ch) 1965, demonstrated a more precise way for White, which until now has been considered as best in the Yugoslav *Encyclopedia of Chess Openings*: 7 cxb6 ♕xb6 8 ♘h3!? (after 8 e5 ♘e8 9 f4 Black attacks White's centre by 9...d6 10 ♘f3 ♘c6 and obtains good counterplay) 8...♘c6 9 ♘f2 e6 10 ♗e2 ♗a6 11 0-0 ♖fd8 12 ♔h1 d5 13 cxd5 exd5 14 exd5 ♗xe2 15 ♕xe2 ♘xd5 16 ♘fe4 and White stands better.

But who knows, perhaps because it was played so long ago, somebody will "harbour a grudge" against it, and will find a way to prove the opposite?

But White can avoid all this and carry on the theme of the Sämisch-System by playing 5 ♗e3 when after 5...d6 we have a simple transposition of moves.

5 f3
The Yugoslav grandmaster's choice of the Sämisch variation came as a surprise to me since Gligorić often plays the Black side of the King's Indian and frequently has to contend with this system himself.

5...0-0 6 ♗e3 ♘c6
I had every reason to choose this particular variation, since Gligorić himself is a devotee of 6...e5 or 6...c6 7 ♗d3 e5.

7 ♘ge2 ♖b8 8 ♕d2

8...a6

In one of my clashes with Polugaevsky (Riga 1975) I chose 8...♖e8. Lev replied 9 ♖b1!? (nowadays the more standard 9 ♘c1 e5 10 ♘b3 is preferred) and after 9...a6 10 b4 b5!? there was some very interesting play: 11 cxb5 axb5 12 d5 ♘e5 13 ♘d4 ♗d7 14 ♘cxb5 (upon 14 ♗xb5 ♗xb5 15 ♘cxb5 ♘c4 the knight's activity fully compensates for the sacrificed pawn while if 14 ♘dxb5 I had prepared 14...e6) 14...e6 15 dxe6 fxe6 16 ♗e2 ♘xf3+?! (more natural was 16...d5 with a double-edged game) 17 gxf3 e5 18 0-0 exd4 19 ♘xd4 d5? (it was necessary to remove the king by 19...♔h8) 20 exd5 ♘xd5 21 ♗c4 ♖e5 22 f4 ♖h5 23 f5 c6 24 b5! and Black's position was in ruins.

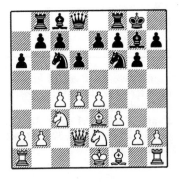

In the diagram position Black is preparing the attack ...b7-b5 and White has a choice how to proceed. This choice is very wide. And it should be mentioned that the roads leading from 9 ♘c1 and 9 h4, which is preferred nowadays, were fraught with danger. I also had to travel these roads as White. And my experience led me to believe that the King's Indian should not only be studied, but also *felt* through one's fingertips. Theory and practice must go hand in hand. Of course this advice does not need to be given to such a keen King's Indian player as Svetozar Gligorić, even if he didn't choose the best continuation here.

9 a4

This goes against the character of the variation. White overextends his front line, and Black's queenside counterplay accordingly gains in strength. Another drawback of this move is that White restricts his possibilities as now he cannot contemplate the plan of queenside castling.

9...e5

A counterthrust which, in conjunction with the following knight maneuvre, secures full equality for Black.

10 d5 ♘a5

Of course not 10...♘e7 11 c5, when the initiative on the queenside lies entirely in White's hands.

11 ♘c1 c5 12 ♖b1

12 dxc6 bxc6 would be playing into Black's hands.

12...b6 13 b4 cxb4

Not 13...♘b7 14 a5.

14 ♖xb4 ♘d7 15 ♗e2 ♘c5 16 0-0 f5

The regrouping 16...♕c7, 17...♗d7 and 18...♖f8-c8, is also worthy of consideration, keeping the break ...f7-f5 in reserve.

17 ♕e1

White does not succeed in transferring his knight to b4, since on 17 ♘1a2 there follows 17...♘ab3 and ...♘b3-d4. But the move played is superfluous, as becomes clear. Another possibility is 17 ♗xc5 dxc5 18 ♖b1 ♕h4 19 d6.

17...♗d7 18 ♕d1

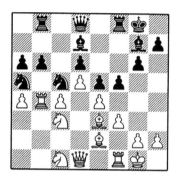

18...♕h4

By exerting pressure on the e4 square, Black pursues a double aim: either to force his opponent to take on f5, after which ...g6xf5 would give him a clear advantage, or to exchange on e4 himself, creating an additional pawn weakness for White. But 18...♗f6 19 ♕d2 f4 20 ♗f2 ♗h4 does not look bad either.

19 ♗f2 ♕g5 20 ♘d3 ♗h6 21 ♕b1!

An excellent manoeuvre. Despite Black's superficial activity, there does not seem to be any concrete way for him to obtain the advantage. On 21...♕d2 there follows 22 ♗e1 ♕e3+ 23 ♗f2 etc.

21...fxe4 22 ♘xe4

Of course not 22 ♘xc5 exf3.

22...♘xe4 23 fxe4 ♖bc8

The tempting 23...♗h3 does not achieve its aim, owing to 24 ♘e1.

24 ♕a2!

With accurate play Gligorić neutralizes Black's initiative and, but for impending time trouble, the game would seem to be heading for a draw.

24...♕d2 25 ♖b2

A mistake. With 25 ♕xd2 ♗xd2 26 ♖xb6 ♘xc4 27 ♖xa6 ♖a8 28 ♖xa8 ♖xa8 29 ♘c5, White would draw easily.

25...♕g5

25...♕c3! is more energetic.

26 ♖c2

White re-evaluates his position. He should not be persistent, but instead play 26 ♖b4.

26...♘b7 27 ♗xb6

A mistake in time trouble. Any prophylactic move was better, for example 27 ♔h1.

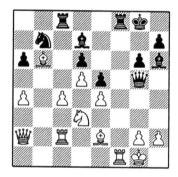

27...♘c5!

The dark-squared bishop finds itself cut off from the king's flank, and White quickly perishes.

28 ♗xc5

28 ♘xc5 is more stubborn, and sets a pretty trap: 28...♕e3+ 29 ♔h1 ♕xe2? 30 ♖g1! and White wins. To be fair, however, I would point out that after 29...dxc5 his position would still remain hopeless.

28...dxc5 29 ♔h1 ♕e3 30 ♖cc1 ♕xe4 31 ♖xf8+ ♖xf8 32 ♖e1 ♗h3 33 ♖g1 ♗e3 0-1

Game 4
Lutikov *White* **Gufeld** *Black*
USSR 1980

**1 d4 ♘f6 2 c4 g6 3 ♘c3 ♗g7 4
e4 d6 5 f3 0-0 6 ♗e3 ♘c6 7 ♕d2
a6 8 ♘ge2 ♖b8 9 d5**

A premature advance since Black
can start an attack on the fixed pawn
chain.

9...♘a5

This idea, which gains a tempo
for organizing counterplay on the
queenside, I have employed numerous times in my career, though in
the present position (where ...e7-e5
has not yet been played) apparently
9...♘e5 10 ♘g3 c6 is also possible,
not fearing 11 f4 ♘g4 with sharp
play.

10 ♘g3 c5 11 ♖c1

Somewhat more accurate is 11
♗e2 followed by kingside castling.

11...♗d7

11...e6 also deserved attention.

12 ♗d3 b5 13 b3 bxc4?!

This inopportune exchange sim-
plifies White's task of planning his
game. 13...e6 was stronger.

**14 bxc4 ♖b4 15 ♘d1 ♕b6 16 0-0
♖b8**

Black has carried out his plan: all
his pieces are activated, but for the
time being they are striking at
empty squares.

White's threats on the kingside
look more real and Lutikov tries to
prove this with his next moves.

17 ♗h6 ♗h8

My reflex action.

18 ♘f5! ♕d8 19 ♕g5

If 19 ♕f4?, then 19...♗xf5 20
exf5 ♘xd5 and a pawn is lost.

19...♖a4 20 f4?!

Anatoly Lutikov was known for
his sharp attacking style, but in
rushing into this attack he apparently underestimated Black's capac-
ity for counterplay. He should have
first defended his pawn with 20 ♖f2.

20...♖xa2 21 e5

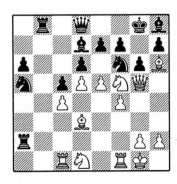

21...♖d2!

Black seizes the initiative. On 22
exf6 there follows 22...♗xf6 23
♕g3 ♖xd3 24 ♘xe7+ ♕xe7 25
♕xd3 ♗d4+ 26 ♔h1 ♗f5 and the
bishops dominate the important
diagonals.

22 ♘f2 ♖xd3! 23 ♘xe7+

Or 23 ♘xd3 ♗xf5 24 exf6 ♗xf6
25 ♕g3 ♘b3 and the knight cap-
tures the d4 square.

23...♕xe7 24 ♘xd3 ♘xc4!

The decisive blow.

25 ♖xc4

If 25 exf6 then 25...♗xf6 26 ♕g3
♗h4 27 ♕f3 ♘e3 is decisive.

25...♗b5 26 ♖c3

If 26 ♖b1 then 26...♖e8! winning.

26...♘xd5 27 ♕xe7 ♘xe7 28 ♖e1 ♘f5 29 ♗g5 ♖e8

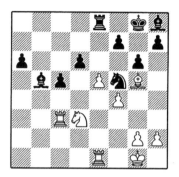

Despite being the exchange up White's position is critical. Because of the pin against the rook it is impossible to hold the e5 pawn.

30 ♔f2 dxe5 31 fxe5 c4 32 g4 cxd3 33 gxf5 ♗xe5 34 ♖xe5 ♖xe5 35 ♖c8+ ♖e8 36 ♖xe8+ ♗xe8 37 f6 ♗b5 38 ♗h6

Staking everything on opposite-coloured bishops and a blockade of the king does not pay off since the white king is forced to run over to the a-pawn.

38...a5 39 ♔e3 a4 40 ♔d2 a3 41 ♔c3 ♗c4 42 h4 a2 43 ♔b2 g5! 44 ♗xg5 h5 0-1

Game 5
Beliavsky *White* **Gufeld** *Black*
Moscow 1979

1 d4 ♘f6

This came as a relief. In all our previous encounters A.Beliavsky had opened with 1 e4, and events had turned out in his favour. So why did he change his weapon? In provoking me to choose my favourite King's Indian he must have had something up his sleeve. It was going to be interesting to see what it was...

2 c4 g6 3 ♘c3 ♗g7 4 e4 d6 5 f3

The Sämisch-System had been my opponent's main weapon against the King's Indian for almost 15 years— ever since he introduced closed openings into his repertoire.

5...0-0 6 ♗e3 ♘c6 7 ♘ge2 ♖b8 8 ♕d2 a6 9 ♘c1

At the time the Yugoslav *Encyclopedia of Chess Openings* gave a certain preference to this move. White focuses on positional play.

9...e5 10 ♘b3

10 d5 was the main line at the time.

10...exd4

The position in the centre is opened to the great pleasure of the bishop on g7.

11 ♘xd4

11...♘e5

The *Encyclopedia* recommends 11...♘xd4 12 ♗xd4 ♗e6 13 ♗e2 c6 as the main continuation. Though the centralized knight is replaced by a powerful bishop, Black has sufficient counterplay based on ...b7-b5.

12 ♗e2?!

The first critical moment. 12 ♖d1 is considered to be the best move, preventing the advance ...c7-c5. Now my task was somewhat simplified as I had the opportunity to go down the beaten track blazed long ago by L.Portisch.

12...c5! 13 ♘c2 ♗e6 14 b3

White has to look to the defence of c4.

14...♛a5!

Black too must display certain caution. 14...b5 comes to mind, but White's position is not yet bad enough to justify such sharp methods. I once analyzed the variation 15 cxb5 axb5 16 ♘xb5 d5 17 ♗xc5 dxe4 18 ♗xf8 ♛xf8 19 ♛d6, but couldn't find sufficient compensation for the sacrifice.

15 0-0 b5 16 cxb5 axb5

There is a constant threat of ...b5-b4 hanging over White's position, followed by ...c5-c4 or ...d6-d5.

17 ♖fd1!

Beliavsky takes measures against Black's incipient initiative. On 17...b4 18 ♘a4 c4 he plans 19 ♘d4, when 19...c3 20 ♛c2 is not dangerous since White has the break a2-a3! in reserve.

17...♖fe8

During the game, this move greatly appealed to me on account of the "x-ray" ♖e8-♗e3. Analysis showed this to be pure speculation, however, unsupported by concrete variations. With 18 ♘d5! White could now have forced simplifying exchanges.

Therefore 17... ♘ed7! deserved preference, not only clearing the path for the g7-bishop but also over-protecting the c5-pawn.

18 ♗f2

White shows excessive optimism in refraining from 18 ♘d5. The point of the text move is not to remove the bishop from the rook's x-ray, since the dose of "radiation" is not yet so great. White's aim, simply, is to free the e3-square for his knight, since from there it will be able to control the important d5 and c4 squares. That these squares are

extremely important is adequately confirmed by the following variation: 18 ♖ac1 b4 19 ♘a4 c4 20 ♖b1 (20 ♘d4 is not good now— 20...cxb3 21 axb3 ♗xb3!) 20...d5! 21 exd5 ♗xd5, and the game opens up in Black's favour. But if the knight gets to e3, then in the event of ...b5-b4, ♘c3-d5 would seem to be good.

However, although the knight is only one step away from the e3-square, it will not find the time to get there.

18...♘ed7!

The knight retreat is based on concrete considerations. Black prevents 19 ♘d5 and himself threatens 19...d5! when 20 exd5 would be met by 20...♘xd5! For example, 21 ♘xd5 ♛xd2 22 ♖xd2 ♗xd5, which is to Black's advantage.

Another idea of this flexible move is that if White still carries on with his planned 19 ♘e3, Black has either 19...♘g4! 20 ♖ac1 ♘xf2 21 ♔xf2 ♗h6, or 19...b4 20 ♘cd5 (20 ♘a4 d5! 21 exd5 ♘xd5) 20...♗xd5 21 exd5 ♗h6, threatening ...♘d7-b6xd5!

Therefore White must move his rook from a1, which weakens not only the a2-pawn but the whole of his queen's flank.

19 ♖ac1

Would 19 ℤab1 have been better? The b3-pawn needs supporting, as soon becomes apparent. On 19 ℤab1 there is the strong 19...b4 20 ♘a4 (20 ♘d5 ♗xd5 21 exd5 ♕xa2 is bad) 20...d5!. For example: 21 exd5 ♗xd5 22 ♘e3 ♗h6!, or 22 ♗f1 ♗c6, or 22 ♘a3 ℤxe2!.

Now, however, if 19...b4 20 ♘a4 d5? is played, there follows 21 exd5 ♗xd5 22 ♘e1! and the rook on c1 gives White valuable service (e.g. 22...ℤbc8 23 ♗c4! and then ♘e1-d3).

I had a long think here about another possibility: 19...b4 20 ♘a4 c4! with threats on the queenside. In this case 21 ♘d4 cxb3 22 axb3 ♗xb3 23 ♘xb3 ♕xa4 would be unacceptable for White. Over the board, however, I couldn't find a clear way to realize the advantage after 21 ℤb1!:

(a) 21...cxb3 22 axb3 ♗xb3 23 ℤxb3 ♕xa4 24 ℤxb4, restoring the material balance;

(b) 21...d5 22 exd5 ♗xd5 23 bxc4 ♕xa4 24 cxd5 ♕xa2 25 ℤxb4 ℤxb4 26 ♘xb4, when 26...ℤxe2 is not good enough as Black simply remains the exchange down;

(c) 21...c3 22 ♕xd6 and the protected passed pawn is no compensation for the pawn sacrificed, with White planning the subsequent break a2-a3;

(d) 21...d5 22 exd5 (22 ♘d4 cxb3! is bad) 22...c3! 23 ♕c1 ♗xd5 24 ♗f1 ♗c6 (24...♗f8 also deserves consideration) 25 a3 bxa3 26 ♕xa3 ♗f8 27 ♕a1!, and White's position, despite its outwardly unattractive appearance, is not lacking in defensive resources. All the same, analysis shows that this variation was objectively Black's strongest, though it may not have given a decisive advantage.

I was trying during the game to extract the maximum possible from the position. The result was a combination several moves deep, which gives a clear win in all variations except two.

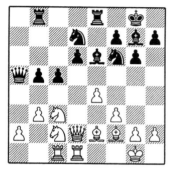

19...♘g4?!

This is not objectively strongest, in comparison with the line already examined: 19...b4 20 ♘a4 c4 21 ℤb1 d5!. White could have now obtained a satisfactory game with correct defence, but this was found only in subsequent analysis, and I have given the move an exclamation mark on account of its practical effectiveness. After all, in the event of 19...b4 White might have saved the game, while the move played presented him with problems which he was unable to solve over the board.

20 ♗e1

The exchange sacrifice could have been accepted: 20 ♘xb5! ℤxb5 (20...♕xd2 is worse, i.e. 21 ℤxd2 ♗h6 22 ♗e1! ♗xd2 23 ♗xd2 ♘ge5 24 ♘xd6!) 21 ♗xb5 ♕xb5 22 fxg4 ♘f6 23 ♕xd6. Although Black has a strong initiative, with accurate defence White's material advantage is sufficient to avoid defeat.

20...b4

Of course nothing is gained by 20...♗h6 21 ♕xd6! ♗xc1 22 ℤxc1 ♘gf6 (22... ♘ge5 is still worse: 23

f4 ♖b6 24 ♕c7 or 23...♘g4 24 f5 gxf5 25 exf5 ♗xf5 26 ♗xg4 ♗xg4 27 ♕g3) 23 ♘a4 b4 24 ♘e3, and the initiative passes to White.

21 ♘a4?

The decisive mistake, although this way of saving the knight is just what I had counted upon when playing 19...♘g4?!.

The point about the position is that if Black had played 19...b4, White could have held the game by moving his knight away to a4, whereas 20 ♘d5 would have lost. Now it is the other way around. 21 ♘d5 is the only saving move: Black cannot take on a2 as his knight is *en prise*, and this tempo allows White to consolidate his position. For instance: 21...♗xd5 (on 21...♘gf6 or 21...♘ge5 White has 22 a3!, ridding himself of his queenside difficulties) 22 ♕xd5 ♘gf6 (on 22...♘ge5, White again has 23 a3!. Nor is anything gained by the piece sacrifice 22...♕xa2 because of 23 fxg4 ♘f6 24 ♕xd6 ♘xe4 25 ♕d3) 23 ♕xd6 ♕xa2 24 ♗c4, and matters are in no way worse for White.

Beliavsky's mistake can be explained primarily on psychological grounds: he seems to have made a subconscious mental note that in the event of ...b5-b4 he should withdraw his knight not to d5 but to a4.

He replied automatically, not delving deeply enough into the details of the new situation.

21...c4!

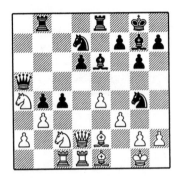

22 ♖b1

Other continuations do not save the situation either:

(a) 22 fxg4 cxb3 23 axb3 ♗xb3 24 ♕xd6 ♗xa4 25 ♗xb4 ♕a7+ 26 ♔h1 ♗f8, and Black wins a piece;

(b) 22 ♕xd6 ♗e5 23 ♗xb4 ♖xb4 24 ♕xb4 ♕a7+! with mate;

(c) 22 ♘xb4 cxb3 23 axb3 ♗xb3 24 ♘c6 ♕xa4 25 ♘xb8 ♕a7+ 26 ♔h1 ♕xb8 27 fxg4 ♗xd1 28 ♖xd1 ♖xe4, and Black remains a pawn up, for 29 ♕xd6? ♕xd6 30 ♖xd6 ♖xe2 costs White even dearer;

(d) 22 ♗xc4 ♗xc4 23 fxg4 ♗b5 (23...♘f6! is not bad either) 24 ♕xd6 ♗xa4 25 bxa4 (25 ♗xb4? ♕a7+ 26 ♔h1 ♖e6!, and Black retains the piece) 25...♘f6! 26 ♗xb4 ♕xa4 27 a3 ♘xg4!, and if 28 ♕f4, then 28...♕a7+ 29 ♔f1 ♖xe4! Thus the weakness of the g1-a7 diagonal is a weight which tips the scales in Black's favour in all the above variations.

But what of the game continuation?

22...c3 23 ♕xd6 ♕a7+!

The same motif, only in another form.

24 ♔h1 ♘f2+ 25 ♗xf2 ♕xf2

Black threatens not only the bishop but also the knight by means of 26...♗e5 and 27...♕h4.

26 ♕d3! ♘c5! 27 ♘xc5 ♕xc5

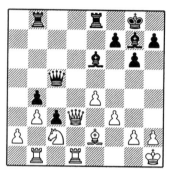

Only now can the combination be considered complete, since the evaluation of the position is no longer open to doubt—White's queenside is defenceless.

28 ♕e3

There is no adequate defence against the threat to double rooks on the a-file.

28...♕xe3 29 ♘xe3 ♖a8 30 ♖a1

30 ♗b5 ♖eb8 31 ♗a4 ♖xa4! loses even more quickly.

30...♖a5 31 ♗c4 c2 32 ♘xc2 ♗xc4!

White could still have put up resistance after 32...♗xa1 33 ♗xe6! Now, however, he can resign immediately, in view of 33 bxc4 ♗xa1 34 ♖xa1 b3 35 axb3 ♖xa1+ 36 ♘xa1 ♖d8. But in a team tournament you fight to the end.

33 ♖ac1 ♗e6 34 ♘xb4 ♖ea8 35 h3 ♗f8 36 ♘d5 ♖xa2 37 ♘c7 ♗xb3! 38 ♖d3 ♖a1 0-1

Game 6
Beliavsky *White* **Kasparov** *Black*
Linares 1990

1 d4 ♘f6 2 c4 g6 3 ♘c3 ♗g7 4 e4 d6 5 f3 0-0 6 ♗e3 ♘c6 7 ♕d2

a6 **8 ♘ge2 ♖b8 9 ♘c1 e5 10 ♘b3 exd4 11 ♘xd4 ♘e5 12 ♖d1 c6 13 ♗e2 b5!**

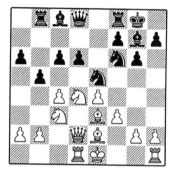

According to A.Beliavsky, writing in his book *Uncompromising Chess*, Kasparov had prepared this variation for one of his forthcoming World Championship matches.

14 cxb5

White should parry the move ...b5-b4 after which his control over d5-square is weakened and Black, if the opportunity presents itself, can rely on the freeing ...d6-d5.

14...axb5 15 b4 c5 16 ♘c2

After 16 bxc5 b4 17 ♘a4 ♕a5 18 ♘b6 dxc5 19 ♘xc8 cxd4 20 ♘e7+ ♔h8 21 ♗xd4 ♖fd8 Black seizes the initiative (G.Kasparov).

16...cxb4 17 ♘xb4 ♗e6

18 0-0

There is no sense in "pushing" the knight by 18 f4 for the sake of winning the exchange 18...♘c4 19 ♗xc4 ♗xc4 20 ♘c6 ♕e8 21 ♘xb8, since after the intermediate 21...b4 the black bishop-pair would have developed too much activity. Therefore White castles, rightly thinking that his opponent can handle any problems arising from the weak d6-pawn.

18...♕a5 19 ♕xd6

"A bird in the hand is worth two in the bush." White is prepared to put up with the initiative Black gains after capturing this pawn—rather then play the miserable endgame reached after 19 ♘bd5 ♘xd5 20 ♘xd5 ♕xd2 21 ♖xd2 ♘c4 22 ♗xc4 bxc4 23 ♖c1 ♗xd5 24 ♖xd5 c3 25 ♗d4 ♖gc8.

19...♘c4

Of course not 19...♖fd8? because of 20 ♗b6!.

20 ♗xc4 bxc4 21 ♘c6

On 21 ♖b1 there could follow 21...♕a3!

21...♕xc3 22 ♗d4

22...♘xe4!

Black's play is based on this tactical possibility. Now, after 23 fxe4 ♗xd4+ 24 ♕xd4 ♕xd4+ 25 ♘xd4 ♗g4 26 ♖c1 ♖fd8 he would have the better endgame.

23 ♗xc3 ♘xd6 24 ♗xg7 ♔xg7 25 ♘xb8 ♘f5 26 ♘d7 ♖c8

Despite the loss of the exchange, the passed pawn on the c-file leaves Black chances of saving himself and so supporting it looks quite natural. Nevertheless, in the game Beliavsky -Loginov, Azov 1991, Black played stronger: 26...♖a8 27 ♘c5 ♖xa2 28 ♖f2 ♖a7 29 ♘xe6+ fxe6 30 ♖e2 ♔f6 31 ♖e4 ♖a6 32 ♖de1 ♖c6 33 ♔f2 c3 34 ♖c1 ♘e7 35 h4 ♘d5 and the centralized knight in tandem with the passed c3-pawn is not inferior to the rook.

27 ♘b6 ♖c6

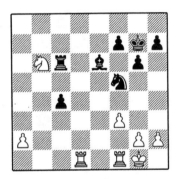

28 ♖b1?

G.Kasparov thought that White should have played 28 ♘a4 c3! (after 28...♘e3 29 ♘c3 the passed a-pawn becomes dangerous) 29 ♖d3! c2 30 ♖c3 ♖a6 31 ♘c5 ♖xa2 32 ♖c1 ♘d4 33 ♔f2 ♖b2 34 ♘d3! (with the idea of winning a pawn after 34...♖b1 35 ♖3xc2, whereas 34 ♔e3 ♖b1 35 ♘d3 ♗f5 36 ♔xd4 ♗xd3 leaves the position drawn) 34...♖b8! 35 ♔e3 ♘f5+ 36 ♔d2 ♘d4 37 ♘c5 ♘b3+ 38 ♘xb3 ♗xb3. But here O.Stetsko showed the way to victory by 39 ♖d3! ♔f6 (or 39...♗a4 40 ♖d4 ♗b3 41 ♔c3 threatening 42 ♖b4) 40 ♖d4 ♔e5 41 ♖e4+ ♔d5 42 ♔c3 ♔c5 43 ♖e5+

♔d6 44 ♖a5 h5 45 ♖a3 and the c2-pawn is lost.

28...c3 29 ♖b4 ♗xa2 30 ♖c1 c2 31 ♔f2 h5! 32 ♔e2 ♗e6 33 ♔d2 ♖d6+ 34 ♔xc2?

34 ♔e2 was necessary. This mistake, which places Beliavsky on the edge of defeat, is explained by time-pressure. But Black too was in time trouble...

34...♘e3+ 35 ♔b2 ♘xg2

If 35...♖d2+? 36 ♔c3 ♖xg2 White saves himself by 37 ♖b2.

36 ♘c4

36...♖d3?

"One good turn deserves another." 36...♖d5! 37 ♘b6 ♖d2+ 38 ♖c2 ♖xc2+ 39 ♔xc2 ♘e1+ 40 ♔d1 ♘xf3 41 ♖b2 g5 would have led to victory (G.Kasparov).

37 ♘e5 ♖e3 38 ♖e4 ♔f6 39 ♖xe3 ♘xe3 40 ♘d3 ♗d5 41 ♘e1 ½-½

Game 7
Kerr *White* **Gufeld** *Black*
Wellington 1988

1 d4 ♘f6 2 c4 g6 3 ♘c3 ♗g7 4 e4 d6 5 f3 0-0 6 ♗e3 ♘c6 7 ♘ge2 a6 8 ♕d2 ♖b8 9 ♘c1 e5 10 ♘b3 exd4 11 ♘xd4 ♘xd4 12 ♗xd4 ♗e6 13 ♗e2 c6

Black follows the main line in the *Encyclopedia* and, depending on the

circumstances, prepares the break ...b7-b5 or ...d6-d5.

The latter is rather effective when White is slow with castling, for example in the case of 14 a4—14...d5! 15 cxd5 cxd5 16 e5 ♘d7 17 f4 f6 18 exf6 ♘xf6 and Black equalizes, Beliavsky-Nunn, Reykjavik 1988.

14 0-0 b5

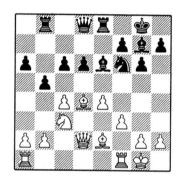

15 cxb5

Here my opponent deviates from the *Encyclopedia*, which considers only 15 b3 bxc4 (15...c5 16 ♗e3 irreparably weakens the d6-pawn, which can be taken after 16...b4 17 ♘a4 ♘d7 18 ♕xd6!) 16 bxc4. Despite the fact that White still controls the central area, Black retains sufficient resources to exert an influence over it. For example: 16...♕a5 17 ♖ac1 ♖fd8 18 ♔h1 c5 19 ♗e3 ♕a3 20 ♖c2 ♘d7 21 f4 ♘b6= Hjartarson-Nunn, Rotterdam 1989, or 16...c5 17 ♗e3 ♘d7 18 ♖ab1 ♕a3= as played in Petursson-Timoshchenko, Moscow 1989.

After the exhange on b5 Black has an easier game.

15...axb5 16 ♖fc1

On 16 b3 also possible is 16...♕e7 or 16...♕a5!?.

16...♕e7

This kind of queen's development in the King's Indian is in a certain way my "favourite dish". Of course 16...b4 17 ♘d1 c5 is also possible, but after 18 ♗f2 White makes way for the knight to head for the d5 square via e3.

17 a3 ♖fd8

Black prepares to undermine White's centre by ...d6-d5.

18 b4 ♖bc8

Bringing up all his reserves before the break in the centre.

The immediate 18...d5 19 e5 ♘d7 was also tempting, when after 20 ♕e3 he can save himself tactically by 20...♘xe5! 21 ♗xe5 d4 22 ♕f4 ♗xe5 23 ♕xe5 dxc3 with good play. But after 20 f4 everything is still not clear. Sometimes it pays off to allow less-experienced players the chance to express themselves...

19 ♘d1?!

That's it. White decides to warn his opponent about the presence of a weak pawn on c6. But it does not matter too much, because it is not so easy to reach it, and retreating the knight away from the centre makes the break ...d6-d5 more effective.

19...d5 20 e5 ♘d7 21 ♕e3 ♖e8

Not an obvious choice, the point of which lies in the idea 22...♗f5 23 g4 ♗xe5!.

22 ♖c3?!

In supporting his queen, White places the rook in a poor position which sets himself up for a ...d5-d4 advance.

22...♗f5 23 f4

It turns out that the bishop on f5 cannot be pushed back by 23 g4 in view of tactical possibilities such as 23...♗xe5 24 ♗xe5 ♕xe5 25 gxf5 d4 or 23...♘xe5!? 24 gxf5 ♕h4! with dangerous threats.

23...f6! 24 exf6 ♗xf6 25 ♗xf6

25 ♕xe7? is no good because of the intermediate 25...♗xd4+.

25...♕xf6

The aim of break 23...f6 now becomes clear. Black has uncovered the line-up of the rook on e8 against the opponent's queen and also cleared the way for the d-pawn.

26 ♕f2 d4!

Not only freeing a square for the knight, but creating an outpost for it to reach c3 or e3.

27 ♖cc1 ♘b6 28 ♘b2 ♘d5 29 g3 ♘c3

Both players were already short of time, and the last move is typical of such a scramble.

30 ♗d3?

A blunder in a difficult position. 30 ♗f3 was necessary.

30...♗xd3 31 ♘xd3 ♘e2+ 32 ♔g2 ♘xc1 33 ♖xc1 ♕e6

After centralizing the queen the game quickly comes to an end.

34 ♘e5 ♖ed8 35 ♕d2 ♕d5+ 36 ♔g1 c5 37 bxc5 ♖xc5 38 ♖d1 d3 39 ♕e3 ♖c2 40 ♖d2 ♖xd2 41 ♕xd2 ♔g7 42 ♔f2 ♕c5+ 0-1

Game 8
Z.Polgar *White* **Gufeld** *Black*
Wellington 1988

1 d4 ♘f6 2 c4 g6 3 ♘c3 ♗g7 4 e4 d6 5 f3 0-0 6 ♗e3 ♘c6 7 ♘ge2 a6 8 ♕d2 ♖b8 9 ♘c1 e5 10 d5

Along with 10 ♘b3, this is one of the main continuations in this variation.

10...♘d4

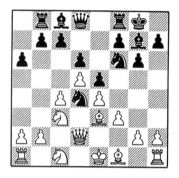

11 ♘1e2

There is an "extra" way as well—11 ♘b3. In this case it is not so easy for Black to play 11...c5, as in the game, since here, on 12 dxc6, the recapture 12...♘xc6 is less logical, while after 12...bxc6 13 ♘xd4 exd4 14 ♗xd4 he has to sacrifice a pawn, which is not to everybody's taste. However, altough Black can reckon on counterplay, being a pawn down makes his task harder. Here is one example:

14...♖e8 15 ♗e2 d5 16 cxd5 cxd5 17 e5 ♘d7 18 f4 f6 19 0-0! fxe5 20 fxe5 ♘xe5 21 ♖ad1 with an initiative for White, Atalik-Golubev, Bucharest 1996.

After 14...♕a5 15 ♖c1 ♗e6 16 ♗e2 ♖fd8 17 0-0 White also retains the better chances.

However, after 11 ♘b3 one has to reckon with the exchange 11...♘xb3 12 axb3 c5!? after which Black has good counterplay after either 13 b4 cxb4 14 ♘a4 b5 15 cxb5 axb5 16 ♕xb4 ♘e8, with the idea of ...♗h6, or 13 g4 h5 14 h3 ♘h7 15 gxh5 (otherwise 15...h4) 15...♕h4+ 16 ♕f2 ♕xf2+ 17 ♔xf2 gxh5 transposing to an endgame.

11...c5!?

I did not want to exchange knights, even though I knew that the *Encyclopedia* preferred 11...♘xe2 12 ♗xe2 ♘h5, assessing Black's position as not worse.

So, continuing with the main line, 13 0-0-0 f5, Black gains good counterplay. For instance, 14 c5 can be met by 14...♘f6 15 ♕c2 f4 16 ♗f2 g5, and Black's attack on the kingside is more dangerous than White's initiative on the queen flank, since 17 ♘a4 is parried by 17...b5!, and the moves ...a7-a6 and ...♖a8-b8 turn out to be rather useful. The idea of exchanging the dark-squared bishops by 14...f4 15 ♗f2 ♗f6! (with the idea of ...♗h4) is also interesting, and if White prevents it by 16 h4, then 16...♘g3! is strong.

12 dxc6 ♘xc6

The weak pawn on d6 is not as tangible a weakness as appears at first glance, since Black gains active piece play in return. Moreover, the pawn sacrifice 12...bxc6 13 ♘xd4 exd4 14 ♗xd4 has its drawbacks, as shown in the annotations to the move 11 ♘1e2.

13 ♖d1

A weaker line is 13 ♘c1 ♗e6 14 ♘b3 ♘a5 15 ♘xa5 ♕xa5 16 ♕xd6 b5 with compensation for the pawn.

Byrne and Mednis recommended a struggle for the initiative by 13 ♘d5 b5 14 ♘ec3, though it is clear that the position is too complicated for precise assessments.

13...♗e6 14 ♘d5

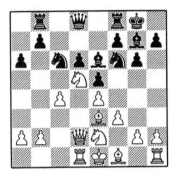

14...b5!

Black extends the diagonal for his light-squared bishop to the pawn on a2. This novelty of mine changes the assessment of the position, whereas 14...♘d7 would leave some advantage to White.

15 cxb5 axb5 16 ♘xf6+ ♗xf6

After 16...♕xf6?? 17 ♗g5 Black's queen is trapped.

17 g3 ♗xa2 18 ♕xd6

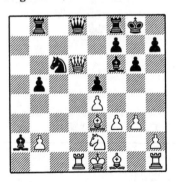

18...♗b3!?

The bold, tempting and attacking 18...♕a5+? 19 ♗d2 ♕b6 20 ♕xf6 ♘b4 fails to 21 ♗g5! (a cold shower for a hot head). Apart from

the text move, another possibility would be 18...♘d4? For example 19 ♕xd8 ♖fxd8 20 ♘xd4 exd4 21 ♗f4 ♖bc8 22 ♗d3 ♗c4 23 ♔e2.

19 ♕xd8 ♖fxd8

The less obvious 19...♗xd8! would be stronger, when Black's position is preferable.

20 ♖xd8+ ♗xd8 21 ♘c1 ♗c4 22 ♔f2 ♘b4?!

Again Black could have obtained the better chances with 22...♘d4.

23 ♗h3!

Only with this move can White's development be completed, at the same time equalising the chances.

23...♘c2 24 ♗c5 ♗b6 25 ♗xb6 ♖xb6 26 b3

White thereby forces off the second pair of bishops.

26...♗e6 27 ♗xe6 ♖xe6 28 ♖d1 ♘d4 29 ♘e2

The most clear-cut path to the draw.

29...♘xb3 30 ♖b1 ½-½

Game 9
Karpov *White* **Cu.Hansen** *Black*
Groningen 1995

1 d4 ♘f6 2 c4 g6 3 ♘c3 ♗g7 4 e4 d6 5 f3 0-0 6 ♗e3 ♘c6 7 ♘ge2 a6 8 ♕d2 ♖b8 9 ♘c1 e5 10 d5 ♘d4 11 ♘1e2 ♘xe2 12 ♗xe2 ♘h5 13 0-0-0 f5 14 ♔b1

14 g3, which does not allow the knight to f4, also deserves attention since after 14...f4?! 15 ♗f2 White threatens to close the kingside by g3-g4 and to switch play to the queenside where he can aim for the advance c4-c5.

14...♘f4 15 ♗f1

Any "gifts" associated with an exchange on f4 are unacceptable.

15...b6 16 g3 ♘h5 17 ♗e2

One of White's typical tricks 17 exf5 gxf5 18 f4 ♘f6 also leaves

Black with some chances. But, for the present, White is threatening 18 f4.

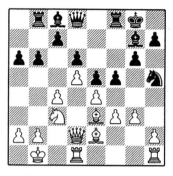

17...♘f6

The fight for control of the d4 square begins. After the preliminary 17...fxe4 18 ♘xe4 ♘f6 White keeps the e4 point under his control by 19 ♗g5 ♕e8 (19...♗f5 20 ♗d3) 20 ♗xf6! thereby retaining an advantage.

18 ♗g5 ♕e8 19 ♗d3

A.Karpov recommends 19 ♖df1!? and 19...fxe4 is still no good, since it loses to 20 ♗xf6! exf3 21 ♗xg7 fxe2 22 ♖xf8+.

19...fxe4 20 ♘xe4

Here, after 20 ♗xf6, Black holds on with the tactic 20...exd3!.

20...♘xe4 21 ♗xe4 ♗f5 22 ♕e2! ♗xe4+ 23 fxe4 ♕f7 24 ♖hf1 ♕d7 25 g4 ♖xf1 26 ♖xf1 ♖f8 27 h3 h6

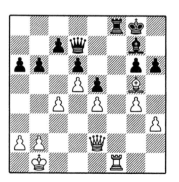

The fight for the e4 square has ended in mass exchanges, but White has retained a minimal advantage thanks to his "better" bishop. The fight for similar little objectives now moves to the f-file. Black does not mind exchanging rooks by 27...♖xf1+ 28 ♕xf1, but he cannot exchange the queens, because he has to keep an eye on the c7 pawn (28...h6 does not help—29 ♗h4!).

Now on 28 ♗h4 there is a deflecting manoeuvre 28...♖f4! since after 29 ♗g3 ♖xf1+ 30 ♕xf1 ♕f7 Black achieves his aim.

28 ♖xf8+ ♗xf8

Of course not 28...♔xf8 29 ♕f3+! ♔e8 30 ♗h4! and the advantage still lies with White.

29 ♗d2

A.Karpov in the 90s is as strong in technical positions as he used to be in his palmy days. This can be seen here by his timely exchange of rooks and technique in preparing for the break c4-c5. After 29 ♗e3 ♔g7 the break 30 c5?! is parried by 30...♕a4.

29...♔g7 30 c5!

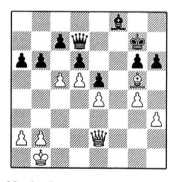

30...dxc5

Small advantages have developed into a more significant one. Black is now forced to allow a deterioriation of his pawn structure. It is obvious that 30...bxc5 31 ♕xa6, presenting

White with an outside passed a-pawn, is no good. And after 30...♕a4 A.Karpov shows two variations which deserve attention:

(a) 31 c6!? ♗e7 32 ♗c3 ♗g5 33 a3! with the threat of ♔b1 and b2-b3;

(b) 31 cxb6 cxb6 32 b3 ♕d4 33 ♕e3 ♕xe3 34 ♗xe3 b5 35 ♔c2 ♗e7 36 ♔c3 with the threat of a break on the queenside.

31 ♕xa6 h5

31...c6? is suicidal after 32 ♗c3 cxd5 33 ♗xe5+ and 34 ♕xb6.

32 ♕e2 hxg4 33 ♕xg4

Maybe he should have kept the queens on by 33 hxg4, since then it would be easier for Black to hold on passively.

33...♕xg4 34 hxg4 ♔f7 35 a4 ♔e8 36 a5 ♔d7 37 axb6 cxb6 38 ♗c3

In case of 38 b4 c4 39 b5 ♗c5 Black has all the holes plugged.

38...♗d6

In case of 38...♔d6 White breaks through with 39 b4 c4 40 b5 ♔c5 41 ♗xe5, creating connected passed pawns.

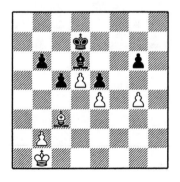

39 b4!

A magnificent temporary pawn sacrifice. Since Black can never transpose to a pawn endgame because of White's passed d5-pawn,

he is forced to continue playing the bishop endgame with isolated pawns.

39...cxb4

Of course not 39...c4 40 b5 ♔e7 41 ♔c2 ♔f6 42 ♗d2 ♗c5 43 ♔c3 and Black loses a pawn.

40 ♗d2 ♔c7 41 ♔c2 b5 42 ♔b3 ♔d7 43 ♗xb4 ♗c7 44 ♗c3 ♗d6 45 ♗b2 b4 46 ♗c1 ♗c5 47 ♗d2 ♗g1 48 ♔xb4

White has won a pawn, but it is not so easy to realize it.

48...♗f2 49 ♔c4 ♗g1 50 ♔d3 ♗c5 51 ♗e3 ♗e7 52 ♔c4

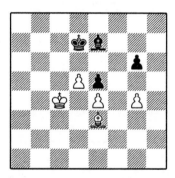

52...♗a3?

This move allows the bishop to be pushed into a passive position. According to Karpov's analysis after 52...♗h4 53 ♗c5 ♗g5 54 d6 ♔c6 55 d7 ♗d8 56 ♗b4 ♔xd7 57 ♔d5 ♗f6 58 ♗c3 ♗g7 59 ♗xe5 ♗h6 White would improve the position of his king but at the cost of reducing the number of pawns on the board, which would leave Black hopes of salvation.

53 ♗d2!

Preparing to hit the e5 pawn.

53...♗e7 54 ♗c3 ♗d6

After 54...♗f6 55 g5! ♗g7 56 ♗b4 leaves the enemy bishop caged in—after which a subsequent infiltration by triangulating the White king does the business.

55 &b4 &b8 56 &b5 &a7
After 56...&c7 57 d6 &xd6 58
&xd6 &xd6 59 g5 White wins the
pawn endgame.
57 &c5 &b8 58 d6! 1-0

Game 10
Peturni *White* **Gufeld** *Black*
Los Angeles 1987

**1 d4 &f6 2 c4 g6 3 &c3 &g7 4
e4 d6 5 f3 0-0 6 &e3 &c6 7 &ge2
&b8 8 &d2 a6**

9 &h6
Before storming the king flank by
h2-h4-h5 White has to "soften up"
the g7 square. A question must be
asked here: why White so rarely
makes up his mind to play the seemingly obvious 9 0-0-0, preferring an
immediate 9 h4 instead?
The point is, that after 9 0-0-0 b5!
it is Black who attacks the king first,
and who meets the h-pawn advance
—10 h4—by 10...h5. Today this operation is carried out automatically
and not only in the King's Indian
Defence (the same reaction can be
seen in the Dragon variation of the
Sicilian Defence). But, apparently,
the "old-fashioned" 10...e5 11 d5
&a5 12 &g3, which occurred in
Knaak-Gufeld 1978, is also possible. Here Black has a choice between 12...&c4 13 &xc4 bxc4 14

h5 or the advance 12...b4. I preferred the latter but after 13 &b1 c6
14 dxc6 b3 15 a3 &e6 16 &xd6, instead of playing 16...&c8? 17 c7!
when Black's position became difficult, I should have exchanged
queens by 16...&xd6 17 &xd6
&xc4. For example: 18 c7 &bc8 19
&b6! &xf1 20 &xa5 &xg2 21 &g1
&xf3 and Black's position is defensible. After a preliminary 10 g4 e5
11 d5 &a5 12 h4 bxc4, White has to
reckon with the fact that Black not
only has a counterattack but also an
extra pawn.
9...&xh6!
After my game with Bagirov, in
which I played 9...b5, I had more
than enough time to prepare myself
for the next attempt to disarm me.
The text exchange is better and allows Black to fight for the initiative.
The white queen is diverted from
the centre which Black now proceeds to undermine.
10 &xh6 e5
The best way to meet a flank attack is by a reaction in the centre.

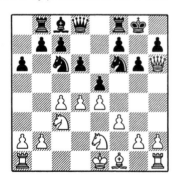

11 d5
According to the *Encyclopedia*
the main continuation is 11 0-0-0 b5
12 h4. Razuvaev-Gufeld, Tbilisi
1973, proceeded 12...&h8 13 &d5
&g8 14 &d2 bxc4 15 dxe5 &xe5
16 &ec3 &f6 17 h5 (17 f4 promised

more for White) 17...♘xd5 18 hxg6 fxg6 19 ♘xd5 ♗e6 20 ♗c4 ♖f7 21 ♗b3 c6 22 f4 cxd5 23 fxe5 dxe5 24 ♗xd5 ♗xd5 25 ♕xd5 ♕g5+ 26 ♕d2 ♕g4 ½-½. Later on it was discovered that it is more accurate for Black to relieve the tension in the centre immediately by 12...exd4 13 ♘xd4 ♘xd4 14 ♖xd4 ♕e7 or 12...bxc4 13 h5 ♕e7 14 g4 exd4 15 ♘xd4 ♘xd4 16 ♖xd4 ♗e6. In both cases Black retains approximately equal chances.

11...♘a5

This corresponds more with the idea of a flank attack than the obvious 11...♘d4, which can be met by the simple 12 0-0-0 c5 13 dxc6 ♘xe2+ 14 ♗xe2 bxc6 15 ♕d2, putting pressure on the weak d6 pawn.

12 ♘g3 c5

13 b4 was threatened.

13 h4 ♗d7

Black is confident that his attack on the queenside will come first, otherwise he would have blockaded the other wing by 13...♔h8 14 h5 ♘g8 15 ♕d2 g5.

14 h5 b5 15 cxb5

Black should not have created a mobile pawn-pair. 15 0-0-0 was more reliable though even here, after a capture on c4, Black's chances would be superior.

15...axb5 16 ♘d1

This retreat shows that White's superficially attractive attack along the h-file needs more support. But it's a long time coming.

16...♔h8!

With the idea of carrying out the manoeuvre pointed out in the note to Black's 13th move.

17 hxg6 fxg6 18 ♘f2

Of course not 18 ♕xg6? because of 18...♖g8.

18...♖f7 19 ♘h3 ♗xh3

Before starting his operations on the queenside, Black liquidates the knight and secures himself a comfortable life on the kingside.

20 ♖xh3 ♖g7! 21 ♗e2 c4

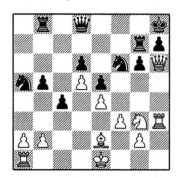

The pawn frees a square for the knight which is now ready to gallop, via b7, to c5 after which the a2-pawn can be attacked by ...♖b8-a8 threatening ...♘c5-b3.

22 0-0-0

Completing his development but of course the white king will find no safe haven on the queenside. Perhaps White was still hopeful that his battery of major pieces along the h-file would bring results.

22...b4 23 ♖dh1 b3

A decisive assault.

24 a3 c3 25 ♗d3

25 bxc3 b2+ 26 ♔b1 ♖b3 wins.

25...♖c8!

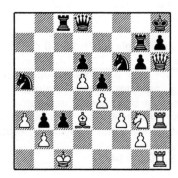

While White's heavy artillery is shooting blanks, Black's infantry has already reached the enemy king and his storm troops are ready to invade.

26 ♕g5 ♘c4!! 27 ♖h6 ♘xb2 28 ♗a6 ♖a8 29 ♖xg6 ♖xg6 30 ♕xg6 ♖xa6 0-1

Game 11
Spassky *White* **Fischer** *Black*
S.Stefan/Belgrade (m/8) 1992

1 d4 ♘f6 2 c4 g6 3 ♘c3 ♗g7 4 e4 d6 5 f3 0-0

It is nice to see that even after 20 years in "retirement" World Champion Robert Fischer remains faithful to the King's Indian, and is still master of the subject—just as he used to be. In the first game of the present match he essayed a rare continuation 5...c5 6 dxc5 dxc5 7 ♕xd8 ♔xd8 8 ♗e3 ♘fd7 9 ♘ge2 b6 (in the 70s Fischer played 9...♘c6 10 0-0-0 b6) 10 0-0-0 ♘a6!? 11 g3 (more active is 11 f4 ♘c7 12 g4 ±) 11...♘c7 12 f4 e6 13 ♗h3 ♔e7 14 ♖hf1 h6! and Black managed to maintain equality.

6 ♗e3 ♘c6 7 ♘ge2 a6 8 ♕d2

In this game B.Spassky links the development of his queen to queenside castling. But despite the favourable impression of his play in this game, he later preferred the positional manoeuvre ♘e2-c1-b3. After 8 h4 h5 9 ♘c1 in the 28th game R.Fischer played 9...e5 10 d5 ♘d4 11 ♘b3 ♘xb3 12 ♕xb3, as he used to do in the past, but ran into opening problems. However already in his next Black game he thought up the brand-new plan of 9...♘d7 10 ♘b3 a5! and obtained equal chances.

8...♖b8 9 h4

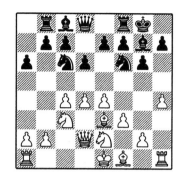

The most popular continuation. With this straightforward attack White threatens to break down the enemy king's fortifications.

9...h5

The most radical way to fight against White's flank attack. 9...b5 10 h5, which entails certain risk, has also been played.

(a) 10...bxc4 11 g4! ♗xg4 12 fxg4 ♘xg4 13 0-0-0! and Black gains no compensation for the piece, Kasparov-Spassky, Niksic 1983

(b) 10...e5 11 d5 ♘a5 12 ♘g3 bxc4 13 0-0-0 ♖b4 14 ♗h6! ♗xh6 15 ♕xh6 ♕e7 (G.Kasparov considers 15...♔h8! better) 16 ♗e2 ♗d7 17 ♘f1! ♖fb8 (suicidal is 17...♘h5 18 g4 ♘f6 19 ♘g3) 18 ♖d2 c5?! (18...♗e8 19 g4) 19 ♗d1! (not yet 19 g4 ♗a4! and ...♕e7-b7) 19...♘e8 20 hxg6 fxg6 21 g4! ♕g7 22 g5! with a strong attack, Kasparov-Loginov, Manila (ol) 1992.

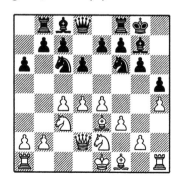

10 ♗h6

Transposing to the theme 10 ♘c1 e5 11 d5 ♘d4 12 ♘1e2 is as harmless for Black as it is in the position without the confrontation of the h-pawns. He can react the same way: 12...c5. An example was provided by the game Ernst-M.Carlson, Stockholm 1995: 13 dxc6 bxc6 14 ♘xd4 exd4 15 ♗xd4 ♖e8 16 ♗e2 d5 17 cxd5 ♖b4! (on 17...cxd5?! 18 e5 ♘d7 19 f4 is unpleasant) 18 ♗c5 ♘xe4! 19 fxe4 ♗xc3 20 ♕xc3 ♖bxe4 21 0-0-0 (or 21 0-0 ♖xe2 22 dxc6 ♕h4 with a double edged game) 21...♖xe2 22 d6 ♗f5 23 ♖he1 ♕h4 24 ♖xe2 ♖xe2 25 d7 ♕f4+ 26 ♗e3 ♕xe3+ 27 ♕xe3 ♖c2+ ½-½.

After 10 0-0-0 b5 Black has sufficient counterplay. For instance, the game Oll-Gelfand, USSR 1984, continued 11 ♘d5 bxc4 12 ♘xf6+ (on 12 g4 or 12 ♗h6 Black would have himself exchanged knights, favourably, by 12...♘xd5 13 exd5 ♘b4 14 ♘c3 c6!) 12...♗xf6 13 g4 ♘b4 14 ♘c3 c5 15 ♗c4 cxd4 16 ♗xd4 ♕c7 17 ♗b3 ♗e6 (17...♗xd4 18 ♕xd4 ♗e6 also has been played) 18 ♗xf6 ♗xb3 19 axb3 exf6 20 gxh5 ♕a5! and Black maintained equality.

After 10 ♘d5 good is 10...b5 11 cxb5 axb5 12 ♖c1 ♗d7 13 ♘xf6+ ♗xf6 14 g4 hxg4 15 fxg4 e5 16 d5 ♘d4 17 ♘xd4 exd4 18 ♗g5 ♖e8 19 ♕f4 ♗xg5!? (19...♗e5 20 ♕f3 ±) 20 hxg5 ♕e7 and Black maintains equal chances. (A.Korolev).

10...e5

The course of this game leads one to believe that this move is premature. I think that 10...b5 is more logical.

11 ♗xg7 ♔xg7 12 d5 ♘e7 13 ♘g3!

Hindering ...b7-b5, which would have been Black's response to 13 0-0-0.

13...c6 14 dxc6 ♘xc6!

The decision of a real King's Indian fan: allowing a backward pawn on d6 for the sake of active piece play. After 14...bxc6 15 0-0-0 ♕b6 Black manages to carry out the idea of ...d6-d5 only in the event of 16 ♘a4?! ♕b4 17 ♕xb4 ♖xb4 18 b3 d5. But, as was shown by Y.Seirawan, after 16 c5!? he has to reckon with a more serious positional drawback in his position: 16...dxc5 17 ♘a4 ♕b4 18 ♕c2!?. White's chances are preferable.

15 0-0-0 ♗e6 16 ♔b1!

16 ♕xd6 can be met by 16...♕b6 17 ♕d2 ♘d4 or 16...♕a5 with active piece play for the pawn.

16...♘e8

Upon 16...♕a5 Black has to reckon with 17 ♘f5+!.

17 ♘d5 b5 18 ♘e3

An immediate 18 ♖c1 was stronger, as shown by Spassky's 21st move.

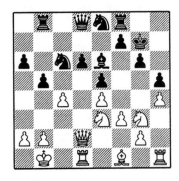

18...♖h8!

Having got into difficult position, R.Fischer displays surprising tenacity, nullifying White's feeble efforts to prepare g2-g4.

19 ♖c1 ♕b6 20 ♗d3 ♘d4 21 ♘d5 ♕a7

Closing the centre by 21...♗xd5 22 cxd5 favours White.

22 ♘f1! ♘f6

After 22...bxc4 23 ♗xc4 ♘f6 Black's position is less stable, and apart from 24 ♘fe3 he also has to reckon with 24 ♘xf6 ♔xf6 25 ♗xe6.

23 ♘fe3

In reply to the tempting opening of the position by 23 ♘xf6 ♔xf6 24 c5 Black has the retreat 24...♔g7 when, after 25 cxd6 ♕e7, he regains the pawn, getting rid of the d6 weakness free of charge.

23...♗xd5 24 cxd5 ♖bc8 25 ♖cf1!

White prepares to open up lines by g2-g4 for which it is useful to keep the rooks on the board.

25...♕e7 26 g4 ♘d7 27 g5 ♔f8?!

Where does the king go? R.Fischer begins a manoeuvre with the king which could have led to unpleasant consequences.

Black stands worse and is confined to passivity. However he might push White into trying an active plan with f3-f4. Therefore 27...♖cf8! was fully in the spirit of the position—with the idea of the break ...f7-f6. For example: 28 f4!? exf4 29 ♖xf4 ♕e5 30 ♖hf1 f6 and Black's chances are not worse (Y.Seirawan).

28 ♖f2 ♔e8?! 29 ♗f1

The bishop is transferred to an active diagonal and joins in the battle for the c-line, but 29 ♖hf1 also deserved attention.

29...♘c5 30 ♗h3

30 ♗g2, protecting the pawn on e4, was rather more solid, after which the f3-f4 break would come to the fore: 30...♖f8 31 f4 exf4 32 ♖xf4 ♕e5 33 ♖hf1 and Black doesn't have an easy life.

30...♖c7 31 ♖c1

"When I moved the rook to the c1 square," recalls B.Spassky, "then I immediately saw the knight sacrifice. I know what a killer instinct Bobby has, and he, of course, would not have missed such a good chance to finish me off in this game. That evening, at home, Yuri Balashov showed me what was probably the best defence—with the queen on c2".

It was still not too late to return to the idea of 31 ♗g2.

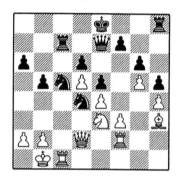

31...♘cb3! 32 axb3 ♘xb3 33 ♖c6?

Having missed the sacrifice on b3, B.Spassky could not pull himself together and quickly lost the game. In time-pressure of course it is not easy to find a move like 33 ♕c2, which puts the queen *en prise*. However it seems that even this move does not solve his problems: 33...♖xc2 34 ♖fxc2 ♘xc1 35 ♖c8+ ♕d8 36 ♖xd8+ (or 36 ♔xc1 ♖f8! and 37...f6) 36...♔xd8 37 ♔xc1 ♖f8! 38 ♔d1 f6 39 gxf6 ♖xf6 40 ♔e2 ♖f7 and White has to watch over the h4 pawn and reckon with the threat of the manoeuvre ...♖f7-c7 followed by ...♔e7-f6 and ...g6-g5, as given by V.Kupreichik and Y.Seirawan.

A computer analysis carried out by the *Deep Thought* program considered 33 ♕c3! ♘xc1! 34 ♕a3 b4 35 ♕a4+ ♔f8 36 ♗f1 b3 (or 36...♔g7 37 ♖xc2 ♖xc2 38 ♘xc2 f6) 37 ♘c4 f6! was a better continuation, but such positions with material inequality are very difficult for precise evaluation.

33...♘xd2+ 34 ♖xd2 ♔f8 35 ♖xa6 ♖a7 36 ♖c6 ♔g7 37 ♗f1 ♖a1+! 38 ♔xa1 ♕a7+ 39 ♔b1 ♕xe3 40 ♔c2 b4 0-1

Now let us examine a few games where White deviates from the general line 7 ♘ge2 a6 8 ♕d2.

Game 12
Seirawan *White* **Gufeld** *Black*
Seattle 1989

1 d4 ♘f6 2 c4 g6 3 ♘c3 ♗g7 4 e4 d6 5 f3 0-0 6 ♗e3 ♘c6 7 ♘ge2 a6 8 d5

After any early closing of the centre it is easier for Black to develop counterplay since he can undermine the advanced pawn without having to lock the pawn chain.

8...♘e5

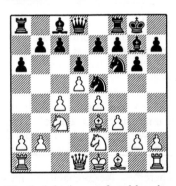

The knight is comfortably placed in the centre, whereas the d5-pawn will become an object of attack.

9 ♘g3 c6 10 a4

White prevents the advance of the b-pawn, which would have followed a placid 10 ♗e2?! b5 11 cxb5 axb5 12 dxc6 b4, whereupon Black already stands better.

On 10 f4 there could have followed 10...♘eg4 11 ♗g1 cxd5 and now 12 h3?! is met by the intermediate 12...d4! 13 ♗xd4 e5 14 fxe5 ♘xe5 and the knight makes a triumphant return to e5. Of course 12 cxd5, with a complex game, is stronger.

10...cxd5

On 10...♕a5 good is 11 ♖a3!.

11 cxd5 e6

The d5 pawn still feels uneasy.

12 ♗e2 exd5 13 exd5 ♖e8 14 ♕d2

Not only protecting the bishop on e3, but also threatening to fix Black's queenside by a4-a5.

After 14 ♗d4?! the d5 pawn is subject to attack by 14...♕a5! 15 ♕b3 ♘d3+ 16 ♔f1 ♘b4.

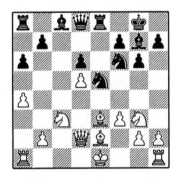

14...♕a5!

An obvious improvement on the game Seirawan-Nunn, Brussels 1988, in which after 14...♕e7?! 15 ♔f2 Black failed to solve his opening problems. Black develops his queenside pieces harmoniously, posting his queen to its "rightful" square a5 and allowing his rook to control the c-file.

Nunn recommends 14...♕c7!? 15 0-0 ♘c4 16 ♗xc4 ♕xc4 17 ♘ge4

②xe4 18 ②xe4 ♕b3! 19 ♗d4!
♕xd5 20 ♖fd1 ♕xd4+ 21 ♕xd4
♗xd4+ 22 ♖xd4 ♖e7 23 ②xd6 with
equal chances.

15 0-0 ♗d7

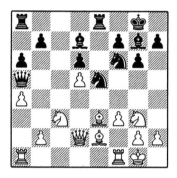

16 b4!?
Seirawan is unsure of Black's
probable initiative after ...♖a8-c8
and himself provokes a crisis on the
queenside, although it is clear that
he cannot count on obtaining any
initiative.

**16...♕xb4 17 ♖ab1 ♕h4! 18
②ge4**
On 18 ♗g5 there is the retort
18...②c4.

18...②xe4 19 ②xe4 ②g4! 20 fxg4
On 20 ♗f4 I had 20...②f6!.

20...♖xe4 21 ♗f3
Of course not 21 ♗g5? because of
21...♖xe2, but now Black gets a
chance to force a draw.

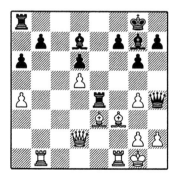

**21...♖xe3! 22 ♕xe3 ♗e5 23 g3
♗xg3 24 hxg3 ♕xg3+ 25 ♔h1
♕h3+ ½-½**

Game 13
Browne *White* **Gufeld** *Black*
New York 1989

**1 d4 ②f6 2 c4 g6 3 ②c3 ♗g7 4
e4 d6 5 f3 0-0 6 ♗e3 ②c6 7 ②ge2
a6 8 a3**
White plans to extend his pawn
front to the b-file. But this allows
Black to get ahead in development
and commence active counterplay
against the advanced pawns.

8...♗d7 9 b4

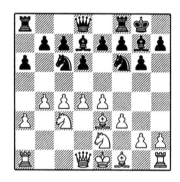

9...e5!
Black reacts according to the classic principle: the best way to meet a
flank attack is by a reaction in the
centre.
An alternative lies in play based
on ...b7-b5 But it is not good to play
this immediately because of the loss
of a pawn after 9...b5 10 cxb5 axb5
11 d5 ②e5 12 ②d4 ②c4 13 ♗xc4
bxc4 14 ♕e2.
Therefore the preparatory move
9...♕b8 is necessary when 10 ②c1
is met by 10...b5 11 cxb5 (after 11
②b3 there is an interesting knight
sacrifice: 11...bxc4 12 ♗xc4 ②xb4!
13 axb4 ♕xb4 when White cannot
unravel his tangled minor pieces

without loss, e.g. 14 ♕d3 d5! and after 15 exd5?! there follows 15...♗f5! so he has to return the piece by 15 ♘c5! dxc4 16 ♕c2 ♗c6 —Vlasak) 11...axb5 12 ♘b3 e5 13 d5 ♘e7 14 ♗d3 (or 14 ♗e2 ♖d8! 15 0-0 c6= Brunner-Xie Jun, match, Berne 1995) 14... ♘h5 15 g3 f5 16 ♕e2 fxe4 17 fxe4 c6 with a double-edged game, Nenashev-Golubev, Alushta 1994

10 d5 ♘e7 11 ♘c1

11 ♕d2!? also deserves attention.

11...♘h5 12 ♘b3 f5 13 ♕d2 ♔h8!

A typical trick in such positions: the king frees a square for the knight manoeuvre ...♘g8-f6, while the second knight is directed towards the outpost on f4.

14 0-0-0 ♘g8 15 ♗d3 ♘gf6 16 ♔b1 fxe4!

The logic of this "illogical" move lies not in the surrender of the central square e4, but in trying to distract the queen's knight from c3 so as then to continue 17...b5!, taking the ground from under the d5-pawn's feet.

17 ♗xe4 ♘xe4 18 fxe4 ♕h4!

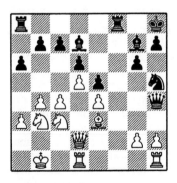

As a result of the operation begun by the move 16...fxe4 Black exerts control over the kingside.

19 ♖df1 ♔g8

Of course not 19...♖xf1+ 20 ♖xf1 ♕xh2?! because of 21 ♖f7. But now this is threatened so...

20 h3 b6 21 ♔a2 ♕g3! 22 ♖fg1?!

He should not have relaxed his control over the f-file. An immediate 23 ♘c1 was better.

22...♖f7 23 ♘c1 ♘f4 24 ♖f1?

Acknowledging that his 22nd move was a mistake. More stubborn was 24 ♗f2 ♕g5 25 ♘d3.

24...♘xg2 25 ♖xf7 ♔xf7 26 ♗f2 ♕f3 27 ♖f1 ♗xh3 and White soon resigned. **0-1**

Game 14
Petursson *White* **Gufeld** *Black*
Hastings 1986/87

1 d4 ♘f6 2 c4 g6 3 ♘c3 ♗g7 4 e4 d6 5 f3 0-0 6 ♗e3 ♘c6 7 ♕d2

White does not waste time developing the g1 knight and hurries to castle queenside. Black's reaction is immediate.

7...a6 8 0-0-0

I can just see the chess pieces talking to each other. Anyone with a perfect ear for chess will surely hear the white king's cue: "I hereby declare war!"

At this moment a thought flashed through my mind, and I couldn't help smiling. Maya Chiburdanidze, playing on a neighbouring table, noticed this and asked me after the game what was so funny. Well, it was this image I had of myself and my opponent. Think of it: a young, good-looking, invariably courteous, slim guy, wearing big glasses, weighing less than 130 lbs—in combat with a super-heavy weightlifter!

8...b5!

On with the game! Strangely enough, this pawn sacrifice for the initiative was a novelty at the time.

The main continuations were 8...♖b8 and 8...♗d7 with the traditional 9...e5 to follow. These ways are quite logical and secure good chances for Black, but in the present position, with White having decided where to place his king, the text move is more critical.

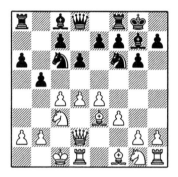

9 cxb5?!

9 ♘ge2 might be an alternative, although after 9...e5 10 d5 ♘a5 Black would have plenty of play.

9 h4 h5 10 ♗h6 e5 11 ♘ge2 bxc4 12 g4 ♗xh6 was a possible alternative (12...hxg4? 13 h5 ♘xh5 14 ♘g3 ♘xg3 15 ♗xg7 is suicidal) 13 ♕xh6 ♗xg4 14 ♖g1 (14 fxg4 ♘xg4 15 ♕d2 ♘f2 16 ♖h2 looks more natural) 14...♗f3 15 ♘f4 and here, instead of 15...♘g4? 16 ♖xg4 ♗xg4 17 ♘xg6! which led to an advantage for White in Dolmatov-Thorsteins, Polanica Zdroj 1987, stronger was 15...exf4 16 ♗xc4 ♗g4 with a double-dged game.

9...axb5 10 ♗xb5 ♘a5!

It is quite possible that, prior to this game, someone had considered the pawn sacrifice on b5, but had not thought of following it up with 10...♘a5. The idea behind this move is to fight for the strategically important c4-square. The alternative 10...♗d7 seems insufficient. For example, 11 ♘ge2 ♘a5 12 ♗d3!.

11 ♘ge2

The attempt to hinder 11...♗a6 by means of 11 ♕e2 looks ugly and the knight on g1 would be appalled by it! This verdict is borne out by the variation 11...c6 12 ♗d3 ♕b6 intending ...♗c8-a6, ...d6-d5, and a struggle for the c4-square. On 11 ♗h6 possible is 11...c6 12 ♗xg7 ♔xg7 13 ♗d3 ♕b6!, with forcing threats.

11...♗a6 12 ♗xa6 ♖xa6 13 ♕d3 ♕a8 14 ♔b1

White has to take care that Black's initiative doesn't develop into a formidable attack on the king. A series of prophylactic moves is called for.

14...♖b8 15 ♗c1

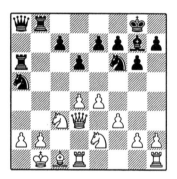

Black's direct threats are temporarily contained, but let's recall the motives behind the pawn sacrifice and the fight for the strategically important c4-square. In this connection, the moves ...e7-e6 and ...d6-d5, with a subsequent jump of the knight to c4, look logical. Turn your attention to the strategic reason for the change in Black's central pawn structure, permitting the "Gufeld bishop" to gain in strength while remaining in place.

15...e6!! 16 h4!

Petursson correctly decides that the best defence is counterattack.

16...d5 17 h5

Black can, of course, continue his attack unhindered after 17 e5 ♘d7 with ...c7-c5 to follow.

17...♘c4

I did not even look at the proffered gift 17...♘xh5.

18 hxg6 hxg6 19 b3!

This move, which brings the game to a crisis and forces White to walk the edge of a precipice, is essentially the strongest in the position.

Taking into account White's initial advantage of having the first move, if Black succeeds in equalizing as a result of his opening experiment he can be considered the moral victor of the theoretical duel.

The outcome of 19...♖xb3+ 20 axb3 ♖a1+ 21 ♔c2 ♖a2+ 22 ♔b1 ♖a1+, or 22 ♘xa2 ♕xa2+ 23 ♔c3 ♕a1+ 24 ♔c2 (24 ♔b4?? ♕a5 mate) 24...♕a2+, with a draw in both cases, can be counted on the credit side for Black. But I decided to pour oil on the fire.

19...c5!

There are many threats. For example: 20...♘a3+ 21 ♗xa3 c4!.

20 dxc5!

The only move, as can easily be verified.

20...♘d7!

Black can again force a draw if he so wishes, by means of 20...♖xb3+

21 axb3 ♖a1+ 22 ♔c2 ♖a2+ 23 ♔b1! ♖a1+.

21 exd5 exd5!

Once again rejecting a peaceful conclusion by ...♖xb3+.

22 ♕xd5!

Again, the only continuation. The following variation indicates the dangers for White: 22 ♘xd5 ♘xc5! 23 ♕xc4 ♖xb3+ 24 axb3 ♖a1+ 25 ♔c2 ♕a2+ winning.

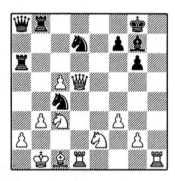

The sharpening of the struggle reaches its climax. White has a large material advantage and the exchange of queens is threatened.

22...♖xb3+ 23 axb3!

White had another possibility: 23 ♔c2. In this case Black would have a pleasant choice: either 23...♘e3+!? 24 ♗xe3 (but not 24 ♔xb3?? ♕b8+ winning) 24...♖xa2+ 25 ♔xb3 ♕a3+ 26 ♔c4 ♕a6+ 27 ♔b3 (but not 27 ♘b5?? ♕a4+ 28 ♔d3 ♕c2 mate) 27... ♕a3+ with a draw, or 23...♖b2+! 24 ♗xb2 ♘e3+ 25 ♔b1 ♘xd5 26 ♖xd5 ♘e5! (but not 26...♘f8 27 ♖hd1 ♘e6 28 ♘f4 with advantage to White) 27 ♖hd1 ♘c6! 28 g4 ♕b8! 29 ♘c1 ♖a8! 30 ♘b3 ♕e8, and Black has the better chances. Black again has ambitions of transferring a knight to c4. If, in the last variation, White were to play the immediate 28 ♘c1, then

28...♕e8! 29 ♘b3 ♖a8, and again Black's chances are preferable.

23...♖a1+ 24 ♔c2

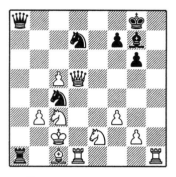

24...♖xc1+!

Many moves before, when preparing to rush into a whirlwind of complications, I couldn't find a satisfactory continuation after 25 ♔d3!?. Later, as an experiment, I offered this position to many colleagues for solving—and was persuaded that the right answer does not lie on the surface. Psychological laws are probably in effect here. The obvious solution comes up for consideration at the last moment or is rejected on the whole as illogical.

Where is the rub, then? Let us examine a situation in which wolves find themselves not the hunters, but the hunted. It is a paradox: if the wolves are driven into an enclosed area surrounded by red flags, most of them will remain "trapped," even though in practical terms there is no barrier. There are undoubtedly psychological parameters in play.

Something similar happens to chess players under certain conditions.

I observed another phenomenon here: Finding the right solution in this example is inversely proportional to the strength of the chess player... And here it is! 25...♕xd5+ 26 ♘xd5 ♘xc5 mate!

So, whence the paradox? It is that strong chess players form certain stereotypes, e.g. that when carrying out a sacrificial attack one should avoid the exchange of pieces.

25 ♘xc1

The only move. If 25 ♔xc1 then 25...♕a3+ 26 ♔c2 ♘e3+ wins.

25...♘e3+ 26 ♔b1

Events now develop along forced lines.

26...♘xd5 27 ♖xd5 ♗xc3 28 ♖xd7

It is as if a tornado is sweeping over the chessboard, carrying away the erstwhile heroes of this remarkable duel.

28...♕a3! 29 ♔c2 ♕xc5 30 ♖hd1?

The tempest abates. Let us calmly attempt to evaluate the position. There is approximate equality of forces on the board, but Black continues to hold the initiative. White should be thinking about a peaceful solution to his problems.

With this in mind, 30 ♖h4!? deserves attention, so that after 30...♕f2+ 31 ♔xc3 ♕xh4 White would have the possibility of setting up an impregnable fortress.

30...♗f6+?

This game was widely acclaimed in chess literature: the Yugoslav *Informant* published it with comments and a number of chess magazines in other countries carried it too. It got on the pages of the London *Times* as well with commentary by British grandmaster R.Keene. And the most surprising thing is that neither Keene, nor I, nor any other commentator saw what was found by one of the scrupulous readers of the newspaper, who informed the editors about his discovery.

So, what was it? If Black carried on with 30...♗d4+ he would win. This bishop move, which severs the coordination of two much stronger rooks, proves how easy it is sometimes (as in real life) to break down well-established links.

Why did it not occur to me at once? Because I could not permit a situation in which my favourable piece—the bishop—would be sandwiched between two enemy rooks. After 31 ♔d3 ♕f5+ 32 ♔c4 ♕xd7 33 ♖xd4 ♕c6+ wins, or 31 ♔b1 ♕f5+ 32 ♖d3 ♕xd7 33 ♘e2, when both 33...♕b5 and 33...♕f5 win.

31 ♔b1 ♕c3 32 ♖7d2 ♔g7

There was a tempting possibility to draw the king out of his sanctuary. For instance, 32...♕a1+ 33 ♔c2 ♕b2+ 34 ♔d3 ♕c3+ 35 ♔e2. But here too, Black's attempt at significantly increasing his advantage does not succeed: 35...♗g5 36 ♘d3! ♕xb3 (36...♗xd2 37 ♖xd2 ♕xb3 leads only to a "moral" victory) 37 f4.

33 f4?

The explanation for this error is the extreme pressure to which my amiable opponent had been subjected. Interestingly, in our post mortem analysis, Petursson insisted

that there is *zugzwang* on the board and White has no other move here.

In fact, though, White has only one acceptable move, and it is not 33 f4 but 33 ♖a2!, after which it would be practically impossible for Black to improve his position.

33...♕a1+ 34 ♔c2 ♕c3+ 35 ♔b1 ♕a1+

With Black running a little short of time, there followed:

36 ♔c2 ♕b2+ 37 ♔d3 ♕d4+ 38 ♔c2 ♕b2+ 39 ♔d3 ♕d4+ 40 ♔c2 ♕xf4

Black's position improves dramatically with the win of this pawn. The realization of his advantage involves the accurate advance of his kingside pawns to the f4 and g4 squares. So the logical continuation here was 41...♕e5 followed by g6-g5, ♔g7-g6, ♗f6-g7, f7-f5, ♗g7-f6, g5-g4 and f5-f4.

41 ♔b1 ♕g4?

It was necessary to advance the pawns, i.e. 41...g5 and ...g5-g4.

In accordance with the playing schedule, this tense game was resumed after a few hours which were allotted to dinner and a short break. To my regret, I spent the whole time on dinner.

The further course of the game—in which, after having every chance of victory, I committed many technical errors and ended up with a draw—patently confirms the truth of scientifically-based deductions that it is difficult to play after a lavish meal.

42 ♖f1! ♕e4+ 43 ♖c2 g5 44 ♖f3 g4 45 ♖d3 ♕e5 46 ♖a2 ♗g5 47 ♖c2 ♗f6 48 ♖a2 ♗g5 49 ♖c2 ♕f5 50 ♖dxc3 ♕f1 51 g3! ♗f6 52 ♖c4 ♕f3 53 ♖f4! ♕xg3 54 ♖cc4 ♕h2 55 ♖xg4+ ♔h6 56 ♖c2 ♕e5 57 ♖a4!

In time trouble I overlooked this move.

57...♗g5 58 ♖ac4 ♗f6 ½-½

Game 15
Kotronias *White* **Gufeld** *Black*
Athens 1985

1 d4 ♘f6 2 c4 g6 3 ♘c3 ♗g7 4 e4 d6 5 f3 0-0 6 ♗g5

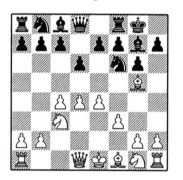

A popular thrust which hinders ...e7-e5. There is something provocative about the bishop's move to g5: White wants his opponent to play ...h7-h6, in order to retreat the bishop to e3 and afterwards gain a tempo for the attack by the move ♕d1-d2.

But here another chess rule comes into force: do not move pawns in the place where you are weak! The g-pawn has already been advanced, and any new advance will make it easier for the opponent to open up lines, undermining the sanctuary of the black king.

But do we need to do anything about the bishop which, for the time being, poses no threat? What kind of defence should Black set up? First of all, it is necessary to understand that building up a "Maginot Line", i.e. an insurmountable defence, amounts to defeat. Sooner or later it will end in a total rout of your combat forces.

That is why the best defence is counterattack. It is clear that any counterattack also involves the opening up of lines. But where? Best of all it should be done in the centre—where the enemy is most vulnerable.

6...♘c6

It is only natural, if White pays no attention to the d4-square, that it should be attacked. Would it be better to use the infantry for this purpose—6...c5 7 d5 e6 8 ♕d2 exd5? After 9 cxd5 there arises a position along the lines of of the Modern Benoni, in which White blocks the d-file and finds a useful function for his queenside bishop. However Black does not have the worse game here. Quite often White takes on d5 with the knight, but in this case it seems to me that Black's play, in connection with his queenside pawn attack, is rather effective. Here is one example: 9 ♘xd5 ♗e6 10 ♘e2 ♗xd5 11 cxd5 ♘bd7 (11...h6 12 ♗e3 is weaker) 12 ♘c3 a6 13 a4 ♕c7 14 ♗e2 c4 15 0-0 b5! 16 axb5 axb5 17 ♗e3 (or 17 b4 cxb3! 18 ♘xb5 ♕b7! with counterplay B.Gelfand) 17...♕b7 18 ♖fb1!? ♖xa1 19 ♖xa1 b4 with complex play, Yusupov-Gelfand, Moscow 1992.

But what can we do? Chess, as with many things in life, is subject to style, and here it appeals to my own taste—I am a staunch supporter of the 6...♘c6 development. If White pays no attention to the d4 square, then it is only natural to attack it.

It should be added that the essence of the move 6...♘c6 is also its peculiar provocation, like White's 6th move. Black invites the pawn forward to attack the knight. But after 7 d5 ♘e5 followed by ...e7-e6 the black pieces, with an opened centre, will gain space for action, and the move f2-f3 will turn out to be useless.

7 ♘ge2

Both development and prophylaxis. With the bishop on g5, the d4 square is more vulnerable and the need to protect it more concrete, because, after 7 ♕d2 e5 8 d5 ♘d4, the enemy knight reaches a vantage point from which it surveys the entire position. Then 9 ♘ge2 is met by 9...c5! intending ...a7-a6, ...♖a8-b8 and ...b7-b5, and if 10 dxc6 then 10...bxc6, when an exchange on d4 would only benefit Black.

7...a6!

I like this move. It is in the spirit of chess, since it sets in motion the hidden springs of the counterattack by ...b7-b5 with threats to the c4 square, as well as to the centre (after ...b5-b4). This counterplay of Black's is no weaker than White's attack on the kingside.

The thrust 7...e5, in view of the pin on the knight, is not in the spirit of the position: 8 d5 ♘e7 9 ♘g3 h5 10 ♗e2 and White stands better.

8 ♕d2 ♗d7

Black has a number of active plans at his disposal, e.g. 8...♖b8 or 8...♖e8. This is the main consequence of White's over-commital move f2-f3

9 h4

Far from amicable behaviour towards the opposing king! Essentially this is the signal for hostilities to commence.

9...h5!

Again the same recipe for maximum activity. It would be dangerous to let the white pawn reach h5, but now, to prepare the g2-g4 break, White has to waste several precious tempi which Black can use for the development of his forces. Very sharp play now gets underway, move by move.

10 ♕e3

On 10 0-0-0 possible is 10...b5. Black is not afraid of 11 ♘d5 bxc4 12 ♘xf6+? (the attacking 12 g4 is better) 12...exf6 13 ♗h6 f5! with advantage to Black. Sadler-Nunn, Hastings 1993.

It would now be disadvantageous for Black to play ...e7-e5, since after castling queenside the confrontation of the rook on d1 and the queen on d8 would be in White's favour. But Black has other resources.

10...b5 11 0-0-0 ♘a5 12 ♘f4 ♘h7

The black knights are rather going against the rules, which enjoin them not to stand on the edge of the board. Their decentralization involves some risk, but this is justified by factors that are no less important. Indeed, even in their seemingly awkward positions, the knights are creating threats against enemy units!

13 e5 ♘xg5

Why not 13...f6? Because the bishop would sell its life too dearly: 14 exf6 exf6 15 ♘xg6 fxg5 16 ♘xe7+ ♔f7 17 ♗d3!. I do not have the slightest wish to consider such variations.

14 hxg5 c5

Black has accomplished the deployment of his forces and is ready for hand-to-hand combat in any part of the board. White has no time to waste, since otherwise his combat formation will collapse.

15 dxc5 ♗xe5!

Of course not 15...dxe5 16 ♘fd5!.

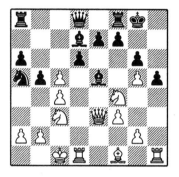

Here Black's position still looks insecure, in view of the possibility 16 g4. How, then, should he defend?

I presented this position to many masters and grandmasters, giving each of them ten attempts. If they found the right move in just one of these attempts I would lose the bet. I can say that none of them managed to find the right solution on the first try. Moves like ...hxg4, ...h4, ...b4 and others caught their eye at once, but these only play into White's hands. When playing 15...♗xe5, I had in mind the far from obvious rejoinder 16 g4 ♖c8!! with the idea of drumming up counterplay against the white king after 17 gxh5 ♖xc5!. All the variations are favourable for Black; all his pieces are participating both in attack and defence. True, his king also gets caught in the crossfire, but he can defend successfully.

I would say that the move 16...♖c8 epitomizes my style. I have been playing like this all my life. Though I sometimes miscalculate and make an aggressive move when the position demands defence or waiting tactics, my decision is justified 80 percent of the time, since it is in accordance with the spirit of chess which proclaims: "Attack!". If we imagine that two generals are playing chess, competing in the depth and precision of their plans, then the general who manages to be more active with fewer forces has the better chances. It is precisely the same as in real combat. The one who defends is in a worse position. That is why the present-day military code calls not for passive defence, but active counter-offence. On the chessboard a model of such counteraction is the move 16...♖c8. I will cite just one variation: 17 gxh5 ♖xc5 18 hxg6 ♘xc4 19 ♗xc4 ♖xc4 20 gxf7+ ♖xf7, with advantage to Black.

16 ♘fd5!

A strong move, which presents Black with fresh problems. f3-f4 is threatened, so that attention must be switched instantly from the flanks to the centre, where major hostilities are about to take place.

16...♖e8?!

This move seems logical, as it repels White's threats, defending the e7-pawn and bringing the rook to the central zone. But it has a defect: it weakens the f7-square, and this, it appears, could have had serious consequences. Therefore 16...♗e6! deserved attention, after which everything would be in order for Black. Maybe the text move is not worse, but this has yet to be proved.

17 g4!

This time the "star" move 17...♖c8 is no good: 18 gxh5 ♖xc5 19 hxg6 ♘xc4 20 ♗xc4 ♖xc4 21 gxf7+ and Black has to capture with the king (not the rook), and tread a dangerous path.

17...hxg4 18 cxd6 exd6

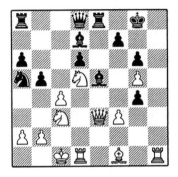

A critical position has arisen, and the result of the game depends on what is decided now. White could play 19 ♘e4! with the threat of check on f6, and what should Black do then?

There is no time for the prophylactic 19...♗f5 in view of 20 ♘df6+ ♗xf6 21 gxf6! with the decisive threat 22 ♖h8+! ♔xh8 23 ♕h6+, and mate next move. Black has other tries at his disposal, it is true —but not very promising: 19...♖c8 20 ♘df6+ ♔g7 21 ♖h7+ ♔f8 22 ♖xd6! ♘xc4 23 ♗xc4 ♖xc4+ 24 ♔b1 ♗xd6 25 ♘xd6!, and White wins. Or 19...♔f8 20 ♘df6 ♕c7 21 ♖h8+ ♔g7 22 ♖h7+ ♔f8 23 f4 ♘xc4 24 ♗xc4 ♕xc4+ 25 ♔b1, and White prevails. Or 19...♖e6 20 ♘df6+ ♖xf6 21 gxf6 ♗xf6 22 ♖xd6 and Black stands badly. 19...♔g7 is not possible because of 20 f4!.

One might suggest other attempts to find defensive resources for Black. But would they bring success?

19 f4?

White follows his projected plan, which turns out to be mistaken.

19...♗g7 20 ♘e4

This is too late now, since the knight does not have pawn support on the e4-square, the bishop solidly defends the king and the rook operates along the e-file. Concealed and highly effective counterplay materializes for Black.

20...♗c6!

The "stock" 20...♖c8 was now also possible. For example, 21 ♘df6+ ♗xf6 22 ♘xf6+ ♕xf6 23 ♕xe8+ ♗xe8 24 gxf6 ♘xc4 25 ♗xc4 ♖xc4+ 26 ♔b1 ♗c6 is to Black's advantage.

21 ♘ef6+ ♔f8

21...♕xf6 was playable straight away, but I had not yet fully worked out this possibility. On the other hand, 21...♗xf6 would fail to 22 ♕xe8+, as if 22...♗xe8 then 23 ♘xf6+ ♕xf6 24 gxf6 ♗c6 25 ♖h2! with a clear advantage to White. And on 23...♔f8 there follows 24 ♖h8+ ♔e7 25 ♖e1 mate!

22 ♘h7+ ♔g8 23 ♘df6+

Forcing Black to make the correct move

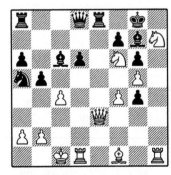

23...♕xf6! 24 ♘xf6+ ♗xf6 25 ♕a3

In this situation 25 ♕b6 warrants consideration, so that after 25...♗d8 this bishop has been deflected from the main thoroughfare. For example: 26 ♕g1 ♗xh1 27 ♕xh1 ♖c8, although even then Black has a comfortable game. But now it is even more comfortable.

25...♗g7 26 ♖h2

26 ♖g1 is possibly better, but would not of course alter the basic evaluation of the position.

26...♘xc4 27 ♗xc4 bxc4 28 ♕g3

Surprisingly, the queen is not in a position to fight successfully against the two bishops and the g-pawn. The whole point is that Black's forces are excellently coordinated—something you cannot say about White's.

28...♗f3 29 ♖xd6

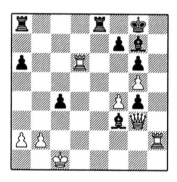

29...c3!

The triumph of Black's strategy. His numerically weaker forces are greatly superior to White's!

30 ♖f6

The "Gufeld bishop" is particularly fearsome: on its own it is worth the enemy queen, so it is not surprising that White hastens to subdue it at any price. However, the white king is now driven into the open, so 30 b4 would have been more stubborn, although Black retains winning chances in that case too.

30...cxb2+ 31 ♖xb2 ♖ed8!

The signal for the mating attack. Naturally, the bishop on g7 disdainfully rejects the offered rook.

32 f5 ♖d1+ 33 ♔c2 ♖c8+ 34 ♔b3 ♖d3+ 35 ♔b4

Of course, if 35 ♔a4 ♗c6+.

35...♗f8+!

To my chagrin, my opponent immediately capitulated, not allowing me to demonstrate the pretty mate on the board: 36 ♔a5 ♖a3+ 37 ♔b6 ♗c5 mate!

0-1

The following game was acknowledged as the best one played in the Hastings international tournament.

Game 16
Mestel *White* **Gufeld** *Black*
Hastings 1986/87

1 c4 g6 2 e4

This kind of trick might just bring a smile to anyone who is an avid King's Indian player.

2...♗g7 3 d4 d6 4 ♘c3 ♘f6 5 f3 0-0 6 ♗g5 ♘c6 7 ♘ge2 a6 8 ♕d2 ♖b8 9 h4

As in similar situations with 6 ♗e3, an early advance 9 d5 is premature. After 9...♘a5 10 ♘d4 c5 11 ♘c2 ♗d7, Black is ready for open hostilities: 12 ♖c1 b5! or 12 ♘a3 e6!. 9...♘e5 has its merits too.

9...h5!

The very case where an exception to the rule applies. Of course the move ...h7-h5 doesn't strengthen the defence of the king, but it does gain valuable time for organizing a counter-offensive.

10 0-0-0

There is no better sanctuary to be found for the white king. The attempt to strengthen the g5-bishop's position by the thrust 10 ♘d5 can be met by the counterstrike 10...b5 11 ♗xf6 exf6 12 cxb5 axb5 13 ♖c1 ♘e7, and Black gains the better play. The retreat 10...♘h7 is also possible, not fearing the exchange 11 ♗h6 ♗xh6 12 ♕xh6 e6 13 ♘e3 b5! and Black again has a successful counterattack, Piket-Nijboer, Groningen 1992.

On 10 ♗h6, Black can play as in the game: 10...b5. In the famous retro-match for the World Championship Spassky-Fischer, S.Stefan/ Belgrade (m/8) 1992, Fischer preferred 10...e5 and after 11 ♗xg7 ♔xg7 12 d5 ♘e7 13 ♘g3! Black ran into difficulties.

10...b5

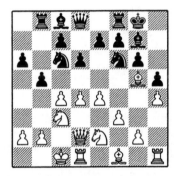

11 ♗h6?!
White's desire to exchange off an important defender is perfectly understandable and fits in with his aggressive plan.

Yet there are two serious objections to this move:

(a) It involves the loss of time. White is exchanging off his bishop in two steps (♗c1-g5 and ♗g5-h6) for a piece which has made just one move (...♗f8-g7). It seems of little importance. But if we compare a chess game 40 moves long with a human life of 80 years, then the loss of one tempo is equivalent to the loss of two years.

(b) It exchanges the "good" bishop for the potentially "bad" one. Botvinnik, in his time, divided all strategic aspects into constant and variable ones, paying more attention to constant factors. Among them is one of the key concepts of chess strategy—the concept of good and bad bishops. When exchanging pieces one should always see the difference in their quality. Let us determine which bishop is better— the one on g5, or the one on g7.

In the endgame it is quite easy to determine how good or bad your bishop is: it is enough to see whether the bishop is on the same colour squares as all or most of its pawns. In the opening or the middlegame the matter is more difficult, and the only true guideline, in my opinion, is the pawn formation in the centre. To be more precise, the deployment of the d- and e-pawns.

Even if one doubted the merits of the g5-bishop (with the pawns on d4 and e4), the g7-bishop (with the pawns on d6 and e7) should certainly be called the "bad" one. Let us recall that in allowing his opponent to occupy the centre, and in playing ...♘b8-c6, Black acknowledged the need to proceed sooner or later with the counterstrike ...e7-e5, which unfortunately would block the path of his own king's bishop.

With the exchange of the bishop this one drawback disappears, so now is the right time for...

11...e5!
With the bishop on g5, here would immediately follow d4-d5. But now after 12 ♗xg7 ♔xg7, the move 13 d5 leaves him uncomfortable, positionally. Above all, White remains with a "bad" bishop on f1 (as his centre pawns are on the light

squares d5 and e4), whereas the bishop on c8 (with pawns on d6 and e5) is perfectly "good." In addition, after 13...♞a5! it appears that White will have to block his own g-pawn with 14 ♞g3, sharply reducing his attacking potential.

We should note, incidentally, that in this kind of position it is highly disadvantageous to reply to d4-d5 by retreating the knight to e7. On this square the knight is restricted by the pawn on e4, and, devoid of any prospects, merely gets under the feet of Black's other pieces, causing havoc in his ranks.

Indeed, in this game something similar happens to the knight on e2.

What should White do, then, if d4-d5 is no good?

12 ♗xg7 ♔xg7 13 dxe5

The only move. On 13 ♞d5 would follow 13...bxc4 with a counterattack, which is even more dangerous because White cannot complete his development. And his bishop is not only "bad" but is "blind" as well: the knight on e2, which is guarding the d4 square, completely obstructs his view.

After all this, the conclusion is that after 11 ♗h6?! e5! Black has a small advantage.

13...dxe5

13...♞xe5 has also been played.

(a) 14 cxb5 axb5 15 ♞f4 b4 (16...c5!? deserved attention) 16 ♞cd5 ♞xd5 17 ♞xd5 c5 18 f4 ♞c6 19 f5 ♞e5 20 g4 and Black comes under attack, Rivas Pastor-Mestel, Marbella (zt) 1982;

(b) 14 ♞d4 b4 15 ♞d5 c5 16 ♞b3 ♞xd5 17 ♕xd5 ♗e6! with equal chances. Solozhenkin-Schmidt, Katowice 1991.

14 ♕g5?!

All in the same spirit of direct aggression—in an inferior position

it is accepted practice to strive for simplification. But Mestel did not play h2-h4, 0-0-0 and ♗g5-h6 to end up fighting for a draw in an inferior endgame with chronically weak dark squares and a bad bishop on f1.

14 ♕e3 ♕e7 15 ♞d5 ♞xd5 16 cxd5 ♞a5 17 ♞c3 is objectively stronger.

14...♕e7

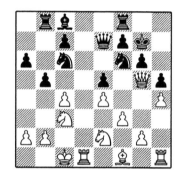

15 ♞d5

This obvious thrust enables Black to seize the initiative.

15 ♞g3 bxc4 was stronger (15...♖e8!?) 16 ♞d5 (on 16 ♗xc4 possible is 16...♕b4 17 ♗b3 ♞d4) 16...♞xd5 17 ♞xh5+ ♔g8 18 exd5 ♕b4 (18...♕xg5 19 hxg5 gxh5 20 dxc6 ♗xc6 21 ♖h5 ±) 19 ♞f6+ ♔g7 20 ♞h5+ and White forces a draw.

The impetuous 15 g4? hxg4 16 h5 would subject him to a "cold shower": 16...♞h7! and if 17 ♕d2, then 17...♕g5, when White's position would collapse.

15...♞xd5 16 exd5?!

A very interesting and debatable move. One must not think that the grandmaster did not consider the more solid 16 cxd5. Mestel saw that in response Black has two promising possibilities:

(a) 16...♕xg5+ 17 hxg5 ♘a5 18 ♘c3 ♘b7 with ...♘b7-d6 to follow, preparing to break with ...c7-c6;

(b) 16...f6 17 ♕d2 ♘d8 followed by ...♘d8-f7, ...♖f8-d8, ...♗c8-d7, ...♖a8-c8 and ...c7-c6. Therefore he gives up the important f5-square, but undertakes a desperate attempt at somehow activating his unfortunate bishop, trusting in the tactical resources of the position.

A gripping duel between the knights now begins. The black knight dreams of getting to d4, while the white knight waits impatiently for his opposite number to leave c6, so that he may at last open the way for the bishop.

16...f6

The only move. In the event of 16...♕xg5+? 17 hxg5, the black knight moves away and the advantage is now with White: he has the e4-point at his disposal, while the e5-pawn, cut off from its base, is left weak.

17 ♕d2

A practically forced reply. After 17 ♕e3? ♘a5! White is not able to coordinate his forces and finds himself subjected to an onslaught. But where does the black knight go now?

17...♖d8!

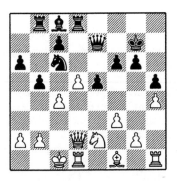

This pin is the *leitmotif* of Black's entire strategy! His knight continues to fight for the key square: if now 18 ♘c3 then 18...♘d4! would follow with great force (and subsequent preparation for ...c7-c6). It turns out that White has no way of completing his kingside development. What is he to do?

Maybe he should move his queen away? But 18 ♕e3 is bad in view of 18...♘a5, and if 18 ♕c2 or 18 ♕c3, then 18...♘b4.

There remains only 18 ♕e1!?

Stop! Here comes the crucial moment of precise calculations. If up to here Black has been guided essentially by general principles, now has come the time to prove the correctness of his play with concrete computations.

And in that case, some kind of unity of theory and practice should appear on the board. As Fischer used to say, the real beauty of the chess game is hidden in the analysis of its variations.

So, 18 ♕e1!? Then of course 18...♘a7 is possible—19 ♘c3 bxc4 20 ♗xc4 ♘b5 with reasonable counterplay. But this is actually too passive. A far more energetic reply is the knight sacrifice 18...♘c5!! It turns out that on 19 dxc6 the underdevelopment of White's kingside lets him down: 19...♕e3+ 20 ♔b1 (20 ♖d2 bxc4, threatening 21...♖xb2 and 21...c3! 22 bxc3 ♗f5 with an unstoppable mate on b1) 20...bxc3 (probably 20...♗f5+ 21 ♔a1 bxc3 leads to the same thing) 21 ♔a1 (21 ♘g3 is met by 21...♕a3! while if 21 ♘xc3 then 21...♖xd1+ 22 ♕xd1 ♕xc3 is decisive. 21 ♖xd8 is met by 21...♗f5+ 22 ♔a1 ♖xd8 and White is helpless) 21...♗f5 22 ♘g3 ♖xd1+ 23 ♕xd1

🖾d8 24 ♘xf5+ gxf5 25 ♕b1 c3 26 ♗xa6 (if 26 b3 then 26...c2 27 ♕xc2 ♕e1+) 26...🖾d2 27 ♕g1 (also on 27 b3 ♕d4 28 ♕g1 ♕b4 White is defenceless) 27...cxb2+ 28 ♔b1 ♕c3, and Black wins.

So the knight cannot be taken, but it would also be disastrous to play 19 ♘c3 ♘d4! 20 ♘e4, since the knight on d4 is more secure than its White counterpart (in addition to being situated in the enemy's camp!). This being the case, White has to do something urgently.

18 g4!

Mestel also heeds the principle "the best defence is counterattack." The text move flows logically from all of White's previous play, and of course I was now expecting it.

Two or three more moves (g4xh5, 🖾h1-g1, etc.) and Black's position would collapse (these are the long-term consequences of the move ...h7-h5!).

18...bxc4!

I never let the initiative slip for the sake of material gains. Moreover, it seemed to me during the game that 18...hxg4 simply loses to 19 h5 g5 20 ♕c2?! (a double attack) 21 ♘g3.

Admittedly, I later ascertained that after 21...♘d4! 22 ♕g6+ ♔h8 the white h-pawn shields the black

king, and there is nothing more to fear.

On 18...hxg4 I was also troubled by 19 fxg4 (with the threat of 20 g5 and h4-h5) 19...♗xg4 20 ♗h3, but this is refuted by 20...♗xh3 21 🖾xh3 ♕c5!. Also dangerous-looking is 20 🖾g1 f5 21 ♕e3! ♘a5 22 ♘d4 🖾b6! 23 🖾e1 ♘xc4 24 ♗xc4 bxc4 25 ♘e6+ with an attack, but 23...🖾e8! is stronger here.

Nonetheless, extensive analysis has established that my intuition—which is fundamental to chess art—did not let me down. In this last line, instead of 22 ♘d4, White has the much more unpleasant 22 ♘f4!, aiming to use the c-pawn as a battering ram. Inadequate replies are 22...♗xd1 23 🖾xg6+ ♔h7 24 🖾e1 ♕xh4 (if 24...♕f7, then 25 ♕xe5 🖾e8 26 ♗d3) 25 ♕xe5, then 22...♘xc4 23 ♗xc4 bxc4 24 ♘e6+ ♔h7 25 ♕xe5 🖾e8 26 🖾xg4! fxg4 27 h5—in both cases with an irresistible attack.

There remains 22...🖾b6, but then 23 c5! 🖾f6 24 🖾e1 🖾e8 25 h5 g5, and White has the choice between the simple 26 ♘h3 and the more vigorous 26 🖾xg4 fxg4 27 ♘e6+ 🖾xe6 28 dxe6 ♕xe6 29 ♕xg5+ ♔h8 30 ♗d3—and in either case Black's position is beyond salvation.

Possibly some defensive players would have taken on g4 all the same, in the hope of repelling the opponent's numerous threats and realizing his material advantage. One must always trust in one's own intuition, however, and I felt there is something not right there! Imagine that you are receiving the serve in tennis. The ball is flying high and seems to be going out of court—but what if it doesn't? Overcoming your doubts, you take the game firmly into your own hands with a power-ful stroke (18...bxc4!).

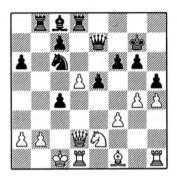

19 ♘c3

The counter-blow 19 gxh5 de-manded delicate calculation. In re-ply I had planned 19...♘b4 (with the threat of 20...♘d3+) 20 ♘c3 ♗f5 21 ♗xc4 (21 hxg6 is not possi-ble due to 21...♖xd5 22 ♘xd5? ♘xa2 mate!) 21...♕c5.

How should White continue now? In the event of 22 ♕e2 ♗d3! 23 ♗xd3 ♘xa2+ 24 ♔c2 ♖xb2+! 25 ♔xb2 ♕xc3+ 26 ♔xa2 ♖b8 27 ♗b5 (if 27 ♕d2, then 27...♕b3+ 28 ♔a1 ♕a3+ 29 ♕a2 ♕c3+) 27... ♕a5+ 28 ♔b3 ♖xb5+ 29 ♕xb5 ♕xb5+ and 30...gxh5, Black obtains a winning endgame.

And what if 22 b3!?. I couldn't sleep for a month thinking about this move: it is clear that Black stands well, but where is the win? I worried and fretted, but believed that, as in a good algebra problem, everything must work out, since once you have found the main solu-tion, the side-lines should also be-come clear. When I woke up one morning, having looked at the posi-tion who knows how many times, I couldn't believe my eyes: it turned out that there is the quite simple move 22...♘xd5!!. If now 23 ♘xd5, then 23...♕xc4+! (24 bxc4 ♖b1

mate), and if 23 ♗xd5 then 23...♖xd5 leads to victory. In the event of 23 ♘e4 general exchanges take place: 23...♖xe4 24 fxe4 ♘e3 25 ♕xd8 ♖xd8 26 ♖xd8 ♘xc4 27 bxc4 ♕xc4+ 28 ♔b2 ♕xe4 29 ♖g1 ♕e2+ and 30...♕xh5 with a win-ning endgame for Black.

My happiness was short-lived: I then and there changed the move 22 b3 to 22 ♗b3 and sank into deep thought...for two more months! It became clear that after 22 ♗b3 ♘d3+ 23 ♔b1, not one discovered check wins. There are many tempt-ing combinations, but nothing better than perpetual check is to be found. For example: 23...♖xb3 (23...♘f2+ 24 ♗c2!) 24 axb3 ♘b4+ 25 ♔a1 ♕a5+ 26 ♘a4 ♘c2+ etc.

You can imagine how happy I was when I discovered the devastat-ing force of the "quiet" move 22...a5!!. This threatens 23...a4 24 ♗xa4 ♘xa2 mate, the only defence being 23 ♕e2 a4 24 ♗c4. Now, 24...♗d3!! This is similar to the combination in the variation with 22 ♕e2, but on a different theme: there Black used the a5 square and the a-file, here he uses the rook's pawn, which has become charged with en-ergy, as a kind of battering ram. Af-ter 25 ♗xd3 ♘xa2+ 26 ♔c2 a3! (but 26...♖xb2+? 27 ♔xb2 ♕xc3+ 28 ♔xa2 ♖b8 does not work on ac-count of 29 ♖b1!) 27 ♖b1 ♖xb2+! 28 ♖xb2 ♕xc3+ 29 ♔b1 axb2 30 ♕c2 ♖b8, White's position is com-pletely hopeless, and he can resign with a clear conscience.

These later discoveries brought me great creative satisfaction, since I value the merits of artistic achieve-ment above everything else in chess. However, let us return to the game. Mestel's move 19 ♘c3 also de-mands the most precise calculation.

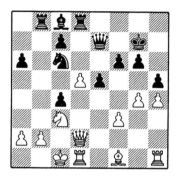

19...hxg4!

Many magazines in which this game was published considered the transposition 19...♘d4 to be playable. In fact, though, White has the remarkable reply 20 ♕g2!, changing the whole complexion of the battle. So 19...hxg4! is the only acceptable solution.

20 ♗xc4

Most serious attention had to be given to 20 h5!? g5 21 ♕c2, which has the dual threat of capturing on c6 and paying an unwelcome visit to the black king's mansion. But 21...♘d4! 22 ♕g6+ ♔f8 23 d6 (23 ♗xc4 ♕g7!) 23...cxd6 24 h6 (if 24 ♖xd4 exd4 25 ♗xc4, then 25...♕g7) 24... ♗f5 25 h7 (the only chance) 25...♗xg6 26 h8=♕+ ♔f7 27 ♗xc4+ d5 28 ♗xd5+ ♖xd5! 29 ♕xb8 ♘e2+! 30 ♘xe2 ♕c5+ 31 ♘c3 ♕e3+, and mate next move. This whole variation had to be calculated when playing 19...hxg4!, because if there were no mate, Black would have to resign.

After 20 ♗xc4 White's attack abates sharply, and his position collapses like a house of cards.

20...♘d4

The knight's dream comes true. It invades the central square with decisive effect.

21 fxg4 ♗xg4 22 ♖df1 ♖b4! 23 h5

A desperate attempt to complicate Black's task. Both 23 b3 ♖xc4 24 bxc4 ♖b8, and 23 ♗xa6 ♖db8 24 b3 ♖xb3 are hopeless.

23...♖xc4 24 hxg6 ♖xc3+! 25 ♕xc3

On 25 bxc3 Black wins with 25...♕a3+ 26 ♕b2 (or 26 ♔b1 ♖b8+ 27 ♔a1 ♘b3+) 26...♘e2+ 27 ♔c2 ♕xb2+ 28 ♔xb2 ♘g3.

25...♘e2+ 26 ♔c2 ♘xc3 27 ♖h7+ ♔xg6 0-1

White resigned. After 28 ♖xe7 ♘xd5 his rook is trapped.

Game 17
Kovikov *White* **Smirin** *Black*
Las Vegas 1999

1 d4 ♘f6 2 c4 g6 3 ♘c3 ♗g7 4 e4 d6 5 f3 0-0 6 ♗g5 ♘c6 7 ♘ge2 a6 8 ♕d2 ♖b8

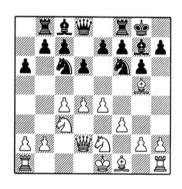

9 d5

As so often happens in similar positions an early advance 9 d5 enables Black to "latch on" to the d-pawn and thereby develop counterplay.

From this point of view 9 ♖c1 ♗d7 10 d5 is more clever:

(a) 10...♘e5 11 b3 b5 (11...♘h5 is weaker 12 ♘g3! f5 13 ♘xh5 gxh5 14 ♗e2 ♘g6 15 exf5 ♗xf5 16 0-0 ♕d7 17 ♘e4 h4 18 ♗d3 and the control over the e4 square secures White a solid advantage, Dreev-Mukhutdinov, St Petersburg 1993) 12 f4!? (on 12 cxb5 axb5 13 ♘d4 Black undermines White's foundations in the centre: 13...♕e8 14 f4 c5) 12...♘eg4 13 ♘g3 h6 14 ♗h4 ♘h7 (Dreev-Golubev, Alusta 1994) 15 ♗e2 ±.

(b) 10...♘a5 (in this position, the knight is more stable here than on e5) 11 ♘d4 c5 12 dxc6 (after 12 ♘c2 b5 arises a position considered in the next note) 12...bxc6 13 b3 c5 (13...♘b7 14 ♗e2 ♘c5 15 0-0 a5 is also interesting) 14 ♘c2 ♘c6 15 ♗e2 ♘e8 (with the idea of ...♘e8-c7-e6-d4) 16 ♘d5 f6 17 ♗h4 e6 18 ♘de3 ♗h6 19 0-0 e5 20 ♗g3 ♘d4 and Black gained some advantage. Tegshsuren-Gufeld, Los Angeles 1998

9 h4 h5 is examined in the previous game Mestel-Gufeld, Hastings 1986/87.

9...♘e5
The choice of which route to take for the knight is a matter of taste, but the text is a favourite continuation of that staunch supporter of the King's Indian, I.Smirin. I am more accustomed to 9...♘a5 and if 10 ♘d4 then, of course 10...c5 11 ♘c2 ♗d7. Now if 12 ♘a3 then 12...e6! is strong, and in case of 12 ♖c1 b5 Black's pieces on the queenside are already in place. This was shown by the game Yusupov-Kovalev, Germany 1992, which continued: 13 b3 bxc4 14 bxc4 ♗c8 (he could have consolidated his grip on the b-file by playing 14...♖b2 followed by ...♕d8-c7 and ...♖f8-b8) 15 ♗h6

♗xh6 16 ♕xh6 e5!. The game is equal.

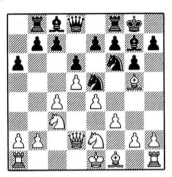

10 ♘g3
An alternative is 10 ♘d4 c5 11 ♘c2 when again the knight is less stable on e5 than on a5, since now on 11...e6 or 11...♗d7 possible is 12 f4. In the game Dreev-Smirin, Biel (izt) 1993, Black launched a flank attack, not afraid to sacrifice: 11...b5 12 cxb5 axb5 13 ♗xb5 ♖xb5 14 ♘xb5 ♘c4 15 ♕e2! ♕a5+ 16 ♔f2 ♘xb2 (16...♕xb5 17 b3 ±) 17 a4!, but did not gain sufficient compensation.

This idea was carried out more successfully in the game Meulders-Kovalev, Belgium 1992: 11...♘e8 12 ♗e2 b5 13 cxb5 axb5 14 ♘xb5 ♘c7 15 a4 f5! 16 0-0 ♘f7 (now the bishop on g7 gets into play, which doubles the effectiveness of the break ...f7-f5) 17 ♗h4 ♘xb5 18 axb5 fxe4 19 fxe4 ♗xb2 20 ♖a7 ♗d7 and a position was reached with equal chances.

10...c6 11 ♗e2 b5
This typical pawn sacrifice, known to any true supporter of the King's Indian, scarcely needs endorsing with an exclamation mark.

12 cxb5 cxd5 13 exd5
There is no need to exchange the bishop, even it is for the sake of

consolidating the position of the knight on d5. 13 ♗xf6 ♗xf6 14 ♘xd5 ♗g7 15 a4 axb5 16 axb5 ♗d7, obviously with good play for Black. Sadler-Vogt, Altensteig 1992.

13...axb5 14 ♘xb5 ♗b7 15 ♗xf6?!

A strange decision. White not only presents Black with the advantage of the two bishops "free of charge", but also dooms himself to the problem of defending the dark squares in his own camp. More natural was 15 ♘c3, in reply to which Smirin was going to play 15...♗a8, parrying 16 0-0? because of 16...♕b6+.

15...exf6!

Apparently White only reckoned on 15...♗xf6 16 ♘e4 ♗g7 17 0-0.

16 f4 ♘d7 17 f5

Practically forced, since Black also intended ...f6-f5.

17...♕b6

Black has an obvious advantage and White faces problems associated with the exchange of his dark-squared bishop: kingside castling is a long way off, while 18 0-0-0? is prohibited due to 18...♗a6 19 ♘c3 ♗h6!.

18 ♘e4 ♗a6 19 ♘bxd6 ♘e5

It would be a bad deal to take the b2 pawn, allowing simplification. So, for the time being, Black activates his knight and prepares to exert pressure on the d-file.

20 b3

The benefits of the manoeuvre 19...♘e5 are illustrated by the following variation: 20 a4 ♗xe2 21 ♕xe2 ♕a5+ 22 ♕d2 ♘d3+ or 22 ♘c3 ♖xb2!.

20...♖fd8 21 ♘c4?

The delay in castling results in material losses. As pointed out by Smirin, it was necessary to simplify by 21 ♗xa6 ♕xa6 22 ♕e2! (22 ♖d1 ♗f8!) 22...♖xd6 23 ♘xd6 ♕xd6 24 0-0 ♕xd5, when he still has hopes of saving the game.

21...♘xc4 22 bxc4 ♖e8 23 c5 ♕a7 24 0-0

Castling costs a knight. Nor does 24 ♕d4 help, because of 24...♗xe2 25 ♔xe2 gxf5.

24...♖xe4 25 ♗xa6 ♕xa6 26 ♖fe1

After 26 d6 the rooks rush in: 26...♖e2 27 ♕d5 ♖bb2.

26...gxf5 27 ♖ac1 ♕a3!

The passed pawns look strong but soon Black's bishop will spring to life and dispel any illusions White may have had... But first of all he has to reckon with Black's major pieces, which are about to invade White's camp.

28 d6 ♖b2 29 ♕d5 ♖be2! 30 ♖xe2 ♕xc1+ 31 ♔f2 ♕f4+ 32 ♔e1 ♖d4 33 ♕a8+

33 ♕f3 ♕c1+ 34 ♔f2 ♕c5 also loses.

33...♗f8 34 ♕a3 ♕xh2 35 ♕e3 ♖e4 36 ♕f2 ♖f4 37 ♕e3 ♗h6!

The bishop makes an appearance —in all its glory! 38...♕h1+ 39 ♔d2 ♖d4+ is threatened.

38 ♕e8+ ♔g7 39 ♔d1 ♕g1+ 0-1

Classical System

The development **1 d4 ♘f6 2 c4 g6 3 ♘c3 ♗g7 4 e4 d6 5 ♘f3 0-0 6 ♗e2 e5** is called the Classical System. This name is derived from the mode of development of the minor pieces.

White has set up a pawn centre, developed his king flank without any delay, and, after castling kingside, plans active play in the centre and on the queenside.

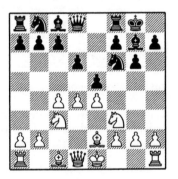

After the capture of the e5 pawn, 7 dxe5 dxe5 8 ♕xd8 ♖xd8 9 ♗g5 (9 ♘xe5 ♘xe4 is not enough) 9....♖e8 10 ♘d5 ♘xd5 11 cxd5 c6 12 ♗c4 cxd5 13 ♗xd5, with accurate play, Black can maintain equality. The most prevalent continuation is **7 0-0 ♘c6** (there is also the "classical" 7...♘bd7).

In my opinion, the development of the knight to c6 in this position, as in many variations of the King's Indian, has a most effective influence over the centre. In particular, the influence over the d4 square forces White to take urgent measures. After the natural 8 d5 ♘e7 we reach the principal position, which occurred for the first time in the game Taimanov-Aronin, 20th USSR Championship, 1952. After this, the variation was called the Taimanov-Aronin System.

It should be noted, that a few decades of practical play with this variation, for which I too have done my bit, has led to the formulation of some kinds of axioms for the youth of today. For example, one of the leading contenders for the chess crown, Vladimir Kramnik, when commenting on one of his games expressed it like this: "I remember a well-known rule: two knights on d7 and f6 are not very mobile—a queen's knight on e7 is much better!".

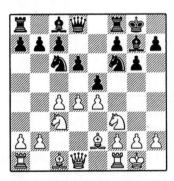

Let us examine the features of this position. The centre is closed and the pawn formation determines the appropriate plans for both sides in the forthcoming struggle. White's chances lie in organizing an attack on the queenside, where developing an initiative is linked to the advance c4-c5 and the opening of the c-file along which he can invade the enemy camp. Black's chances lie in launching an attack on the kingside which usually follows the pawn advance ...f7-f5-f4 followed by ...g6-g5-g4, and, if the opportunity arises, ...g4-g3 as well.

There is a broad spectrum of continuations for White. Apart from the immediate 9 b4, he has preparatory-prophylactic moves such as 9 ♘e1, 9 ♗d2 and 9 ♘d2 at his disposal. I have had to stand up and defend Black in all of these continuations.

Lately, White has tried various ways to counter the Classical System, by anticipating the development of the knight on c6, directly with 7 d5, or indirectly with 7 ♗e3—since after 7...♘c6 8 d5 ♘e7 9 ♘d2 the presence of the bishop on e3 gives White a clear-cut advantage in the forthcoming play with attacks on opposite flanks.

Illustrative Games
Taimanov-Aronin-System

Game 18
Taimanov *White* **Gufeld** *Black*
28th USSR Championship,
Moscow 1961

1 d4 ♘f6 2 c4 g6 3 ♘c3 ♗g7 4 e4 d6 5 ♘f3 0-0 6 ♗e2 e5 7 0-0 ♘c6 8 d5 ♘e7
In the 60s the chess paths of myself and Mark Taimanov frequently crossed and it took a fair amount of audacity, even impudence, to use this variation against him, as in

those days he played it quite masterfully.

Of course I knew Taimanov's games from the USSR Championship 1952, against Aronin and Bronstein, where Taimanov played 9 ♘e1, clearing the f3 square for the pawn and then moving his bishop to e3. But ten years later his priorities were different and I could hardly have challenged him on his own territory if I had not had prepared —with the help of Leonid Stein— one or two new ideas.

9 b4

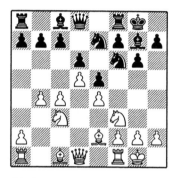

This is the very continuation that was Taimanov's "staple diet." Still fresh in my mind was an interesting game he had played against Gligorić in a tournament at Santa Fe. Of course that game, together with several others, had been thoroughly analyzed by us. We came to the conclusion that in reply to White's rapid pawn offensive on the queenside Black should counter with immediate operations on the opposite wing.

9...♘h5
The main reply for Black. The threat c4-c5 is met by speedy preparation for a counterattack on the kingside. But Black often postpones this plan and instead continues with a prophylactic 9...a5 on the

queenside, reducing the support of the c4 pawn by exchanging its neighbour, which White frequently replaces with the bishop after 10 ♗a3 axb4 11 ♗xb4.

10 g3

Before advancing the c-pawn White parries the knight's thrust to f4, from where it attacks the bishop on e2. Lately, White has often essayed 10 ♖e1, freeing the f1 square for his bishop.

10...f5 11 ♘g5

It is precisely because of this possibility that Black's plan was then considered somewhat risky: the visit of the knight to e6 is scarcely in the "spirit of mutual understanding." Black will have to give up his light-squared bishop for this knight.

Here I should reveal one of my little professional secrets (there is no point in hiding it now). The g7-bishop has for a long time been described as the "Gufeld bishop," and so many of my opponents have instinctively tried to separate me from my friend, even to the detriment of their own position. What they do not know is that I have also made a secret contract with my light-squared bishop, without whose services Black is often in even more trouble in the King's Indian Defence than he is without its renowned colleague.

Maybe it is easier to retreat 11 ♘d2? I hardly think so!

Black would feel much better then. For example, the game Yudovich-Gufeld, Moscow 1966, proceeded 11...♘f6 12 f3 ♗h6! (let someone blame me for callously parting with my beloved one!) 13 ♘b3 ♗xc1 14 ♖xc1 f4 15 g4 g5 16 c5 ♘g6 17 a4 h5 18 h3 ♖f7 19 ♔f2 ♘h4 20 ♕d3 hxg4 21 hxg4 ♗xg4! and Black was ahead in the race for the initiative. Of course more stubborn was 12 c5, but after 12...f4 13 ♘c4 ♗h3 14 ♖e1 ♘c8! Black starts his attack on the king's flank.

11...♘f6 12 f3

The pawn needs some support here, since on 12 exf5 possible is 12...♘xf5! with a transfer of the knight to d4.

12...f4

In the above-mentioned game, Taimanov-Gligorić, after 12...h6 13 ♘e6 ♗xe6 14 dxe6 c6 15 b5!, White seized the initiative on the queenside. Since Stein and I did not see how Black could later have improved, we opted for a different continuation here.

But a long time has passed since then and nowadays, along with the natural text move, 12...c6 and 12...♔h8 are both considered playable.

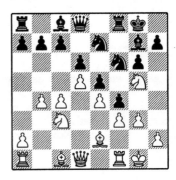

13 b5

Our own experience concurs with the fact that nowadays the prophylactic 13 ♗d2 is more frequently preferred.

But in those days the move b4-b5 looked rather pretty. White hinders ...c7-c6 and develops a queenside offensive. Its drawback, however, is that it does not create any concrete threats, thanks to which Black obtains a tempo in which to organize counterplay. The big question is how effective this counterplay will turn out to be. Before our game it was considered that White had nothing to fear, so Taimanov went into this position full of confidence. If only he had known what an original combination had entered the head of Leonid Stein! But in that case, alas, this fine game would not have occurred.

13...fxg3 14 hxg3 ♘h5

Now how should White defend the g-pawn? It does not seem to matter—say, with 15 ♕e1. In that case, however, 15...c6 16 bxc6 bxc6 is possible, and it is not clear that there is anything better than 17 ♔g2, to make h3 available to the knight, since the invasion of e6 is no longer so clear as it was with the queen on d1.

One thought arises: won't it be easier to move the king to g2 directly? That's the way Taimanov played...

15 ♔g2?

White should after all have played 15 ♕e1, which would have prevented Black's stunning combination. The variation indicated in the preceding note leads to an approximately level game. Now, however, White's position has only a superficial appearance of solidity...

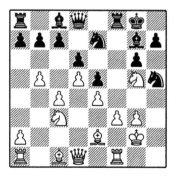

15...♘f4+!!

A textbook example of a purely positional piece sacrifice.

The price of the knight is high: the white king is deprived of its pawn cover and the black pieces spring to life. Stein had no doubt on this score. Nor had I.

16 gxf4 exf4

What is threatened? In the first place, obviously, the capture of the knight on c3. If White defends it, Black's knight on e7 will jump forward. For example: 17 ♗d2 ♘f5! or 17 ♕e1 ♘xd5! Therefore White is practically forced to give up a second pawn in order to free the e4-square for his pieces.

17 e5 ♗xe5 18 ♘ge4 ♘f5

19...♗xc3 20 ♘xc3 ♕g5+ is threatened.

19 ♖g1 ♘g3! 20 ♗d2 ♗xc3 21 ♗xc3 ♘xe4 22 fxe4

22...♕g5+!

An accurate continuation of the attack. It seemed to many during the game, that 22...f3+ was stronger, with the idea of 23 ♗xf3 ♕g5+ 24 ♔f2 ♗g4, and if 25 ♖xg4 ♕xg4 26 ♔e3, then 26...♕f4+ 27 ♔f2 ♖f7 with the decisive threat of 28...♖af8. However, post-mortem analysis quickly established that instead of 25 ♖xg4 White has 25 ♖g3!. Then Black gains nothing by either

25...♗xf3 26 ♖xg5 ♗xd1+ 27 ♔e3, or 25... ♕h4 26 ♔g2!—not to mention 25...♖f7? 26 ♕d4!.

Admittedly, Black does have the favourable continuation: 25...♖xf3+! 26 ♕xf3 ♖f8, emerging with queen and a pawn for two rooks. But the exchanges involved in this line would weaken Black's onslaught.

23 ♔f1 ♗h3+

Quite a rare case of the light-squared bishop instead of the dark-squared one playing the leading role in a King's Indian-type attack.

24 ♔f2 ♕h4+ 25 ♔f3 ♕h5+ 26 ♔f2 ♕h4+

By no means with the intention of giving perpetual check. With time trouble impending it is useful to get nearer the control without spending time deliberating.

27 ♔f3 g5! 28 ♗f1 g4+ 29 ♔e2 f3+ 30 ♔d3 g3 31 ♗xh3 ♕xh3

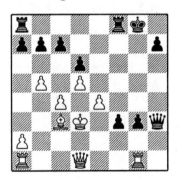

With the forcing play finally over, we can take stock.

White has retained his extra piece, which occupies a highly attractive position on the long diagonal, and his king has escaped the direct threats. All well and good, but how is White to stop his opponent's duo of passed pawns? If he does not create counterplay, he will have to give up a rook for one of these pawns.

32 ♕d2

White creates a threat for the first time in the whole game, but so what? It is hardly a mating attack! Black has to find moves which combine attack with defence.

32...♕g4 33 ♕f2 g2

The passed pawns are now securely blockaded, but a third infantryman is presently coming to help. How does White oppose its march, while the e4-pawn may also come under attack?

34 ♖ae1

He could have tried to regroup by way of 34 ♕d4 ♕g6 35 ♗e1 ♖ae8 36 ♗f2 ♖f4 37 ♖ae1, but then White's pieces would be tied up, with the h-pawn deciding the issue.

34...♖ae8!

There is no need to hurry with the advance of the pawn. It is useful to finish developing first, at the same time preventing any active notions such as e4-e5.

35 ♔c2 ♖f4 36 ♔b3 ♖fxe4 37 ♖xe4 ♖xe4 38 ♕xa7 ♕g6 39 ♕f2 ♕g4

Repeating moves so as to gain time on the clock.

40 ♕a7 ♖e8

The game was adjourned here, with Taimanov sealing his move. Home analysis did not present any special difficulties.

41 ♗e1

Attempting to erect a barrier in front of the pawns, White abandons his king to its fate.

41...♕e4 42 ♗f2 ♕d3+ 43 ♔b4 ♕d2+ 44 ♔b3

Black has more than one road to victory, but he chooses the simplest.

44...b6! 0-1

White must give up a piece for each of the pawns. As you see, the turn of the h-pawn has not even come.

The most sincere heartfelt congratulations that I received for this victory, as you might guess, were from Leonid Stein. For my part, I thanked him for his imaginative contribution, though I lamented the fact that it was only me who had been rewarded. However, it so happened that fate was to balance the scales...

This happened eight years later, at the USSR Team Championship in Grozny. Yes, in the well-known capital of rebellious Chechnia. Today it hardly seems possible, but in those days we were living in the "common family of Nations". I was playing for the Georgian team for the first time, and in the Ukraine-Georgia match I had Black against Stein. Of course I played the King's Indian Defence, and...my game with Taimanov was repeated up until move 13! Here Leonid diverged with **13 c5**, but I dogmatically remained true to the precedent! There followed **13...fxg3 14 hxg3 ♘h5 15 ♕e1** (again a slight difference Stein took into account Taimanov's mistake) **15...♘f4?**

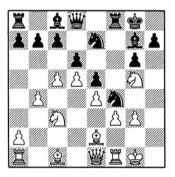

Alas! This sacrifice is not so effective in the present situation, since the knight on c3 is now defended. I should have restricted myself to 15...c6 Now, after **16 gxf4 exf4 17**

♖f2! ♗d4 18 ♔h1 ♘f5 19 exf5 ♕xg5 20 ♖g2 ♕xf5 (more stubborn is 20...♕h6+ 21 ♖h2 ♕g7 22 ♗d2 ♗xf5 with some initiative) **21 ♗d2 ♗d7 22 ♘e4**, White retained both the attack and a material advantage. By the 30th move it was my turn to congratulate Stein. It was as if in this game I involuntarily "showed my gratitude" to Leonid for his help in my win over Taimanov. But in the end, of course, it was opening theory that gained the most, being enriched with two valuable games.

As to an evaluation of an advance 13 c5 Black could have played stronger. For example, simply 13...h6 14 ♘e6 ♗xe6 15 dxe6 d5!.

Game 19
Van Wely *White* **Cvitan** *Black*
Moscow (ol) 1994

1 d4 ♘f6 2 c4 g6 3 ♘c3 ♗g7 4 e4 d6 5 ♘f3 0-0 6 ♗e2 e5 7 0-0 ♘c6 8 d5 ♘e7 9 b4 ♘h5 10 g3 f5 11 ♘g5 ♘f6 12 f3 f4 13 ♔g2

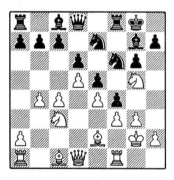

Since it is impossible to do without this move, nowadays players prefer to make it right away.

13...♘h5

Black carries on with his pressure on the king flank. If Black tries to oppose White's plans on the queenside first by 13...a5 14 bxa5 ♖xa5, then the game would have assumed an entirely different character: 15 ♕b3! ♘e8 16 ♗d2 ♖a8 17 c5 ♔h8 18 cxd6 ♘xd6 19 ♘e6 ♗xe6 20 dxe6 ♘c6 21 ♘d5 ♖e8 and Black has a quite stable position, Lobron-Gelfand, Munich 1992

14 c5

To get ahead in the race. But maybe it was worth getting rid of the "headache" ...g3 by 14 g4 and, though linked to a pawn sacrifice, 14...♗f6 15 ♘e6 ♗e6 16 dxe6 ♘g7, after 17 c5 White's initiative offers full compensation. The game Van Wely-Zapata, Matanzas 1995, continued: 17...♔h8 18 cxd6 cxd6 (18...♕xd6 19 ♗c4 ♕b4 20 ♕b3 is weaker) 19 ♘b5 ♘c8 20 ♗c4 ♖e8 21 ♗d5 and here, as was shown by Z.Krnić and S.Velicković, Black could resist by 21...♕e7! 22 ♗b2 a6 23 ♘c3 ♘xe6 24 ♗xe6 ♕xe6 25 ♘d5 ♕f7.

14...fxg3 15 hxg3

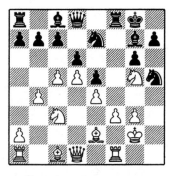

15...♘f4+!

The experience of the previous generation in action! The reader again has spectacular proof of the seriousness of Black's counterplay. In this situation the combination is based on the unprotected state of the knights on c3 and g5.

16 gxf4 exf4 17 ♕e1 ♘f5

As shown by L.van Wely, after 17...♗xc3 18 ♕h4 (18 ♕xc3 is met by 18...♘f5) 18...h5 19 ♗xf4 Black should have evaluated the consequences of capturing the rook on a1 —19...♘xd5 20 ♗c4 ♗xa1 21 ♗xd5+ ♔g7 22 ♖xa1 ♕f6 23 ♗e3 ♕xa1 24 ♕f2 etc. But if Black declines the sacrifice by 19...♗xb4 20 cxd6 cxd6 or 20...♗xd6!? it is not so easy to punch his position.

18 ♗xf4 ♗xc3 19 ♕xc3 ♘h4+

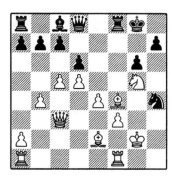

20 ♔f2

The only reply. On 20 ♔g3? would have followed anyway 20...♖xf4! 21 ♔xf4 ♘g2+! 22 ♔g3 ♕xg5+ with an irresistible attack.

20...♖xf4 21 ♘e6 ♗xe6 22 dxe6 ♕e7

The pawn should be blocked, since after the desired 22...♕g5 there could have followed 23 e7 ♕xe7 24 ♗c4+.

23 cxd6 cxd6 24 ♖ac1 ♖af8 25 ♔e1

On 25 ♕c7 Black can play 25...♕f6 threatening the sacrifice 26...♖xf3+.

25...b5!

This move on the side enables Black to take control of the c4 square—with the intention of capturing on e6.

26 ♕b3 ♖4f6 27 ♖c6 ♔g7 28 ♔d2 h5 29 ♕d5 ♖xe6 30 ♕xb5 ♖e5?!

An impetuous move which enables White to create threats against the enemy king and seize the initiative. 30...♘g2, followed by ...♘g2-f4 and ...h5-h4, would have been the logical turn of events.

31 ♕c4

31...♕g5+?

Far too optimistic. 31...d5 suggested itself and, in order to parry 32...dxe4, White has only one move—32 ♕c3.

32 ♔c3 ♘g2 33 ♕d4 ♘f4 34 ♗c4 d5

This move is already too late and leads to the loss of a pawn.

35 ♖g1! ♕e7 36 exd5 ♔h6 37 ♔b3 a5 38 d6 ♕f6 39 ♖c5!

Depriving Black of any last illusions.

39...a4+ 40 ♔xa4 ♖a8+ 41 ♔b3 ♘e6 42 ♕xe5 ♕xf3+ 43 ♔b2 ♕f2+ 44 ♗e2 1-0

Game 20
Henley *White* **Gufeld** *Black*
Tbilisi 1983

1 d4 ♘f6 2 c4 g6 3 ♘c3 ♗g7 4 e4 d6 5 ♗e2 0-0 6 ♘f3 e5 7 0-0 ♘c6 8 d5 ♘e7 9 b4 ♘h5 10 c5

With the present pawn formation, à la Nimzowitsch, White has an inbuilt favourable exchange on the queenside—and his eagerness to make it is quite natural. Moreover the advance of the c-pawn frees the c4 square for the knight. But Black also has the opportunity to transfer his knight to an active position.

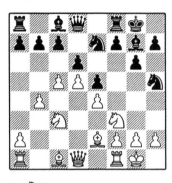

10...♘f4

By attacking the bishop Black forces his opponent to make a decision, which usually results in an exchange of bishop for knight and a transfer of the white knight from f3 to d2 and c4. But if Black is cunning he can make the useful preliminary move 10...h6 and, only after 11 ♘d2, 11...♘f4 12 ♘c4 f5 (after 12...♘xe2+?! 13 ♕xe2 f5 14 f3 f4 15 a4! g5 16 ♗a3 ♖f6 17 b5 ♘g6 18 b6! it is White who takes the lead with his attack on the queenside, M.Gurevich-Gelfand, Belgrade 1991) 13 f3 g5 The race goes on—and Black is still not trailing behind even after 14 ♗e3 ♘eg6 15 cxd6 cxd6 16 ♘b5 ♘h4. The game Tukmakov-Reinderman, Antwerp 1993, proceeded here 14 ♗a3 ♖f6 15 ♖c1 ♖g6 16 ♘b5 g4? 17 fxg4 fxe4 18 ♘e3! and Black's attack already ran out of steam. As was shown by V.Tukmakov, instead of 16...g4? the right way was 16...a6 and the forced variation 17 ♘c7! ♕xc7 18 cxd6 ♖xd6 19 b5 ♖d7! 20

d6 ♕d8 21 dxe7 ♖xd1 22 ♖fxd1! ♘e2+ 23 ♔f2 ♕e8 24 ♖d8 ♗d7 leaves Black with chances for counterplay.

Apparently an immediate 10...f5 is also possible, and playing "à la Taimanov" by 11 ♘g5, is met by 11...♘f4 12 ♗c4 h6! 13 ♘e6 ♗xe6 14 dxe6 fxe4 15 g3 ♘h5 16 ♗e3 ♘f6 with nice play for Black.

11 ♗xf4

If he turns down the exchange of this bishop 11 ♗c4 he has to reckon with 11...♗g4 12 h3 ♗h5 13 ♖e1 g5 14 ♗f1 and after 14...g4 or 14...f5 Black has a good chances on the kingside. But now the black bishop comes to life, which is to the liking to every King's Indian fan.

11...exf4 12 ♖c1

White frees his rook from the pin, intending to utilise it on the c-file. In the event of 12 ♕d2 Black can exchange the knight on f3: 12....♗g4 13 ♖ac1 ♗xf3 14 ♗xf3 g5 followed by 15...♘g6 and Black obtains formidable chances on the kingside. Black can carry out the same manoeuvre also after 12 ♕b3.

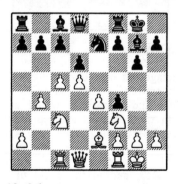

12...h6

Black prepares an attack on the kingside. The break 12...a5 13 a3 is also useful (in the game Kamsky-Kasparov, New York 1994, White sacrificed a pawn: 13 ♘b5 axb4 14 cxd6 cxd6 15 ♕d2 ♗g4! 16 ♖c7 ♗xf3 17 ♗xf3 ♗e5 18 ♖xb7 ♕a5 19 ♘d4 ♕xa2 20 ♕xa2 ♖xa2 21 ♖b4 and the game transposed to an approximately level endgame) 13...axb4 14 axb4 f5 (sometimes Black protects the f4 pawn—14...h6 15 ♘d4 g5 16 ♗h5 c6! with complex play, Beliavsky-Spasov, Manila (ol) 1992, but 15 ♕d2 g5 16 ♖a1! with an initiative on the queenside looks more logical) 15 ♖e1 ♗xc3 16 ♖xc3 fxe4 17 ♘g5 f3 18 gxf3 exf3 19 ♗xf3 ♘f5 with an equal game, Tukmakov-Smirin, Burgas 1993

13 a4

a4-a5 is foreshadowed. Another possibility would be to transfer the knight by means of 13 ♘d2 g5 14 ♘c4 (after 14 ♗h5 c6 15 ♘b3 cxd5?! 16 exd5 a5 17 ♘b5 a4 18 ♘a5 in the game Beliavsky-Romero Holmes, Leon 1994, White achieved an advantage, but 15...dxc5 16 bxc5 cxd5 17 exd5 ♗xc3 18 ♖xc3 ♕xd5 was stronger, though in fact, here too, White has compensation for the pawn) 14...a6 15 ♘a4 ♘g6 (with the idea of ...♘g6-e5) 16 cxd6 cxd6 17 ♘ab6 ♖b8 18 ♗g4 and White's position is preferable.

13...g5 14 h3 ♘g6 15 cxd6

15 a5 ♖e8 16 ♘d2 is weaker because of 16...♗xc3! (premature is 16...♘e5 17 cxd6 cxd6 18 ♘b5! to White's advantage) 17 ♖xc3 ♕f6 18 ♕c2 ♘e5 19 ♖e1 ♔g7 20 ♕d1 with approximately level play. Malich-Bukić, Vrnjacka Banja 1972. On 15 ♘b5 possible is 15...a6 16 ♘bd4 ♖e8 17 ♖c4 ♖xe4 18 ♘e6 ♖xe6 19 dxe6 ♗xe6 20 ♖c1 d5 with compensation for the exchange (S.Cvetković).

15...cxd6 16 ♘b5 ♘e5 17 ♘fd4

The exchange of knights is in Black's favour, since after 17 ♘xe5

♗xe5 he is all set to storm the enemy king's fortress.

17...♕f6 18 ♗h5

An interesting idea. White does not allow the queen on to the important post g6.

18...♗d7 19 ♕b3 a6

19...♔h8 is worth considering.

20 ♘c7 ♖ab8

On 20...♖ac8 White would have the interesting possibility 21 ♘de6!?.

21 ♖fd1

The two knights are good when in contact with one another, but now the one on d4 has lost the support of its colleague and, for this reason, a direct queenside assault fails. For example: 21 b5 ♘d3!?, and if the flashy 21 ♘de6, simplest would be 21...♖fc8 22 ♘xg7 ♔xg7 with a level game.

21...♔h8 22 b5 g4! 23 hxg4 ♘xg4

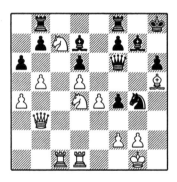

It is evident to the naked eye that, with play on both wings, when it comes to creating threats Black is ahead of his opponent. Thus, on 24 ♘ce6 he has the strong 24...♘xf2!; equally after 24 ♘de6 ♘xf2! 25 ♘xf8 ♖xf8 Black has the initiative.

24 ♘f3 ♖g8

Attempting to win the bishop does not work: 24...♕e7 (intending

25...♘f6) 25 ♘e6! ♘f6 26 ♘xf8 ♖xf8 27 bxa6 bxa6 28 ♖c7 ♘xh5 29 ♕b7 ♘f6 30 ♖e1 and White's position is preferable. On the other hand 24...♘e5 was possible.

25 ♘e6!

The only move in what is now a difficult situation.

25...♘xf2 26 ♔xf2 fxe6 27 ♖c7!

Again the best decision. On 27 ♗g4 there is the strong 27...exd5! 28 ♗xd7 dxe4.

27...♗e8 28 ♗xe8 ♖bxe8 29 dxe6

Events now made a kaleidoskopic impression due to severe time-trouble.

29...♖xe6 30 ♕d3 axb5 31 axb5 ♕g6 32 ♘h4

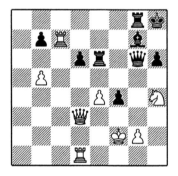

32...♕g4?

Black has achieved a marked advantage but now begins to play at "give-away." After 32...♕h5 33 ♘f5 ♖g6 a position would arise with nice combinational possibilities: 34 ♕f3 ♕h2!. Now there is the threat of 35...♖xg2+ 36 ♕xg2 ♗d4+. On 35 ♖g1 there follows 35...♖g3, and in the event of 35 ♖xg7 ♖8xg7 36 ♘xg7 the winning move is 36...♖g3!. Now let us examine 34 ♘e7. 34...♖g3 35 ♕d5 is followed by 35...♖xg2+ 36 ♔xg2 ♕e2+ 37 ♔h1 ♕f3+ 38 ♔h2 ♕g3+ 39 ♔h1 ♕h3+ 40 ♔g1 ♗d4 mate.

Instead of 35 ♕d5 a cleverer try is 35 ♕c4. A draw is achieved by 35...♖xg2+ 36 ♔xg2 ♕g4+ 37 ♔f2 ♕g3+ 38 ♔e2 ♕e3+ 39 ♔f1 ♕f3+ 40 ♔e1 ♕e3+ 41 ♔f1 (but not 41 ♕e2?? ♗c3+ and 42 ♖g1 mate). But there is an excellent move which leads to victory: 35...d5!! For example: 36 ♕xd5 ♖xg2+; 36 ♘xd5 ♖xg2+ 37 ♔xg2 ♗d4+, or 36 ♖xd5 ♕h1. The only sequel after 32...♕h5 33 ♘f5 ♖g6 is 34 ♖xg7 ♖8xg7 35 ♘xg7 ♔xg7, and Black is a pawn up.

Now a circus gets under way which requires no commentary.

33 ♘f5 ♗f6? 34 ♕f3 ♗h4+? 35 ♔f1 ♖xe4? 36 ♘xh4 ♕xh4 37 ♕xe4 ♕h1+ 38 ♔f2 ♕h4+ 39 ♔g1 f3! 40 ♕h7 mate.

Game 21
A.Schneider *White* **Gufeld** *Black*
Helsinki 1992

1 d4 ♘f6 2 c4 g6 3 ♘c3 ♗g7 4 e4 d6 5 ♘f3 0-0 6 ♗e2 e5 7 0-0 ♘c6 8 d5 ♘e7 9 b4 ♘h5 10 c5 ♘f4 11 ♗xf4 exf4 12 ♕b3

A rather rare continuation. White gives his rooks time to choose a square.

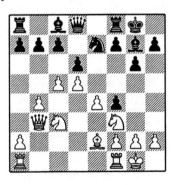

12...♗g4

It is considered important to exchange this knight, which will otherwise head for c4. But 12...h6 13 ♖ad1 g5 is also possible. In the game Stickler-Uhlmann, Germany 1992, White tried to break through the centre: 14 e5 ♘f5 (in the event of 14...dxe5 one has to consider the pawn sacrifice 15 d6!? ♘f5 16 dxc7 ♕xc7 17 h3 ♗e6 18 ♗c4 ♗xc4 19 ♕xc4 and White gains control over the central squares) 15 exd6 cxd6 16 h3 h5 17 ♘h2 ♘d4 and Black obtains good play.

13 ♖ad1 ♗xf3! 14 ♗xf3 g5 15 ♗h5 ♘g6 16 ♗xg6 hxg6

After the exchange of three sets of minor pieces the advantage of the "King's Indian" bishop over the knight leaves the position in Black's favour, though the limited amount of remaining material allows White to defend himself.

17 ♘b5 ♖e8 18 ♖fe1 a6

I should not have pushed the knight to a better position. 18...g4 is more accurate.

19 ♘a3! g4 20 ♘c4 ♗e5 21 f3 ♕h4 22 fxg4 ♕xg4

The impulsive 22...f3? 23 ♕xf3 ♗xh2+ 24 ♔f1 favours White.

23 ♖f1 ♖e7

23...♔g7!?, aiming at the h-pawn by ...♖a8-h8, is worth considering.

24 ♕f3 ♕xf3

After the avoidance of the exchange 24...♕g5?! one has to reckon with 25 cxd6 cxd6 26 ♘xe5 dxe5 (26...♕xe5 27 ♕xf4) 27 ♖c1.

25 gxf3 ♔g7 26 ♔g2 ♖h8 27 ♖f2

The thrust 27 ♘a5 is parried by 27...♗c3!.

27...♖h5 28 ♖c2

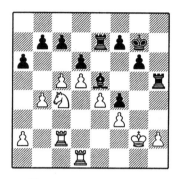

28...Ⓡe8

Sometimes it's a fine line between "better" and "worse". If Black is too slow, White manages to open up the position and immediately exploit the c-file. More active is 28...♔f6!? 29 cxd6 cxd6 30 ♘b6 g5, intending to open the g-file.

29 ♔h1 Ⓡeh8 30 ♘xe5 Ⓡxe5 31 cxd6 cxd6 32 Ⓡc7 Ⓡeh5 33 Ⓡd2 ♔f6!

Black has to be vigilant. In the event of direct play against the f3-pawn he would have lost the pawns on b7 and a6: 33...Ⓡh3 34 Ⓡf2 Ⓡg3 35 Ⓡxb7 Ⓡhh3 36 Ⓡb6 Ⓡxf3 37 Ⓡxf3 Ⓡxf3 38 Ⓡxa6.

34 Ⓡxb7 Ⓡh3 35 Ⓡf2 g5! 36 ♔g1

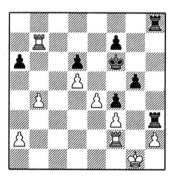

When it comes to attacking the weak pawns the black king becomes a really powerful piece. For instance 36 Ⓡd7 ♔e5 37 Ⓡxf7 ♔d4 or 36 Ⓡb6 ♔e5 37 Ⓡxa6 g4. However, even now the black monarch reveals his ambitions by sending forward his brave infantry.

36...g4! 37 fxg4 f3 38 Ⓡc7

The rook lends a hand in the defence and both sides are happy with a peaceful outcome.

38...Ⓡ8h4 39 g5+! ♔g6! 40 Ⓡc3 Ⓡf4 41 a4 ♔xg5 42 b5 axb5 43 axb5 Ⓡxe4 44 Ⓡcxf3 ½-½

Game 22
Kramnik *White* **Kasparov** *Black*
Novgorod 1997

1 ♘f3 ♘f6 2 c4 g6 3 ♘c3 ♗g7 4 e4 d6 5 d4 0-0 6 ♗e2 e5 7 0-0 ♘c6 8 d5 ♘e7 9 b4 ♘h5 10 Ⓡe1

This continuation, which somehow acknowledges the sufficiency of Black's counterplay after 10 g3, has lately became popular. The rook frees a place for the bishop and g2-g3 is postponed until an appropriate moment.

10...♘f4 11 ♗f1

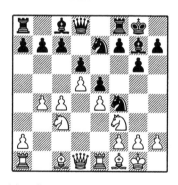

11...a5

Modern methods of development in typical King's Indian positions are not confined to straightforward attacks, dictated by the peculiarities of the pawn formation. Before starting an offensive on the kingside, Black often reinforces as much as he can—with a bridgehead of pawns—his position on the queen-side where White's forces are poised to attack. That's exactly the aim of the text advance, which at the same time gets the rook into play.

Regarding the characteristics of positions like this, with the knight on f4, those players who like immediate play on the kingside have to reckon not only with the advance c4-c5, but also with a possible exchange of the knight in association with the break e4-e5.

All these factors come into play after the programmed 11...f5 12 ♗xf4 exf4 13 e5 dxe5 14 ♘xe5 when after ♕d1-d2 and ♖a1-d1 White clenches his "fist" of major pieces along the central files. Therefore it is preferable to protect the knight on f4 first, starting with 11...h6 12 c5 (also the preliminary 12 ♘d2 and now 12...f5 13 c5 g5 leads only to a transposition of moves; if he switches play to the queenside by 12...a5 13 bxa5 ♖xa5 the knight appears at the right place at the right time: 14 ♘b3 ♖a8 15 c5 f5 16 cxd6 cxd6 17 ♘d2! g5 18 ♖b1 g4 19 ♕b3 ±, Karpov-Kamsky, Elista (m/7) 1996) 12...g5 13 ♘d2 f5 14 g3! ♘fg6 15 a4. Here, in the game Anand-Almasi, Groningen (m/2) 1997, after the optimistic 15...♘c4 Black landed in a difficult position. As was shown by V.Anand, 15...fxe4 16 ♘dxe4 ♘f5 is stronger, though here too, after supporting his knight on e4 by 17 ♗g2, White stands better.

12 bxa5 ♖xa5 13 ♘d2

On 13 a4, the text move 13...c5 is possible since after 14 ♖a3 ♖a6 15 ♘b5 ♗d7 Black has a stable position; more active is 14 ♖b1 h6 15 ♘d2 ♖a6 16 ♘b3 g5 17 a5 f5 18 g3 ♘gf6 19 exf5 ± I.Sokolov-Glek,

Wijk aan Zee 1997. An immediate 13...f5 14 ♖a3 is not bad (Spasov also recommends 14 ♘d2!? g5 15 g3! ♘fg6 16 exf5 ♘xf5 17 ♘de4 ±) 14...h6 15 exf5 ♘xf5 16 ♘e4 g5 17 g3 ♘g6 with chances for both sides, Bareev-Spasov, Elista (ol) 1998.

13...c5 14 a4 ♖a6 15 ♖a3

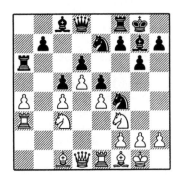

15...g5

The world champion sacrifices a pawn, counting on being able to exploit the weakening of the light squares in the enemy's camp. After a preliminary 15...h6 16 ♘b5 g5 (in the game Topalov-Nijboer, Wijk aan Zee 1998, was played the weaker 16...♗d7 17 g3 ♘h5 18 ♗b2 ±) 17 g3 ♘fg6 18 ♗e2 f5 19 exf5, White has a minimal advantage. It is now Black who has to reckon with the weakening of the light squares in his camp.

16 g3

A crucial decision—V.Kramnik accepts the challenge. But in his annotations to the text move, he also recommends 16 ♘b5. Now if 16...g4?! already good is 17 g3 ♘h3+ 18 ♗xh3 gxh3 19 f4, opening the game in his favour. But Black, of course, could play 16...h6 or even 16...f5.

16...♘h3+ 17 ♗xh3 ♗xh3 18 ♕h5 ♕d7

Cutting off the bishop by 18...g4? would be a mistake if only because of 19 ♘f3 with the idea of ♘f3-h4-f5.

19 ♕xg5

An attempt to capture the bishop by 19 f3 g4 20 ♘d1 was rejected by V.Kramnik because of possible active counterplay by 20...f5! 21 ♘f2 (21 ♘e3? gxf3! 22 ♕xh3 f2+! is no good) 22...♖xa4.

19...h6

It seems that an immediate 19...f5 is also possible.

20 ♕e3 f5 21 ♕e2 f4

The attempt to gain a foothold on d4 for the knight after 21...fxe4 22 ♘dxe4 ♘f5 leads only to its exchange—23 ♘b5! ♘d4 24 ♘xd4 exd4 25 ♕h5 ♗g4 26 ♕h4 and White's pieces quickly become active. (V.Kramnik).

22 ♘b5 ♔h7

This allows White to open up the g-file favourably. Later on it turns out that he attacks on that side of the board which traditionally is Black's hunting ground.

Therefore more accurate is 22...♘g6 (protecting the f4 pawn with the knight), on which V.Kramnik planned 23 ♔h1 ♔h7 24 ♖g1.

23 gxf4 exf4

This is stronger than 23...♖xf4, since at least the dark-squared bishop comes to life.

24 ♔h1 ♗g4 25 ♘f3!

Better than allowing the pin after 25 f3 ♗h5 when the white rooks' prospects are considerably reduced.

25...♘g6 26 ♖g1

Indirectly protecting himself against the pin in view of the possible 27 ♘g5+.

26...♗xf3+?

This exchange to gain permanent control of the e5 square gives White

a free hand since his major pieces can start an assault on the enemy king. The threat of check on g5 could be avoided by the prophylactic 26...♔h8!, so that on 27 ♗b2 possible is 27...♖g8 or even 27...♗xb2 28 ♕xb2+ ♔h7 and White still has to take care of his knight on f3.

27 ♕xf3 ♘e5 28 ♕h5 ♕f7

Black certainly cannot take the pawn and allow White's major pieces to attack his king along the open files—28...♘xc4 29 ♕g6+ ♔g8 30 ♖h3.

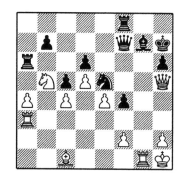

29 ♕h3!

All the same! White threatens 30 ♗b2, finally pinning down Black's pieces.

29...♘xc4 30 ♖f3 ♗e5

On 30...♕e7 possible is 31 ♕e6! ♕xe6 32 dxe6 and because of the threat ♘b5-c7 the passed e-pawn becomes dangerous.

31 ♘c7!

White exploits the combinational theme of deflection (the knight cannot be captured because of the two rooks mate after a queen sacrifice on h6) to transfer his knight on e6.

31...♖xa4 32 ♗xf4!

Now after 32...♗xf4 33 ♘e6 Black is defenceless.

1-0

Game 23
Kramnik *White* **Shirov** *Black*
Linares 1998

1 ♘f3 ♘f6 2 c4 g6 3 ♘c3 ♗g7 4 e4 d6 5 d4 0-0 6 ♗e2 e5 7 0-0 ♘c6 8 d5 ♘e7 9 b4 ♘h5 10 ♖e1

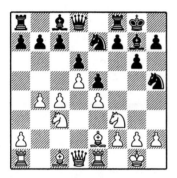

10...f5

The most logical follow-up to the move 9...♘h5. Sometimes 10...a5 11 bxa5 is played. But now, on 11...f5, besides 12 ♘g5 ♘f6 in the spirit of the text game, White can play 12 ♘d2, transferring the knight to b3 if Black plays 12...♖xa5. And 12...♘f4 involves a pawn sacrifice: 13 ♘b3 ♘xe2+ 14 ♖xe2 f4 15 ♖c2 f3 16 gxf3 h6 17 c5 ± Kanstler-Smirin, Givatayim 1998

11 ♘g5

A principled continuation. The knight heads for the weak e6 square, on which White is ready to sacrifice a pawn in order to increase the dynamic potential of his pieces.

The game Gelfand-Shirov, Wijk aan Zee 1998, provides a good illustration of the retreat 11 ♘d2— 11...♘f6 12 c5 ♗h6 13 ♗d3 fxe4 14 ♘dxe4 ♘xe4 15 ♗xe4 ♗xc1 16 ♖xc1 ♘f5 17 ♕d2 ♘d4 18 ♘e2 ♘xe2+ 19 ♖xe2 ♗f5 20 f3 ♕f6 21 ♖c4 ½-½.

If 11 c5 is played at once, then the knight lands on f4 in a more favourable situation: 11...fxe4 12 ♘xe4 ♘f4 13 ♗xf4 ♖xf4 14 ♘fd2 dxc5 15 ♗c4 ♔h8 16 ♘xc5 ♘xd5 17 ♘de4 c6 18 b5 ♖f8 (or 18...♗g4 19 ♕b3 ♕e7 20 f3 ♗f5= Lalić-Oll, Szeged 1997) 19 ♖b1 and here, in the game Kramnik-Gelfand, Novgorod 1996, instead of 19...♘b6?! 20 ♕xd8 ♖xd8 21 ♘g5, as played, with the better game for White, Black should have kept the queens on by 19...♕c7.

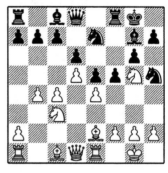

11...♘f6

The subject of the knight thrust 11...♘f4 12 ♗f4 exf4 13 ♖c1 was also discussed by Kramnik and Shirov: 13...♗f6 14 ♘e6 ♗xe6 15 dxe6 ♗xc3 16 ♖xc3 fxe4 17 ♗g4 (in Tilburg 1997, Kramnik retreated 17 ♗f1 e3 18 fxe3 fxe3 19 ♖cxe3 c6 20 ♕d2! d5 21 cxd5 cxd5 22 ♕d4! and White obtained the better chances, but after the game it was pointed out that 19...a5!? 20 b5 c6 led to a draw) 17...♘c6 (here 17...a5 18 b5 is already in White's favour) 18 ♖xe4 ♘e5 19 g3 ± Kramnik-Shirov, Monaco (blindfold) 1998.

An early 13...a5 14 b5 has also been played, but then 14...♗h6!? (14...♗f6 may lead to variations already examined) 15 h4 (W.Browne also recommends 15 ♘e6 ♗xe6 16 dxe6 f3 17 ♗xf3 ♗xc1 18 ♕xc1 ±) 15...fxe4 16 ♘cxe4 ♘f5 17 ♖c3!

♞h4 18 ♞e6 ♝xe6 19 dxe6 ♕e7 20 ♝g4 is considered advantageous for White. Browne-Peters, Los Angeles 1997.

12 ♝f3

On 12 f3 good is 12...h6 13 ♞e6 ♝xe6 14 dxe6 c6 with an approximately level game.

12...c6

The exchange 12...fxe4 13 ♞cxe4 ♞f5 14 ♝b2!? is in White's favour.

13 ♝e3

The bishop aims at the queenside. In case of 13 ♝b2 h6 14 ♞e6 ♝xe6 15 dxe6 fxe4 16 ♝xe4 Black creates a pawn centre in a more favourable situation:

(a) 16...♕b6 17 ♕b3 (on 17 ♕xd6? there follows 17...♕f2+!) 17...d5= S.Ivanov-Avrukh. Beer-Sheva 1998;

(b) 16...d5 17 cxd5 cxd5 18 ♝c2 e4 19 ♝b3 ♕b6= (A.Delchev).

13...cxd5

A.Shirov takes into account his knowledge of the game Kramnik-Nijboer, Wijk aan Zee 1998, in which after 13...h6 14 ♞e6 ♝xe6 15 dxe6 g5 16 exf5! ♞xf5 17 ♕d3 ♞xe3 18 ♜xe3 ♕e7 19 ♜d1 White had obtained the better position. Here he relieves the tension in the centre before placing the knight on e6.

If Black drives back the bishop first by 13...f4, then 14 ♝c1 favours White. For example, the game Kramnik-Gelfand, Belgrade 1997, proceeded 14...h6 15 ♞e6 ♝xe6 16 dxe6 ♞c8 17 b5! ♕e8 18 bxc6 bxc6 19 c5 ♕e6 20 ♝a3 dxc5 21 ♞a4! ♞b6 22 ♞xc5 ♕f7 23 ♕c1! and, because of the threat ♝d1-b3, White gains the advantage.

If 13...♚h8, then 14 ♕b3 when simplification is good for White since his pieces are better developed: 14...h6 (playing 14...cxd5 15 cxd5 just strengthens the role of the queen on b3) 15 ♞e6 ♝xe6 16 dxe6 fxe4 17 ♞xe4 ♞xe4 18 ♝xe4 ♕c8 19 b5 with an initiative for White. Zontakh-Shulman, Belgrade 1998.

14 cxd5 h6 15 ♞e6 ♝xe6 16 dxe6 fxe4

16...f4 is worth considering.

17 ♞xe4 ♞xe4 18 ♝xe4 d5 19 ♝c2

19 ♝c5 dxe4 20 ♕xd8 ♜fxd8 21 ♝xe7 is also possible, with a slightly better endgame for White.

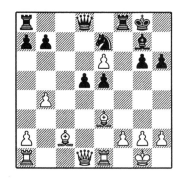

A year earlier this same position arose in Linares, in the game Kramnik-J.Polgar. Black endeavoured to mobilise the centre pawns, but after 19...e4?! 20 ♜c1 d4?! 21 ♝d2 e3 (or 21...d3 22 ♝b3±) 22 fxe3 d3 23 ♝b3 ♕d6 24 ♕g4 ♝e5 25 ♜f1! ♝xh2+ 26 ♚h1 ♕g3 27 ♕d4 was no better off than before. Commenting on this game, V.Kramnik suggested 19...b6, as played by A.Shirov.

19...b6 20 ♕g4 ♜f6 21 ♝b3

White sacrifices the e6-pawn, preferring to give the light-squared bishop an active role rather than sit by passively with 21 ♝a4 h5 22 ♕h3 ♕d6 23 ♝d7 ♜af8!? (this is more productive than 23...♕xb4 24 ♝g5) 24 b5 d4 (I.Zaitsev).

21...♕d6 22 ♜ad1 ♜d8 23 b5!

Not only to block the a7/b6 pawn-pair, but to broaden the sphere of action of his own pieces.

23...♕xe6 24 ♕xe6+

This decision to transpose to a promising endgame is more in the style of a veteran, wiser with experience, than a 22-year-old title contender. In a "Veterans v Juniors" match-tournament, held approximately at the same time in Cannes, 75-year-old S.Gligorić, playing against Nataf, preferred to keep the queens on by 24 ♕a4 and after 24...♖d7 25 f4! e4?! (necessary was 25...exf4) 26 ♗c1! ♕f5 27 ♕xe4 his strategy bore fruit.

24...♖xe6

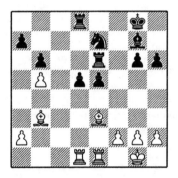

25 ♗c1!

The bishop is transferred to the more active a3-f8 diagonal, after which Black faces problems in protecting the pawn on d5. It becomes clear that, despite being a pawn down, White has the better endgame.

25...♔f7 26 ♗a3 e4

Black is ready to part with his centre pawns in order to activate his bishop.

27 g3 ♖d7 28 ♗xe7 ♔xe7 29 ♖xd5 ♖xd5 30 ♗xd5 ♗c3 31 ♖e2

The e4 pawn won't run away but, with rooks on the board, any "guaranteed draw" because of the opposite-coloured bishops is out of the question.

31...♖e5 32 ♗xe4 g5 33 a4 ♔d6 34 ♔g2 ♔c5

Bearing in mind White's possibility of creating a passed f-pawn, it is better for the king to remain nearer to it.

35 f4 gxf4 36 gxf4 ♖e6 37 ♔f3 ♖d6 38 ♔g4

Allowing the exchange of rooks after which Black's task is simpler. After 38 ♗f5 ♖d2 39 ♖e7 ♖xh2 40 ♖xa7, Shirov would have encountered more difficulties.

38...♖d2 39 ♖g2

More clever is 39 ♗f3 ♖xe2 40 ♗xe2 and Black would have to find 40...♔d5! 41 ♔h5 ♔e4! as pointed out by S.Dolmatov.

39...♔d4 40 ♗c6 ♖xg2+ 41 ♗xg2 ♗d2 42 ♗f3 ♗c1 43 ♗d1 ♗d2 44 ♗c2 ♗c1 45 f5 ♔e5 46 ♔h5 ♔f6 ½-½

Game 24
Van Wely *White* **Ivanchuk** *Black*
Wijk aan Zee 1999

1 d4 ♘f6 2 c4 g6 3 ♘c3 ♗g7 4 e4 d6 5 ♘f3 0-0 6 ♗e2 e5 7 0-0 ♘c6 8 d5 ♘e7 9 b4 a5

Black diverts his attention to get his rook into the action.

10 ♗a3

From this square the bishop supports the c4-c5 advance.

Black's task is simpler after 10 bxa5 ♖xa5 (after 10...c5 11 ♗d2 ♖xa5 12 ♕c2 h6 13 ♘e1 ♖a6 14 ♖b1 ♘d7 15 ♘d3 f5 16 f3 White stands better) 11 ♘d2 c5 12 ♘b5 (or 12 ♘b3 ♖a6 13 a4 ♘d7 14 ♗d2 f5 with chances for both sides) 12...♖a6 13 ♗b2 ♘d7 14 a4 ♗h6 15 ♖a3 f5 with active counterplay for Black. Skembris-Nikolaidis, Greece 1996.

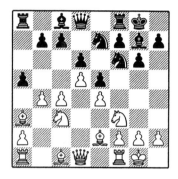

10...♘d7

The knight prepares to take control of the c5 square, which is an object of White's attack. Here we see a sort of "knights' castling", typical for such positions: the king's knight gallops to the queenside while his counterpart heads for the kingside. Accordingly their routes are ...♘g8-f6-d7-c5 and ...♘b8-c6-e7-g8-f6. This might seem long-winded but practical reasons associated with the logic of the Classical System dictate why the King's Indian knights have to travel this way.

Black can also hinder the advance c4-c5 by 10...axb4 11 ♗xb4 b6, intending to retreat the knight to e8. For example, the game Gelfand-Istratescu, Erevan (ol) 1996, proceeded 12 a4 ♘e8 13 ♘d2 f5 14 ♕b3 ♔h8 14 ♕b3 ♔h8 15 a5! c5 16 axb6! (a positional piece sacrifice—with the pawn on b6 it is more difficult for Black to unravel his tangled pieces, packed together on the first two ranks) 16...♖xa1 17 ♖xa1 cxb4?! (17...♕xb6 18 ♗a5 ♕xb3 19 ♘xb3 ± was better) 18 ♕xb4 ♗b7 19 ♘b3 ♘c8 20 ♘a5 with a dangerous initiative for White.

After this game A.Istratescu came to the conclusion that it would have been more logical to commence operations on the queenside: 13...c5!? 14 dxc6 ♘xc6 15 ♗a3 ♘c7 16 ♘b3

♘d4 and Black has sufficient counterplay. However, with due respect, probably 13 ♕b3, played in the game I.Sokolov-Kindermann, Nussloch 1996, is stronger. That game proceeded 13...♖b8 14 ♘b5 f5 15 a5 fxe4 16 ♘d2 bxa5 17 ♗xa5 ♘f5 18 ♘xe4 and White retained the initiative.

Taking into account future events it should be mentioned that, before the knight retreats to d7, usually 10...axb4 11 ♗xb4 is played, but it does not change matters. 11...♘d7 leads to a transposition to the game, but only after the 12th move.

11 bxa5 ♖xa5 12 ♗b4 ♖a8 13 a4 ♗h6

13...♘c5 14 ♘d2 has also been played (insufficient is 14 ♗xc5 dxc5 15 a5 ♗d7 and Black has quite a stable position) 14...♗d7 15 a5 ♘c8 16 ♘b3 (or 16 ♕c2 ♕e7 16 ♖fb1 ±) 16...♕e7 and here in the game T.Petrosian-Stein, USSR (ch) 1969, instead of 17 ♗f3 b6=, White retained somewhat better chances by 17 f3.

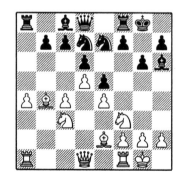

14 a5

White conquers space on the queenside. After 14 ♘d2 f5 Black prevents White's initiative by a timely ...b7-b6. Here are some examples:

(a) 15 &f3 b6! 15 a5 &c5 16 axb6 &xa1 17 &xa1 cxb6?! 18 &a2 ± Gelfand-Schebler, Germany 1996; 17...&xd2 18 bxc7 &d7 with unclear play.

(b) 15 &b3 b6! 16 a5 &c5 17 exf5?! (17 &c2 =; 17 &a3 =) 17...gxf5 18 &b5 &g6 19 &e1 e4! 20 &f1 &e5 ∓ I.Sokolov-Gelfand, Groningen 1996

14...f5 15 &d3

The alternative is 15 &d2 &f6 (15...&h8 16 &f3 &a6 16 &e1 b6 17 &b5 &c5 18 axb6 cxb6 19 &c2 fxe4 20 &xe4 &f5 21 &f3 ± Bareev-Vl.Georgiev, Erevan (ol) 1996) 16 c5 (15 exf5 &xf5 16 c5 &d4 =) 16...&xd2 17 &xd2 &xe4 18 &xe4 fxe4 19 &c3 &f5 20 &a4 &h4 21 cxd6 cxd6 22 f4 e3 23 &d1 &d7 and Black equalizes. Babula-Istratescu, Krynica (zt) 1998.

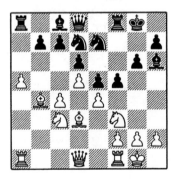

15...&h8

Those who learn the Classical System have probably noticed that Black frequently plays this move at an early stage of the game. The idea is that the king vacates the g8 square for the e7-knight in order that it may transfer to f6.

After other continuations Black fails to maintain equality. If Black brings up his reserves by 15...&f6 then White seizes the initiative by

16 c5 fxe4 17 &xe4. The pawn assault on the kingside starting with 15...&f7?! leads nowhere after 16 &b3 g5 17 &fd1 g4 18 &d2 b6 19 &b5 bxa5 20 &e2 &c5 21 &xc5 dxc5 22 &b3 f4 23 &xc5 since White's queenside attack comes first, Van Wely-Piket, Monaco (m/4) 1997.

16 &d2 &g8

The move 16...&f6 was hotly debated in games between Kramnik and Topalov: 16 &a4 &f7 17 c5 dxc5 18 &c3 fxe4 19 &xe4 &f5 20 &c4. In Las Palmas 1996, Topalov retreated 20...&g7, but after 21 &xf5 &xf5 22 d6 he failed to achieve equality. In 1997, in Dortmund, he managed to strengthen his position by 20...&d6 21 &xe5 &xe5 22 &xe5 &g7 and gained an equal game.

17 &e1

A new idea. 17 &b3 or 17 &c2 is met more often.

17...&f7

The pawn on f5 has to be taken care of.

18 &b5

18 &c2 followed by 19 &ad1 looks stronger. Then Black has more problems with controlling White's objects of attack—c5 and f5.

18...&a6 19 &c2 &df6

Indirectly protecting the pawn on f5 (20 exf5 gxf5 21 &xf5 &xd5!).

20 c5 fxe4 21 &xe4 &d7

V.Ivanchuk's intuitive refusal to accept the pawn sacrifice after 21...dxc5 22 &xc5 (unclear is 22 &xc5 &xe4 23 &xe4 &xd5 24 &ad1 &c6, but simply 22 &c3 is possible) 22...&f8 23 &c4 &xe4 24 &xe4 &xb4 25 &xb4 &xd5 26 &ad1, can be trusted—the position is opened and White's pieces display too much activity.

22 ♘c3 ♗f5 23 ♗xf5 gxf5 24 ♘c4 ♘e7 25 cxd6 cxd6 26 ♘b5 ♘e8 27 ♖ed1

27 ♘b6 is more active, keeping the rook out of play. Then, sooner or later, Black would probably have to sacrifice it on b6.

27...f4?!

Black's pawn sacrifice proves to be ineffective and therefore 27...♖g7 followed by ...♘e7-g6 looks more natural.

28 ♖a3

And here it is not too late to play 28 ♘b6.

28...f3 29 ♖xf3 ♖xf3 30 gxf3 ♕d7

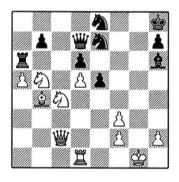

31 ♘bxd6!

An exchanging operation, based on the power of the passed d-pawn.

32...♘xd6 32 ♗xd6 ♖xd6 33 ♘xd6 ♕xd6 34 ♕b2?!

This natural desire to aim his sights at the b7 and e5 pawns proves to be insufficient for maintaining an advantage, which, according to Van Wely, could have been achieved by the more subtle 34 ♕b1! (preventing an activation of the queen by ...♕d6-g6+) 34...♕d7 (or 34...♗f4 35 ♕xb7 ♕g6+ 36 ♔f1 ♕c2 37 ♕b1!±) 35 ♕b6 ♗g5 36 ♕e6 ♕xe6 37 dxe6 ♘c6 38 ♖d7 ♔g8 39 f4! etc.

34...♕g6+ 35 ♔f1 ♕f5 36 d6 ♕xf3!

Setting up the drawing mechanism ...♕h1+ and ...♕e4+.

37 ♕xe5+ ♗g7 38 dxe7 ♕xd1+ 39 ♔g2

White cannot avoid the perpetual check after 39...♕g4+, since 40 ♕g3?? loses the e7 pawn to 40...♕e4+.

½-½

Game 25
Vogt *White* **Gufeld** *Black*
Baku 1980

1 ♘f3 ♘f6 2 c4 g6 3 ♘c3 ♗g7 4 e4 d6 5 d4 0-0 6 ♗e2 e5 7 0-0 ♘c6 8 d5 ♘e7 9 ♗d2

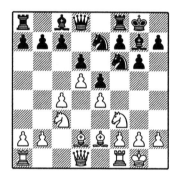

Today this continuation is met less often than other lines, but in the 70s it was quite popular. As in many other cases it was Mark Taimanov who provided the impulse by using it as his main weapon in his Candidates match against Robert Fischer (Vancouver 1971).

White completes the deployment of his pieces, frees a square for his rook and retains the possibilities of both a pawn offensive and a piece assault on the queenside.

9...♘h5

An active continuation, which virtually forces White to weaken his queenside by 10 g3. R.Fischer preferred 9...♘e8, and Taimanov carried out the queenside attacking plan: 10 ♖c1 f5 11 ♕b3 (in the first game he played his favourite manoeuvre 11 exf5 gxf5 12 ♘g5 h6 13 ♘e6 ♗xe6 14 dxe6 ♕c8 15 ♕b3 c6 and landed in a worse position) 11...b6 12 exf5 gxf5 13 ♘g5 ♘f6 14 f4 h6 15 fxe5 dxe5 16 c5!? ♘fxd5 16 ♘xd5 ♘xd5 17 cxb6 axb6 19 ♖c6 ♔h8 and a complicated struggle followed, Taimanov-Fischer, Vancouver (m/3) 1971. After the match it was pointed out that an immediate 11 ♘g5 h6 12 ♘e6 ♗xe6 13 dxe6 ♕c8 14 ♕b3, leaving White with the better position, was stronger. Therefore after 10 ♖c1 Black should close the queen flank at once by 10...c5. For example, the game Ribli-Torre, Alicante (m/8) 1983, proceeded 10 ♖c1 c5 11 dxc6 bxc6 12 b4 ♘c7 13 b5 d5 14 cxd5 cxd5 15 ♘xd5 ♘cxd5 16 exd5 ♘xd5 with equal chances.

After the retreat 9...♘d7, Black leaves the e6 square unprotected and after 10 b4 f5 11 ♘g5 he has to move his knight back. 11...♘f6 12 f3 ♘h5 13 g3 when the position favours White.

10 g3
White prevents the penetration of the knight to f4. Another main line is 10 ♖c1.

10...f5
A decisive move, which is backed up by tactics. In case of 10...c6?! White is first to take the initiative: 11 ♖c1 f5 12 dxc6 bxc6 13 c5!.

11 exf5
11 ♘g5 is not dangerous 11...♘f6 12 f3 c6 13 ♕b3 h6 14 ♘e6 ♗xe6 15 dxe6 ♕c8 and the knight's epic is over.

11...♘xf5

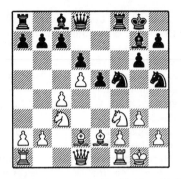

Black is not afraid of 12 g4? in view of 12...♘d4! 13 gxh5 ♘xe2+ 14 ♕xe2 ♗g4 regaining the material with interest.

12 ♘e4
It is useful to occupy the central square with a view to proceeding to g5.

In the game Eingorn-A.Kuzmin, USSR (ch) 1991, there followed 12 ♗d3 ♘f6 13 ♘g5 ♘d4 14 f3 c6 15 ♔g2 ♗d7 16 ♘ge4 ♘xe4 17 ♗xe4 c5 with good play for Black.

12...♘f6 13 ♗g5
It is clear that White is eager to keep his knight on e4, even at the cost of conceding the two bishops. However 13 ♗d3 can be met by 13...♗h6.

13...h6 14 ♗xf6 ♗xf6 15 ♗d3 ♗g7 16 h4
16 ♔g2 would have been met by the same reply as in the game.

16...c6!
The character of the position enables Black to display activity on the kingside and play for the advance ...g6-g5-g4. On the other hand, White will not stand idly by, but prepare an attack on the queenside by c4-c5. By breaking up the centre Black prevents these possibilities and at the same time increases the sphere of activity of his queen. With White's dark-squared

bishop off the board, Black's influence on the dark squares is most effective on the queenside. The previously played 16...b6 17 ♔g2 ♗b7, trying to exploit the long light-squared diagonal, is less effective and leaves White with the better chances.

17 ♔g2 ♗d7 18 ♕d2 cxd5 19 cxd5 ♕b6 20 ♖ad1

More logical is 20 ♖ac1, seeking compensation for Black's pressure on the f-file by play along the c-file.

20...♖f7 21 ♗b1?! ♖af8 22 g4?!

The second poor move in succession. Even though he pushes back the active black knight, White should not have weakened f4 which now becomes a very important square for Black's attack.

22...♘e7 23 ♘h2 ♗b5!

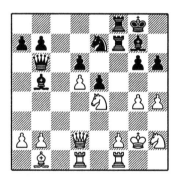

Now we see the drawbacks of White's 21st and 22nd moves. After 24 ♗d3 possible is 24...♘xd5! 25 ♗xb5 ♘f4+ 26 ♔g1 ♕xb5 27 ♘xd6 ♕c6 with the double threat of mate and ...♖f7-d7, exploiting the pin against the queen.

24 ♖g1

It seems that, having strengthened his position in the centre, White should have sacrificed the exchange with 24 f3, since after the fall of the d5 pawn his king is also vulnerable to attack.

24...♗c4 25 h5 ♗xd5 26 f3 g5

The f4 square won't run away but, if an immediate 26...♖f4, White's pieces might become more "lively" after 27 g5!?.

27 b3 ♖f4 28 ♖gf1 ♖d8! 29 ♖fe1 ♗f7 30 ♘f1 d5

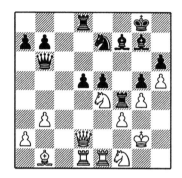

Now comes the turn of the centre pawns—and the dark pieces behind them are also beginning to show their strength.

31 ♘e3 ♘c6 32 ♘g3 e4! 33 ♘ef5

The exchange 33 fxe4 dxe4 reveals new defects in White's position.

33...♖xf3 34 ♘xg7 ♔xg7 35 ♕b2+ ♔g8 36 ♘f5 ♖xf5! 37 gxf5 ♕c7!

Despite being the exchange up, the position of the naked white king is a sorry sight. Its vulnerability can probably be exploited by the simple advance of Black's central pawn pair. However, first it is necessary to parry the threat of the white queen to invade to f6, which would prove quite unpleasant after, say, an immediate 37...♗xh5?!.

38 ♕f6?!

An impetuous move in time-trouble. However, White is doomed anyway.

**38...Ξd6 39 ♕c3 ♗xh5 40 Ξd2
♗f3+ 41 ♔f1 ♕f7**

After the fall of the f5 pawn it becomes impossible for White to hold back the avalanche of black pawns.

**42 ♕c5 Ξd7 43 Ξh2 ♔g7 44 Ξe3
♘e5 45 ♕d4 ♕f6 46 Ξd2 ♕xf5 47
♔e1 ♕f6 48 Ξc3 ♗g4 0-1**

Game 26
Piket *White* **Gelfand** *Black*
Dos Hermanas 1995

**1 d4 ♘f6 2 c4 g6 3 ♘c3 ♗g7 4
e4 d6 5 ♘f3 0-0 6 ♗e2 e5 7 0-0
♘c6 8 d5 ♘e7 9 ♗d2 ♘h5 10 Ξc1**

A consistent manoeuvre: White completes the deployment of his pieces.

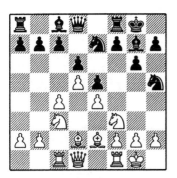

10...h6

A routine plan. Black prevents the lunge ♘f3-g5 and prepares an assault on the kingside by the g- and h-file pawns. However, there is still no convincing proof of any drawbacks to 10...f5.

(a) 11 exf5 ♘xf5 12 ♘e4 (stronger is 12 g3! with chances for both sides) 12...♘f4 13 Ξe1 ♘xe2+ 14 ♕xe2 b6 15 b4 h6 and Black obtains good play, Taimanov-Spassky, USSR (ch) 1973;

(b) 11 ♘g5 (considered as best) 11...♘f4 12 ♗xf4 exf4 13 ♗f3 fxe4

14 ♗xe4 ♘f5 15 ♘e6 ♗xe6 16 dxe6 c6 17 Ξe1 ♕e7 and Black's position is not inferior, Korchnoi-Spraggett, Montpellier (ct) 1985.

11 Ξe1 ♘f4

The blockading move 11...c5 deserves attention. For example: 12 g3 b6 13 a3 f5 14 ♘h4 ♘f6 15 exf5 g5 16 ♘g6 ♘xg6 17 fxg6 ♗f5 with level chances, Vaganian-Piket, Groningen 1993.

12 ♗f1 g5

Not only for attacking purposes, but also to free a square for the second knight.

13 h4 g4!

This is more stubborn than 13...gxh4, played in the game Geller-Van Wely, Tilburg 1993, in which after 14 ♘xh4 f5 15 g3 the knight was forced to retreat because the position has assumed an open character: 15...♘fg6 16 ♘xg6 ♘xg6 17 exf5 (also interesting is 17 ♕h5 Ξf6 18 exf5 ♗xf5 19 ♗xh6 ♗xh6 20 ♕xh6 ♘f4! 21 ♕g5+ ♔f7 noted by L.van Wely) 17...♗xf5 18 ♘e4 ♘e7!, though here too the play is of a double-edged character.

14 ♘h2 h5 15 c5

In the event of 15 g3 the knight should not retreat—stronger is 15...♘eg6!.

15...dxc5 16 ♗e3 ♘eg6

On 16...b6 possible is 17 b4.

17 ♗xc5 Ξe8 18 g3

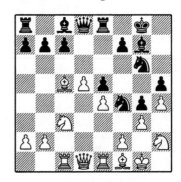

18...a6!

That the f4-knight cannot be taken is obvious, since after 19 gxf4 exf4 20 ♗d4 ♕xh4 Black's attack is too strong.

19 ♕b3 b6 20 ♗e3

After 20 ♗a3 possible is 20...♗h6 with the threat of a knight sacrifice on h4.

20...♗f8 21 ♘d1!

A clever manoeuvre: the knight strives to take the weak f5 point under its control, which is achieved, for example, in the variation 21...♗d6 22 ♗d2 f5 23 ♘e3.

21...♗d7 22 ♗d2 ♗c5 23 ♘e3 a5?!

A blunder, since now, as noted by J.Piket, White could have developed an unpleasant initiative by sacrificing the exchange: 24 ♖xc5!? bxc5 25 ♖c1 ♕e7 26 ♕a3 ♖eb8 27 ♘f5!.

Therefore 23...♗d4!? deserves attention.

24 a4?! ♕f6 25 ♖xc5

Here the aforementioned sacrifice is less effective since it allows Black to exploit the b-file.

25...bxc5 26 ♖c1 ♖eb8 27 ♕a3

27...♔h7?

Apparently an overestimation of his own chances. As shown by J.Piket, Black could have retained good play by the counter-sacrifice of the exchange 27...♖b4! 28 ♗xb4

axb4 29 ♕b3 ♗xa4 30 ♕c4 ♖a5! etc.

28 ♖xc5 ♖b7 29 ♕c3!

Obliging Black to watch out for a capture on f4.

29...♗xa4

For the time being preventing 30 gxf4 because of 30...♖b3!.

30 ♖xc7 ♖b3 31 ♕c1 ♗e8?

It is difficult to explain such a weak-willed move played by a dynamic grandmaster like B.Gelfand. Even after 31...♘xh4 32 gxh4 g3 33 fxg3 ♖g8 the situation is not as clear as after White's reply in the game.

32 ♘f5!

Now the threat to capture the knight becomes real and Black is forced to open the locks on the king's flank.

32...♘xd5 33 ♗g5 ♕e6 34 ♗c4 ♘xc7 35 ♗xe6 ♘xe6 36 ♗f6

Under threat of mate, Black is forced to suffer further losses.

36...♘gf4 37 gxf4 ♘xf4 38 ♔h1 ♖a6 39 ♗xe5 ♘d3 40 ♕g5 1-0

Game 27
Polugaevsky *White* **Gufeld** *Black*
Sochi 1981

1 c4 g6 2 d4 ♘f6 3 ♘c3 ♗g7 4 e4 d6 5 ♗e2 0-0 6 ♘f3 e5 7 0-0 ♘c6 8 d5 ♘e7 9 ♘e1

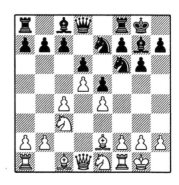

The aim of the manoeuvre ♘f3-e1-d3 is to increase the pressure on the c5 square. In addition, the useful move f2-f3 is made possible—to counter the forthcoming pawn attack ...f7-f5-f4.

9...♘d7

After 9...♘e8 one of the protectors of the e5 square is removed and, along with the traditional attack on the queenside 10 ♗e3 f5 11 f3 f4 12 ♗f2 g5 13 c5, White can attack the e-pawn by 10 f4 immediately or after the preliminary 10 ♘d3. Having a passion for the generally accepted 9...♘d7, contemporary theory has not made any particular claims for the continuation 9...♘e8.

10 ♘d3

After this move Black anticipates that White's bishop will be developed on d2.

10...f5 11 ♗d2 ♘f6 12 f3

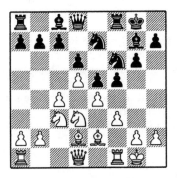

Polugaevsky had introduced this system into his armoury not long before our game. It brought him a string of convincing victories, for example in his quarter-final Candidates match against Tal (Alma Ata 1980). The forcing play after 12...f4 13 c5, where White develops a rapid queenside attack, had been thoroughly studied by my opponent, and I did not wish to test his home

analysis over the board which is why I had chosen the less-studied continuation...

12...♚h8

Almost two decades later I can add that my intuition did not let me down. Nowadays the *Encyclopedia* considers this move quite solid.

13 g4

No, this is not an attempt to seize the initiative: White's aim is rather to establish his kingside defences in a forward position. The idea of the move is to set up a blockade, for example: 13...f4? 14 h4! and all Black's pieces are deprived of mobility, whereas White's queenside initiative develops automatically (exchanges on e4 or g4 would also be mistaken).

But this distraction on the kingside secures Black's play on the queenside.

In the game Kozul-Gufeld, Tbilisi 1988, was played 13 a4 a5! 14 g4 c5 (14...c6!? also deserved attention) 15 ♖f2 b6 16 h4 ♖a7 17 ♖h2 ♚g8 (with the king on h8 the idea to exchange the dark-squared bishops was possible 17...♘eg8!? 18 h5 gxh5 19 gxf5 ♗h6) 18 h5 and here, instead of 18...fxg4?! 19 fxg4 gxh5 20 g5 ♘e8 21 ♗xh5, which appeared to favour White, Black should have played 18...f4.

Nowadays 13 ♖c1 is considered as the main continuation.

(a) 13...c5 14 g4 a6 (or 14...♗d7 15 ♘f2 ♘eg8 16 ♚h1 f4 17 b4 b6 18 ♘b5 a6 19 ♘a3 ♘e8 20 ♖b1 ♕h4= Ftacnik-Geller, Sochi 1977) 15 ♘f2 h6 (or 15...♗d7 16 a3 ♘eg8 17 b4±) 16 h4 fxg4 17 fxg4 ♘eg8 18 ♚g2 ♘h7 19 ♖h1 ♗f6 20 g5! hxg5 21 h5 ♕e8 22 b4 cxb4 23 ♘a4 ♗d8 24 ♗xb4 ♗d7 with complex play, Gelfand-Kasparov, Linares 1990;

(b) 13...c6 14 ♗e3 a6 (14...c5 15 g4 ♘eg8 16 ♔g2 ♘e8! 17 ♖h1 and here 17...♗f6!? left Black sufficient counterplay in Gelfand-Wahls, Munich 1992; stronger was 15 b4 b6 16 ♖b1 h5 17 a4 f4 18 ♗f2 g5 19 a5 ±) 15 c5 (on 15 b4 possible is 15...cxd5 16 cxd5 ♗d7 17 ♘b2 b5 with complex play. Gelfand-Topalov, Amsterdam 1996) 15...cxd5 16 cxd6 ♕xd6 17 ♗c5 ♕d8 18 ♘xe5 ♘h5! 19 f4 ♘xf4 20 ♖xf4 ♗xe5 21 ♗d4 ♘c6! 22 ♗xe5+ ♘xe5 23 ♘d5 and White stands slightly better, Gelfand-Nijboer, Wijk aan Zee 1998.

13...c6!

One of the classic rules of chess strategy states: "Don't move pawns where you are weaker!" The queenside is White's sphere of influence —he has a space advantage there. However, in the present specific case, the continuation chosen by Black is not even an exception to this rule, but rather a consequence of White being the first to break the "convention" with the move 13 g4.

Also possible is 13...c5 and, on 14 ♖b1, 14...fxg4 15 fxg4 h6.

14 ♔h1

Maybe White should prefer 14 a4, but after 14...a5! he would have to reckon with the fact that his opponent could close the queenside at will by ...c6-c5.

14...b5! 15 b3

After 15 dxc6 bxc4 the knight, which was miserably placed on e7, would have fine prospects of establishing itself on d4.

15...♖b8

With the threat against e4, Black wants to force his opponent to make a concession on the kingside.

16 a3 a5 17 ♘f2

The e4-pawn is defended, but White's position is now cracking in its seemingly most fortified place.

17...b4! 18 axb4 axb4 19 ♘a2 fxe4 20 fxe4 cxd5 21 cxd5

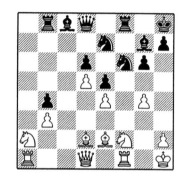

21...♕b6??

Trying to have my cake and eat it too. I wanted to strengthen my position still further, so that after 22 ♔g2? (as if there were no other moves!) I could play the combination 22...♘fxd5 23 exd5 ♘xd5 with decisive effect.

Instead, I should have carried out the long-prepared strike on d5 without delay. In this case Polugaevsky would have had to apply his defensive skill to the full. Here are some sample variations: 21...♘fxd5!! 22 exd5 ♘xd5 23 ♔g1 ♕b6 or 23 ♗f3 ♗b7 24 ♗g5? ♖xf3! 25 ♗xd8 ♘e3, or 23 ♘e4 ♗b7 24 ♖xf8+ ♕xf8 25 ♗f3 ♖a8! 26 ♘g5 h6! (26...e4 27 ♗xe4 ♕f6 28 ♕f1 ♕xa1 29 ♘f7+ ♔g8 30 ♘h6+ with a draw) 27 ♘e6 ♕f6, with a great advantage to Black in all cases.

22 ♘xb4 ♘fxd5

22...♗b7 is better.

23 ♘xd5 ♘xd5 24 ♗a5!!

I had underestimated this move. The advantage now swings over to White and, although I count myself the winner of the theoretical argument, my opponent became the actual victor in the tournament table.

24...♕e3

It was here that I noticed the "hole" in my calculations.

On my planned 24...♘e3 White has the decisive 25 ♗xb6 ♘xd1 26 ♘xd1! ♖xb6 27 ♖xf8+ ♗xf8 28 ♖a8 ♖c6 29 ♗c4. However, this particular continuation should have been crossed out since after 29...♔g7 30 ♘e3 ♗e7 Black could still resist.

25 exd5 e4

Hastening the end.

26 ♗d2 ♕d4 27 ♗h6!! ♗b7 28 ♕xd4 ♗xd4 29 ♗xf8 e3 30 ♘h3 ♗xd5+ 31 ♔g1 ♗xa1 32 ♗xd6 ♖a8 33 ♖f8+ ♖xf8 34 ♗xf8 ♗xb3 35 ♗c5, and **White won**.

Game 28
Atalik *White* **Gufeld** *Black*
Waikiki 1997

1 d4 ♘f6 2 c4 g6 3 ♘c3 ♗g7 4 e4 d6 5 ♗e2 0-0 6 ♘f3 e5 7 0-0 ♘c6 8 d5 ♘e7 9 ♘e1 ♘d7 10 ♗e3

White moves his bishop on to the g1-a7 diagonal, from where it supports the break c4-c5.

10...f5 11 f3 f4

Nowadays this move is made without any thought, but in the primary source game Taimanov-Aronin, Moscow 1952, the "founders" were in uncharted territory. Aronin played 11...h5?! 12 ♘d3 f4 13 ♗f2 g5 14 c5 ♘f6 15 ♖c1 g4 16 ♕b3 ♗h6 17 cxd6 cxd6 18 ♘xe5! and White obviously succeeded in realizing his plan. It turns out that the advance ...h7-h5 is merely a loss of time and already in the next game in this tournament D.Bronstein, playing against Taimanov, made an

amendment: 11...f4 12 ♗f2 g5, which then became one of the main lines of the variation.

12 ♗f2 g5

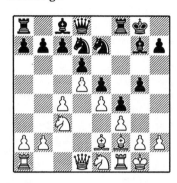

13 ♖c1

Nowadays a very routine continuation. White prepares the advance of the c-pawn.

Here it is useful to return to the history of the variation. In the aforementioned game, Taimanov-Bronstein, White played 13 b4 ♖f6 14 c5 ♖h6 15 cxd6 cxd6 16 ♘b5 and his initiative on the queenside turned out to be more real. Soon after, the rook manoeuvre was refined by Boris Spassky. In his game against Laszlo Szabo (Bucharest 1953) he played 14...♖g6! and, as becomes clear, from here the rook provides a more effective support to the advance of the g-file pawn. I'd like to remind you that in my "primary source" from 1954 (game 1), Khasidovsky played 13 ♘d3, upon which I resorted to the same plan, 13...♖f6 14 c5 ♖g6, and here too it is not bad.

Nowadays, a generation on, 13 b4 suggests another deployment of pieces: 13...♘f6 14 c5 ♘g6 15 ♖c1 ♖f7, clearing the f8 square for the bishop. Here are some examples:

(a) 16 cxd6 cxd6 17 a4 ♗f8 18 a5 ♗d7 19 ♘b5 g4 with good play for

Black, Piket-Kasparov, Tilburg 1989;

(b) 16 a4 ♗f8 17 cxd6 ♗xd6 18 ♘d3 h5 19 ♘c5 ♖g7 20 ♘e6 ♗xe6 21 dxe6 ♕e7! 22 ♘d5! ♘xd5 23 exd5 ♗xb4 24 ♕b3 with a double-edged game, in which the protected e6 pawn fully compensates for the material deficit. Tukmakov-Atalik, Tilburg 1993.

Looking at the character of the position on the board, one may ask a question: why can't the g-pawn be blocked by 13 g4? But this continuation contradicts one of the classic rules of chess strategy—don't move pawns where you are weak, and I have already drawn your attention to this rule. And indeed, after 13...fxg3 14 hxg3 ♘g6 15 ♘g2, or 15...h5 or 15...a5, Black gains good counterplay.

It remains to mention that the *Encyclopedia* considers 13 a4 as the main continuation.

13...♘g6 14 c5

This pawn sacrifice was made for the first time in the game Kozul-Fedorowicz, Wijk aan Zee 1991. Before this game, 14 b4, 14 ♘d3 or 14 ♕d2 were played.

14...♘xc5

On 14...dxc5 there would follow 15 b4! and now 15...cxb4 16 ♘b5 or 15...b6 16 ♘d3 is to White's advantage.

15 b4 ♘a6 16 ♘b5

White hurries to win back the pawn. This knight swoop is based on White's previous play. The dark side of this move is that it introduces a forcing character to the game.

An alternative is 16 ♘d3.

16...♗d7

On 16...♖f7 possible is 17 ♕a4 followed by 18...♕a5

17 ♘xa7

The game Kozul-Fedorowicz, Wijk aan Zee 1991, proceeded 17 ♕a4 g4! 18 fxg4 (18 ♕a5? g3∓) 18...f3 19 gxf3 ♘f4 20 ♕d1 h5! with excellent play for Black.

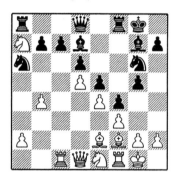

17...♕b8

In a series of subsequent games on this theme Black did not waste time pushing back the knight, but started active measures on the king-side at once—17...h5;

(a) 18 a3 g4? 19 fxg4 f3 20 ♗xf3 hxg4 21 ♗xg4 ♖xf2 22 ♖xf2 ♖a7 23 ♖c3 and White repels Black's onslaught, Korchnoi-M.Ivanov, Enghien 1997; more flexible is 18...♖f7 with the idea of 19 ♕c2 g4 20 ♗xa6 bxa6 21 ♕c7 ♕f8 22 ♕b6 h4 and Black has active counterplay (M.Ivanov).

(b) 18 a4 ♖f7 19 ♘b5 ♗h6 (19...♗f8 20 ♘c3 deserves attention) 20 ♘c3 ♖g7 21 ♘d3 ♔h8 with sufficient counterplay for Black, Yermolinsky-Fedorowicz, North Bay 1998) 20 ♖c4 ♖g7 21 ♔h1 ♘f8 22 g3 fxg3 (or 22...♖g6 23 gxf4 exf4 24 ♖g1 ♗g7 ±) 23 ♗xg3 ♘g6 24 ♘d3 ♘f4 (24...♔h8 is considered by A.Yermolinsky as better) 25 ♗xf4 (after 25 ♘xf4 gxf4 26 ♗f2 ♗e8 the game is equal) 25...gxf4 26 ♖g1 ♗g5 27 ♗f1! ♗h4 28 ♖xg7 ♔xg7 29 ♕c2?! ∓ Atalik-G.Timoshchenko, Romania 1998

According to G.Timoshchenko, White would have retained some advantage by 29 ♕c1.

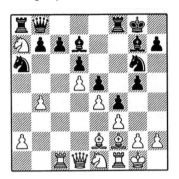

18 ♘b5

On 18 ♗xa6 I would have played 18...♖xa7!.

V.Korchnoi at first recommended an exchange of bishops: 18 ♗b5!? ♖f7 19 ♗xd7 ♖xd7 20 ♕a4 ♖f7 21 ♔h1 (21 ♘b5 is too soon in view of 21...♕e8 ∓) 21...♖f8 (21...♖xa7? loses to 22 ♗xa7 ♕xa7 23 b5 ♕e3 24 bxa6 ♕xc1 25 a7 and the pawn cannot be stopped) 22 ♕a3 with ♘a7-b5 to follow.

18...♖f7

Preparing an attack on the kingside is more to my taste than striving for unclear prospects on the queenside: 18...♘xb4 19 ♘xc7 ♖xa2 20 ♗xb5!.

19 a4 h5

19...♘xb4 is also possible.

20 ♘d3 ♗h6 21 ♖c4 ♖g7 22 ♔h1 ♕d8!

The threat of an attack on the kingside is quite real, whilst White's play on the queenside is exhausted.

23 g3

A crucial move. White should have also considered 23 ♕c2.

23...fxg3 24 ♗xg3 ♘f4

An ideal square for the black knight! And it is clear that White cannot tolerate it.

25 ♗xf4 gxf4

Gaining space.

26 ♖g1 ♖xg1+ 27 ♕xg1+ ♔h7 28 ♗f1 ♕e7?!

28...♗f8! should definitely be considered.

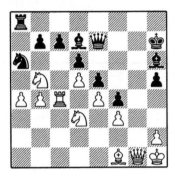

29 ♘xc7

The concentration of White's forces on the queen flank is at its maximum and he can't help capturing the pawn. But the knight falls into a pin and the play becomes very forcing.

29...♖c8 30 ♕b6 ♗xa4 31 ♘b2 ♗b3

Weaker is 31...♘xc7 32 ♗h3! and White is one step ahead of his opponent: 32...♗b3 33 ♗f5+ ♔h8 34 ♗xc8 ♗xc4 35 ♘xc4±.

32 ♘xa6 ♗xc4 33 ♘xc4 bxa6 34 ♕xa6 ♖g8

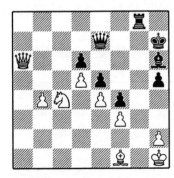

35 ♕b6?

White has got rid of the pin along the c-file (with quite small material losses), but not the threats on the kingside. Apparently that is why S.Atalik subconsciously cannot make up his mind to play 35 ♕xd6 and prefers to keep his king in view. Nevertheless, the pawn capture is possible, since on 35...♕a7 there is the reply 36 ♕c5. But now Black falls into a critical situation. But, regrettably, I had no virtually no time left to look for a way to realize the advantage. Otherwise I would have found 35...♕h4!, and Black can look forward to a comfortable game, 36 ♕a7+ ♖g7.

35...♕g7? 36 ♕f2?

Mistake is met by mistake. 36 ♘xd6! sems to have some merit: 36...♗g5 37 ♗h3. In fact, though, my chances are still preferable. Seeing that I had a catastrophically small amount of time left, with my next move I offered a draw, which was immediately accepted.

36...♕b7 ½-½

Game 29
Piket *White* **Kasparov** *Black*
Linares 1997

1 d4 ♘f6 2 c4 g6 3 ♘c3 ♗g7 4 e4 d6 5 ♘f3 0-0 6 ♗e2 e5 7 0-0 ♘c6 8 d5 ♘e7 9 ♘e1 ♘d7 10 ♗e3 f5 11 f3 f4 12 ♗f2 g5 13 ♖c1 ♘g6 14 c5 ♘xc5 15 b4 ♘a6 16 ♘d3

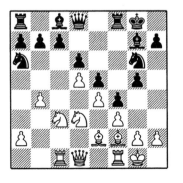

This calm move, stabilizing the situation in the centre, looks quite natural. White is in no hurry to win back the pawn and leaves the thrust ♘c3-b5 in reserve.

16...h5

The game Piket-Ivanchuk, Wijk aan Zee 1999, proceeded 16...♖f7 17 ♘b5 ♗d7 18 a4 ♕e8! 19 ♘b2 (on 19 ♖c3 possible is 19...h5 20 ♕b3 g4) 19...♕b8 20 ♕c2 and here, as J.Piket noted, 20...♗xb5 21 axb5 ♘xb4 22 ♕b3 a5 maintained equality.

17 ♘b5 ♗d7 18 a4 ♗h6

The plan ...c7-c6, ...♖f7, ...♗f8 with the idea of reinforcing the d6 pawn, definitely deserves attention.

19 ♖c3 b6

A radical way of protecting the pawn on a7. After 19...♕b8, the tangle of black pieces in the corner looks unproductive and White could have exploited it by transferring the knight from b5 to a5 after 20 ♘a3!, threatening b4-b5.

In Korchnoi-Cvitan, Pula 1997, Black regained the pawn after 19...♖f7 20 ♘xa7 and developed an initiative on the kingside: 20...♖g7 21 ♘b5 ♘f8 22 h3 ♘h7 23 ♗e1 ♘f6 24 ♘f2 ♘xb4 25 ♖xc7 ♘a6 26 ♖xb7 ♘c5 27 ♖c7 g4 28 hxg4 hxg4 29 fxg4 ♘fxe4 with approximately equal chances.

20 ♗e1!

The battle lines of the position are drawn: Black has a weak pawn on c7 which he hopes to offset by a pawn assault ...g5-g4. White prevents this by posting his knight on f2.

20...♖f7

Protecting the knight on a6 by 20...♗c8 would mean "freezing" a number of his queenside pieces. Such a way of playing is not in the style of the world champion.

Kasparov prefers to return the pawn and make his pieces more dynamic.

21 ♘f2 ♘h4 22 ♘xd6 cxd6 23 ♗xa6 ♕e8! 24 ♕e2

White ignores 24...♗xa4? because of 25 b5, but a surprise awaits him.

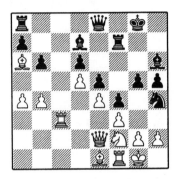

24...g4!

A breakthrough on what seems the most protected square, but regrettably this attacking idea does not reach its logical culmination.

25 fxg4 ♖g7?

As noted by G.Kasparov, Black could have sacrificed a knight: 25...♘xg2!! 26 ♔xg2 hxg4 27 ♕c2 (on 27 ♔h1? there would follow 27...f3 28 ♕c2 g3 29 hxg3 ♗e3! followed by...♖f7-h7 and ...♕e8-h5) 27...♖h7!. Black threatens to attack with his major pieces along the h-file (27...f3+ 28 ♔g1 already does not work here) and White has to give back the piece: 28 ♘h1 ♕h5 29 ♘g3 fxg3 30 ♗xg3 with unclear consequences.

But now, just in time, White manages to erect a barrier and Black fails to obtain compensation for the sacrificed pawn.

26 h3 ♕g6 27 ♗b5! ♗xb5 28 axb5 ♖f8 29 ♘d1

Despite the full mobilization of forces on the kingside it is not easy to break through White's position,

while the dangers to Black's queenside have been neutralised.

29...hxg4?!

The champion pursues a "sacrificial" line, counting on an attack on the g2 square, but he should have restricted himself to 29...♕g5.

30 ♗xh4 f3 31 ♕c2 gxh3 32 g3??

Fear makes mountains out of molehills! White removes the threat to the g2 square, but overlooks a new resource for Black.

The simple 32 ♖fxf3 ♕xg2+ 33 ♕xg2 ♖xg2+ 34 ♔h1 would leave Black just a piece down.

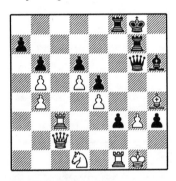

32...♖f4! 33 ♘e3?

Out of the frying pan into the fire! In protecting himself against 33...♖xh4 (34 ♘f5), J.Piket underestimates another threat by the rook. He should have chosen the defence 33 ♖fxf3 ♖xh4 34 ♘f2 h2+ 35 ♔h1.

33...♖xe4! 34 ♘f5?! ♕xf5 35 ♖cxf3 ♕g4 36 ♔h1

It turns out that 36 ♖f8+ ♔h7 37 ♖e1 which, though leading to the win of the exchange by 37...♕xh4 38 ♕xe4+ ♕xe4 39 ♖xe4, does not save White after 39...♖xg3+ 40 ♔h2 ♖b3! with the unpleasant threat of ...♗h6-f4.

36...♖f4! 37 ♖3f2 ♖xf2 38 ♖xf2 e4! 39 ♖f6 e3 40 ♖e6 ♕f3+

As noted by J.Piket, after 40...♖c7! 41 ♖g6+ ♗g7 42 ♖xg4 ♖xc2 43 ♗f6 e2 44 ♖xg7+ ♔f8 White could not avoid defeat, but it is not so easy to calculate such manoeuvres at the moment of the time control.

41 ♔g1 ♖f7 42 ♕g6+ ♗g7 43 ♖e8+ ♖f8 44 ♖xf8+ ♔xf8

On 44...♕xf8 White protects himself by 45 ♕e6+ ♕f7 46 ♕xe3 ♕xd5 47 ♕e2! followed by ♔h2. But now he finds a curious perpetual check.

45 ♗e7+! ♔g8

Or 45...♔xe7 46 ♕e6+ ♔f8 47 ♕c8+.

46 ♕e6+ ♕f7 47 ♕c8+ ♗f8 48 ♕g4+ ♗g7 49 ♕c8+ ♔h7 50 ♕xh3+ ♗h6 51 ♗g5 ♕f2+ ½-½

Game 30
Atalik *White* **Gufeld** *Black*
Los Angeles 1999

1 d4 ♘f6 2 c4 g6 3 ♘c3 ♗g7 4 e4 0-0

In my practice, I have often played this flexible move which provokes White into premature activity in the centre. It seemed to me that 5 e5 would now follow and we would immediately begin hand to hand fighting; Black would retreat 5...♘e8 and then he would organize a traditional break in the centre.

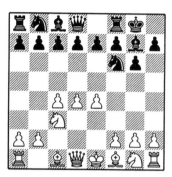

After 5 e5?! ♘e8 6 f4 d6! (weaker is 6...c5 7 dxc5 ♕a5 8 ♗e3) 7 ♗e3 c5! 8 dxc5 ♘c6 the white centre collapses. The game Letelier-Fischer, Leipzig (ol) 1960, proceeded 9 exd6?! (the careful 9 ♘f3 is better) 9...exd6 10 ♘e4 ♗f5! with a dangerous initiative for Black.

However, White usually pays no attention to Black's "suggestion" and prefers to play his favourite line.

5 ♘f3 d6 6 ♗e2 e5 7 0-0 ♘c6 8 d5 ♘e7 9 ♘e1 ♘d7 10 ♗e3 f5 11 f3 ♘f6

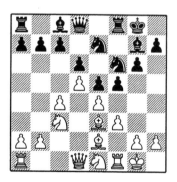

This move allows c4-c5 without any further preparations.

12 c5 f4 13 ♗f2 g5 14 a4 ♘g6 15 a5 h5

So now we see that, with the centre closed, White intends to expand on the queenside while Black counterattacks on the kingside.

Atalik was moving so fast and confidently here that I felt he had calculated in advance his entire plan.

16 cxd6 cxd6 17 ♘b5 g4 18 ♗xa7

After 18 ♘xa7 ♗d7 we have an unclear position in which, in my opinion, Black has sufficient initiative for the pawn.

18...g3 19 ♗b6 ♕e7 20 ♘c7

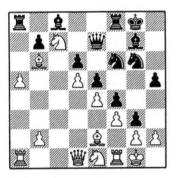

20...♘d7!!

A very important theoretical novelty. When I saw how visably it upset Atalik, I became convinced of its effectiveness. And this was confirmed by Fritz 5.32, when I asked it to analyse the move after the game. The computer attached two question marks to the move because it could not find anything like it in its database and did not understand the ideas behind it.

I want to mention how such discoveries take place. It was not a move found in home preparation, but a sudden inspiration of an intuitive nature. Of course I could not calculate all the consequences of the

move, but my intuition prompted me to make way for my queen to h4 after which I would get a dangerous attack.

21 h3

Of course, more spectacular was 21 ♘xa8 ♕h4 22 h3 ♘xb6 23 ♘xb6 ♗xh3 24 gxh3 ♕xh3 25 ♖f2 gxf2+ 26 ♔xf2, but in this case the white king could get trapped. My intuition told me Black has sufficient compensation for the sacrificed material. I am not a computer and as a human being it is more important to assess a position correctly than to calculate all the variations. In order to satisfy the reader's curiosity, out of the possible continuations 26...♕g3+, 26...♗f6, 26...♖f6, 26...♕h2+, let us examine just the last one: 27 ♘g2 (after 27 ♔f1 Black can force a draw by 27...♕h1+) 27...♘h4 28 ♕h1 (or 28 ♕f1 ♖f6 29 ♘c8 ♗f8 30 ♕h1 ♕g3+ 31 ♔f1 ♘xf3 32 ♖d1 ♖g6) 28...♕g3+ 29 ♔f1 ♘xf3 30 ♗xf3 (after 30 ♖d1 ♘h2+ 31 ♔g1 f3 32 ♕xh2 fxe2 Black wins) 30...♕xf3+ 31 ♔g1 ♕xe4 32 ♕h4 ♕d4+ 33 ♕f2 e4 34 ♖a4 ♕d1+ 35 ♕e1 ♕xe1+ 36 ♘xe1 f3 37 ♘c2 ♖f4 etc.

21...♘xb6 22 axb6 ♖xa1 23 ♕xa1 ♘h8

Black heads with his knight to g5 in order to increase the power of the threatened sacrifice on h3, since an immediate 23...♗xh3? 24 gxh3 ♕h4 25 ♔g2 clearly favours White.

24 ♗c4

After 24 ♘e6 Black can restore material equality with 24...♗xe6 25 dxe6 ♕xe6 when he has quite a comfortable game: he can take aim at the pawn on b6, prepare ...♘h8-f7-g5, or play 24...♘f7 as in the game.

24...♘f7 25 ♘e6 ♘g5!

25...♗xe6? 26 dxe6 ♘d8 27 ♗d5 favours White. The knight on e6 is a mighty piece and it could well be good to give a rook for it.

After 26 ♘xf8?! ♗xf8 Black seizes the initiative thanks to a possible sacrifice on h3. For example: 27 ♘d3 h4 28 ♗b5 ♗xh3 29 gxh3 ♘xh3+ 30 ♔g2 ♘g5 etc.

The only chance for White is to recover his pawn and transpose to the endgame which is usually considered in his favour.

But, everything is not so simple!

26 ♕a2 ♘xe6 27 dxe6 ♖e8 28 ♘d3

So the knight is heading for d5, counting on "sealing" the position and then getting down to realizing a positional advantage. Therefore, when playing 20...♘d7, I might have made an evaluation of precisely this position. But the main feature here—the black pawn on g3 —gives grounds to think that Black's chances are not worse. And look...the white king is not secure and in any endgame the g2 pawn would become an object of attack. And if the g2 pawn falls, followed by the collapse of its neighbours, the Black infantry will sweep the field.

28...♗xe6 29 ♗xe6+ ♕xe6 30 ♕xe6+ ♖xe6 31 ♘b4 ♖e8 32 ♖c1

Of course, the white rook could seize either open file but he can't have both of them. Atalik chooses the more important c-file. Otherwise, after 32 ♖a1 ♖c8 Black would be a little better.

32...♖a8

Threatening 33 ♖a2 White does not want to deactivate his rook by putting it on b1. He should free his king from danger area and use his rook to penetrate the black camp.

33 ♔f1 ♗f6!

Good! If 33...♔f7, then after 34 ♘d5 the black bishop faces difficulties.

34 ♘d5 ♗d8

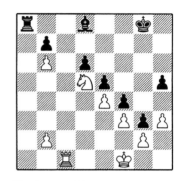

The key position.

35 ♔e2

Trying to force the situation with 35 ♖c7 does not change the assessment of the position. Of course 35...♗xc7? 36 bxc7 wins for White, but, after 35...♖a1+! 36 ♔e2 ♖g1 37 ♖xb7! (on 37 ♖c8?! ♖xg2+ 38 ♔d3 ♖f2 39 ♖xd8+ ♔g7 40 ♖d7+ ♔h6 41 ♖d8 ♔g5 it is Black who obtains winning chances) 37...♗xb6! 38 ♖xb6 ♖xg2+ 39 ♔d3 ♖f2 40 ♖b7 g2 41 ♖d7 f1=♕ 42 ♘f6+ ♔f8 43 ♘h7+ ♔e8 44 ♘f6+ the position is drawn.

35...♔f7 36 ♔d3 ♖a6

After the tempting 36...♔e6? 37 ♘c7+ ♗xc7 38 ♖xc7, in spite of the even material, I did not like this endgame at all. Therefore attacking the b6 pawn is the only way to hold the position, otherwise White simply marches his king to the queenside and wins.

37 ♖c8 ♗xb6 38 ♖b8 ♗g1 39 ♖xb7+ ♔g6 40 ♖d7 ♔g5 41 h4+ ♔g6 42 ♔c2 ♗d4 43 ♔b1

Atalik's king crawls to b1, not making real progress but preventing the black rook from occupying the a1 square.

43...♗c5 44 ♖b7

It is clear that 44 b4? ♗xb4 45 ♘xb4 ♖b6 is not in White's favour.

44...♖a4 45 ♖b3 ♔f7 46 ♖c3 ♔e8 47 ♖d3 ♖a7 48 ♔c2 ♔d7 49 b4 ♖a2+!

The most stubborn reply, but 49...♗d4 is also possible.

50 ♔b3 ♖xg2 51 bxc5 ♖f2 52 ♘c3

Now it is White who has to find ways to neutralize Black's passed pawn, since after 52 cxd6? g2 it cannot be stopped. Now on 52...g2 there is 53 ♖xd6+ and 54 ♖g6.

52...♔c6!!

What a revelation! In its profound effect the sacrament of this move's birth has something in common with 20...♘d7!!.

Aesthetically moves like this have such a great emotional influence, that, when discovering them, one can just rejoice over the incredible opportunities in chess.

And what is the idea of the king's move—which after 53 cxd6 seems to allow a free run to the passed pawn? The point is that the king returns by 53...♔d7!!, but the g3 pawn queens quicker than its counterpart on d6 and White loses: 54 ♘a4 g2 55 ♘c5+ ♔c6 56 d7 g1=♛ 57 d8=♛ ♛b1+ with two echo-mates 58 ♔c4 ♖c2+ 59 ♖c3 ♛b5

mate or 58 ♔a4 ♖a2+ 59 ♖a3 ♛b5 mate.

53 ♖xd6+ ♔xc5 54 ♖d5+

Otherwise the black pawns cannot be stopped.

54...♔c6 55 ♖xe5 ♖xf3

All the subsequent events took place in the turmoil of severe time-pressure and the final stage of the game was played in a state of high tension.

56 ♖g5

If 56 ♖xh5?, then 56...♖xc3+! 57 ♔xc3 g2 58 ♖g5 f3 and Black wins.

56...♖f2

The attempt to queen by 56...♖e3 57 ♔c4 f3 58 ♖xg3 f2 fails to 58 ♖g6+ ♔d7 59 ♖f6.

57 ♘d5

In severe time pressure 57 e5!? no doubt looks more active. If Black doesn't take serious measures against the e-pawn, he risks losing the game:

(a) 57...♖h2 58 e6 ♔d6 59 ♖e5 winning;

(b) 57...♔d7 58 ♔c4! ♖d2 (58...♖c2 59 ♔d3 ♖c1 60 ♘e2 or 58...♔e6 59 ♘e4 ♖h2 60 ♘c5+ ♔e7 61 ♖g7+ would lead to a quick loss) 59 ♘e4! ♖d1 60 ♘f6+ ♔e6 61 ♘xh5 with a great advantage to White;

(c) 57...g2 58 ♖g6+ ♔d7 (58...♔c7 59 e6 f3 60 ♖g7+) 59 e6+

♔e8 60 ♘e4! ♖e2 (60...♖f3+ 61 ♔c4 ♖g3 62 ♘xg3 g1=♕ 63 ♖g8+ ♔e7 64 ♔f5 winning) 61 ♘f6+ ♔f8 (61...♔d8 62 ♖g8+; 61...♔e7 62 ♘d5+) 62 ♖g8+ ♔e7 63 ♘d5+ ♔d6 (63...♔xe6 64 ♘xf4+) 64 ♘xf4 ♖e3+ 65 ♔c2 ♖e4 66 ♘xg2 ♔xe6 67 ♔d3 and White wins.

However Black saves himself by placing his rook behind the passed e-pawn: 57...♖f1! 58 ♔c4 ♖e1 59 ♖g6+ ♔d7 60 ♔d5 f3 61 ♖g7+ ♔e8 62 ♔e6 ♔d8 63 ♘b5 ♔c8 64 ♘a7+ ♔b8 65 ♘c6+ ♔c8 66 ♘e7+ ♔b8 ½-½.

57...g2 58 ♘b4+ ♔d6 59 e5+

Or 59 ♖g6+ ♔e7 60 ♘c6+ ♔f8 61 ♘d4 f3 draw.

59...♔d7 60 ♖g7+ ♔e8 61 ♘d3 ♖f3 62 ♖xg2 ♖xd3+ 63 ♔c4 ♖g3 64 ♖a2 f3 65 ♔d5 ♖g2 66 ♖a3 f2 67 ♖f3 ♔e7 68 ♖f4 ♖g4 69 ♖xf2 ♖xh4 70 ♖a2 ♖b4 71 ♖a7+ ♔e8 72 ♔c6 h4 73 ♖h7 ♖d4 74 ♔c5 ♖d1

I decided to go for the theoretically drawn position rather than retain material equality—which also draws: 74...♖a4=.

75 ♖xh4 ♔e7

The rest is of no interest. The game was **drawn** on the 89th move.

Game 31
Ivanchuk *White* **Shirov** *Black*
Tilburg 1993

1 d4 ♘f6 2 c4 g6 3 ♘c3 ♗g7 4 e4 d6 5 ♘f3 0-0 6 ♗e2 e5 7 0-0 ♘c6 8 d5 ♘e7 9 ♘d2

A well-known theoretical position. Recently 9 ♘d2 has become very popular. The idea is easy to understand: White wants to strengthen the pawn structure on the kingside without changing it by playing f2-f3, and to transfer the burden of the battle to the queenside. As the centre is locked, Black

naturally seeks his fortune on the kingside.

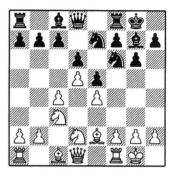

9...c6

This continuation, undermining the centre, along with 9...c5, is considered the principal reaction to 9 ♘d2. The traditional response in such positions, 9...♘d7, allows White the possibility of getting ahead in the race by 10 b4 f5 11 c5. On the other hand, 9...♘e8 is weaker, since the knight does nothing to forestall the c4-c5 advance.

10 dxc6

Black must also be prepared for this exchange when playing 9...c5.

When trying to retain the tension in the centre, White should always reckon on a possible undermining of his bridgehead of pawns.

On 10 ♖b1 good is 10...b5! 11 dxc6 b4 12 ♘d5 ♘xc6 13 ♘xf6+ ♗xf6 14 ♘f3 ♗g4 15 ♗e3 ♗xf3 16 ♗xf3 ♘d4 and Black equalizes. Gligorić-A.Kuzmin, Moscow GMA 1989.

On 10 b4, instead of 10...b5, stronger is 10...a5!, which was the topic of a discussion between A.Shirov and Z.Lanka:

(a) 11 bxa5 ♕xa5 12 ♕c2 c5 13 ♘b3 ♕d8 14 a4 (or 14 f4 exf4 15 ♗xf4 h6! 16 ♖ae1 g5 with a double-edged game, Shirov-Lanka, USSR 1988) 14...♘d7! 15 ♗e3 f5 16 f3 f4

17 ♗f2 g5 18 a5 h5 19 ♘a4 ♔h8 20 ♖fb1 ♖g8 21 ♕b2 ♘g6 and here, in the game Shirov-Lanka, USSR 1989, instead of 22 h3?!, which would give Black better play after 22...♖a6, A.Shirov indicates as strongest 22 ♘axc5! dxc5 23 ♘xc5 ♘xc5 24 ♗xc5 g4 25 ♕b6! with active play which compensates the sacrificed piece.

(b) 11 dxc6 axb4 12 cxb7 ♗xb7 13 ♘d5 ♘exd5 14 cxd5 ♘d7! 15 ♕b3 ♘c5! 16 ♕xb4 ♖a4 17 ♕b1 ♕a8 ∓ Shirov-Lanka, USSR 1989.

10...bxc6 11 b4

The idea of attacking the centre by 11 ♘b3 ♗e6 (after 11...d5 and general exchange on d5 White plays ♗e2-f3 and obtains an advantage) 12 f4 certainly deserves attention.

11...d5

Undermining by ...f7-f5 is not effective in the present semi-open position: 11...♘e8 12 ♘b3 f5 13 ♗a3 fxe4 14 ♘xe4 and White stands better.

The move 11...♘h5 is linked to a pawn sacrifice: 12 ♗xh5 (after 12 g3 a6! 13 ♖e1 f5 14 ♗f3 ♘f6 Black carries out the idea ...f7-f5 without material loss) 12...gxh5 13 ♕xh5 f5 14 ♖d1! (14 ♘f3 fxe4 15 ♘xe4 ♗f5 is weaker) 14...♖b8!? (before playing ...d6-d5 it is useful to bring up the reserves—in this respect 14...♕c7!? is not bad) 15 a3 (on 15 b5 there is 15...♕a5!) 15...d5 16 cxd5 cxd5 17 ♘xd5 ♘xd5 18 exd5 ♕xd5 19 ♗b2 a5 ± (A.Guseinov).

12 a4

White creates a solid pawn mass on the queenside, intending 12...d4 13 ♘a2 ♗e6 14 ♗a3 followed by b4-b5, because after 12 ♗a3 a6 it is more difficult to carry out the advance b4-b5: 13 ♖e1 h6 (or 13...♗e6 14 ♗f1 h6 15 cxd5 cxd5 16 exd5 ♘exd5 17 ♘a4 ±

K.Grigorian-Gufeld, Vilnius (zt) 1975) 14 ♖b1 ♖e8 15 ♗f1 ♗g4 with approximately equal chances, Sinkovics-Uhlmann, Stary Smokovec 1985.

An immediate 12 b5 can be met by 12...d4 13 ♘a4 ♘h5 (or 13...cxb5 14 cxb5 d3 15 ♗f3 ♗d7 or 13...♗h6! 14 ♘c5 a6 15 a4 ♘d7 and Black maintains equality) 14 ♘c5 ♘f4 15 ♘db3 ♔h8 16 a4 ♘xe2+!? (16...♘g8?! 17 ♗xf4 exf4 18 ♘d3± is weaker, Lputian-A.Fedorov, Elista (ol) 1998) 17 ♕xe2 ♘g8 with chances for both sides (A.Fedorov).

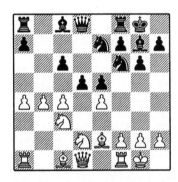

12...♘h5

Taking into account White's lag in development, Black sacrifices a pawn to open up the position.

In Ftáčnik-Lanka, Germany 1994, there followed 12...g5 13 cxd5 cxd5 14 exd5 ♘fxd5 15 ♘xd5 ♘xd5 16 ♘e4 and, after the careless 16...g4? 17 ♗g5 f6 18 ♗c4, White achieved an advantage; more natural is 16...♘f4!? 17 ♗xf4 exf4 (or 17...gxf4 18 ♗c4 ±) 18 ♕xd8 ♖xd8 19 ♖ad1 ♗d7 20 b5 and White retains some initiative (L.Ftáčnik).

13 exd5

Upon the acceptance of the sacrifice 13 ♗xh5 gxh5 14 ♕xh5 f5 15 exd5 cxd5 16 cxd5 ♘xd5 17 ♘xd5

♕xd5 18 ♖a3 f4! Black gains an aggressive e- and f-pawn pair (A.Shirov).

13...cxd5 14 cxd5 ♗b7 15 d6!

White returns the pawn and transposes to a favourable endgame in which he can count on creating an outside passed pawn on the queenside.

15...♕xd6 16 ♘de4 ♕xd1

Otherwise after 17 ♗xh5 Black would not have sufficient compensation for the lost pawn.

17 ♖xd1 ♘f5?

A tactical miscalculation. It was necessary to consolidate the position by 17...♘f6 ±.

18 ♘c5 e4 19 ♖a3 ♖ac8 20 g4 a5

The alternative 20...♘d4 21 gxh5 a5 does not make the situation easier: 22 ♘xb7 axb4 23 ♖a2 etc.

21 ♘xb7 axb4 22 ♖b3 ♘d4 23 ♖xb4 ♖xc3 24 ♖bxd4 ♗xd4 25 gxh5 ♖c2 26 ♔f1

The advantage of the white minor pieces over the rook is increased further by the presence of the passed a-pawn.

26...♖a8! 27 a5 ♗e5! 28 a6

He should have removed the h-pawn from attack but stubbornly continues to ignore it.

28...f5 29 ♗e3

Here too, 29 h3 is not too late.

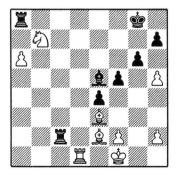

29...♖xe2

A.Shirov prefers to play on a piece down rather than be tied down by the passed pawn.

30 ♔xe2 ♖xa6 31 ♖d8+?!

White is carried away by cleaning up behind enemy lines, and leaves the h2-pawn unprotected.

31...♔f7 32 ♖d7+ ♔f6 33 ♖xh7 ♖a2+ 34 ♗d2 gxh5 35 ♘c5

Of course not 35 ♖xh5?? in view of 35...♗f4, but here there is a last chance to play 35 h3, though in a less favourable situation than previously: 35...♗f4 36 ♖d7 ♗xd2 37 ♖xd2 ♖a3 ±.

35...♗xh2 36 ♖xh5 ♗g1!

An unexpected resource: White cannot avoid the loss of the last pawn.

37 ♘b3 f4 38 ♔d1

On 38 ♔f1 would follow 38...e3.

38...♗xf2 39 ♗xf4 e3 40 ♗xe3 ½-½

Game 32
Sherbakov *White* **Gufeld** *Black*
Hastings 1994/95

1 d4 ♘f6 2 c4 g6 3 ♘c3 ♗g7 4 e4 0-0 5 ♘f3 d6

Besides my favourite King's Indian reply, sometimes I used to play successfully 5...c6!? with the idea of ...d7-d5 which is in the spirit of the Grunfeld Indian Defence:

(a) 6 h3 d5 7 e5 ♘e4 8 ♗d3 ♘xc3 9 bxc3 c5 10 0-0 ♘c6 11 cxd5 ♕xd5 12 ♖e1 cxd4 13 ♗e4 ♕c4 14 cxd4 ♖d8= Chernin-Gufeld, Palma de Mallorca GMA 1989;

(b) 6 ♗e2 d5 7 e5 ♘e4 8 0-0 ♗f5 9 ♕b3 ♕b6 10 ♕xb6 axb6 11 cxd5 ♘xc3 12 bxc3 cxd5= Imocha-Gufeld, Calcutta 1992.

6 ♗e2 e5 7 0-0 ♘c6 8 d5 ♘e7 9 ♘d2

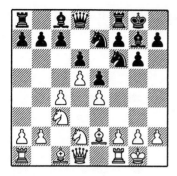

9...c5

Recently 9...a5 has become popular—ever since Kasparov started using this method. Certainly ...a5 slows down White's queenside play a little but Black must still create counterplay on the other flank. There are quite a few people imitating Kasparov, and in respect of the 9...a5 variation, he resembles the famous designer Christian Dior. I hate to copy anyone which is why I prefer the move 9...c5. I consider it no worse than the fashionable 9...a5.

10 dxc6

The alternative—launching an attack on the c5-pawn by b2-b4—is examined in the next game.

10...bxc6 11 b4 d5

With the position now being of a semi-open character, a return to the theme of undermining the white pawn centre by ...f7-f5 is not effective: 11...♘e8 12 ♘b3 f5 13 ♗a3 fxe4 14 ♘xe4 and White stands better.

The move 11...♘h5 is linked to a pawn sacrifice: 12 ♗xh5 (after 12 g3 a6! 13 ♖e1 f5 14 ♗f3 ♘f6 Black carries out the ...f7-f5 idea without losses) 12...gxh5 13 ♕xh5 f5 14 ♖d1! (weaker is 14 ♘f3 fxe4 15 ♘xe4 ♗f5) 14...♖b8!? (before playing ...d6-d5 it is useful to bring up reserves—in this respect 14...♕c7!? is also not bad) 15 a3 (if 15 b5

♕a5!) 15...d5 16 cxd5 cxd5 17 ♘xd5 ♘xd5 18 exd5 ♕xd5 19 ♗b2 a5 ⩲ (A.Guseinov).

12 ♗a3 ♖e8

I like this logical move. Black moves his rook away from the bishop's x-ray, the effect of which can be clearly seen, for example, after 12...d4?! 13 ♘a4 ♘e8 14 b5.

In the USSR Zonal tournament, held in Vilnius 1975, I played against Karen Grigorian 12...a6 13 ♖e1 ♗e6 (The *Encyclopedia* recommends 13...h5 14 ♖b1 ♖e8 15 ♗f1 ♗g4=) 14 ♗f1 h6 15 cxd5 cxd5 16 exd5 ♘exd5 17 ♘a4 ♕b8 18 ♘c5 ♗f5 19 ♕b3 and still White's chances proved to be preferable.

13 ♖e1

According to R.Knaak's analysis White could have maintained the initiative by 13 b5! ♗e6 (no better is 13...♕a5 14 ♗b2 ♘e4 15 ♘dxe4 dxe4 16 ♘xe4) 14 bxc6 d4 15 ♘b5 ♘xc6 16 ♘d6 ♗e7 17 ♕a4 with the idea of the clamping c4-c5. But now Black equalizes by a knight swoop to d4.

13...dxe4

In the game Ulibin-Bologan, Chalkidiki 1992, there followed 13...♗e6 14 ♗f1 dxe4 15 ♘dxe4 ♘xe4 16 ♘xe4 ♘f5 17 ♗b2 and here, instead of 17...♕e7?!,

17...♕b6! 18 a3 ♖ed8 19 ♕a4 a5! would have maintained equality (V.Bologan).

14 ♘cxe4 ♘f5

This knight is *en route* to d4. Black has solved all his opening problems. My opinion is that Black has equalised in the opening.

15 ♗b2 ♖b8 16 a3

16 ♕a4 a5 17 b5 cxb5 18 cxb5 ♗b7 is unclear.

16...a5 17 ♗c3 axb4 18 axb4 ♘d4 19 ♘xf6+ ♕xf6 20 ♘e4 ♕e7

21 ♗xd4?!

A small mistake. Now the position swings more and more in Black's favour, 21 c5!? ♖d8 22 ♘d6 ♘f5 23 ♘xc8 ♖bxc8 would have maintained equality.

21...exd4 22 ♗d3 ♗e6

The pawn is poisoned because of ♘f6+.

23 ♘c5 ♖xb4 24 ♘xe6 fxe6 25 ♖a2 ♖f8

White might try to exploit the opposite-coloured bishops and attack along the b1-h7 diagonal in conjunction with an advance of the h-pawn, but nevertheless Black retains the advantage.

26 g3 e5 27 h4 ♕f7 28 ♔g2

This move is too optimistic. Better is 28 ♕e2 ♔h8 with a slight advantage to Black. But 28 h5 is met by 28...gxh5!

28...♖xc4! 29 ♗xc4 ♕xc4 30 ♖c2 ♕d5+?!

Much better was 30...♕b5! The c-pawn is very difficult to stop and Black retains the check as a future possibility.

The text move allows White to blockade the pawns.

31 f3 c5?

Still it is not too late to return to 31...♕b5! and White would not have sufficient defensive resources: 32 ♕b1 ♕d3! 33 ♖f2 (or 33 ♕d1 ♖xf3!) 33...♕xb1 34 ♖xb1 c5, followed by ...♖c8, ...♔f7-e6-d5, ...♗f8-d6 But now White manages to block the passed pawns.

32 ♕d3 ♖c8 33 ♖c4!=

I had only prepared for 33 ♕c4? ♕xc4 34 ♖xc4 ♔f7 with the idea of ...♔e6-d5, but now, having lost my advantage, I fell into time trouble.

33...♗h6

Black would have retained some chances after 33...♗f8!? with ...♗d6 to follow.

34 ♖e2 ♖f8

Threatening to capture on f3.

35 ♖e4 ♖f7 36 ♖a4 ♖c7 37 ♖c4 ♖f7 38 ♖a4 ♖c7 39 ♖c4 ♖f7 40 ♖a4 ♖c7 ½-½

Game 33
Kamsky *White* **Yurtaev** *Black*
Manila (ol) 1992

1 d4 ♘f6 2 c4 g6 3 ♘c3 ♗g7 4
e4 d6 5 ♘f3 0-0 6 ♗e2 e5 7 0-0
♘c6 8 d5 ♘e7 9 ♘d2 c5

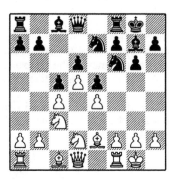

10 ♖b1
White declines to capture the c-pawn and prepares an advance of the b-pawn.

The old method of attacking the c5-pawn—10 a3 ♘e8 11 b4 has "collected dust" in the archives of theory after the game Korchnoi-Tringov, Kapfenberg 1970, which proceeded 11...b6 12 bxc5 (or 12 ♖b1 f5 with equal chances) 12...bxc5 13 ♘b3 f5 14 f3 ♔h8! 15 ♗d2 ♘g8 16 ♖b1 ♘gf6 17 ♕c2 ♘h5 18 g3 ♘ef6 19 exf5 gxf5 when the game is equal.

10...♘e8
Considered a main line.

11 b4 b6 12 bxc5 bxc5
In case of 12...dxc5 13 a4 White's chances are preferable.

13 ♘b3
In the 70s, 13 ♕a4 f5 14 ♘b3 was preferred—but this is also no good.

13...f5
A natural consequence of the retreat 10...♘e8. However, taking into account the problems which arise after the pin by 14 ♗g5, some

specialists of this variation wait with the advance ...f7-f5 until the c1 bishop has been developed, preferring to make the useful move 13...♔h8!?. For example: 14 ♗d2 f5 15 f3 (after 15 ♘b5 good is 15...fxe4! 16 ♗a5 ♕d7 17 ♘d2 ♕f5! 18 ♘c3 ♘f6 with level play for Black, Shirov-Lanka, Torcy 1990) 15...f4 (weaker is 15...♘g8 16 exf5 gxf5 17 f4±) 16 ♘b5 h5 17 ♗a5 ♕d7 18 ♘c1 ♘g8 19 ♕a4 ♖f7 20 ♘d3 g5 with sufficient counterplay for Black. Chernin-Belotti, Reggio Emilia 1994/95.

14 ♗g5!
Rather an unpleasant pin, since Black has to reckon with the threat 15 ♘a5.

14 f3 is also possible, on which 14...f4?! is premature, since after 15 ♕e1 g5 16 g4 Black has to exchange on g3 with better play for White. Therefore making a useful move, 14...♔h8, freeing a square for the e7-knight, is better.

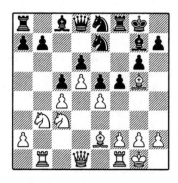

14...♗f6
(a) 14...h6 (this radical way of eliminating the pin does not save Black from his problems, since the knight reaches c6 anyway: 15 ♗xe7 ♕xe7 16 ♘a5 ♘f6 (16...♗d7?! 17 ♖b7±) 17 ♘c6 ♕d7 (a loss of time is 17...♕e8 18 ♘b5 ♕d7 19 exf5

gxf5 20 罝b3! 罝f7 21 罝a3± Cosma-A.Fedorov, Romania 1995) 18 f3 h5! 19 豐e1 奧h6 20 奧d1 奧a6 21 奧a4 豐h7! 22 奧b5 奧c8 23 罝b3 h4 and here, instead of 24 exf5 gxf5= Hertneck-Wahls, Munchen 1991, as noted by Hertneck, White retains the initiative by 24 罝a3 a6 25 奧a4 奧f4 26 奧c2! with the idea of 心a4.

(b) 14...心f6 (allowing the position to be opened up by a tactical stroke based on the unprotected a8 rook) 15 心xc5! dxc5 16 d6 奧e6 17 dxe7 豐xe7 18 f3! 罝ab8 19 心d5 豐f7 20 奧e3 罝xb1 21 豐xb1 罝c8 22 豐b5 奧f8 23 豐a6! with a serious positional advantage for White, Shirov-Zarnicki, Timisoara 1988

(c) 14...含h8 (Black moves his king away to neutralise the effect of the knight sacrifice on c5) 15 exf5 gxf5 16 f4 (possible here is 16 心xc5!? dxc5 17 d6 心xd6 18 心d5 罝e8 19 心xe7 罝xe7 20 豐d5 奧b7 21 罝xb7! 心xb7 22 豐xd8+ 罝xd8 23 奧xe7 罝d2 24 奧h5 e4 25 罝b1 罝xa2 and here in the game Farago-Watson, Beer-Sheva 1987, White could have retained the initiative by 26 奧xc5! 心xc5 27 罝b8+ 奧f8 28 罝xf8+ 含g7 29 罝f7+ 含h6 30 g4 ± L.Ftacnik) 16...h6 17 奧h4 exf4! (17...e4 18 豐c2 ±) 18 豐d2 心f6 19 奧xf6! 奧xf6 20 奧h5! 奧a6! 21 心e2 奧xc4 22 豐f4 奧xd5?! 23 豐h6+ 含g8 24 心f4 and White has the initiative, Polugaevsky-Timoshchenko, Moscow GMA 1990.

15 奧d2 含h8 16 f3
More energetic is 16 心b5! 心g8 17 心a5 奧d7 18 奧f3! and White stands better. Kishnev-Hausrath, Dortmund 1993.

16...心g8 17 心a4?!
Black would have faced a more complicated task after 17 豐c1. But now he can exchange his passive bishop and activate his queen.

17...奧g5!
A typical trick in such pawn formations.

18 奧xg5 豐xg5 19 豐c1 豐h5!
There is no reason for Black to exchange the active queen.

20 豐e1 豐h6 21 豐c3
He should have offered the exchange again by 21 豐c1, since 21...f4 can be met by the blockading 22 g4. But now the initiative passes to Black.

21...心ef6! 22 exf5 奧xf5 23 罝be1 罝ae8 24 心b2 心h5 25 心d1 心f4 26 心e3 心f6 27 g3

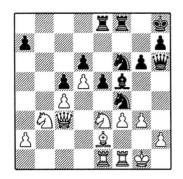

27...心e4?!
This combination is only sufficient to force a draw. Stronger is 27...心h3+ 28 含g2 心g5, retaining attacking chances.

28 fxe4 心h3+ 29 含h1
The only move. 29 含g2? 奧xe4+ 30 奧f3 罝xf3! 31 罝xf3 心g5 loses.

29...奧xe4+ 30 心g2 心f2+ 31 含g1 心h3+ 32 含h1 心f2 33 罝xf2 心xf2+ 34 含g1 心h3+ 35 含h1 罝f8 36 罝f1 心f2+ 37 含g1 心h3+ 38 含h1 罝xf1+ 39 奧xf1 豐f8 40 豐e1 ½-½

Game 34
Browne *White* **Gufeld** *Black*
Los Angeles 1995

1 d4 ♘f6 2 c4 g6 3 ♘c3 ♗g7 4 e4 0-0

This game was played in the last round of the Los Angeles Open when I was leading by half a point. If he beat me, Browne would at least tie for first. On the other hand I was happy to draw and become joint champion. This was my third encounter with Browne over the 64 squares. Time and again in in my chess career I have succeeded in creating something on the chessboard when my opponents were strong. With weaker opponents, as a rule, I cannot create anything—they, on the other hand, have frequently gained even full points from me.

5 ♗e2 d6 6 ♘f3 e5 7 0-0 ♘c6 8 d5 ♘e7 9 ♘d2 c5

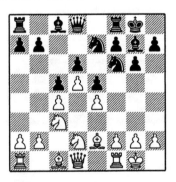

10 ♖b1

This move, along with 10 dxc6, is considered the main continuation.

10...♘d7

Forcing White into long and deep thought. After the game Browne told me that he was familiar with 10...♘d7, but was trying to remember what the *Encyclopedia* recommended. In fact the 1998 *Encyclopedia*, based on my game

with Li Wenliang (which is considered later) is very dubious about the move 10...♘d7 and recommends instead 10...♘e8 as the main line.

An immediate 10...b6 11 b4 cxb4 12 ♖xb4 has also been played, when the move 12...♘d7 is fully justified:

(a) 13 ♖b1 ♘c5 14 ♘b3 f5 15 ♘xc5 bxc5 16 ♗d2 fxe4 17 ♘xe4 ♘f5 18 ♗d3 ♘d4 with an equal game. Bukić-Gligorić, Yugoslavia 1971;

(b) 13 a4 ♗h6! 14 a5 bxa5 15 ♖b1 ♗a6 with complex play, Psakhis-Loginov, Manila (ol) 1992

11 ♘b5

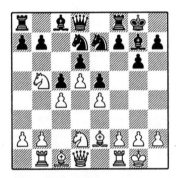

11...♘b8!?

Browne said that the recommendation in the *Encyclopedia* was 11...♕b6. To be honest, I was not aware of that recommendation but in any case it would not occur to me to place my queen opposite the long-range rook on b1. When preparing this book I looked through the *Encylopeadia* and was not disappointed, since 11...♕b6 is condemned, and as an example they give the game Lputian-Khalifman, USSR (ch) 1987, which proceeded as follows 12 b4! cxb4 13 a3 bxa3 14 c5! ♘xc5 (14...dxc5 15 d6 ♘c6 16 ♘c7 is in White's favour) 15 ♗a3 ♕d8 16 ♘xd6! with advantage to White.

I do not exclude the fact that experts might regard the theoretical novelty 11...♘b8 as a paradox. The knight from b8 transferred to e7 and later on to g8, and the knight g8 journeyed to b8. The knights "work in mysterious ways". And indeed this is all quite remarkable—maybe some kind of "first" in tournament play. The knight is heading for a6 in order to take the critical c5 square under its control.

12 a3 f5 13 b4 ♘a6 14 ♘b3 b6

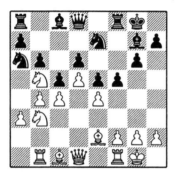

15 f3

This move seems inaccurate to me. Of course at this point White should dare to open the b-file. What does it mean to "dare"? This was in his plans: 15 bxc5 ♘xc5 16 ♘xc5 bxc5 and only then 17 f3. A complicated position arises that is very hard to balance out. To my regret I failed to prove the pluses for Black in future practice. The game Li Wenliang-Gufeld, Beijing 1996, continued 17...♔h8 18 ♗d2 ♘g8 19 ♕a4 a5 20 ♕c2 ♘f6 21 ♘c3 f4 22 ♘a4 ♘d7 23 ♖b5 g5 24 ♖fb1 ♖g8 25 ♖1b3 ♗f8 26 ♗e1 with an initiative for White.

15...cxb4!

An uncompromising solution. War is declared.

16 axb4 ♘xb4 17 ♘3d4

This move was probably the result of detailed consideration. I imagine that Walter came to the conclusion that 17 ♗a3 a5 18 ♕d2 ♗a6 19 ♗xb4 axb4 20 ♕xb4 ♗xb5 21 ♕xb5 ♗h6 was dangerous for White, as the bishop breaks out to freedom by seizing the most important diagonal.

17...exd4

Browne thought that 17...a5 was stronger, but I didn't agree with him. Evidently he was considering the continuation 18 ♘c6 ♕d7. It is true that in this variation there might not be sufficient compensation for a pawn. However, after 17...a5, I feared 18 ♘e6 ♗xe6 19 dxe6. This traditional strategy, linked to the d5 square and the two bishops, is promising for White and such a position did not appeal to me.

Now a forced sequence of moves follows.

18 ♖xb4 fxe4 19 fxe4 ♖xf1+ 20 ♗xf1

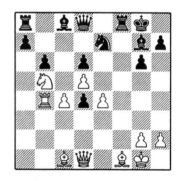

20...♗d7!

The white knight on b5, which has entered my territory without invitation, is in my way. It must go away or it will be destroyed. The technical justification: White cannot take, 21 ♘xd6, because after 21...♗e5! Black seizes the initiative.

21 ♘xd4 ♕c7

To complete the development of his pieces is a mandatory, strategical requirement.

22 ♗e3 ♖e8

Black has a defect in his camp—the poor position of the knight e7. On this square it has no prospects. But now there appears the threat of ...♘e7-f5. This move, though not winning anything, helps to get rid of this defect. So White has to take measures...

23 ♕d2 ♔h8

The king himself starts to show concern for the wretched knight by freeing a square from where it has prospects of reaching f6.

24 ♘f3!

My opponent realizes that it takes time to breathe fresh air into the black knight, so he immediately tries to exploit his superior activity.

24...♘g8

If Black manages to post the knight on f6, he will have reason to be more optimistic about his position. but Browne doesn't want to give Black any chances.

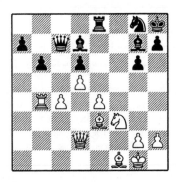

25 e5!

An original pawn sacrifice. Taking advantage of the fact that Black, essentially, has not completed his development and has lost time in the mobilisation of his forces, White launches an attack.

25...dxe5 26 d6 ♕c6 27 c5

An absolutely correct strategy. Upon 27 ♘g5 ♘f6 28 c5 bxc5 29 ♖h4 ♖f8, Black would repel the hasty flank attack. Walter's action in the centre seemed more dangerous for me.

27...♘f6!

Probably the only move, since otherwise I could fall under a strong attack. By returning the Greek gift of a pawn, I complete the development of my pieces...

28 cxb6 axb6 29 ♖xb6 ♕d5!

Any piece in the centre is always a force to be reckoned with. Essentially this was the only move. At this point my opponent, experiencing serious time pressure, made a mistake.

30 ♖a6?

Were there any other possibilities? During the game I was considering 30 ♕c2 followed by ♗c4 and, after 30...♖c8, I discovered an interesting queen sacrifice. 31 ♕xc8+ ♗xc8 32 ♖b8.

The first impression was quite unpleasant, but later on I found out that I would be able to buy my way out with a bishop. 32...h6 33 ♖xc8+ ♔h7 and Black gains an obvious advantage.

In my opinion, the only continuation where White could maintain a precarious balance was 30 ♗g5 with the threat of 31 ♗xf6. Probably Black should trade queens, 30...♛xd2 31 ♘xd2 e4, when his position seems preferable. Browne's choice in time pressure leads to the loss of a piece. The following swift pawn advance sweeps everything in its path.

30...e4 31 ♘e1 ♛xd2 32 ♗xd2 e3 33 ♗c3 e2 34 ♗xe2 ♖xe2 35 ♘f3 ♘d5! 36 ♖a8+ ♖e8 37 ♗xg7+ ♔xg7 38 ♖a7

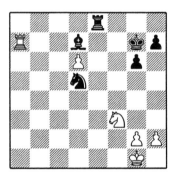

38...♘f6?

Here I made a mistake—after winning the piece I failed to play the strongest move. I managed to find this only during the post mortem analysis—38...♖d8 39 ♘e5 ♘b6! 40 ♖b7 ♔f6 would lead to an easy victory. One does not always have to play defensively. At times, as here, attack is the best defence. A most elementary win—although the chosen continuation still preserves Black's advantage.

Recently it has been ascertained that endgames with a king, rook and two minor pieces against king, rook and minor piece are winning most of the time. In the majority of cases this is achieved by creating an attack on the king. This game may be of interest to those who study

positions with such an alignment of forces.

39 g4 g5 40 h4!

40 ♘xg5 ♔g6 is obviously in Black's favour.

40...h6 41 hxg5 hxg5 42 ♘xg5 ♖e3 43 ♔f2 ♘xg4+ 44 ♔f1 ♘f6 45 ♔f2 ♖e5 46 ♘f3 ♖d5 47 ♖a6 ♔f7 48 ♔e3

Theoretically this is winning for Black.

48...♗f5 49 ♘d4 ♘g4+ 50 ♔f4 ♗c8 51 ♖a7+ ♔f6 52 ♔e4 ♖xd6 53 ♖c7 ♗d7 54 ♖c1 ♖a6 55 ♔d5 ♘e3+ 56 ♔c5 ♖a8 57 ♖e1 ♘f5 58 ♘xf5 ♗xf5

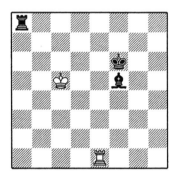

So I have transposed into an endgame of rook and bishop against rook. Chess is an amazingly profound game. Although it appears to have been exhaustively analysed, there are still grey areas. I don't know anybody today who would be brave enough to state categorically whether this position is a win or a draw.

Many years ago, my friend and colleague, Efim Geller, was analyzing the position of rook and bishop against rook. It proved impossible to reveal all the possibilities and he came to the conclusion that most of the positions could be won in practice. My own practice also confirms this: I have won all the games for the stronger side and lost all for the weaker one!

59 ♖f1 ♔e5 60 ♖e1+ ♗e4 61 ♔b6 ♖c8 62 ♖e2 ♖c1 63 ♖e3 ♔d4 64 ♖e2 ♖b1+ 65 ♔c7 ♔e5 66 ♖d2 ♖b7+ 67 ♔c8?

In my opinion the white king is going in the wrong direction.

He should have gone to the centre —67 ♔d8 with the idea of ♔e8-f8. When the stronger side has a white-squared bishop, the position is considered drawn if the king of the weaker side is on f8 and his rook controls the f7 square.

67...♖h7 68 ♔b8 ♗d5 69 ♖d1 ♔d6 70 ♖d2

At this point there was a minor interruption of the game.

Browne had only two minutes left and I about forty minutes. All of a sudden my opponent engaged the tournament directors in a persuasive argument. They then brought out a chess arbiter's reference book and bgean explaining something to me.

"Are you going to call it a draw here?", I asked them with a smile and showed them the position. This misunderstanding was quickly resolved, the tournament directors apologized to me for some incorrect interpretation and we returned to the game. After a few moves it was all over.

70...♖b7+ 71 ♔c8 ♖b1 72 ♖d4 ♖h1 73 ♔b8 ♖h8+ 74 ♔a7 ♔c5 0-1

Illustrative Games—7 d5

After **1 d4 ♘f6 2 c4 g6 3 ♘c3 ♗g7 4 e4 d6 5 ♘f3 0-0 6 ♗e2 e5** White often closes the centre by **7 d5**, and denies Black of the possibility of developing his knight on c6.

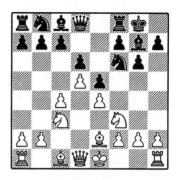

By immediately closing the centre White determines the further course of the struggle. His open structure looks ideal for a queenside offensive. However, with such an early stabilisation of the centre, Black is entitled to seek counterplay on the opposite side of the board. He will have the opportunity to occupy the c5 square temporarily, so as to impede White's queenside attack while also preparing his traditional play based on the break ...f7-f5. For this reason the early advance of the white d-pawn may be viewed as a definite achievement for Black, not only objectively but also psychologically—since White appears to have demonstrated his unwillingness (maybe due to timidity?) to conduct a serious dispute in the sharp Taimanov-Aronin System.

One drawback of such an early definition of a position is that Black obtains the possibility of temporarily halting White's attack on the queenside by 7...a5 (sometimes 7...c5 is also played) or he can proceed with his development by 7...♘bd7. A radical way to hinder Black's counterplay is the Petrosian System, which is characterized by the move 8 ♗g5. By developing the bishop White pins down the queen and transfers the knight (♘f3-d2) to the queenside to attack it.

Theory considers the obvious 7...♘h5, preventing the pin, as being unfavourable, based on an old game of mine with Tigran Petrosian. Since there was an unexpected echo of the consequences of this game a few decades later, I think it is useful to show it to the reader.

There has been a tendency among chess writers to present the "King's Indian" g7-bishop as a prime example in demonstrating the notion of "bad bishop". In 1994, Boris Gulko, in his article *The Mystery of "Bad" Bishops,* analysed my game against Petrosian, which had in fact already been annotated by Isaak Boleslavsky, the former world champion's coach. The analyst, presumably proceeding from the result, had given a wrong evaluation of the position. Try to imagine my feelings when I read Gulko's article and found the same mistake of principle.

Game 35
T.Petrosian *White* **Gufeld** *Black*
USSR (ch) Leningrad 1960

1 d4 ♘f6 2 c4 g6 3 ♘c3 ♗g7 4 e4 d6 5 ♘f3 0-0 6 ♗e2 e5 7 d5 ♘h5

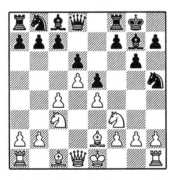

It is clear that Black's reaction to the closing of the centre will be to undermine it by ...f7-f5. However, in the present position this obvious move is not the best. Black will not manage to advance ...f7-f5 without making positional concessions. But I did not want to play 7...♘bd7 8 ♗g5 against Petrosian, whose "King's Indian" conception was to limit Black's kingside counterplay with a pin on the knight in conjunction with a closed centre—a line that was officially named the Petrosian System.

8 g3 ♘a6

On 8...f5?! would follow simply 9 exf5 when both 9...gxf5? 10 ♘xe5 and 9...♗xf5 10 ♘g5 are bad for Black.

The game T.Petrosian-I.Zaitsev, Moscow 1966, proceeded 9...♕f6 10 ♘g5! ♕xf5 11 0-0 ♘f6 12 f3 and White consolidated his hold on the e4 square with an occupation by one of his pieces.

On 8...a5 possible is 9 ♘d2 ♘f6 10 h4, as in the game.

9 ♘d2 ♘f6 10 h4

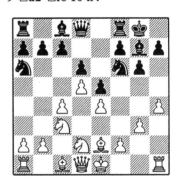

"An important part of White's plan. Now, on 10...♗h6 with the aim of exchanging the dark-squared bishops, there follows 11 h5 and Black stands badly. Besides, the threat of further advancing the pawn deters Black from playing ...f7-f5 for a long time", is the way I.Boleslavsky commented on the move 10 h4. Nevertheless, White still has not completed the development of his pieces and it seems to me that Black's problems are rather exaggerated...

10...c6 11 ♘b3 ♘c7 12 ♗g5

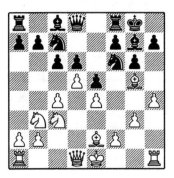

12...cxd5

"In spite of clarifying the situation in the centre, I think this move was a decisive mistake", Gulko writes. It is surprising how easily the famous grandmaster passes sentence on a standard exchange in the opening!

13 cxd5 h6

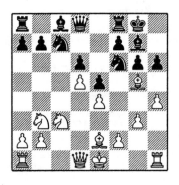

14 ♗xf6?

Neither Boleslavsky nor Gulko had explained this exchange, which aims to leave Black with a "bad" bishop. To this end, White does not spare the life of his..."good" one! I associate this idea with the joke about the man who decided to pull

out his eye because he wanted his mother-in-law to have a one-eyed son-in-law. I hope that Petrosian with his good sense of humour wouldn't have been offended at my making such a comparison.

14...♕xf6 15 ♗g4?

A serious mistake (given an exclamation mark by Gulko).

The only way to cast doubt on Black's strategy was 15 h5!, because 15...g5 makes the bishop on g7 look rather dumb.

Therefore I would have been forced to weaken my pawn structure on the kingside and allow the opening of the h-file for White. But even in this case Black's prospects after 15...♕g5 16 hxg6 f5!? are not worse. Now my position is simply better.

15...h5 16 ♗xc8 ♖axc8 17 ♕e2 ♗h6

According to Gulko, this bishop "does not attack anything and does not take part in active operations".

Nevertheless, it controls the c1 square, which White uses to build up his major pieces on the only open file! Let's imagine: two armies are fighting and one of them is forced to take up a position in a ravine—but this ravine is then ambushed by the other side.

18 ♘a5 ♖b8 19 0-0

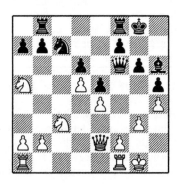

19...♖fc8?

My main error in this game lay in a stereotyped approach to the position. Rightly believing that my position was better, I considered myself obliged to take the c-file. But the idea behind this plan has no future. I absolutely agree with Boris—I should have launched an offensive on the kingside (which, as a matter of fact, has been deserted by the white army): 19...♕e7, followed by ...♘c7-e8-g7 and ...f7-f5, and, later, if the opportunity arises, ...f5-f4, ...g6-g5 etc. After the death of both bishops, the position of the far advanced pawns that had to stand guard over their king is quite miserable. The attack seems so natural that I still wonder why I had been so timid. It is amusing however that, while showing the right plan for Black, Gulko does not see the position in its proper perspective and evaluates it in White's favour.

Over the next few moves I was marking time and only understood what I had to do when it was too late; meanwhile my opponent created decisive pressure on the queenside. Unfortunately time in chess is irreversible. Petrosian demonstrated his genius by finding a brilliant way of outflanking the enemy's artillery (the dark-squared bishop). His plan, a2-a4, b2-b3, ♖a1-a2-c2 and ♖f1-b1-b2, is indeed awesome! He simply narrowed the board to 7 ranks, going around the ill-fated c1-square, after which my bishop really did stare into emptiness.

20 a4 ♕d8 21 ♘c4 ♘e8 22 ♖a2 ♕c7

Here and later on, albeit with loss of time, I should have transferred the knight to g7, and the rook to f8 in order to prepare ...f7-f5, since Black has no prospects if he plays a

waiting game. But, regrettably, I reverted to the necessary plan far too late.

23 b3 ♕d7 24 ♔g2 ♖c5 25 ♖b1 ♖cc8 26 ♖c2 ♘c7 27 ♖bb2 ♖f8 28 b4 ♘e8 29 a5 ♘g7

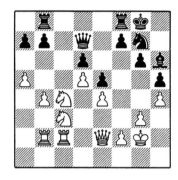

30 a6! bxa6

Insufficient is 30...b6 31 ♘a3 f5 32 ♘cb5 f4 33 ♖b3.

31 ♘a5 f5 32 ♘c6 ♖be8 33 ♘b1 ♔h7 34 ♖b3 fxe4 35 ♕xe4 ♖f5 36 ♖a3 ♕b7 37 ♘c3 ♖ef8 38 ♕c4

Freeing the central e4 square for the knight.

38...♖f3 39 ♖xa6 ♗e3

An attempt to stir up trouble, which was simply ignored by the wise Tigran.

40 ♘e4 ♗h6 41 ♖xa7 1-0

Game 36
Petkevich *White* **Gufeld** *Black*
USSR 1975

1 d4 ♘f6 2 c4 g6 3 ♘c3 ♗g7 4 e4 d6 5 ♘f3 0-0 6 ♗e2 e5 7 d5 ♘bd7

This continuation, along with 7...a5, for a long time has been considered as the main line. Lately 7...♘a6 has also been added.

8 0-0

White abides by classical principles of the deployment of forces: having settled down on the king's flank, he intends to launch an assault on the opposite side.

8...♘c5 9 ♕c2 a5 10 ♗g5

The most active move. The manoeuvre 10 ♘d2, with the idea of posting the knight on c5, is no longer played because of E.Geller's recommendation 10...♗h6!, when White cannot avoid an exchange of dark-squared bishops and after 11 ♘b3 ♗xc1 12 ♖axc1 ♘fd7 13 ♘d2 f5 Black obtains fine counterplay.

10...h6 11 ♗e3

After 11 ♗h4 g5 12 ♗g3 ♘h5 arises the typical Petrosian-System formation, but here the setup favours Black, since the white queen does not control the h5 square.

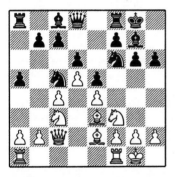

11...♘h5

The pawn formation requires that Black organize a break ...f7-f5 and this move fully corresponds to the spirit of the position.

This knight is also used as a way to influence the bishop on e3—11...♘g4, not fearing 12 ♗xc5 dxc5 13 h3 ♘f6 14 ♘xe5 because of 14...♘xd5 15 cxd5 ♗xe5 16 f4 ♗d4+ 17 ♔h2 g5 18 e5 gxf4 19 ♕e4 ♕e7 20 e6 fxe6 21 ♗c4 ♗d7 22 ♘e2 b5! and Black maintains equality. Ruban-Oll, USSR 1984.

Sometimes Black prefers a preliminary 11...b6, waiting for 12 ♘d2, and now 12...♘g4 forces an exchange of the light-squared bishop 13 ♗xg4 ♗xg4, but in order to advance ...f7-f5, Black has to take care of his light-squared bishop in view of the possible f2-f3. Therefore 12...♗g4 also seems promising to me, with the idea, after 13 f3 ♗d7, to provoke a further weakening of the king's flank by ...♘f6-h5.

12 g3

On 12 ♕d2 Black can sacrifice a pawn by 12...♘f4!? 13 ♗xf4 exf4 14 ♕xf4 f5, and favourably open the position.

12...b6

12...f5? does not work at the moment due to 13 ♘h4 and Black suffers material losses: 13...♘f4 14 ♗xf4 exf4 15 ♘xg6.

The line 12...♗h3 13 ♖fe1 b6 14 ♘d2 leads to a transposition of moves.

13 ♘d2 ♗h3 14 ♖fe1 ♕d7

14...f5 is also possible, since there is no risk of Black conceding the e4 square: 15 exf5 ♗xf5 16 ♘de4 ♘xe4 17 ♘xe4 ♘f6 etc.

15 b3

After the exchange of the bishop-pair, 15 ♗xh5 gxh5 16 ♗xc5 bxc5 17 ♘f3 f5, Black's control over the light squares fully compensates for his weak pawns. But maybe White no longer has anything better?

15...♖ae8 16 a3 f5

17 f3

The struggle has reached its climax and White has to admit that Black is ahead of him in developing an initiative, since if he converts the pawn centre to a piece centre by 17 exf5 ♗xf5 18 ♘de4 ♘xe4 19 ♘xe4, he has to reckon with 19...♘f4!.

Parting with the dark-squared bishop would be senseless: 17 ♗xc5 bxc5 and on 18 exf5 Black has the reply 18...e4! with a nice mate after 19 fxg6? ♖xf2! 20 ♔xf2 ♗d4 mate!

17...f4

It is impossible to predict the outcome of this position without thorough analysis—the more so that Black has to go into action on both flanks.

18 ♗f2 fxg3 19 hxg3 ♕e7

It is necessary to vacate a square for the knight, but it may be better to do it differently—19...♕d8!?, giving the knight on c5 the chance to retreat to d7.

20 ♔h2 ♗c8 21 ♘b5

On 21 b4 there is the retreat 21...♘d7.

21...g5?!

A hasty move. It is not very difficult to find 21...♕d7 22 ♗f1 a4! and now after the best reply 23 bxa4, (after 23 b4 ♘b3 24 ♘xb3 ♖xf3 White's position is in ruins) 24...g5 gains in strength.

22 b4 ♘b7 23 ♔g2 g4?

In the excitement of the struggle it was not easy to tear myself away from the g-pawn. 23...♖f7 looks more cautious.

24 fxg4 ♘f6 25 ♕d1 ± ♕f7

If you say "A" you should add "B" as well: 25...h5! 26 gxh5 ♗h6 27 ♗f3 ♕g7, and the kingside pressure compensates for the loss of the pawns. Now White could have

blocked this idea, but fate dictated otherwise...

26 ♗g1?

A strange decision, to say the least. Instead of occupying the vitally important c1-h6 diagonal with the bishop, White puts it out of play. Much stronger was 26 ♗e3 ♕g6 27 g5! and if 27...♘xe4, then after 28 ♗d3 ♗f5 29 g4! White has a serious advantage. Black could have played stronger—27...hxg5, but after 28 ♘xc7 White's position is quite defensible. But now events settle down in Black's favour.

26...h5! 27 gxh5 ♕d7 28 g4 ♘xh5!

Despite his defensive efforts, White still gets hit on the same critical h5 square.

29 ♘a7

White tries to destroy Black's queen and bishop battery, but it is too late.

29...♘f4+ 30 ♔g3

After 30 ♔h1 ♕e7 31 ♘xc8 ♕h4+ 32 ♗h2 ♘h3 White cannot save himself from the decisive threats.

30...♗f6!

Intending to "call out" the king by 31...♗h4+!.

31 ♗f1 ♕h7 32 ♘f3 ♗xg4! 33 ♔xg4 ♕g6+ 0-1

Game 37
Naumkin *White* **Smirin** *Black*
Ischia 1995

1 d4 ♘f6 2 c4 g6 3 ♘c3 ♗g7 4 e4 d6 5 ♘f3 0-0 6 ♗e2 ♘a6 7 0-0 e5 8 d5 ♘c5 9 ♕c2 a5 10 ♗g5

By transposition of moves we have reached the Petrosian-System.

10...h6 11 ♗e3 b6

Along with 11...♘h5, which is examined in the game Petkevich-Gufeld, this is one of the most logical continuations.

Black makes a useful wait-and-see move. Since White has nothing better than 12 ♘d2, before playing ...♘f6-h5 Black prepares to neutralize the bishop on e2.

12 ♘d2

In the event of 12 ♘e1, the knight does not control the e4 square and the break ...f7-f5 becomes more effective: 12...♘e8 13 ♘d3 f5 14 ♘xc5 dxc5!? and, after the knight's transfer to d6, Black has good play.

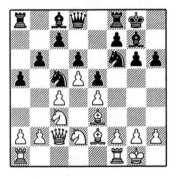

12...♗g4

12...♘g4 13 ♗xg4 ♗xg4 forces an exchange of light-squared bishops but, when preparing the break ...f7-f5 Black has to be careful having a bishop on g4. For example, the game Gavrikov-Kozul, Biel 1991, proceeded 14 a3 ♘a6 (after 14...♗d7 15 b4 ♘b7 16 ♘b3 f5 17 exf5 gxf5 18 f4 White's chances are preferable) 15 ♖ab1 f5! (played without prejudice, after 15...♗d7 16 b4 axb4 17 axb4 f5 18 exf5! gxf5 19 f4 White retains the initiative) 16 f3 (or 16 exf5 gxf5 17 f4 e4 with chances for both sides) 16...♗h5 17 b4 axb4 18 axb4 f4 19 ♗f2 g5 with complex play.

13 f3 ♗d7 14 b3

The game Azmaiparashvili-Gufeld, USSR 1985, proceeded 14 ♖fe1 ♘h5 15 g3 f5 16 exf5 gxf5 17 f4 ♕e8 18 fxe5 dxe5 19 ♗xc5 bxc5 20 ♘b3 f4! 21 ♕d1 ♘f6 22 ♗d3 ♘g4 23 ♘e4 ♕h5 and Black creates dangerous threats.

14...♘h5 15 ♖fe1?!

White vacates a square for the knight, but the e-file is far too overloaded to realize the rook's potential energy.

Therefore more stubborn is 15 ♖fb1, preparing b3-b4, though after 15...♘f4 16 ♗f1 f5 17 a3 fxe4 18 fxe4 ♕g5 Black doesn't have any particular problems, Grünberg-Vogt, East Germany (ch) 1984.

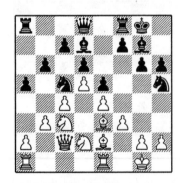

15...♗f6!

A spectacular pawn sacrifice, which secures Black control over the important weakened g1-h7 diagonal.

16 ♗xh6 ♗g5 17 ♗xg5

Forced, since after 17 ♗xf8? ♗e3+ 18 ♔h1 (or 18 ♔f1 ♕h4 19 ♘d1 ♘g3+) 18...♘g3+! 19 hxg3 ♕xf8 Black creates decisive threats along the h-file.

17...♕xg5 18 ♘f1

On 18 ♗f1 possible is 18...♘f4 followed by ...♔g8-g7 and an attack by the heavy artillery along the h-file.

18...f5 19 exf5

On 19 ♕c1 Black carries on his attack by 19...♘f4 20 g3 ♘h3+ 21 ♔g2 f4

19...gxf5 20 a3 a4!

In this formation, a typical counter to White's preparations for a pawn advance to b4.

21 b4 ♘b3 22 ♖a2 ♖f7

The queen and the knight on b3 have full control of the dark squares in White's camp. For example it is not possible to exchange the knight by 23 ♘d2 in view of 23...♘f4 24 g3 ♘d4 and Black intensifies his threats.

23 g3 ♔h8!

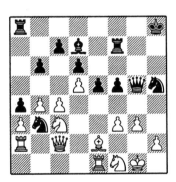

The second rook joins the attack.

24 ♗d1 ♖g8 25 ♕b1 ♕h4?!

25...♘d4, retaining the knight and preparing ....f5-f4, is stronger.

26 ♗xb3 axb3

Nothing is achieved by 26...♕d4+ 27 ♔h1, because after 27...♕xc3?

28 ♖e3 ♕d4 29 ♖d2 the queen is lost.

27 ♖g2

White goes over to deep defence, since after 27 ♕xb3? f4 his position would have been shattered.

27...♕d4+ 28 ♖e3 f4 29 ♘e2 ♕xc4 30 gxf4

30 ♕xb3 loses to 30...♕a6 31 gxf4 ♖xg2+ 32 ♔xg2 exf4 33 ♖e3 ♘f6! 34 ♕b2 ♖g7+ (I.Smirin).

30...♖xg2+ 31 ♔xg2 exf4? 32 ♖e4

Also after 32 ♕xb3 ♖g7+ 33 ♔h1 ♕a6 34 ♖e4 ♘f6 White suffers material losses.

32...♕xd5 33 ♔f2 ♕g5?!

I.Smirin considers 33...c5! 34 ♘c3 ♕g5 35 ♕xb3 ♖g7 36 ♔e1 ♕h4+ to be the strongest.

34 ♔e1 ♘f6 35 ♕b2 ♔g8 36 ♖xf4 ♗b5 37 ♘fg3 ♗xe2 38 ♘xe2 ♖e7!

Now the king knows no rest even on his original square.

39 ♕xb3+ ♔g7 40 ♖c4 ♕g1+ 41 ♔d2 ♕xh2 42 ♕d3

42...c5!

With the creation of a central pawn-pair the game quickly comes to an end.

43 ♖c1 ♔f7 44 bxc5 bxc5 45 a4

On 45 ♖e1 decisive is 45...d5.

45...♖e5! 46 ♕b5 ♕f2 47 ♖c3 d5

0-1

...c5-c4 is threatened, while the capture of the c5-pawn would cost a piece (48 ♖xc5 ♖xe2+ 49 ♕xe2 ♕xc5).

Game 38
Ivkov *White* **Gufeld** *Black*
Belgrade 1988

1 ♘f3 ♘f6 2 d4 g6 3 c4 ♗g7 4 ♘c3 0-0 5 e4 d6 6 ♗e2 e5 7 d5 ♘bd7 8 ♗g5

On the board we have the Petrosian-System formation, where White hinders Black's counterplay on the kingside and prepares the manoeuvre ♘f3-d2 to launch an attack on the queenside.

8...h6 9 ♗h4 g5

This weakening of the kingside pawn cover is considered the most radical way of dealing with the pin on the f6-knight. Waiting for castling by 9...♖e8 10 0-0 ♘f8 11 ♘e1 g5 12 ♗g3 ♘g6 13 ♘c2 would leave White with the better chances.

10 ♗g3 ♘h5

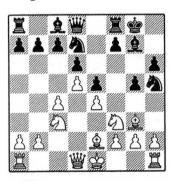

11 h4

Only with this break can White count on retaining the initiative. After 11 0-0 ♘f4 12 ♘e1 this hope disappears. The game Stein-Gufeld, USSR (ch), Moscow 1961, proceeded: 12...♘f6 13 ♘c2 ♔h8 14 h3 ♘xe2+ 15 ♕xe2 g4 16 ♗h4 gxh3 17 g3 ♕d7 18 f3 ♘g8 19 g4 ♘e7 20 ♕h2 ♘g6 21 ♕xh3 ♘xh4 22 ♕xh4 ♕d8 23 ♕h5 ♕f6 24 ♘e3 ♕g6 25 ♕h3 f5 with equal chances.

The problem of the f5 square can also be solved by 12...♘xe2+ 13 ♕xe2 f5 14 exf5 ♘f6 15 ♘f3 ♗xf5 with equal chances. Wexler-Fischer, Mar del Plata 1960.

11...g4

The exchange 11...♘xg3 12 fxg3 g4 amounts to a transposition of moves, while 12...gxh4 13 ♘xh4 ♕g5 14 ♗g4! concedes the f5 square to White and gives him some advantage.

12 ♘h2

Also possible is 12 ♘d2 f5 13 exf5 ♘df6 14 ♗xg4 ♘xg3 15 fxg3 ♘xg4 16 ♕xg4 ♗xf5 17 ♕e2 e4 18 0-0 ♕d7 19 ♕e3 c5 20 dxc6 bxc6 21 ♘b3 c5 22 ♖ad1 ♕e6 23 ♘d5 with a slight edge for White, Hort-Vogt, Leipzig 1973.

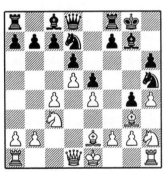

12...♘xg3

The alternative is 12...f5 13 exf5 ♘c5 14 0-0 ♗xf5 15 ♘xg4 (on 15 ♗xg4 possible is 15...♘xg3 16 fxg3 ♗d3! 17 ♗e2 e4! 18 ♗xd3 exd3 19 ♕g4 ♔h8 20 ♘f3 c6! with a double-edged game, Lyrberg-Lanka, Gausdal 1994) 15...♘xg3 16 fxg3 ♕e7 (or 16...e4) 17 ♘e3 ±) 15...♘xg3 16 fxg3 e4 17 ♕d2 ♗xg4 18 ♗xg4 and White retains the somewhat better chances. Bukić-Gligorić, Budva 1967.

13 fxg3 h5 14 0-0

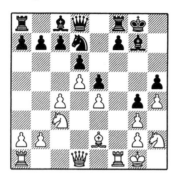

We have reached a complex position in which theory slightly prefers White, first and foremost because of the weakness of the f5 square—since Black has to reckon with the possibility of the knight manoeuvre ♘h2-f1-e3-f5.

14...♗h6

Black activates his "King's Indian" bishop, vacating the g7 square for the knight, from where it will cover the weakness of the f5 square. It should be noted that this manoeuvre had already been used for two decades prior to this game.

Nowadays the recommendation of the *Encyclopedia*, 14...a5 15 ♗d3 (on 15 ♖f5 possible is 15...♘f6) 15...♘c5 16 ♕e2, favours White. He will transfer his knight by the route ♘h2-f1-e3 when his control over the f5 square will guarantee him a slight, but enduring advantage.

The attempt to "cut the Gordian knot" by 14...f5, examined in the next game, is insufficient.

15 ♗xg4

This piece sacrifice was made for the first time in the game Heyns-Bouaziz, payed in the Olympiad at Lugano 1968. It does not entail particular risk for White, but Black exploits the opportunity to return the piece at an appropriate moment as a defensive resource.

The positional strategy, 15 ♗d3 ♘c5 16 ♗c2 a5 17 ♕e2 f6 18 ♖f2, looks more solid and, in view of the threat of transferring the knight from h2 to e3, White's chances are preferable, Hort-Janosević, Wijk aan Zee 1970.

15...hxg4 16 ♘xg4 ♗g7 17 ♘e3

The primary source game Heyns-Bouaziz, Lugano (ol) 1968, proceeded 17 ♕f3 f5 18 exf5 ♘c5 (more cautious is 18...♘f6) and here 19 f6! ♗xg4 20 ♕xg4 ♖xf6 21 b4 ♘d7 22 ♘e4 would have given White a slight edge.

17...c6 18 ♘f5 ♘f6 19 g4

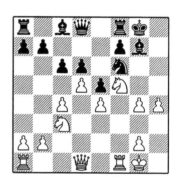

19...cxd5?

This intermediate exchange is parried...by an intermediate move! It was necessary to complete his development by 19...♗d7, not fearing 20 g5 ♘h7 since it won't be easy to punch a hole in Black's position,

20 g5! ♘xe4 21 ♘xd5

With the knight appearing on d5 the problem of defence becomes more complicated.

21...♗xf5 22 ♖xf5 ♖c8!?

The rook hurries over to help (23 ♕g4? ♖xc4). It would be difficult to hold out after the passive 22...f6 23 ♕g4.

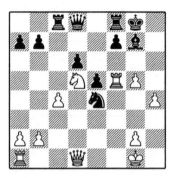

23 ♕e2!

This excellent combination of attack and prophylaxis is based on the black king's inadequate pawn cover. Black is forced to give back a piece. In the event of more "utilitarian" moves Black will find a defence: 23 ♕d3 ♘c5 24 ♕g3 ♘e4 or 23 b3 ♖c5, intending to eliminate the knight.

23...♘g3 24 ♕g4 ♖xc4

On 24...♘xf5 White wins by 25 ♘f6+! ♔h8 (or 25...♗xf6 26 gxf6+ ♔h8 27 ♕xf5) 26 ♕xf5 ♗xf6 27 gxf6 ♕b6+ 28 ♔h1 ♕e3 (nothing is achieved by 28...♖fd8 29 ♕g5!) 29 ♕h5+ ♔g8 30 ♕g4+.

25 ♕xg3

After 25 ♕xc4? ♘xf5 26 ♕g4 ♘e7! Black is a piece up. But the deflection of the queen from the c5 square enables Black to hold on.

25...♖d4 26 ♘f6+ ♔h8

At this moment both of us were in serious time-pressure and if the reader finds other ways of attack or defence, he should bear in mind that we had no time to consider them.

27 ♖af1 ♕b6 28 ♘d7!! ♖g4+ 29 ♘xb6 ♖xg3 30 ♘d7 ♖c8 31 ♖xf7?!

Of course with the flag "hanging" you take everything. After 31 ♔h2! Black is left a pawn down and in a

more difficult situation. But now the activity of his rooks increases considerably.

31...♖g4 32 ♘f6 ♖xh4 33 ♖xb7 a5 34 g3 ♖b4 35 ♖a7 ♖xb2 36 ♖f2

White cannot allow the rooks to double on the second rank, but now a drawn rook endgame is reached.

36...♖xf2 37 ♔xf2 ♗xf6 38 gxf6 ♖f8 39 ♖xa5 ♖xf6+ 40 ♔e3 ♔g7 41 a4 ♔g6 42 ♔e4 ♖f1!

The rook must play actively.

43 ♖d5 ♖e1+ 44 ♔f3 ♔f5 45 ♖xd6 ♖f1+ 46 ♔g2 ♖a1 47 ♖a6 ♖a2+ ½-½

Game 39
Kramnik *White* **Kasparov** *Black*
Linares 1994

1 ♘f3 ♘f6 2 c4 g6 3 ♘c3 ♗g7 4 e4 d6 5 d4 0-0 6 ♗e2 e5 7 d5 ♘bd7 8 ♗g5 h6 9 ♗h4 g5 10 ♗g3 ♘h5 11 h4 g4 12 ♘h2 ♘xg3 13 fxg3 h5 14 0-0 f5

Strange as it may seem, this conceptual break was played for the first time only in this game. Previously 14...♗h6 was played.

15 exf5

Also interesting is 15 ♖xf5!?.

15...♘c5 16 b4 e4 17 ♖c1

17 ♕d2!? certainly deserves attention.

17...♘d3 18 ♗xd3 exd3

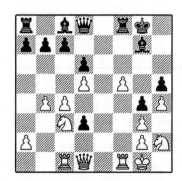

19 f6!

A subtle move which prevents the capture on f5 by the bishop—which would occur after 19 ♕xd3?! ♕f6.

19...♖xf6 20 ♕xd3 ♕f8 21 ♘b5

White's extra pawn does not make any practical difference, while the black bishop-pair is ready to display activity. Therefore White endeavours to transfer his knight to e4, from where it can control the important e6 and f5 squares.

After the obvious 21 ♘e4 Black centralizes his forces by 21...♖xf1+ 22 ♘xf1 ♗f5 23 ♘e3 ♗xe4 24 ♕xe4 ♖e8 and faces the future with optimism...

21...♗f5 22 ♖xf5! ♖xf5 23 ♘xc7 ♖c8 24 ♘e6 ♕f6 25 ♘f1

The knight on e6 offers White sufficient compensation for the exchange and he can think about promoting the advance c4-c5. But firstly he should manoeuvre his knight into play. On 25 ♖f1 V.Kramnik intended to return the exchange by 25...♖f8! 26 ♘xf8 ♕d4+ 27 ♕xd4 ♗xd4+ 28 ♔h1 ♖xf8 with prospects of a king raid in the centre.

25...♖e5!

Black prepares an exchange of queens in order to neutralize the threat of c4-c5 in the endgame.

26 ♖d1

On 26 c5 there would follow not 26...♕f5?! 27 ♕xf5 ♖xf5 in view of 28 ♖d1 and the pawns are safe, but 26...♖xe6! 27 dxe6 ♕d4+ 28 ♕xd4 ♗xd4+ 29 ♔h2 dxc5 with advantage to Black.

26...♕f5

Otherwise White will provide massive support for the advance c4-c5.

27 ♕xf5 ♖xf5 28 c5 ♗f8

Of course not 28...dxc5? in view of 29 d6, but the bishop's ambitions

should be restricted, since after 28...♗e5 29 ♘e3 ♖f7 30 ♔h2 the knight is quickly transferred to c4.

29 ♘e3 ♖f6

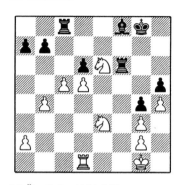

30 ♘c4! dxc5 31 b5!

White's last two moves are part of the same plan. White intends to support his knight by 32 ♖e1, after which the d-pawn will get the green light. Therefore Black cannot do without 31...♖e8 thratening to return the exchange, since on 32 ♖e1 possible is 32...♖f5 33 ♖d1 ♖f6. If White tries to play for a win by 32 ♘f4, Black, apart from the exchange sacrifice 32...♖e4 33 d6 ♖fxf4! 34 gxf4 ♖xc4 35 d7 ♗e7 36 d8=♕+ ♗xd8 37 ♖xd8+ ♔f7, transposing to an equal rook endgame, has the blockading 32...♗d6!? 33 ♘xh5 ♖h6 34 ♘f4 ♖e4 (V.Kramnik).

After his next "blank move" G.Kasparov gets into a difficult situation.

31...♗h6? 32 ♖e1 ♖e8 33 ♖e5

Here the weakness of the g4 and h5 pawns is only too evident. The pawns become the prey of the rook.

33...♖e7 34 ♖xh5 ♖ef7 35 ♔h2 ♗c1 36 ♖e5 ♖f1 37 ♖e4 ♖d1 38 ♖xg4+ ♔h7?

After this move the king succumbs to a mating attack. 38...♔h8 was forced, then 39 ♖e4 ♖xd5 40

♘e5 ♖f6 repels the direct threats, but 41 ♘f3 followed by g4-g5 would still offer White chances for victory.

39 ♘e5 ♖e7 40 ♘f8+

Leaving Black with the choice between losing the rook by 40...♔h8 41 ♘g6+ or getting mated after 40...♔h6 41 ♖g6+ ♔h5 42 g4+ ♔xh4 43 g3+ mate.

1-0

Game 40
Antoshin *White* **Gufeld** *Black*
USSR 1981

1 d4 ♘f6 2 c4 g6 3 ♘c3 ♗g7 4 e4 d6 5 ♘f3 0-0 6 ♗e2 e5 7 d5

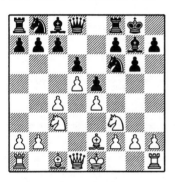

7...a5

This move hampers White's queenside play. 7...♘a6 is not bad either. Then, after 8 ♗g5 h6 9 ♗h4 g5 10 ♗g3 ♘h5 11 h4 ♘xg3 12 fxg3 gxh4 13 ♘xh4 ♕g5 Black obtains a level game. On 8 ♗e3 possible is 8...♘g4 9 ♗g5 f6 10 ♗h4 ♘h6 11 ♘d2 ♕e8 12 g4 f5 or 12...c5!? with complex play. But after 8 0-0 ♘c5 9 ♕c2 a5 10 ♗g5 we reach a position from the Petkevich-Gufeld game, analysed above.

8 0-0

Contemporary practice prefers another order of moves: 8 ♗g5 h6 9 ♗h4 ♘a6 10 ♘d2 ♕e8 11 0-0 ♘h7,

which leads to a simple transposition.

Incidentally, it should be noted that 10 ♘d2 can be met by an activation of the dark-squared bishop by 10...h5 11 0-0 ♗h6 when, after 12 f3 ♗e3+ 13 ♔h1 g5 14 ♗f2 ♗xf2 15 ♖xf2 h4 16 ♘f1 ♘c5, Black gains an active position.

8...♘a6 9 ♗g5 h6 10 ♗h4 ♕e8

Breaking the pin. The radical 11...g5 12 ♗g3 ♘h5 weakens the light squares too much. A slower way to break the pin is by 10...♗d7 11 ♘d2 ♘c5 followed by ...♕d8-c8.

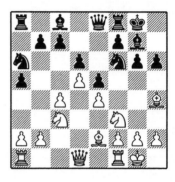

11 ♘d2

After the retreat 11 ♘e1, the knight loses control over the e4 square, which can be immediately exploited by Black, as was shown in the game Polugaevsky-Bukić, Skopje 1971: 11...g5 12 ♗g3 ♘xe4! 13 ♘xe4 f5 14 ♗h5 ♕e7 15 f3 fxe4 16 fxe4 ♖xf1+ 17 ♔xf1 ♘c5 18 ♕e2 g4! 19 ♗xg4 ♗xg4 20 ♕xg4 ♕g5 ½-½..

A.Karpov considers this agreement to a draw premature, since after the exchange of the queens 21 ♕xg5 hxg5 22 ♘f3 the endgame reached is slightly preferable for White. However, the placid 11...♗d7 12 ♘d3 ♘h7 13 f3 h5 14 ♗f2 b6 15 a3 ♘c5 16 ♘xc5 bxc5 17 a4 ♗h6 18 ♘b5 ♕d8 with equal chances looks good, Polugaevsky-Cvitan, Sarajevo 1987.

11...♘h7

A typical recipe in this kind of position. The black knight makes way for the f-pawn.

12 a3

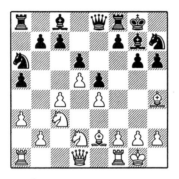

12...♗d7

The main continuation, after which there arises one of the standard modern formations of the Classical System.

12...f5 suggests itself but it had not been used since the game Veingold-Kasparov, USSR 1979: 13 exf5 ♗xf5 (13...gxf5!? 14 ♗h5 ♕d7 with idea of ...♘h7-f6 has not been tested in practice) 14 g4 ♗d7 15 ♘dxe4 and White gained an enduring advantage due to his firm control of the e4 square. But obviously everything is not so clear in this position, since Kasparov, playing against Kramnik in a crucial game in the final match of the "Grand Prix" tournament, Paris 1995, revived 12...f5. White chose another plan: 13 f3 ♗d7 14 b4! axb4 15 axb4 ♘xb4 16 ♕b3 c5 17 dxc6 ♘xc6 18 c5+ ♔h8 19 cxd6 ♘d4 20 ♕xb7 ♖b8 and now 21 ♕a7! (in the game followed 21 ♕a6?! ♖c8 22 ♗c4 ♖c6 and Black regained the pawn) forces Black to solve difficult problems.

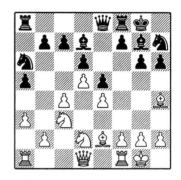

13 ♘b5

This thrust has not been seen much lately, since it does not promise anything special for White—the knight cannot hold on to its active position.

The *Encyclopedia* suggests 13 b3 h5 (sometimes 13...f5 14 exf5 gxf5 15 ♗h5 ♕c8 16 ♗e7 ♖e8 17 ♗xe8 ♕xe8 18 ♗h4 e4 is played, after which Black has sufficient compensation for the exchange) 14 f3 ♗h6 as the main continuation. One of the first games on this theme was Petrosian-Stein, USSR 1967, which went 15 ♗f2 ♕e7 16 ♕c2 h4 17 ♖fd1 f5 18 ♖ab1 ♕g5 and Black easily maintained equality. More recently, preference has been given to moving the king away by 15 ♔h1 which, by transposition of moves, leads to the popular continuation 13 ♔h1 h5 14 f3 ♗h6 15 b3—the last word in modern prophylactic technique.

13...h5

A typical trick in such positions—Black activates the dark-squared bishop.

14 f3 ♗h6 15 b3

White seems to be afraid of 15 ♗f2 ♗xd2 16 ♕xd2 a4. But after the exchange of dark-squared bishops Black has no difficulties.

The game Illescas Cordoba-Gelfand, Wijk aan Zee 1993, went

15 ♕c2 f5 16 exf5 gxf5 17 ♔h1 ♘f6 18 ♖ad1 ♘xd5 19 ♘xd6 cxd6 20 cxd5 b5?! 21 ♘b3! and White gained the advantage.

However, according to M.Illescas Cordoba, Black could have retained equal chances by 20...♘c5! 21 b3 b5! 22 b4 axb4 23 axb4 ♘a4 24 ♕c7 ♖a6.

15...♗e3+

The pawn sacrifice 15...f5!? 16 exf5 gxf5 17 f4 ♘f6! (17...♗xf4?! 18 ♗xh5 favours White) certainly deserves attention 18 ♗xf6 ♖xf6 19 ♗xh5 ♕e7 20 ♕e2 ♕g7 and the activity of the black pieces, in conjunction with the advantage of the two bishops, fully compensates for the sacrificed pawn (A.Lugovoi).

16 ♗f2

After 16 ♔h1 Black could have launched a pawn assault: 16...g5 17 ♗f2 ♗xf2 18 ♖xf2 f5.

16...♗xf2+ 17 ♖xf2 ♕e7 18 ♖b1 ♘f6

After the exchanging operation it is useful to consolidate the positions of his pieces.

19 ♘f1 h4 20 ♕d2?!

Wasting time. The immediate 20 b4 is more accurate, not allowing the knight to c5.

20...♗xb5 21 cxb5 ♘c5

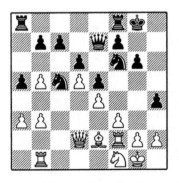

22 b4?!

This move allows Black to carry out a simple combination, which gives him a slight ('half a pawn') material advantage. He should have been satisfied with 22 ♕e3, though after 22...a4 23 b4 ♘b3 followed by ...♘b3-d4 Black's position is preferable.

22...axb4 23 axb4 ♘cxe4!

The knight does not have to retreat.

24 fxe4 ♘xe4 25 ♕e3 ♘xf2 26 ♕xf2 ♖a2

After the exchanging operation and the rook's invasion to the second rank, Black, in addition to having a slight material edge, has also obtained an obvious positional advantage, which I eventually managed to realize.

Game 41
Kramnik *White* **Gelfand** *Black*
Linares 1994

1 ♘f3 ♘f6 2 c4 g6 3 ♘c3 ♗g7 4 e4 d6 5 d4 0-0 6 ♗e2 e5 7 d5 a5 8 ♗g5 h6 9 ♗h4 ♘a6 10 0-0 ♕e8 11 ♘d2 ♘h7 12 a3 ♗d7 13 ♔h1

Contemporary practice has shown that White cannot do without this prophylactic move and so he often prefers to make it at once.

13...h5 14 f3

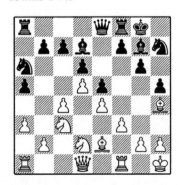

14...♗h6

14...♗f6 15 ♗xf6 is also played (after 15 ♗f2 ♗g5 the bishop is transferred to an active position, as in the game Iskusnykh-Dolmatov, Kemerovo 1995, which proceeded 16 b3 c5! 17 dxc6 bxc6 18 ♖b1 ♕e7 with approximately equal chances) 15...♘f6 16 b3 ♕e7 17 ♕e1 ♔g7 18 ♕f2?! h4! and Black obtains excellent play, Gulko-Kasparov, Novgorod 1995. Stronger was 18 h4.

15 b3

On 15 ♘b5, in the game Damljanović-Sorin, Linares 1994, Black optimistically attacked by 15...g5 16 ♗f2 f5, but after 17 exf5 ♗xf5 18 c5! dxc5 19 d6 c6 20 ♘c7 ♘xc7 21 dxc7 b5 22 ♗xc5 ♖f7 23 ♘e4 he found himself in a difficult position. More cautious would have been 15...♕b8 followed by forcing the knight back.

15...♗e3

In the game Shirov-J.Polgar, Madrid 1994, was played 15...♕b8 16 ♕c2 ♗e3 17 ♗f2 ♕a7 18 ♗xe3 ♕xe3 19 f4 exf4 20 ♖ae1 ♕c5 21 ♕c1 ♕d4 22 ♖f4 ♖ae8 23 ♖ff1 ♕g7 and Black obtained a slight edge.

A few months later V.Kramnik playing against Nunn, Germany 1994, played more accurately for White: 17 ♖ae1 ♕a7 18 ♘d1 ♗c5 19 ♕c1 ♖ae8 20 ♗d3! c6 21 ♘b1! and, after posting the knight on c3, White stood better.

16 ♕c2

On 16 ♖b1 in the game Illescas Cordoba-Gelfand, Linares 1994, Black played 16...c6 17 ♗f2 ♗xf2 18 ♖xf2 ♕d8 and achieved a level game. Black can also play 16...f5 17 b4 f4 or 16...♗c5

16...f5 17 exf5 gxf5

After 17...♗xf5 18 ♗d3 White occupies the e4 square.

18 ♗f2 ♗xf2 19 ♖xf2 ♘f6 20 ♖g1

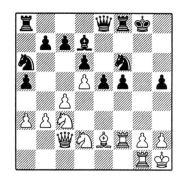

21...♔h8

Despite his apparent well-being, Black has to be vigilant. On 20...♕g6? unpleasant is 21 g4!, when after 20...c6 21 ♗d3! e4 22 fxe4 ♘xg4 White obtains the advantage by 23 ♖e2. However, even on this diagonal the king cannot feel at ease.

21 ♕b2

On 21...c6 White intends to remind Black of his king's poor cover by continuing 22 f4.

21...♘c5 22 b4 axb4 23 axb4 ♘a4 24 ♘xa4 ♖xa4 25 ♗d1 ♖a8 26 f4 exf4 27 ♖e2

Of course not 27 ♖xf4?! ♕e5.

27...♕g6

Since it is not easy to stop the f4 pawn, maybe he should have played 27...♕f7!? 28 ♕d4 (or 28 ♖ge1 ♖ae8! 29 ♖xe8 ♖xe8 30 ♖xe8+ ♗xe8 and 31 ♗xh5? ♕e7! is no good), intending 28...♕g7 29 ♕f4 b5!? with equal chances, B.Gelfand. However, Black is in no hurry to part with the pawn and, on 28 ♕d4, intends 28...♕h6.

28 ♖e7 ♖f7 29 ♖xf7 ♕xf7 30 ♕d4

After 30 ♗xh5?! White has to reckon on 30...♕g7 31 ♗f3 ♘g4.

30...♕g7 31 ♕xf4

31...♔h7?!

And in this position strong is 31...b5! 32 c5 dxc5 (32...♘xd5 33 ♕f3 c6 34 cxd6 is risky, since White supports the d6 passed pawn by the manoeuvre ♘d2-b3) 33 bxc5 (or 33 ♕c7 cxb4) 33...♘xd5 34 ♕f3 c6 35 ♕h5+ ♕h7 with sufficient counterplay (B.Gelfand).

32 ♖e1?!

White misses an opportunity to liquidate Black's main resource by 32 b5! (threatening b5-b6) when after 32...b6 33 ♖e1 he retains the advantage.

32...♖a1 33 h3

And, here too, it is not too late for 33 b5.

33...b5!

Now the worse is over for Black.

34 ♔h2

Also after 34 c5 dxc5 35 bxc5 ♘xd5 36 ♕f3 c6 37 ♘b3 ♖a2 38 ♕h5+ ♕h6 Black would be able to defend. (B.Gelfand).

34...bxc4 35 ♘xc4

On 35 ♕xc4? unpleasant is 35...♗a4 36 ♘b3 ♘e4∓.

35...♘xd5 36 ♕h4 ♘f6

36...♕h6, with the idea of exchanging the queens by 37...♕f4+, is also good.

37 ♗xh5 ♖xe1 38 ♗e2+! ♕h6 39 ♕xe1 ♘e4 40 ♗f3 ♕f4+ 41 ♔g1 ♗e6 ½-½.

Game 42
Zvjagintsev *White* **Beliavsky** *Black*
Yugoslavia 1995

1 d4 ♘f6 2 c4 g6 3 ♘c3 ♗g7 4 e4 d6 5 ♘f3 0-0 6 ♗e2 e5 7 d5 a5 8 h3

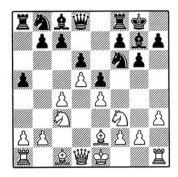

This continuation is regularly played by the young Russian Grandmaster Zvjagintsev. White prepares a retreat of the bishop to e3, which would be unfavourable after 8 ♗g5 h6 9 ♗e3 ♘g4.

And, in connection with the plan with queenside castling, the h3-pawn supports an attack by g2-g4 It is not easy for Black to find an antidote—as shown by the way Beliavsky conducts this part of the game. Incidentally, I have always regarded Beliavsky as a player who tried to refute the King's Indian Defence so, I am pleased to think that "our numbers have grown".

8...♘h5

It is not favourable to Black to allow the knight to be pinned. This is proved by the game Poluljahov-Beliavsky, Igalo 1994, where, after 8...♘a6 9 ♗g5, Black faced difficulties: 9...♘c5 10 ♘d2 c6 11 0-0 ♕e8 12 b3 ♗d7 13 a3 cxd5 14 cxd5 b5 15 b4 axb4 16 axb4 ♘a4 17 ♖a3 (also after 17 ♘xa4 bxa4 18 ♕c2 ♗b5 19 ♗xb5 ♕xb5 20 ♖fb1 ♖fc8

21 ♕d1 ♖c3 22 ♕f1 ♕d3 23 ♕xd3 ♖xd3 24 b5 White has a clear advantage—A.Beliavsky) 17...♘xc3 18 ♖xc3 h6 19 ♗e3 ♘h7 20 ♖c7 and White stands better.

In Zvjagintsev-Beliavsky, Budva 1995, played earlier, Black managed to avoid the pin by pulling back his knight with 8...♘fd7, but it was met by a dangerous attack by White on the king flank: 9 h4! f5 10 h5 ♘f6 (10...f4 11 hxg6 hxg6 12 g3 g5 13 ♘h2 favours White) 11 hxg6 hxg6 12 ♗g5 ♘a6 13 ♘d2 ♘c5 14 ♘b3 b6 15 ♘xc5 bxc5 16 exf5! ♗xf5 (after 16...gxf5 17 ♗h5! the threat is ♗g6) 17 g4 ♗d7 18 ♕d3 ♕e8 and here, by playing 19 ♘e4!, White could have strengthened his advantage.

The text move is more natural and stable. Its aim is to provoke g2-g4, after which kingside castling becomes problematic.

9 ♘d2

After 9 g3 the king flank would be weakened and Black can switch to the queenside by playing 9...♘a6 and then ...c7-c6 which can be useful if White castles long. It should be noted that 9...f5?! is risky before White castles, in view of 10 exf5 gxf5 11 ♘g5! ♘f6 12 g4, revealing the weakness of the b1-h7 diagonal.

However, 9 ♘d2 can also be regarded as an achievement for Black, since with the bishop on e3 this retreat would have looked much better.

9...♘f4 10 ♗f1 ♘a6 11 g3 ♘h5 12 ♘b3

After 12 ♗e2, I.Boleslavsky's famous idea, 12...♘c5 13 ♗xh5 ♘d3+ 14 ♔f1 gxh5 15 ♕xh5 f5, looks tempting, but White could have rejected the pawn sacrifice by 13 ♘b3! and obtained reasonable play. More reliable is 12...♘f6

(intending ...c7-c6), since White fails to open the h-file after 13 h4 h5.

12...c6

The alternative is 12...f5.

13 ♗e3 ♗d7 14 a4

In view of the threat ...a5-a4, White has to go for weakening of the queen's flank.

14...♘b4

Now he is ready for the undermining 15...f5 when, after 16 exf5, Black would capture the pawn with the bishop, threatening ...♗f5-c2.

15 ♖c1

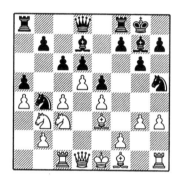

15...♕e7!

A clever move. Now after 16 ♗g2 f5 17 exf5 ♘f4! the knight joins the play most effectively.

16 c5 cxd5 17 cxd6 ♕d8

White's attack achieves its aim only upon 17...♕xd6? 18 ♗c5 ♕f6 19 ♘xa5! ♖xa5 20 ♗xb4.

18 ♘xd5

After 18 exd5 b6 19 ♗b5 ♖b8 20 ♗xd7 ♕xd7 21 ♘b5 ♘f6 22 ♖c7 ♕f5 the initiative passes to Black.

18...♘xd5 19 ♕xd5 ♘f6 20 ♕d3 ♗xa4 21 ♘c5

With the king's unprotected state this kind of activity just gives White more problems. Simpler is 21 ♗g2 ♗xb3 22 ♕xb3 ♕xd6 23 0-0 and the advantage of the two bishops to a certain extent compensates for the lost pawn.

21...♗c6 22 ♗g2 ♛b8!

No wonder that this sort of move can be overlooked. It turns out that the d6 pawn is doomed. On 23 0-0 there follows 23...♖d8 24 ♖fd1 ♗f8.

23 f4 ♘h5 24 ♗f3 ♖d8 25 ♗xh5 ♖xd6 26 ♛c4 gxh5 27 0-0

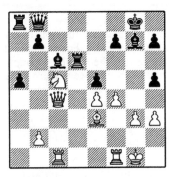

27...♛e8

At last White has castled, but already with his pawn cover has been weakened. True, the straightforward 27...♖g6 is, for the time being, premature since White could have met it by the decisive 28 f5! ♖xg3+ 29 ♔f2 h4 30 ♖g1, obtaining reasonable counterplay. Therefore Black moves his queen up to protect the f7 pawn, at the same time threatening 28...♗b5 winning the exchange.

28 fxe5 ♖g6 29 ♖f5 ♗xe5

Stronger was 29...b6 30 ♘b3 (if 30 ♘d3 there follows 30...b5 31 ♛d4 ♖d8 32 ♛c3 ♗e4) 30...♗d7 31 ♖xh5 ♖xg3+ 32 ♔f2 ♖g6 33 ♗f4 ♗e6 34 ♛d3 ♖d8 35 ♛e3 ♛b5, winning the b2 pawn and obtaining two connected passed pawns on the queenside.

30 g4 hxg4 31 h4 ♖d8 32 h5 ♖gd6 33 ♛e2 ♔h8 34 ♛xg4 f6?

After the simple 34...b6 35 ♘b3 (or 35 ♗g5 bxc5 36 ♗xd8 ♖xd8) 35...♗xe4 36 ♖xe5 ♛xe5 37 ♗f4 ♛g7 38 ♛xg7+ ♔xg7 39 ♗xd6 ♖xd6, Black would have won easily (A.Beliavsky).

35 ♗f4

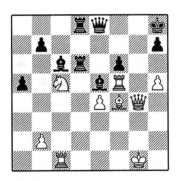

35...♛g8?

Of course it is nice to transpose to an endgame with extra material, but he could have carried on with the attack:

35...♗d4+ 36 ♔h2 ♗xc5 37 ♖fxc5 ♛xe4 and White suffers obvious losses:

(a) 38 h6 ♖g8 39 ♛xg8+ ♔xg8 40 ♖g1+ ♔h8 41 ♗xd6 ♛h4 mate;

(b) 38 ♖5c2 ♖g8 39 ♛xg8+ ♔xg8 40 ♗xd6 ♛h4+ 41 ♔g1 ♛d4+.

36 ♛xg8+ ♖xg8+ 37 ♔f2 ♗xf4 38 ♖xf4 b6 39 ♘b3 ♗e8 40 ♖c4 ♗xh5 41 ♘d4 ♗g6 42 ♘f3 ♖e8 43 ♘h4 ♔g8 44 ♖c7 ♖de6!

If he wins a third pawn by 44...♗xe4 45 ♖g4+ ♔f8 46 ♖gg7 the white rooks boss the seventh rank, while after 45...♔h8 46 ♖xe4! ♖xe4 47 ♖c8+ ♔g7 48 ♘f5+ ♔g6 49 ♘xd6 White even wins a knight —although after 49...♖d4 he loses his last pawn.

45 ♘xg6 hxg6 46 ♔f3 ♖8e7 47 ♖c8+ ♔g7 48 ♖h4 ♖e8 49 ♖c7+ ♖6e7 50 ♖c6 g5 0-1

Illustrative Games—7 ♗e3

Besides closing the centre in the Classical System, after **1 d4 ♘f6 2 c4 g6 3 ♘c3 ♗g7 4 e4 d6 5 ♘f3 0-0 6 ♗e2 e5**, White can instill a completely different character into the game by **7 ♗e3**

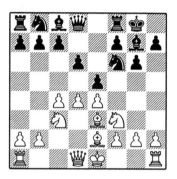

By not spending a tempo on castling, White, to a certain extent, nullifies Black's possibilities after 7...♘c6 8 d5 ♘e7 9 ♘d2, since he manages to carry out a useful knight manoeuvre with the bishop already on e3. Now, after 9...♘d7 10 b4 f5 11 f3 ♘f6 12 c5 ♖f7 13 ♘c4, White comes first in the race for the initiative.

In days gone by I used to play my own concept, 7...♕e7 (I stick to my own opinion on the value of having the queen on e7 in King's Indian positions of a semi-open nature). Black intends to capture on d4 and forces White to make up his mind what to do about the pawn tension in the centre. After 8 d5 the thrust 8...♘g4 gains in strength: 9 ♗g5 f6 10 ♗h4 ♘h6 11 ♘d2 a5 12 f3 ♗d7 13 g4 ♘f7 14 ♗d3 ♘a6 and Black has an easy game.

I managed to reveal the drawbacks of 8 0-0 in the 34th USSR Championship (Tbilisi 1966/67) in my game against Stein: 8...♘xe4!? 9 ♘xe4 exd4 10 ♘xd4 ♕xe4 11 ♘b5 (11 ♗f3 or 11 ♕d2 would have been more cautious) 11...♘a6 12 ♗f3 ♕xc4 13 ♘xa7 ♘c5 14 ♘xc8 ♖axc8 15 ♖c1 ♕b4 16 b3 ♘e6 17 ♖c4 ♕b5 18 ♕d2 ♖b8 19 ♖b4 ♕a6 20 ♖a4 ♕b5 21 ♖b4 and White forced a draw by repetition of moves.

Contemporary theory gives preference to reducing the tension by 8 dxe5 dxe5 9 ♘d5. For example, the 3rd game of the World Championship Match between Karpov and Kasparov, New York/Lyon 1990, proceeded 9...♕d8 10 ♗c5 ♘xe4 11 ♗e7 ♕d7 12 ♗xf8 ♔xf8 13 ♕c2 ♘c5 14 ♖d1 ♘c6! 15 0-0 ♘e6! 16 ♘b6 axb6 17 ♖xd7 ♗xd7 with a slight advantage to White.

Black might also remove the bishop from the e3 square by a preliminary 7...♘g4 8 ♗g5 f6

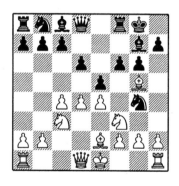

...when both 9 ♗c1 and 9 ♗h4 can be met by 9 ... ♘c6.

The continuations 7...exd4 or 7...c6, preparing the undermining ...d6-d5 represent a different theme of organizing counterplay in the centre.

Game 43
Sahović *White* **Gufeld** *Black*
Yurmala 1978

1 d4 ♘f6 2 c4 g6 3 ♘c3 ♗g7 4 e4 d6 5 ♘f3 0-0 6 ♗e2 e5 7 ♗e3 ♘g4

The latest opinion is that this is the most principled reaction to the bishop's development on e3.

8 ♗g5 f6 9 ♗c1

The alternative is 9 ♗h4.

9...♘c6

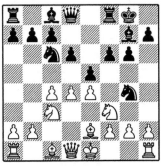

As a result of driving back the bishop, the knight gets the chance to attack the d4 pawn, with the difference (compared to 7 0-0 ♘c6) that after 10 d5 ♘e7 11 ♘d2 his colleague has to retreat to h6. Subsequently this knight re-enters the game via the g8 square, for example, after 12 b4 f5 13 f3 ♔h8 when ...♘h6-g8, ...♗g7-h6 and ♕d8-h4 gives Black sufficient counterplay.

The theme of this variation was actively discussed in the Candidates Match at Wijk aan Zee 1994 between Van der Sterren and Kamsky. In the 1st game G.Kamsky removed the tension from the centre by 9...exd4 10 ♘xd4 f5 11 0-0 ♘c6 12 ♘xc6 bxc6 13 exf5 gxf5 14 h3 ♘f6 15 ♗f3 ♗d7 16 ♗g5 ♖b8 17 ♕d2 ♕e8 18 ♖ae1 ♕f7 19 b3 and

White's chances turned out to be preferable. In the 3rd game Kamsky played 9...♘c6 and after 10 0-0 f5 11 ♗g5 ♗f6 12 ♗xf6 ♕xf6 13 exf5 ♗xf5 obtained reasonable play.

10 h3

It should be noted that the position in the diagram shows how very complicated it is to classify modern opening theory. With a pawn on h3 the line is listed in the *Encyclopedia* as E92. After 10 0-0 it is identical to the position arising after the moves 7 0-0 ♘c6, in the variation 8 ♗e3 ♘g4 9 ♗g5 f6 10 ♗c1, and is classified as E97.

10...exd4

Thanks to this intermediate move the knight is not obliged to retreat on h6, after which Black has to reckon on 11 g4.

11 ♘xd4 ♘ge5

After the exchange 11...♘xd4 12 hxg4 (12 ♕xd4 ♘e5 13 ♕d5+ ♔h8 14 ♗e3 leaves White with a slight advantage in space) 12...♘xe2 13 ♕xe2 White's chances are preferable, since now the undermining 13...f5 leaves the black king too exposed after 14 gxf5 gxf5 15 ♗h6!.

12 ♘xc6

Upon 12 ♗e3 the break 12...f5! is rather effective.

12...bxc6

If Black recaptures by 12...♘xc6 then 13 0-0 f5 14 exf5 ♗xf5 15 ♗e3 leaves White in control of the important d5 square while retaining some tension on the centre.

13 f4 ♘d7

After 13...♘f7 he has to reckon with the advance c4-c5.

14 0-0 ♖b8!

An important move for organizing pressure on the queenside. Black is not afraid of 15 ♕a4?! on account of 15...♘c5, when 16 ♕a7? is no good because of the loss of the queen after 16...♗a6. And 16 ♕xc6 ♗b7 is also bad for White.

15 ♕c2 f5

A well-timed "livening-up" of the famous bishop, whereas after 15...♘c5 16 ♗e3 f5 there is 17 e5.

16 exf5 gxf5 17 ♗e3 c5

Finally the pawns on c5 and f5 control the e4 and d4 squares—which leaves only the d5 square needing to be taken care of.

18 ♖ae1

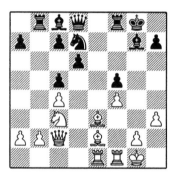

18...♕h4?

A typical positional error. It is clear that, psychologically, it is not easy to part with one's beloved piece, but it is precisely the manoeuvre 18...♗xc3! 19 ♕xc3 ♕f6, eliminating the main "enemy" in fighting for the d5 square, that secures Black a reasonable game.

19 ♗d3 ♘f6 20 b3 ♘h5?

Such persistence deserves better application.

Correct is 20...♕h5, not ceding the centre, although after 21 ♘b5 ♖b7 22 ♗f2 White retains a positional advantage.

21 ♘d5 ♕d8 22 ♗f2 ♔h8 23 ♕d1

After 23 ♕e2?! ♘f6, meeting 24 ♘e7 with 24...♖e8.

23...c6 24 ♕xh5 cxd5 25 cxd5 ♕f6

Black's positional blunders have cost a pawn, but he has managed to activate his queen.

26 ♔h2 ♗d7 27 ♗h4 ♕d4

It should be noted that the previous complicated struggle demanded from my opponent not only an expenditure of energy, but also time on the clock. By now he was already in time-trouble and because of this he now lets his advantage slip. Nevertheless, my play was also not at a very high level.

28 ♕f3 ♗f6 29 ♗xf6+ ♕xf6 30 ♕d1 a5 31 ♕a1 ♕xa1 32 ♖xa1 a4?!

He should have waited for a better moment before playing this move, and gone 32...♔g7 instead.

33 ♗c4 ♔g7 34 ♖fe1 ♔f6

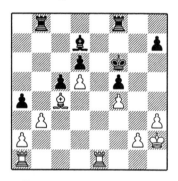

35 ♖e3?!

In time pressure White misses an opportunity: 35 bxa4! ♖b4 36 ♗b5!, since the rook endgame is clearly in his favour. But now, after the exchange of a couple of rooks, it is much easier for Black to resist by opening lines.

35...♖fe8 36 ♖ae1 ♖xe3 37 ♖xe3 a3

Far too optimistic. With a material deficit in the endgame it would have been more logical to hold on to the material by exchanging 37...axb3.

38 ♔g3 ♖g8+ 39 ♔f2 h5?!

More accurate is 39...h6, not creating undesirable weaknesses.

40 ♖g3 ♖xg3?

A typical error for the control move. After 40...♖h8 it is not easy to break through Black's position.

41 ♔xg3 ♗e8 42 ♔f2 h4 43 ♔e3 ♔e7 44 ♔d2 ♔d8 45 ♔c3 ♔c7 46 b4 ♔b6 47 ♔b3 cxb4 48 ♔xb4 ♗d7 49 ♗e2?!

Fighting against shadows. There is no reason to fear 49 ♔xa3 ♔c5 50 ♔b3 ♔d4 in view of 51 ♔b4 followed by ♗c4-b3 and a2-a4.

49...♗c8 50 ♗f3?

My opponent still does not see the above manoeuvre and misses his chance. He should have repeated the position by 50 ♗c4.

50...♗a6! 51 ♔xa3 ♔c5 52 ♔b2 ♔d4

In this situation, compared with the missed opportunity on the 49th move, the white bishop is far more passive and does not have time to help its passed pawn.

53 a4 ♔e3 54 ♔c3 ♔xf4 55 ♔b4 ♔g3 56 ♔a5 ♗f1

Black forces a transposition to a drawn queen endgame.

57 ♔b6 ♗xg2 58 ♗xg2 ♔xg2 59 a5 f4 60 a6 f3 61 a7 f2 62 a8=♕ f1=♕ 63 ♕g8+ ♔h2 64 ♕e6 ♕xh3 65 ♕xd6+ ♕g3 66 ♕c5 ½-½

Game 44
Van der Sterren *White*
Kamsky *Black*
Wijk aan Zee (m/3) 1994

1 d4 ♘f6 2 c4 g6 3 ♘c3 ♗g7 4 e4 d6 5 ♘f3 0-0 6 ♗e2 e5 7 ♗e3 ♘g4 8 ♗g5 f6 9 ♗c1 ♘c6 10 0-0 f5

From the possible continuations, G.Kamsky chooses the sharpest one. Also played are 10...exd4 and 10...♘h6.

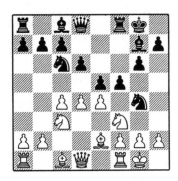

11 ♗g5

The alternative is to close the centre by 11 d5 ♘e7 12 ♘g5 ♘f6 13 exf5 gxf5 (also possible is 13...♘xf5 14 ♗d3 ♘d4 15 ♘e2 ♘f5 16 ♘g3 c6= Farago-J.Polgar, Hungary (ch) 1991) 14 f4 e4 15 ♗e3 h6 16 ♘e6 ♗xe6 17 dxe6 c6 18 ♔h1 ♔h7 (or 18...♘g6 19 g4 ±) 19 g4 ♘xg4! 20 ♗xg4 fxg4 (the preliminary 20...♗xc3!? 21 bxc3 fxg4 22 ♕b1 d5 with a double-edged game also deserves attention —L.B.Hansen) 21 ♘e4 ♘f5 22 ♗f2 d5 23 ♘c5 with somewhat better chances for White, L.B.Hansen-Jakobsen, Denmark 1991.

11...♗f6

The alternative is 11...♕e8 12 ♘d5 (weaker is 12 dxe5 dxe5 13 h3 ♘f6 14 ♗d3 ♗e6 15 ♖e1 ♕f7 16 c5 ♘d7 17 ♗b5 ♘d4!∓ I.Sokolov-Shirov, Las Vegas 1999) 12...♕f7 (12...♖f7 is also possible) 13 dxe5 dxe5 (or 13...♘gxe5 14 exf5 ♗xf5 15 ♕d2 ♖ae8 16 ♖ae1 ♔h8 17 b3 a6! 18 ♔h1 ♘xf3 19 ♗xf3 ♘d4 and Black maintains equality, San Segundo-Topalov, Madrid 1997, but the continuation suggested by P.San Segundo, 18 ♘h4 b5 19 ♘e3! bxc4 20 ♘xc4 ± is stronger) 14 ♗d2 ♘f6 15 ♘g5 ♕d7 16 exf5 gxf5 17 f4 e4 18 ♗c3 h6 19 ♘xf6+ ♗xf6 20 ♕xd7 ♗xd7 21 ♗xf6 ♖xf6 22 ♖ad1

♖d8! with equal chances, Vera-Van Wely, Matanzas 1994

12 ♗xf6 ♘xf6

12...♕xf6 13 d5 ♘d8 14 ♘d2 also deserves attention.

13 exf5

In Portisch-Kasparov, Linares 1990, there followed 13 dxe5 dxe5 14 ♕xd8 ♖xd8 15 ♘d5 (or 15 exf5 e4!∓) 15...♘xe4! 16 ♘xc7 ♖b8 with an equal game.

13...♗xf5

13...gxf5 also suggests itself. Then Black has to reckon with the possibility of transposition to an endgame with "hanging" pawns: 14 dxe5 dxe5 15 ♕xd8 ♖xd8 16 ♘d5!, which is in White's favour. Now after 14 dxe5 dxe5 15 ♕xd8 ♖xd8 16 ♘d5 e4! 17 ♘h4 ♘d4 the initiative passes to Black.

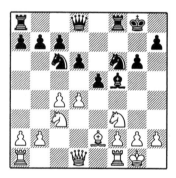

14 d5

Closing the centre in such situations is not dangerous for Black, who has not only carried out the break ...f7-f5, but also exchanged the g7-bishop—which in blocked positions might turn out to be "bad".

G.Kasparov recommends 14 ♕d2 ♘e4 15 ♘xe4 ♗xe4 16 dxe5 dxe5 17 ♕e3, rather preferring White's position.

14...♘e7 15 ♘g5 h6

In inviting the knight to be exchanged on e6, Black counts on winning the resulting pawn on the sixth rank, cut off from its main forces. Previously 15...c6 used to be played, on which after 16 ♗d3! White threatens to gain a foothold on the e4 point. The game Rajković-Nunn, Germany 1990, proceeded 16...♗g4 17 ♕d2 ♕b6 18 h3 ♗d7 19 dxc6 bxc6 (stronger is 19...♘xc6! ±) 20 ♖ae1! with advantage to White.

16 ♘e6 ♗xe6 17 dxe6 ♘f5

More solid is 17...♔g7, protecting the weak pawns.

18 ♗d3 ♘d4

After Black's inaccuracy on the 17th move there was no choice. The threat was 19 ♗xf5 gxf5 20 ♕f3, and 18...♕c8 or 18...♕e8 is met by the unpleasant 19 ♘d5.

19 f4?!

Striving to open the position, Van der Sterren obviously overestimates his position, otherwise he would have chosen 19 ♗xg6 ♘xe6 20 ♘d5.

19...♔g7 20 ♕e1 ♘xe6 21 ♕g3

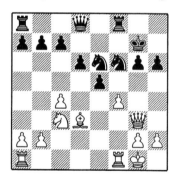

21...g5

According to established chess laws one should not move the pawns in front of a king which is subject to an attack. However in this case this move is forced. 21...♘xf4? loses to 22 ♖xf4 exf4 23 ♕xg6+ ♔h8 24 ♕xh6+ ♔g8 25 ♘d5, and on 21...e4?! Kamsky was afraid of 22 f5! ♘g5 23 ♘e4.

22 fxe5?

In the heat of the battle Van der Sterren underestimates Black's 23rd move. He should have played 22 fxg5 hxg5 23 ♗f5 and Black has nothing better than a repetition of position: 23...♘h5 24 ♕g4 (weaker is 24 ♕h3?! ♘ef4 25 ♕g4 ♔h6 ∓) 24...♘f6 25 ♕g3 ♘h5.

22...dxe5 23 ♕xe5?!

In taking the pawn, White obviously counted on carrying on the attack after 23...♘f4 24 ♖xf4! gxf4 25 ♕f5 ♕e8 26 ♖f1, but Black followed Botvinnik's advice—to make simple moves. Therefore 23 ♖ad1 would have been smarter, on which 23...♘f4 or 23...♕g6 are not bad.

23...♕xd3! 24 ♕xe6

Here 24 ♖ad1 already does not help 24...♕xc4 25 ♖d7+ ♔g6 26 ♕f5+ ♔h5 and White suffers material losses (G.Kamsky).

24...♖ae8 25 ♕f5 ♘e4! 0-1

Game 45
Azmaiparashvili *White*
Fedorov *Black*
Elista (ol) 1998

1 d4 ♘f6 2 c4 g6 3 ♘c3 ♗g7 4 e4 d6 5 ♘f3 0-0 6 ♗e2 e5 7 ♗e3 ♘g4 8 ♗g5 f6 9 ♗h4

It looks more logical to retreat the bishop here than to its original square.

9...♘c6

Also played is 9...g5 10 ♗g3 ♘h6 11 h3 (hindering ...g5-g4, since after 11 c5 g4! 12 ♘d4 ♘c6 13 cxd6 cxd6 14 d5 ♘d4 15 0-0 f5 Black achieves counterplay) 11...♘c6

(a) 12 dxe5 dxe5! (after 12...fxe5 in the game Ehlvest-Van Wely, Reykjavik 1994 13 ♕d2 ♘f7 14 ♘h2! ♘d4 15 ♗g4 ♘h8 16 ♘b5 ♘e6 17 ♘f3 ♘f4 18 ♗xf4 gxf4 19

c5 a6 20 ♘c3 dxc5 21 ♕xd8 ♖xd8 22 ♘d5 White obtained the initiative, but more decisive is 12 c5! ♘f7 14 cxd6 cxd6 15 ♗c4 ±) 13 0-0 ♗e6 with a level game.

(b) 12 d5 ♘d4 (12...♘e7 13 ♕d2 ±) 13 ♘xd4 exd4 14 ♕xd4 f5 15 ♕d2 f4 16 ♗h2 ♗e5 and, with ...c7-c5 to follow, Black has fully sufficient compensation for the sacrificed pawn.

10 d5 ♘e7 11 ♘d2

11...h5

The Byelorussian Grandmaster Aleksei Fedorov is renowned for his sharp style of play. More often played is 11...♘h6 12 f3 g5 (apparently also possible is 12...c5 13 dxc6 bxc6 14 b4 ♗e6 15 ♘b3 ♘f7 16 ♗f2 f5= Gavrikov-Nemet, Switzerland (ch) 1997) 13 ♗f2 f5 14 c5 ♘g6 15 g3 (or 15 0-0 ♘f4 16 cxd6 cxd6 17 ♘c4 ♖f6! 18 a4 ♖g6 19 exf5 ♘xf5 20 ♗d3 ♖h6! with a double-edged game, Shipov-Pavlović, Athens 1997) 15...g4 16 fxg4 f4!? (an interesting pawn sacrifice; after 16...♘xg4 17 ♗xg4 fxg4 18 ♘c4! White's chances are preferable, Ehlvest-van Wely, Groningen 1993) 17 cxd6 cxd6 18 ♘c4 ♕f6! with chances for both sides, Kiselev-Polulyahov, Russia (ch) 1994.

12 h3

On 12 0-0 good is 12...c5.

12...♘h6 13 g4

Azmaiparashvili accepts the challenge. The position is so sharp that half-measures are not enough here. Thus, in the game Timoshchenko-Atalik, Nova Gorica 1999, White played 13 0-0, but after 13...c5 14 ♖b1 ♗d7 15 b4 cxb4 16 ♖xb4 b6 Black's chances are not worse.

13...hxg4 14 hxg4 ♘f7 15 ♘f1

In the game Ehlvest-A.Fedorov, Calcutta 1999, occurred 15 ♕b3 c5 followed by a sacrifice of the b7-pawn (16...♗d7!?).

15...c5 16 ♘e3 ♗d7 17 ♗d3 ♕a5?!

This thrust is not effective here. He should have limited himself to 17...♘c8, intending 18...♗h6.

18 ♘c2 a6?!

This plan reaches a deadlock. Since the idea of advancing ...b7-b5 is not real, he should have moved back the queen, not waiting for the advance of the a-pawn.

19 a4! ♘c8 20 f3 ♕d8 21 a5 ♗h6

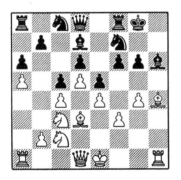

Black gets back on the right track, but at the cost of positional concessions.

22 ♗f2 ♔g7 23 ♔f1 ♖h8 24 ♘e2

24 ♔g2 ♘e7 25 b4 is stronger.

24...♘e7 25 ♘g3 ♕c7 26 b4 ♗f4 27 ♔g2 ♖xh1 28 ♕xh1 ♖h8 29 ♕b1

After losing control over the h-file White should have been more cautious and kept his queen nearer to the king by 29 ♕g1.

29...♕c8 30 ♘e3

Suddenly roles are reversed: Black activates his pieces and a bishop sacrifice on g4 has to be taken into account.

30...♘g5 31 bxc5

31...♖h3!

What a surprise! On 32 cxd6 there would follow 32...♕h8 33 ♕g1 ♗xg3 34 ♗xg3 ♖xg3+! 35 ♔xg3 ♕h3+ with a decisive attack (A.Fedorov).

32 ♗e2 ♕h8 33 ♕g1 dxc5 34 ♖b1 ♗c8 35 ♖d1

Underestimating Black's threats. White should have taken care of his king: 35 ♘ef1 ♘g8 36 ♗xc5 and now, as pointed out by A.Fedorov, the attack 36...♖xg3+ 37 ♘xg3 ♕h3+ 38 ♔f2 ♕h4 39 ♕g2 ♗xg3+ 40 ♕xg3 ♘h3+ is sufficient only for a draw, but 36...♘h6!?, with the threats 37...♘xg4 and 37...f5, deserves attention.

35...♘g8 36 d6 ♗d7 37 ♘d5?

This is neither the time nor the place to display activity. 37 ♘ef1 was necessary.

37...♘h6 38 ♖b1

38...♘xg4!

Black pounces on the exposed king with all his might. On 39 fxg4 there would follow 39...♖xg3+! 40 ♗xg3 ♕h3+ 41 ♔f2 ♗xg3+ 42 ♕xg3 ♘xe4+.

40 ♘xf4 exf4 41 fxg4 fxg3 42 ♗xg3 ♖xg3+ 43 ♔xg3 ♕h3+ 44 ♔f2 ♘xe4+ 45 ♔e1 ♕c3+ 46 ♔f1 ♘d2+ 47 ♔f2 ♕d4+ 48 ♔g3 ♕e5+ 49 ♔f2 ♕f4+ 50 ♔e1 ♘xb1 51 ♕xc5 ♕g3+ 0-1

Systems with the development of the bishop on g5

In this chapter we will examine methods of play which are linked to the development of White's dark-squared bishop on g5.

The most popular of these is the system of development **1 d4 ♘f6 2 c4 g6 3 ♘c3 ♗g7 4 e4 d6 5 ♗e2 0-0 6 ♗g5**, which is called the Averbakh System after the name of its author Yuri Averbakh, who played it for the first time in 1954.

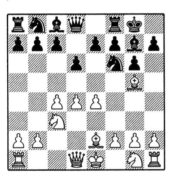

The main reason for developing the bishop in this way is to hinder Black's counterplay based on ...e7-e5 and ...f7-f5.

As an "honoured lover of the King's Indian" I know that there are "creative" and "destructive" variations—and chessplayers. I won't have a dig at anyone in particular, but, frankly speaking, the latter style is not to my liking. Some

players research somebody's ideas, borrow somebody's variations—and for whatever reason most of these variations tend to be destructive. One such "spoiling" variation is the Averbakh-System in which, first and foremost, White strives to suppress Black's initiative, as if to say: I am not up to playing today and I will not let you play either. So, he nips all the opponent's possibilities in the bud and pins down his forces. For many years this variation has been a set course for a number of players and no doubt it has provided them with some relief.

The Averbakh Variation is good for beating inexperienced King's Indian players. True, Black has no obvious weaknesses but neither does he have active play. Therefore I am quite pleased to have found ways to combat those players who seek an easy chess life. The most aggressive of these counterattacking plans are linked to the break 6...c5, which is either played immediately or after pushing back the bishop by 6...h6 7 ♗e3 c5.

Game 46
Polugaevsky *White* **Gufeld** *Black*
USSR (ch) Tbilisi 1966/67

1 c4 ♘f6 2 ♘c3 g6 3 d4 ♗g7 4 e4 d6 5 ♗e2 0-0 6 ♗g5 c5

The main continuation. Black attacks the centre, exploiting the fact that it is insufficently defended.

In the 60s Lev Polugaevsky had a reputation for his expert handling of the White side against the King's Indian Defence and so it is only natural that our duels bore a principled character. One of our "battlefields" was the Averbakh System. Apart from the logical 6...c5, I also tried against him the plan involving the advance ....e7-e5—6...♘bd7 7 ♕d2 e5. In fact, though the *Encyclopedia* considers this to be quite reliable, I know from my own experience that it is not easy to play against the pinning bishop on g5. The game Polugaevsky-Gufeld, Moscow 1969, proceeded 8 ♘f3 c6 9 ♖d1! ♕b6 (it is easier to play according to the generally accepted scheme 9...exd4 10 ♘xd4 ♖e8 11 f3 a5 12 0-0 a4 13 ♖fe1 ♕a5 etc.) 10 0-0 ♖e8 (and here 10...exd4 was necessary since now White closes the centre after which the queen on b6 and the rook on e8 are out of business) 11 d5 cxd5 12 cxd5 ♘c5 13 ♕c2 ♗d7 (13...♗g4!? is stronger) 14 ♘d2 ♖ec8?! (14...h6 15 ♗e3 ♘g4 was stronger) 15 ♕b1 h6 16 ♗e3 ♕d8 17 ♖c1 ♘g4? (the right way is 17...♘e8) 18 ♗xg4 ♗xg4 19 ♘c4 and White's positional advantage is obvious.

7 d5
More principled than 7 dxc5, which is examined below.

7...e6
Those who like sharp play can try the gambit 7...b5 8 cxb5 a6 9 a4 ♕a5 10 ♗d2, in which Black, though living on the edge, can keep his balance.

Undermining the centre by ...e7-e6 is more logical. Since White is late with castling, it is useful to open up the e-file. However, the experience of many games played with the variation has shown that this break is more effective after a preliminary 7...h6 which has the aim of clarifying the position of the bishop.

Therefore I am showing this game in order to demonstrate the problems which Black might face when organizing both defence and counterattack.

8 ♕d2
White reinforces the position of his bishop on g5. On 8 dxe6 good is 8...♗xe6 9 ♘f3 ♘c6 10 0-0 ♘d4! since 11 ♘xd4 cxd4 12 ♕xd4 fails to 12...♘xe4!.

8...exd5 9 exd5
The capture 9 cxd5 ♖e8 10 f3 leads to a position from one of the variations of the Modern Benoni—which favours Black.

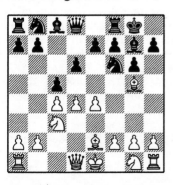

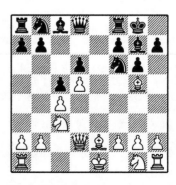

9...♖e8

In the previous USSR Championship (Tallinn 1965) I played against Polugaevsky 9...♕b6—the queen not only gets out of the pin but also attacks the pawn on b2. There followed 10 ♘f3 (as was known from the game Borisenko-Boleslavsky, Moscow 1956, after 10 0-0-0 ♖e8 11 ♗d3 a5 12 h3 ♕a5 13 ♘f3 b5 Black has excellent play) 10...♗f5 (or 10...♗g4 11 0-0 ♘bd7 12 ♖ac1 ♖ae8 13 h3 ♗f5!? 14 ♖fe1 with better chances for White) 11 ♘h4! ♘e4 12 ♘xe4 ♗xe4 13 f3! (M.Tal showed the dark side of 13 0-0-0— 13...♘a6 14 f3 ♘b4!) 13...♕xb2 14 ♖c1 h6! (otherwise the bishop would have to retreat to f5, when ♘xf5 ruins White's kingside pawn structure) 15 ♗xh6 ♕xd2+ 16 ♗xd2 ♗f6 17 g3 (this is stronger than 17 fxe4 ♗xh4+ 18 g3 ♗f6=) 17...g5 (also possible is 17...♗xh4 18 gxh4 ♗f5 19 ♗f4 ±) 18 fxe4 gxh4 19 ♗f4 ♘d7!? (by means of a pawn sacrifice Black eliminates the advantage of the two bishops and activates his knight) 20 ♗xd6 ♖fe8 21 ♗d3 ♗e5 22 ♗xe5 ♘xe5 23 ♔e2 hxg3 24 ♖cg1 ♖ad8 25 ♖xg3+ ♔f8 26 ♖b1 b6 27 h4 ♖d6 28 h5 ♖h6 29 ♖g5 f6 30 ♖f5?! (White should have played 30 ♖f1! and after 30...♘f7, 31 ♖g6) 30...♘f7 31 ♖bf1 ♔e7 32 ♔e3 (here White had the chance to create strong threats by sacrificing material: 32 e5!? ♘xe5 33 ♖xe5+ fxe5 34 ♗g6, and 34...♖f8 is no good in view of 35 d6+) 32...♘d6 33 ♖5f4 ♖g8 34 ♗e2 ♖g3+ 35 ♔f2 ♖a3 36 ♖g1 ♖xa2 37 e5 fxe5 38 ♖g7+ ♔e8 39 ♖g8+ ♔e7 ½-½.

10 ♘f3 ♗g4 11 0-0 ♘bd7 12 h3 ♗xf3 13 ♗xf3 a6

In the game Polugaevsky-Gligorić, Skopje 1968, 13...♕b6

was played, but after 14 ♕c2 a6 15 ♗d2 ♖e7 16 ♖ae1 ♖xe1 17 ♖xe1 ♖e8 18 ♖f1 ♕d8 the queen was forced to retreat and, by playing 19 a4, White gained a slight, but enduring advantage.

14 a4 ♕c7

On 14...♕a5 possible is 15 ♕c2 ♖e7 16 ♗d2 ♕c7 17 ♖ae1 and White's position is preferable.

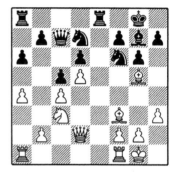

15 ♕c2

The most natural position for the queen as here it avoids any sudden attacks by the f6-knight.

In such positions one always wonders about the expediency of the clamp 15 a5. Apart from the pluses (the weakness of the b6 square), this move also has its minuses (the weakness of the a5 pawn and the possibility of opening up the b-file by ...b7-b6 at an opportune moment). Which side will come out on top is often down to matters of style. In this respect, the game Kaidanov-Kamsky, USA (ch) 1993, is interesting. This proceeded 15 a5 h5 16 ♕c2 ♘h7 17 ♗d2 h4?! 18 ♗e2 ♗d4 19 ♔h2 ♖ab8 20 ♖a3 and White obtained the better game.

15...♖e7

Worth considering is 15...h5!? 16 ♖ae1 ♖xe1 17 ♖xe1 ♖e8, maintaining equality.

16 ♖ae1 ♖ae8 17 ♖xe7 ♖xe7

Psychologically it is not easy to play such positions. In spite of the exchange of rooks, Black has not achieved equality since there are no ready-made targets for organizing counterplay (the most natural one—connected with the break ...b7-b5—is, for the time being, firmly ruled out). On the other hand, White has resources for developing an initiative as Polugaevsky shows by skilful play.

18 ♗e2

Also interesting is 18 b3 ♖e8 19 ♗d1, preparing an advance of the f-pawn.

18...h6 19 ♗d2 ♘e8 20 g4!

Having restricted Black's possibilities on the queenside, White commences an attack on the other flank.

20...♘df6 21 f4 ♕d7 22 ♕d3 b6 23 ♕f3 ♕b7

Black prepares the break ....b6-b5, for which it is useful to place the d5 pawn under surveillance.

24 ♗d3 ♘c7

25 g5! hxg5 26 f5!

A typical break for such a kingside pawn formation. The sphere of activity of White's light-squared bishop is now widened.

26...b5 27 cxb5?!

Until now Polugaevsky has carried out his plan rather brutally, but here he loses the thread of the attack—which could have been intensified by 27 fxg6 bxc4 28 ♗xg5!. After the text his pawn centre collapses and Black obtains powerful counterplay.

27...c4! 28 ♗b1

White does not want to lose his influence over the b1-h7 diagonal.

28...♘cxd5 29 fxg6 axb5 30 ♘xb5 ♕b6+ 31 ♕f2 ♖e2!

Roles are reversed and after this rook invasion the initiative passes to Black. It now becomes clear that 27 cxb5?!, which ceded the centre, was a mistake.

32 gxf7+ ♔f8 33 ♕xb6 ♘xb6 34 ♗c3?

Suddenly, having found himself in the role of defender, made more difficult by a shortage of time, Polugaevsky becomes flustered. In time pressure, providing there are no obvious contra-indications, it is always useful to capture material—in this case the g5 pawn. The f4 square now becomes an outpost for the attack.

34...♘bd5! 35 ♗d4 ♘f4

Even the departure of the queens cannot save the white king from the threats.

36 ♘xd6 ♘6h5

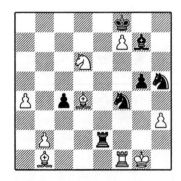

37 ♗c5?

Either flag might have dropped in the time scramble—but finally Polugaevsky blunders into mate. He should have brought up another defensive resource by 37 ♗xg7+ ♔xg7 38 ♗f5.

37...♖g2+

Even today I wish I had given another mate: 37...♘xh3+! 38 ♔h1 ♘g3 mate.

38 ♔h1 ♘g3 mate!

Incidentally, at that time filmmakers were keen on a trick called "candid camera." None of the participants of the championship suspected that a camera was hidden behind one of the curtains in the playing hall. Later this film was used in a documentary entitled *Chessplayers* (screenplay by Beilin). It turned out that the camera showed the episode when I mated Polugaevsky. At that moment Polugaevsky's hair was practically standing on end!

Game 47
Lputian *White* **Gufeld** *Black*
Moscow 1983

1 d4 ♘f6 2 c4 g6 3 ♘c3 ♗g7 4 e4 d6 5 ♗e2 0-0 6 ♗g5 c5 7 d5 h6

Black pushes back the bishop and denies White the possibility of taking the c1-h6 diagonal under his control by ♕d2.

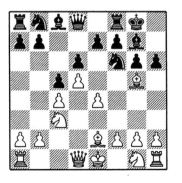

8 ♗e3

If he retreats 8 ♗h4, then after 8...a6 9 a4 ♕a5 the e4 pawn becomes more vulnerable. On the obvious 10 ♕d2?! in the game Kristinsson-F.Olafsson, Reykjavik 1966, there followed 10...♘bd7 11 ♘f3 and Black blew up White's pawn centre with a rather well-known trick: 11...b5! 12 cxb5 axb5 13 ♗xb5 ♘xe4! 14 ♘xe4 ♕xb5!. The immediate 10...b5!? 11 cxb5 axb5 12 ♗xb5 ♕b4! 13 f3 ♗a6 is also possible with good counterplay for the sacrificed pawn.

The *Encyclopedia* recommends 10 ♗d3, but here too the e4 pawn remains vulnerable, which was shown in the game Mirković-Poluljahov, Yugoslavia 1996, which proceeded 10...g5 11 ♗g3 ♘xe4!? 12 ♗xe4 ♗xc3+ 13 bxc3 ♕xc3+ 14 ♔f1 f5 15 ♘e2! ♕f6 16 ♗c2! f4 17 ♖a3 fxg3 18 ♖f3 ♕g7 19 ♖xf8+ ♔xf8 20 ♘xg3 with sharp play.

8...e6 9 h3

To secure the position of the bishop on e3.

9...exd5 10 exd5 ♖e8

The "provocative" move 10...♗f5 is examined in Hort-J.Polgar, Munich 1991.

11 ♘f3

11 ♕d2 ♔h7 12 ♗d3, which prevents the deployment of the bishop on f5, also deserves attention. Upon the stereotyped scheme of development 12...a6 13 a4 ♘bd7 14 ♘f3 ♘e5 15 ♘xe5 ♖xe5 16 0-0 ♘h5 17 ♖ae1 White has a small advantage, Beliavsky-Vogt, USSR 1970, but it would be interesting to check out 12...♘a6.

In Spassky-J.Polgar, Budapest (m/3) 1993, after 11 ♕d2 Black sacrificed a pawn: 11...a6? 12 ♗xh6 ♗xh6 13 ♕xh6 b5 14 ♘f3 ♕e7 15 ♘g5! ♗f5 16 g4! ♗d3 17 0-0-0

♗xe2 18 ♖he1 but failed to get any sort of compensation.

11...♗f5!

It is important to take the e4 square under his control.

12 g4

With this energetic move White strives to maintain the initiative, since after 12 0-0 ♘e4 13 ♘xe4 ♗xe4 Black achieves equality. On 12 ♕d2 I intended 12...♘e4! 13 ♘xe4 ♗xe4, when after 14 ♗xh6?! ♗xh6 15 ♕xh6 ♗xf3 16 gxf3 Black would have the better chances.

12...♗e4 13 ♕d2 ♘bd7 14 0-0

14 0-0-0!? also deserved attention.

14...♗xf3!

After 14...h5 15 ♘g5 the bishop might have got into trouble.

15 ♗xf3 h5! 16 g5

If 16 gxh5, then 16...♘e5 17 ♗e2 ♘xh5, and 18 ♗xh5 is bad because of 18...♘xc4.

16...♘h7 17 ♔h1

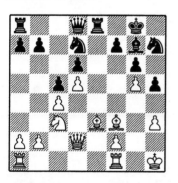

17...♗xc3!

One of the most difficult exchanges for me.

18 bxc3 ♘e5 19 ♗e2 ♕d7 20 ♔h2 ♕f5

But not 20...♕a4? 21 ♕d1.

21 f4

White has to force events because of the threat 21...♕e4.

21 f3 is bad: Black doubles his rooks on the e-file and White's bishops, deprived of support, are helpless.

21...♕e4! 22 ♖ae1

After 22 fxe5 ♕xe5+ Black would take off the "fatter" bishop on e3 or the light-squared one: 23 ♗f4 ♕xe2+ 24 ♖f2 ♕xd2 25 ♖xd2 ♖ad8.

22...♘xc4 23 ♗xc4 ♕xc4 24 ♗f2

White's intention is to launch an attack on the kingside, opening up the f-file with f4-f5. Incidentally, while Lputian was pondering the situation, I went to the press room to get a cup of coffee. There I ran into my friend Kiknadze, a writer. He shook his head and reproached me: "What have you done with your knight?" In order not to hurt his feelings I quickly moved the knight to the centre.

24...♘f8 25 ♗g3 ♖ad8

25...♘d7? 26 f5.

26 h4

Now 26 f5 is met by 26...h4! 27 ♗f4 gxf5 and ...♘f8-g6.

26...♘d7 27 f5 ♖xe1! 28 ♕xe1

If 28 ♖xe1 ♘e5!.

28...♘e5 29 fxg6 fxg6

29... ♘xg6 would be a mistake because of 30 ♖xf7!.

30 ♖f6!

The best chance.

30...♕xa2+!

On 30...♕xd5 I had calculated the variation 31 ♗xe5 ♕xe5+ 32 ♕xe5 dxe5 33 ♖xg6+ ♔f7 34 ♖h6 ♔g7 35 ♖xh5 ♖e8 and made sure that it led to draw: 36 ♔g3 b5 37 ♔f3 a5 38 ♔e4 b4 39 cxb4 cxb4 40 ♖h6!.

31 ♔g1 ♕xd5 32 ♕b1!

32...♕d3

Black was already in time pressure. Instead of 32...♕d3 he should have played 32...♖d7. But I did not see that, in the event of 33 ♗xe5 ♕xe5 34 ♕xg6+ ♖g7 35 ♕xh5, Black could take the rook with 35...♕xf6. And after 35 ♕h6 ♕e1+ and 36...♕xh4 White is in serious trouble.

33 ♕xd3 ♘xd3 34 ♖xg6+ ♔f7 35 ♖h6

Having made the move, Smbat offered me a draw in a low conspiratorial voice. I had about a minute and a half left, and this diplomatic trick all but paralyzed me. I treated my talented colleague with great respect and decided that his offer meant that I had overlooked something. I looked for this "something" for about a minute but, failing to find it, I glanced at my clock and the rising flag and agreed to a draw. But as a matter of fact there was a simple way to victory with natural moves: 35...a5 36 ♖h7+ (36 ♖xh5 b5) 36...♔g8 37 ♖xb7 ♖a8 38 ♗xd6 a4 39 ♖b1 a3 40 ♖a1 a2 41 ♔f1 ♖a6 42 ♗g3 (42 ♗e7 ♖e6) 42...♘c1 etc.

½-½

Game 48
Hort *White* **J.Polgar** *Black*
Munich 1991

1 d4 ♘f6 2 c4 g6 3 ♘c3 ♗g7 4 e4 d6 5 ♗e2 0-0 6 ♗g5 c5 7 d5 h6 8 ♗e3 e6 9 h3 exd5 10 exd5 ♗f5 11 g4 ♗c8 12 ♕d2

12...b5!?

An interesting pawn sacrifice, stimulated by the lack of development of White's pieces. On 12...♔h7 White could play 13 a4.

13 ♗xh6

On 13 cxb5 possible is 13...♔h7 14 ♘f3 a6 with sharp play, in which

the weakness of the white pawn formation would show itself.

13...b4 14 ♗xg7 ♔xg7

Of course not 14...bxc3?? 15
♕h6!.

15 ♘d1 ♘e4 16 ♕f4 ♖e8!

The activity of the black pieces
fully compensates for the sacrificed
pawn.

17 h4

After 17 ♘e3 Black can fix the
kingside pawns by the confident
17...g5! 18 ♕h2 (or 18 ♕f3?! b3!
19 axb3 ♕b6!) 18...b3! 19 axb3
♘a6 with more than sufficient compensation for the pawn (V.Hort).

17...♕f6!

A deep penetration into the position. After an exchange of the queen
—White's only active piece—the
weakness of his pawn formation becomes more obvious.

**18 ♕xf6+ ♘xf6 19 f3 ♘bd7 20
♘f2**

20 ♖h2! is stronger.

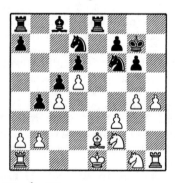

20...♗a6?!

I often used to draw my pupils'
attention to the fact that in positions
of a semi-open character the
queen's bishop, when standing on
its original square, is in fact a developed piece. More frequently this applies to the bishop on c1. In this
position it is the bishop on c8—on
a6 it is deadlocked. 20...a5

suggested itself, after which Black's
position is clearly preferable.

21 b3 ♖e3

More accurate is 21...♖e7.

22 ♘d1 ♖e5 23 ♖h2 ♖ae8

A stereotyped move. The only
thing Black will achieve from his
control of the e-file is a series of exchanges. In fact his rook could have
played a role without leaving its
original square—by retreating the
bishop to b7 and advancing the
a-pawn.

24 ♔f1 ♖8e7

For the time being Black fails to
find the correct plan of preparing
the advance of the a-pawn.

25 ♖c1 ♖e8 26 ♖c2 ♗b7

At last!

**27 ♘h3 a5 28 ♘f4 ♘b6 29 ♘f2
a4**

If he had played 29...♖a8 first,
Black would not have had to sacrifice material, since on 30 g5 he has
30...♘e8.

30 g5

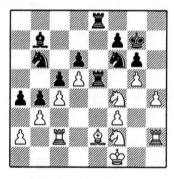

30...♘fxd5

A practically forced sacrifice. After 30...♘fd7 31 ♘e4 ♘c8 32 ♗d3
Black can only sit back and watch
passively as White attacks by h4-h5.
Nor is the exchange sacrifice
31...♖xe4 32 fxe4 ♖xe4 33 ♖f2
very comforting, since Black is
deadlocked again.

31 cxd5 axb3 32 axb3 ♘xd5 33 ♘xd5 ♗xd5 34 ♘g4

White quickly prevents a rook invasion on e3, possible after 34 ♖b2.

34...♖f5?!

As the Russian proverb says: "Misfortunes never come on their own". As noted by V.Hort, he should have carried on sacrificing by 34...♗xb3! 35 ♖b2 ♖xe2! 36 ♖bxe2 ♗c4 37 ♘f6 ♗xe2+ 38 ♖xe2 ♖b8 39 ♘d5 c4 40 ♖b2, even if two pawns for a piece is a bad deal.

35 ♘f6 ♖e3 36 ♘xd5 ♖xd5 37 ♖b2 ♖de5 38 ♖f2 f6 39 gxf6+

Stronger is 39 f4! ♖5e4 40 ♗c4.

39...♔xf6 40 ♔g2 ♖h5 41 ♖d2 ♖xb3 42 ♖xd6+ ♔e5 43 ♖c6 ♔d5 44 ♗b5! ♖xh4 45 ♖xg6 ♖e3 46 ♔g3 ♖d4 47 ♖c2!

White sets up a road block for the c-pawn (47...c4? 48 ♖g5+). Any attempt to remove the blockade leads to new material losses.

47...♖c3? 48 ♖h2 1-0

In order to avoid the mate along the rank, the d4 square has to be vacated, but then a rook will be lost.

Game 49
Kaidanov *White* **Gufeld** *Black*
Reno 1995

1 d4 ♘f6 2 c4 g6 3 ♘c3 ♗g7 4 e4 0-0 5 ♗e2 d6 6 ♗g5 c5 7 d5 h6 8 ♗f4

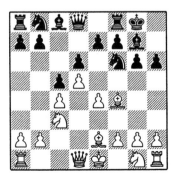

Originally it was thought that, by retreating to f4, White prevents the move 8...e6, but this is not so: 9 dxe6 ♗xe6 10 ♗xd6 ♖e8 11 ♘f3 ♕b6 12 ♗xb8 (12 e5 ♘fd7 13 ♘b5 ♘c6 14 ♗c7 ♕a6=) 12...♖axb8 13 ♕c2 ♘h5 14 g3 ♗xc3+ (also possible is 14...♗h3 15 ♘d2 f5 16 ♗xh5 gxh5 17 0-0-0 fxe4 18 ♘dxe4 ♗f5! with complex play, Piket-Van Wely, Wijk aan Zee 1997; Piket considers 15...♘f6 to be better) 15 ♕xc3 (or 15 bxc3 ♗g4 16 h3 ♗xf3 17 ♗xf3 ♕e6 18 0-0-0 b5! 19 ♖he1 b4! with better prospects for Black, Yermolinsky-Kindermann, Groningen (m/2) 1997) 15...♗h3 16 e5 ♗g2 17 ♖g1 ♗xf3 18 ♗xf3 ♕d6 with equal chances. Tukmakov-Gufeld, USSR 1983

But nowadays I prefer to make sorties with my queen.

8...♕a5

The game Tukmakov-Gufeld, USSR 1981, continued 8...♕b6 9 ♕d2 ♔h7 10 h4 e6 11 dxe6 ♗xe6 12 ♘f3 (on 12 h5 possible is 12...g5 13 ♗xd6 ♖d8 with sharp play) 12...♘e8 (12...♘c6 is weaker in view of 13 ♘g5+! hxg5 14 hxg5+ ♔g8 15 gxf6 with advantage to White) 13 0-0 ♘c6 14 ♖ab1 ♘f6 15 ♘d5 ♗xd5 16 exd5 ♘d4 17 ♘xd4 cxd4 18 ♗d3 a5 19 b4 ♖fd8 20 bxa5 ♕xa5 21 ♕xa5 ♖xa5 22 ♖xb7 and White has a somewhat better endgame.

9 ♗d2 e6 10 ♘f3 exd5 11 exd5 ♗f5

A routine continuation for this variation—White usually responds 11 exd5 with the idea of restricting the opponent's pieces to the maximum. If Black plays passively, White gradually develops his pieces and starts a typical attack on the queenside by a2-a3 and b2-b4. Here he gains a space advantage, leaving his opponent with quite a difficult endgame.

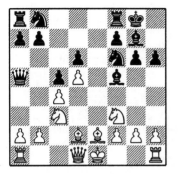

If Black tries to launch a kingside offensive, White constructs a fortress of pawns by f4, g4, and h3, restricting the mobility of the opposing army and at the same time striving to increase his space advantage on the queenside. Sometimes in these variations White crosses the demarcation line on the kingside, preparing f4-f5.

For those who like the development of the bishop to g4, I can draw their attention to the game Uhlmann-Andersson, Skopje (ol) 1972, which proceeded 11...a6 12 a4 ♕c7 13 0-0 ♗g4 14 a5 ♘bd7 15 h3 ♗xf3 16 ♗xf3 ♖fe8 17 ♕a4 ♘e5 18 ♗e2 and White has the initiative.

12 ♘h4

White's reaction is justified, although it does leave the knight standing on the sidelines.

However, if White does not react to the bishop on f5, Black plays ...♘f6-e4, exchanges knights and obtains definite play on the kingside.

12...♗d7 13 ♕c1 ♔h7 14 0-0 ♕d8 15 g3

Allowing Black's queen's bishop to take up a new position. On d7 the bishop takes away the only suitable square for the queen's knight—which would have had an unpromising future on a6. But now Black is able to move his bishop and complete his development naturally.

15...♗h3 16 ♖e1 ♘bd7

Black has probably solved his opening problems.

17 ♕c2 ♖e8 18 ♗f1 ♗xf1 19 ♖xf1

Now follows a series of virtually forced events. Maybe 19 ♖xe8 and 20 ♔xf1 was preferable but, then again, if White had played this and failed, the commentator might well have said that 19 ♖f1 was the right choice. It is hard to say. The position is approximately equal although at this point I considered it in Black's favour.

19...♘e5 20 b3 ♕d7

The black queen makes clear its intention to penetrate the enemy camp via the weakened white squares.

21 ♔g2

Forced. White has to get his king involved in order to head off his opponent's threats.

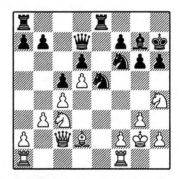

21...b5!

This typical stroke emphasizes Black's aggressive intentions and should be regarded as a formal declaration of war.

22 cxb5

On 22 ♘xb5 Black had planned 22...♘xd5 23 ♖ad1 ♘c7 with a good position.

22...♕b7 23 ♔g1

All this is forced. Back to safety... Now I certainly cannot recover the sacrificed pawn by 23...♘xd5 because of 24 ♕e4, when Black would face material losses. However, in order to attack one should commit to battle all the troops—in other words, the only good orchestra is one in which *all* the instruments are involved.

23...c4!

Once again 23...♘xd5 would be wrong because of 24 ♕e4. If fortune smiles upon him, Black will exploit the d3 square with his knight. However the main idea is to open the c-file, as the ♖a8 is still not in play. The rook was begging to get into the action and its request was being considered.

24 ♗e3 ♖ac8 25 ♖ad1 cxb3 26 ♕xb3 ♖c4! 27 ♗d4 ♖ec8

How can we evaluate this position? It is useless to do it by calculating variations. I felt intuitively that I had full compensation for the sacrificed pawn.

28 b6

Kaidanov realized that Black's initiative was taking a dangerous turn so decides to give back the pawn in order to change the course of events and frustrate his opponent's plans.

28...axb6 29 ♘b5 ♕d7 30 f4

General considerations are giving way to calculations. Yes, sometimes a chess game can be divided up into parts. Half of the game, good chessplayers (pardon me if I include myself in this category) play on understanding. They carry out manoeuvres which often do not require deep and accurate calculation.

There will always come a point, however, when calculation becomes necessary. This game, too, has reached the stage for concrete measures.

30...♘eg4!

A critical moment has been reached. There was one other tempting move—30...♕h3, but I did not like 31 fxe5 dxe5 followed by the counter-sacrifice 32 ♖xf6! ♗xf6 33 ♕f3. 30...♕h3 is probably a hasty, over-aggressive move, lacking rationale.

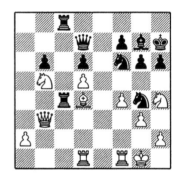

31 ♘f3

The main move to consider and to calculate was 31 h3. Note that the ♘g4 has no retreat. It has crossed the threshold to the point of no return—it must now open up ways for an offensive and give the 'green light' to all the other black pieces.

The question arises: how to sell the knight for the best possible price? The first plan that comes to mind is 31...♖c2. Even here everything is not so obvious: 32 hxg4 ♕xg4 33 ♕f3 ♕h3 34 ♖f2 ♘g4 35 ♖g2 and the black offensive reaches deadlock.

There are no obvious ways of increasing the pressure. All the pieces are doing everything in their power, yet the "fly-wheel" won't spin. But sacrificing the knight by 31...♘e3 is much more effective. Now, after 32 ♕xe3 ♕xb5. Black has an indisputable positional advantage.

In the event of 32 ♗xe3 ♕h3 White is likely to experience serious problems. At least Kaidanov admitted after the game that he did not see how to defend this position. Meanwhile I started getting worried about the fate of the g4-knight.

31...h5

The prospect of the transfer ...♘g4-h6-f5 is wonderful, but there is also the need to take care of the king. A safe haven should be found for it. 31...h5 is an interesting move. If I succeed in relocating the knight from g4 to f5, the position would clearly be in Black's favour.

I also considered 31...♘e4. Why did I reject it? I would like to remind the reader that, in most cases, a chessplayer who has the initiative should avoid trading pieces. I always stress this principle during my lectures and classes, and it is this thought that prevented me from playing 31...♘e4, although it was objectively better. Possibly the position is dynamically balanced. So after 31...♘e4 White should think of equalizing, but after 31...h5 the problem changes sides. The irrational 31...h5 could have led to head-spinning complications.

32 ♖fe1 ♘h6 33 ♘g5+ ♔g8

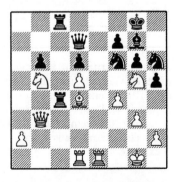

34 ♘e6?!

White also had 34 ♗xf6 at his disposal. I did not pay any particular attention to this move as I came to believe that in most cases the bishop was stronger than the knight. However, the tactical opportunity 34 ♗xf6 ♗xf6 35 ♘e4 should be considered. How is Black to proceed? Both the natural 35...♗g7 and 35...♗e7 will be followed by 36 ♘bxd6, and the knights start to interact. The abundance of tempting continuations gives reason for optimism.

So, 34 ♗xf6 ♗xf6 35 ♘e4 ♗g7 36 ♘bxd6 ♖c3! is the only way to maintain the initiative—as well as the balance of the position. 37 ♘xc3 ♖xc3. Now White has a choice between 38 ♕b4 and 38 ♕xb6 against both of which Black reacts in the same manner: 38...♖c2. So, 38 ♕xb6 ♖c2 39 ♕b8+ ♗f8 (the only move, after 39...♔h7 40 ♘e4, Black is unable to penetrate to the desired h3 square) 40 ♖e8 ♕h3 with an unusual draw after 41 ♖f8+ ♔g7 42 ♘e8+ ♔f8 43 ♕d6+ ♔g8 (the ♘e8 is untouchable) 44 ♘f6+ ♔g7 45 ♘e8+.

After 38 ♕b4 ♖c2, 39 ♕e4 seems good (after 39 ♖e8+? ♔h7 40 ♕e4 ♖xa2 41 ♘c4 ♕h3 Black even wins) 39...♕c7! 40 ♕e8+ (40 ♘e8 ♕c5+ 41 ♕e3 ♕c4! 42 ♘xg7 ♘g4! would have been to Black's advantage) 40...♔h7 41 ♘e4 ♘g4 42 ♖e2 (or 42 ♘g5+ ♔h6 43 ♘xf7+ ♔h7=) 42...♕c4! 43 ♖de1 ♔h6! with unclear prospects.

So, 34 ♘e6 should be regarded as a mistake. The nature of this inaccuracy can be explained. The beautiful onslaught was carried out during the opponent's time pressure. Risky? Of course, but the risk is justified by the opponent's lack of time.

Kaidanov did not resort to the exchange of the bishop for the knight, having come to believe that it was dangerous to leave Gufeld's dark-squared bishop with no opposition. After 34 ♗xf6 ♗xf6 35 ♘e4 it would have been a quite different cup of tea.

34 ♘e6 suggested itself because both the queen and king were posted on the a2-g8 diagonal. If the diagonal is opened, the d5-pawn will become dynamite.

34...fxe6 35 dxe6 ♕e7 36 ♗xf6 ♗xf6 37 ♘xd6 ♖c3! 38 ♕b1

38 ♘xc8 ♕c5+ leaves no chances for White.

38...♖c2! 39 ♕xb6

Here again 39 ♘xc8 ♕c5+ leads to victory for Black.

39...♖8c6

A few more moves in time pressure.

40 ♕b8+ ♔h7 41 f5

Both 41 ♘e4 ♖xe6 42 ♘xf6+ ♕xf6 43 ♖d7+ ♔f7 and 41 ♘e8 ♖xe6 do not save him.

41...gxf5 0-1

Game 50
Zilbermann *White* **Gufeld** *Black*
Kirovobad 1973

1 d4 ♘f6 2 c4 g6 3 ♘c3 ♗g7 4 e4 d6 5 ♗e2 0-0 6 ♗e3

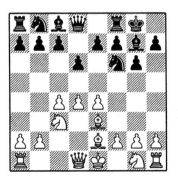

I ask the reader not to be surprised by some deviations from the main theme. Though in this game the bishop did not move to g5, the present position differs from the Averbakh System (6 ♗g5 h6 7 ♗e3) only in that there is no black pawn on h6.

6...c5!

Even with the bishop on e3, this is the most energetic way of influencing the centre, as after 7 dxc5 ♕a5 8 cxd6 ♘xe4 9 dxe7 ♖e8 10 ♔f1 ♘xc3 11 bxc3 ♘c6 Black's pieces develop great activity.

7 d5

Another principled reply is 7 e5 dxe5 (weaker is 7...♘e8 8 dxc5 ♗xe5 9 ♘f3 ♗g7 10 0-0 ±) 8 dxe5 ♘fd7 (also possible is 8...♕xd1+ 9 ♖xd1 ♘g4 10 ♗xc5 ♘xe5 11 ♘d5 ♘c6=) 9 f4 f6 10 exf6 exf6 11 ♘f3 ♖e8 12 ♔f2 ♘a6 13 ♖e1 ♕e7 14 ♗d3 ♘b6 15 a3 ♗g4 with complex play, Miles-Van der Wiel, Groningen 1994.

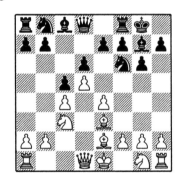

7...b5

A pawn sacrifice in the style of the Benko Gambit. In return for the pawn, Black remains ahead in development and can organize pressure along the semi-open a- and b-files. The alternative is 7...e6.

8 cxb5 a6 9 bxa6

On 9 a4 I would have proceeded with 9...♕a5.

9...♕a5 10 ♗d2

10 ♕d2!? deserves attention.

10...♗xa6 11 ♘f3?!

An inaccuracy after which White fails to get castled. The correct way is 11 ♕c2, intending 11...♗xe2 12 ♘gxe2 and if 11...♕b4 possible is 12 a3.

11...♕b4!

An important resource in such positions—the queen, by attacking the e4 pawn, is quickly transferred to a more active position.

12 ♕c2

If 12 e5 possible is 12...♘e4 13 ♗xa6 ♘xa6 14 ♕c2 ♘xd2 15 ♕xd2 ♕c4.

12...♗xe2 13 ♔xe2 ♘a6

Taking into account the "centralized" king he should have seriously considered 13...e6!?, striving to open the centre.

14 a3

White is already experiencing unmistakable difficulties. An attempt to evacuate the king by 14 ♖he1 fails after 14...♕c4+ 15 ♕d3 ♕xd3+ 16 ♔xd3 ♘b4+ 17 ♔e2 ♘c2.

14....♕c4+ 15 ♕d3 ♕b3! 16 ♖hc1 c4 17 ♕c2 ♘c5

White's queenside is totally blockaded.

18 ♘d4 ♕b6

18...♕b7 deserves attention, with ...e7-e6 in mind.

19 ♗e3 ♘g4!

This cavalry attack takes out the support from the centralized knight on d4. The break ...e7-e5 is threatened.

20 ♘cb5

After 20...e5 White intends 21 dxe6 fxe6 22 ♕xc4 But, all the same, 20 ♖d1 was better.

20...♘d3 21 ♕xc4?!

And here 21 ♖d1 is more stubborn.

21...♘xc1+ 22 ♖xc1 ♘xe3 23 fxe3 ♗xd4 24 exd4 ♖fb8!

After the heavy artillery moves up to the front line, material losses are inevitable.

25 a4 ♕a6!

This manoeuvre paralyses White.

26 b3 ♖c8 27 ♘c7 ♕b7 28 ♕c6

Black has to repel the threat of 28...♖a7.

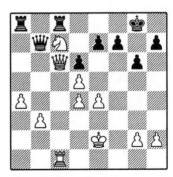

28...♕xb3!

Avoiding the false trail 28...♖a7? 29 ♘b5! ♖xc6 30 dxc6 or 28...♕xc6? 29 ♖xc6 ♖a7 30 ♘b5. Now the queen gathers in the bountiful pawn harvest.

29 ♘xa8 ♕b2+ 30 ♔d1 ♕xd4+ 31 ♔e2 ♕xe4+ 32 ♔d2 ♕f4+ 33 ♔d3 ♖xc6 34 ♖xc6 ♕xa4 35 ♘b6 ♕a2 0-1

Game 51
Zaitshik *White* **Gufeld** *Black*
USSR 1981

1 d4 ♘f6 2 c4 g6 3 ♘c3 ♗g7 4 e4 d6 5 ♗e2 0-0 6 ♗g5 c5 7 dxc5

This continuation is, of course, less thematic than d5, but nevertheless sometimes occurs in practice.

7...♕a5 8 ♗d2

The threat ...♘f6xe4 can also be parried by 8 ♕d2, but after 8...dxc5 Black is not afraid of 9 e5 ♖d8 10 ♕e3 ♘g4 11 ♗xg4 ♗xg4 12 h3 ♗e6 13 ♗xe7 ♖e8 14 ♕xc5 ♕xc5 15 ♗xc5 ♘d7 and in the game Prins-Geller, Amsterdam 1954, Black easily re-established material parity.

8 cxd6 ♘xe4 9 dxe7 ♖e8 favours Black.

8...dxc5

Also possible is 8...♕xc5 9 ♘f3 ♗g4 10 ♗e3 (or 10 0-0 ♗xf3 11 ♗xf3 ♘c6=) 10...♕a5 11 0-0 ♘c6 with equal chances.

9 e5 ♘fd7

It should be noted that in contrast to the variation where 6...h6 has been played (as in my game with G.Garcia) the knight cannot go back to h7. On the other hand, here the kingside has not been weakened in this way, which raises the question of ...f7-f6, undermining the centre.

10 f4 ♘c6 11 ♘f3

11...f6

A typical trick in these sort of positions. It is important for Black to open up the diagonal for the bishop on g7.

12 exf6

White is practically forced into this exchange, since his initiative after 12 e6 is only temporary and reaches a deadlock: 12...♘db8 13 ♘a4 (13 ♘d5 ♕d8 14 f5 gxf5 15 ♘f4 ♘d4 favours Black) 13...♕c7 14 ♘xc5 b6 and Black wins back the pawn with a more favourable position.

12...♘xf6

12...exf6 is more passive.

13 0-0 ♔h8

The game Ubilava-Gufeld, USSR 1981, proceeded 13...♗f5 14 ♘d5 ♕d8 15 ♗c3 ♕d6 16 ♗e5 ♕d8 17 ♘xf6+ exf6 18 ♗d6 ♖e8 19 ♗xc5 ♕xd1 20 ♗xd1 ♗d3 21 ♖f2 ♗xc4 22 ♖c1 ½-½.

14 ♘e5 ♘d4

Here 14...♗f5 15 ♘xc6 bxc6 leads to an unclear position.

15 ♗d3

An immediate exchange of the centralized knight by 15 ♘b5!? ♘xe2+ 16 ♕xe2 is not bad either.

15...♗f5 16 ♘e2?!

And here it would be worth looking at 16 ♘b5 ♕d8 17 ♗c3.

16...♕d8 17 ♗c3 ♘g4!

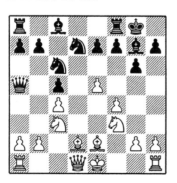

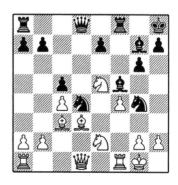

Black liquidates his opponent's only active piece and seizes the initiative.

18 ♗xd4 ♗xd3! 19 ♕xd3 ♘xe5 20 fxe5 ♖xf1+ 21 ♖xf1 cxd4

The exchanging operation is over and very accurate play is required from White to secure equality.

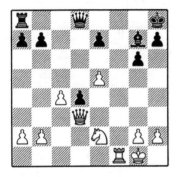

22 ♖f7!

Black's active play has not only demanded absolute accuracy from White but also denied him the possibility of matching the exchanges blow for blow. For example, the prosaic 22 ♕xd4 would now be followed by 22...♕c7! and Black wins the pawn back, gaining an active bishop in the process. So he plays to the 7th rank where surprises can always be expected from a rook...

22...♕a5 23 e6 ♗f6

Not giving White any additional chances by 23...♕xa2 24 ♖xe7 ♕a1+ 25 ♔f2 ♖f8+ 26 ♖f7. But White has another resource at his disposal.

24 ♘f4!

Accurate to the end! The threat of a knight sacrifice on g6 forces a draw.

24...♕e1+ 25 ♕f1 ♕e3+ 26 ♕f2

Of course not 26 ♔h1 in view of 26...d3.

26...♕c1+ 27 ♕f1 ♕e3+ 28 ♕f2
½-½

Game 52
G.Garcia *White* **Gufeld** *Black*
Camaguey 1974

1 d4 ♘f6 2 c4 g6 3 ♘c3 ♗g7 4 e4 d6 5 ♗e2 0-0 6 ♗g5 h6

Before undermining the centre, Black deprives his opponent of the chance to take control of the c1-h6 diagonal and maintain his bishop on the active square g5. Although, in doing this, Black allows a certain weakening of his kingside, the move 6...h6 has been looked upon quite favourably until very recently.

7 ♗e3

White's main reply. On 7 ♗f4 the "old fashioned" 7...♘c6!? 8 d5 e5 is possible when, after 9 ♗e3, Black can sacrifice a pawn 9...♘d4!? 10 ♗xd4 exd4 11 ♕xd4 ♖e8 with comfortable counterplay. After 7 ♗h4 also good is 7...c5, with 8 d5 a6 9 f3 b5! in mind.

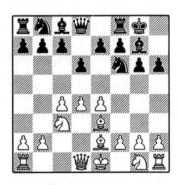

7...c5

In reply to the quite popular 7...e5 White usually closes the centre by 8 d5 ♘bd7 9 ♕d2 and retains the somewhat better chances:

(a) 9...h5 10 f3 ♘e8 11 g4 f5 12 gxf5 gxf5 13 exf5 ♘b6 14 ♗g5 ♕d7 15 ♘h3 ♕xf5 16 ♘f2 c6 17 0-0-0 ± Seirawan-Nunn, Lucerne (ol) 1982;

(b) 9...♘c5 10 f3 a5 11 ♗d1 ♘h5 12 ♘ge2 f5 13 ♗c2 ♕h4+ 14 ♗f2 ♕g5 15 ♖g1! ♘f6 (weaker is 15...♘f4 16 ♘g3! h5 17 ♗e3! h4 18 ♘xf5! gxf5 19 g3 and White gains an advantage—Petrosian) 16 ♘g3! f4 17 ♘ge2 ± A.Petrosian-Shirov, Daugavpils 1989.

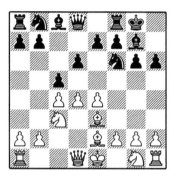

8 dxc5
This exchange permits Black to mobilise his forces by means of a temporary pawn sacrifice.

The onslaught 8 e5 leads to tactical simplification: 8...dxe5 9 dxe5 ♕xd1+ 10 ♖xd1 ♘g4 11 ♗xc5 ♘xe5 12 ♘d5 (after 12 ♗xe7 ♖e8 White's uncastled king's position speaks for itself—if the bishop reteats the c4 pawn is lost, and on 13 ♘d5 possible is 13...♗e6) 12...♘bc6 13 f4 (13 ♘f3 ♗e6 14 b3 ♖fd8 leads to equal play) 13...♘g4 14 ♗f3 (or 14 h3 ♘f6 15 ♗f3 ♗f5=) 14...♗f5 15 ♘e2 ♖fd8 16 h3 (after 16 0-0?! ♗xb2 17 h3 ♘f6 White is a pawn down) 16...♘f6 17 ♘g3 ♗c2! 18 ♖d2 ♗b1 19 b3 ♘xd5 20 cxd5 ♗c3 and Black maintains equality. Bareev-Yurtaev, Moscow 1990.

The continuation 8 d5 is examined in the game Lputian-Gufeld, Moskow 1983.
8...♕a5

Now the threat of ...♘xe4 forces White to break the pin.
9 ♕d2
Not only defending—but at the same time also attacking the h6 pawn. The alternative is 9 ♗d2 ♕xc5 with reasonable play for Black.
9...dxc5 10 ♗xh6

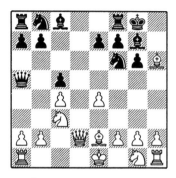

10...♗xh6
An automatic response. He should instead have brought the rook into play at once: 10...♖d8 11 ♕e3 ♗xh6 12 ♕xh6 ♘xe4 13 ♖c1 ♘c6 and Black's pieces display far more activity, whereas White needs some time to develop an attack. The game Seirawan-Timman, Tilburg 1990, proceeded 14 ♘f3 ♘d4 15 h4 (if 15 0-0 then possible is 15...♘xe2+ 16 ♘xe2 ♗g4) 15...♘xe2 and here, instead of 16 ♘g5? ♘f6 17 ♔e2 ♗f5 as played in the game, after which Black repelled the threats, Seirawan showed the way to prosecute the attack: 16 h5! g5! 17 ♘xg5 ♘f6 18 ♔e2, though its consequences demand a thorough analysis of Black's possible replies, 18...♕b6, 18...♗f5, 18...♕a6, and 18...♕b4.
11 ♕xh6 ♘xe4 12 ♖c1 ♘c6
Black's position is already preferable. The white king is detained in the centre and the pin on the ♘c3, aggravated by the activity of the

black knights on the e4 and d4 squares, is much more unpleasant than the queen on h6—which is in accordance with the proverb: "the voice of one man is the voice of no one".

13 g4?!

Maybe White was counting on bringing up the rook along the third rank to join the attack. But it would have been more realistic to adopt the plan indicated in the previous note.

13...♖d8 14 ♘h3 ♘d4 15 ♗d1 ♘f6! 16 ♘g5 ♘e6!

The mobility of Black's cavalry is impressive—the knights retreat harmoniously and...reveal the weakness of the enemy's rear.

17 h4 ♘f8!

Unexpectedly, it turns out that the queen is trapped (the threat is 18...♖xd1+ with ...♘f6xg4 to follow) and in order to save it White has to suffer material losses. G.Garcia is not satisfied by the "prosaic" 18 ♖g1 ♖xd1+ 19 ♖xd1 ♘xg4 20 ♖xg4 ♗xg4 and finds a better practical chance—a sacrifice of the queen.

18 h5! ♖xd1+ 19 ♖xd1 ♘xg4 20 ♕xf8+ ♔xf8 21 hxg6 f6?

An error, after which it is Black who has to think about saving

himself. Of course 21...fxg6 should have been played.

22 ♖d8+ ♔g7?!

It would be easier to give back the queen: 22...♕xd8 23 ♖h8+ ♔g7 24 ♖xd8 in the interest of new material gains: 24...fxg5 25 ♘d5 b6 26 ♘c7 (26 ♘xe7 ♗b7 27 ♖d7 ♗f3 loses a piece) 26...♖b8 27 ♘a6 ♗xa6 28 ♖xb8 ♘e5 29 ♖a8 ♘c6 etc.

23 ♖h7+ ♔xg6 24 ♖g8+ ♔f5 25 ♘f3 ♔f4!

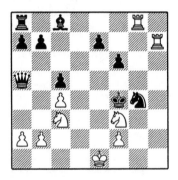

The king not only feels comfortable in enemy territory but, if the opportunity arises, he is ready to take part in any future attack.

26 ♘d2 ♘e5! 27 ♘d5+ ♔f5 28 ♔e2

Black is given a respite, since White has to reckon on the threat of ...♘e5-f3+ (after 28 ♘xe7+ ♔e6).

28...♘c6 29 a3 b6!

Black makes a decision to give up his rook in order to coordinate his disjointed forces.

30 ♘c7 ♘d4+ 31 ♔e3 ♔e5!

His majesty the king himself leads the black army!

32 ♘xa8 ♘f5+ 33 ♔e2 ♗b7 34 ♘c7 ♕a4 35 ♖h5 ♕c2

White is satisfied with his material situation. But now the immobile black queen rushes into the enemy camp in order to clinch victory against the disjointed enemy forces. However this is still a long way off.

36 ♖d8 ♔f4 37 ♘e6+ ♔g4

Now the threat is 38...♗f3+ and he has to sacrifice the exchange.

38 ♖xf5

The only practical chance to re-establish coordination with the knight.

38...♔xf5 39 ♘g7+ ♔g6 40 ♖d7 ♔xg7?

Quite a familiar occurrence: a mistake right on the time-control. The intermediate 40...♗a6 would have put a quicker end to White's resistance.

41 ♖xe7+ ♔g6 42 ♖xb7 ♕xb2 43 ♖xa7 ♔f5

Of course Black has the advantage, as before, but giving up his bishop has clearly made his task more difficult.

44 ♖b7 ♔f4

45 ♖e7

White moves his rook nearer to the king, hoping to construct a "fortress", since Black has resources for strengthening his position by ...f6-f5 and ...b6-b5.

45...♕xa3 46 ♖e3 ♕a7 47 ♖b3 f5 48 ♖f3+

White has succeeded in creating a defensive wall along the third rank, and it is not so simple to break it down.

48...♔e5 49 ♖e3+ ♔f6 50 ♖b3 ♕b7 51 ♔e1 ♔g5 52 ♔d1 f4 53 ♔e2 ♔g4 54 ♔d1

White has to reconcile himself to wait-and-see tactics.

54...♕c6 55 ♔c1 ♕g6 56 ♔d1 ♔h4 57 ♘f3+ ♔h5 58 ♘d2 ♔g4 59 ♔c1 ♔f5 60 ♔c2 ♔e5+

This check allows the queen to penetrate behind enemy lines.

61 ♖d3 ♔e6 62 ♔c3 ♕g1 63 f3

Black has infiltrated White's camp. Now the game ends quickly.

63...♕c1+ 64 ♔b3 ♔f7 65 ♘e4 ♕b1+ 66 ♔c3 ♕b4+ 67 ♔c2 ♕xc4+ 0-1

Game 53
Beliavsky *White* **Yurtaev** *Black*
Elista (ol) 1998

1 d4 ♘f6 2 c4 g6 3 ♘c3 ♗g7 4 e4 d6 5 ♗e2 0-0 6 ♗g5 h6 7 ♗e3 c5 8 dxc5 ♕a5 9 ♗d2

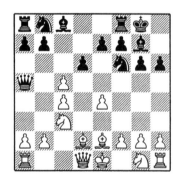

9...dxc5?!

After this exchange White has more chances of reaping dividends from the d-file than Black, since now the bishop on g7 will be switched off from the play for a long time. More logical and stronger is 9...♕xc5 10 ♘f3 ♗g4 11 ♗e3 (rushing around with the bishop, ♗e3-d2-e3, looks rather artificial, but White wants to vacate the d2

square for the queen or the knight)
11...♕a5 12 ♘d2 (or 12 0-0 ♗xf3
13 ♗xf3 ♘bd7 14 ♕d2 ♔h7=)
12...♗xe2 13 ♕xe2 ♘fd7 14 ♖c1
♖c8 15 0-0 ♘c6 16 ♖fd1 h5 17 a3
♕a6! with reasonable play for
Black, Gulko-Ivanchuk, Biel (izt)
1993.

10 e5 ♘h7

One of the merits of the prudent
move 6...h6 is that the knight now
has the possibility to retreat to h7.
After 10...♘fd7 11 f4 ♘c6 12 ♘f3
the undermining 12...f6, to liven up
the g7 bishop, is risky in view of the
excessive weakening of the king's
pawn cover. After 13 ♘h4 ♔h7 14
e6! White obtains a definite
advantage.

11 f4 ♘c6 12 ♘f3 ♗f5

Yurtaev recommended this move
ten years previously. But, taking
into account the course of events,
maybe he should have risked playing 12...f6.

13 0-0 ♖ad8 14 ♕e1

Sometimes the threat is stronger
than its execution and it is better to
wait with the knight swoop to d5
until a more appropriate moment.
After 14 ♘d5 ♕a6 followed by
...e7-e6, the knight would have been
forced to retreat.

14...♖d7 15 ♕f2 ♕d8 16 ♗e3

16...♘d4

Black has managed to complete
his development and even takes the
d-file under his control, but nevertheless his position is worse, since
after 16...b6 17 ♖fd1 the d-file will
pass into White's hands. And the
minor pieces on the kingside are not
in good shape. Even an exchange of
a couple of minor pieces does not
change this assessment of the
situation.

**17 ♖fd1 ♘xe2 18 ♕xe2 b6 19
♖xd7 ♕xd7 20 ♖d1 ♕b7 21 ♕d2**

21 h3! is more clever, depriving
the f5 bishop of the g4 square.

21...♖e8

Black vacates a square for the
knight, having ...♘h7-f8-e6 in
mind.

22 ♕d5 ♕c8

Of course not 22...♕xd5? 23
cxd5, when he is totally clamped.

23 ♘b5

To provoke a weakening of the
queenside after 23...a6 24 ♘c3
when he can dismantle it by ♘c3-a4
and b2-b4.

23...♗e6 24 ♕d3 ♗g4! 25 ♔f2

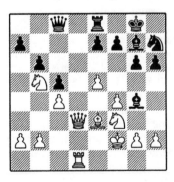

25...g5!

It is not in Yurtaev's style to sit
on the fence and with this energetic
counterattack he forces Beliavsky
—if he wants to maintain his advantage—to decide on a risky venture
with his king.

26 h3 ♗xf3 27 ♔xf3 gxf4 28 ♗xf4 ♘f8

After the obvious 28...♘g5+ 29 ♗xg5 hxg5 30 ♕e4 a6 31 ♘c3 ♕e6 32 ♖e1 ♖d8 33 ♘d5 White retains the initiative in the centre (A.Beliavsky).

29 ♔g3

A clever move. On 29...♘e6 White had prepared 30 ♕f5!.

29...♘g6 30 ♕e4 ♘xf4 31 ♔xf4!

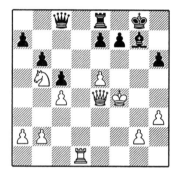

31...a6 32 ♘c3 e6 33 ♖d6 f6?!

It was very difficult for Black to free himself from the allure of this break, about which he has been dreaming for the last twenty moves but, as noted by A.Beliavsky, he should have confined himself to the cool 33...♕c7 and kept ...f7-f6 in reserve after 34 ♕c6 ♕e7.

34 ♕c6! fxe5+ 35 ♔e3 ♕xc6 36 ♖xc6

The game transposes to an endgame, obviously favouring White, in which it is difficult for Black to counter the invading rook, dominating the 6th rank.

36...e4

This move is dear to the hearts of those who support the King's Indian Defence (the bishop on g7 must be brought to life), but it is too late. Of course after 36...♖b8 37 ♖xe6 ♔f7 38 ♖c6 followed by 39 ♘d5 there is nothing left for Black to play for.

37 ♖xb6 ♗xc3 38 bxc3 ♔f7 39 ♔xe4 ♔f6

Black still holds some shadowy illusions in the rook endgame.

If 40 ♖xa6? is suddenly played, then 40...♖b8! and the rook springs to life. But White creates a more promising passed pawn.

40 ♖c6! ♖d8 41 ♖xc5 ♖d2 42 g4 ♖e2+ 43 ♔d3 ♖xa2 44 ♖h5 a5 45 c5 a4

After 45...♔g6 the c6-pawn cannot be stopped, but now Black has to deal with two connected passed pawns.

46 ♖xh6+ ♔e7 47 ♖h7+ ♔d8 48 ♔c4 a3 49 ♔b3 ♖a1 50 g5 a2 51 h4 1-0

Deviations from the Averbakh-System

In this chapter we will look at possible deviations from the Averbakh System, in which White develops the bishop to g5 first, keeping in reserve a more active deployment of his light-squared bishop.

Game 54
Minev *White* **Gufeld** *Black*
Kiev 1962

1 d4 ♘f6 2 c4 c5 3 d5 g6 4 ♘c3 ♗g7 5 e4 d6 6 ♗g5

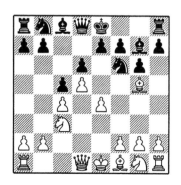

White choses a sharp variation with the development of his bishops on g5 and d3 (unlike the Averbakh System). In those days this way of playing was thoroughly analysed by Bulgarian players.

6...h6 7 ♗h4 ♕a5

Taking advantage of the fact that the bishop has left the queenside, Black creates counterplay there. In the 11th game of the Spassky-Fischer match of 1992, there followed 7...g5 8 ♗g3 ♕a5 and here, according to Minev, White retains rather better chances by 9 ♕d2 ♘h5 10 ♗e2 ♘xg3 11 hxg3 a6 12 ♘f3 ♘d7 13 0-0 ♖b8 14 a4.

8 ♗d3 ♘bd7 9 f4 0-0 10 ♘e2 b5

With this typical pawn sacrifice, Black simultaneously opens up lines for his rooks, shatters White's centre and obtains chances to pressurise the b2 square.

11 cxb5 a6 12 bxa6 c4

Taking into account the fact that the pawn cannot be taken because of ...♘f6xe4, Black vacates c5 for his knight and creates a stronghold on the d3 square.

13 ♗c2 ♘c5 14 0-0 ♗xa6 15 e5 dxe5 16 fxe5 ♘g4 17 ♗xe7

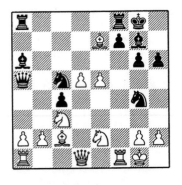

17...♗xe5!
In such positions the dark-squared bishop is not weaker than a rook.

On 18 ♗xf8 would follow 18...♖xf8 with a dangerous initiative.

18 ♘g3 ♘e3 19 ♕e2 ♗d4 20 ♔h1

In his turn, White offers an exchange sacrifice, in order to be rid of the dangerous alien on e3.

20...♕b6!
Black is not tempted by the material offered and takes aim at the important strong-point on b2.

21 ♘ge4 ♘xe4
21...♘d3 is dangerous because of 22 ♘f6+ and 23 ♘d7.

22 ♗xe4 ♘xf1 23 ♖xf1 ♖ab8 24 d6!
The passed pawn, supported by the bishops, gives Black the most trouble.

24...♕xb2 25 ♕xb2 ♖xb2 26 d7
An alternative is 26 ♘d5 ♖fb8 27 d7 f5 or 27 ♘f6+ ♗xf6 28 ♗xf6 ♖d2 with a decisive advantage.

26...♗xc3 27 ♗xf8
27 ♗d5 ♖d2 28 ♖xf7 ♖d8! does not work.

27...♖d2 28 ♗xh6 ♖xd7
The complications are over. Black has won the strategic phase of the game: he has eliminated the main enemy—the d7 passed pawn—and re-established material equality.

29 ♗c1 ♗d2 30 ♗xd2 ♖xd2 31 h3 f5!
Forcing the bishop to leave the b1-h7 diagonal and thereby enabling the passed pawn to advance.

32 ♗c6 c3 33 ♖c1 c2 34 ♔h2 ♗d3 35 ♗f3
The threat was 35...♖d1.

35...♗c4 36 ♗c6
The pawn cannot be stopped, since both 36 a3 and 36 a4 are followed by 36...♗b3 and 37...♖d1.

36...♗xa2 37 ♗a4 ♗b1 38 ♔g3 ♔g7 39 h4 ♔f6 40 ♔f3 ♔e5 41 ♖e1+ ♔d4 42 g4 ♖d3+ 43 ♔f4 ♖e3! 0-1

Game 55
Parker *White* **Gufeld** *Black*
Hastings 1994/95

1 d4 ♘f6 2 c4 g6 3 ♘c3 ♗g7 4 e4 0-0 5 ♗g5 c5 6 d5 h6 7 ♗f4 d6 8 ♕d2

The continuation 8 ♗e2 leads to one of the variations of the Averbakh System.

8...g5!?

Black immediately seizes the chance to exchange the dark-squared bishop. As shown by experience it is not easy for White to exploit the subsequent weakness of the king's flank.

9 ♗g3 ♘h5 10 ♗d3 e6 11 ♘ge2

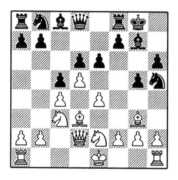

11...f5

A preliminary exchange on d5 was also possible.

12 exf5 exf5 13 f4!? ♘xg3 14 ♘xg3

After 14 hxg3? g4! the strategical gains of Black's position are obvious: it is difficult for White to display any kind of activity, whereas Black can prepare an attack on the queenside: ...♘b8-a6-c7, ...♗c8-d7, ...♕d8-f6, ...♖a8-b8, ...a7-a6, ...b7-b5.

14...♕e8+ 15 ♔d1?!

White is in too much of a hurry to commit his king. Apparently he does not like the position after 15 ♗e2 gxf4 16 ♕xf4 and decides to avoid the pin. However, he could have chosen a sharper continuation 16 ♘h5!? f3 17 ♘xg7 fxg2 18 ♖g1 ♔xg7 19 ♖xg2+ ♔h7.

15...gxf4 16 ♕xf4

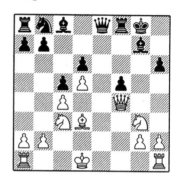

16...♘d7!

When the game assumes an open character and the enemy king is in a precarious position, a trifle such as a pawn is not too high a price to pay to develop one's pieces.

17 ♘xf5

White goes for mass exchanges, since after 17 ♕xd6 ♘e5 he would face an uncertain future.

17...♘e5 18 ♘xg7 ♖xf4 19 ♘xe8 ♘xd3 20 ♔d2 ♘xb2 21 ♘xd6 ♖d4+!

An important intermediate check.

22 ♔c2 ♘xc4 23 ♘xc4 ♖xc4 24 ♖hf1 b5! 25 ♔b2

The play transposes to an endgame which favours Black. However, there is no real reason for him to play for a win.

25...♖b4+ 26 ♔c2 ♖c4 27 ♔b2 ♖b4+ 28 ♔c2 ♖c4+ ½-½

Game 56
Conquest *White* **Gufeld** *Black*
Hastings 1994/95

1 d4 ♘f6 2 c4 g6 3 ♘c3 ♗g7 4 e4 0-0 5 ♗g5 c5 6 d5 d6

Thinking that Conquest may have prepared something after my game against Parker, I decided to vary my play. I have written a book about the Benko Gambit and decided to follow some of the ideas found in that opening.

7 ♕d2

White does not allow his bishop to be pushed back.

7...b5!?

This pawn sacrifice has became a kind of panacea, especially in positions when White is lagging behind in development, for instance after the move 7 h3. As an example I can give the game Yermolinsky-Gufeld, USA 1999, which proceeded 7...b5!? 8 cxb5 a6 9 a4 ♕a5 10 ♗d2 (with the idea of ♖a1-a3) 10...axb5 11 ♗xb5 ♗a6 12 ♖a3 ♘bd7 13 ♘f3 ♗xb5 14 ♘xb5 ♕b6 15 0-0 e6 16 dxe6 fxe6 17 ♕c2 d5 18 exd5 exd5 19 b4 ♖fc8 with sharp play.

8 cxb5

After 8 ♗xf6 exf6 9 ♘xb5 f5 Black's position is already looking impressive.

8...a6

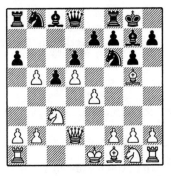

9 h4?!

It's easier for me to criticise this move after my opponent has already done so after the game!

A more natural continuation is 9 ♘f3 ♕a5 10 b6 (or 10 bxa6 ♗xa6

11 ♗xa6 ♕xa6! with good counterplay—O.Stetsko) 10...♘bd7 11 ♗d3 ♘b6 12 0-0 ♗g4 with complex play, Yusupov-Balashov, USSR (ch) 1983.

9...♕a5! 10 b6

A radical way to avoid the opening of files on the queenside. After 10 h5 possible is 10...axb5 and if 11 ♗xb5, then 11...♘xe4. On 10 bxa6 I had prepared 10...♘bd7.

10...♘bd7 11 ♘f3 ♘xb6 12 ♗d3 ♗g4

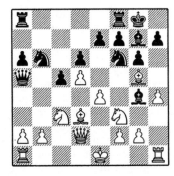

Now the thrust 9 h4?! is shown to be a blank shot.

13 ♔f1?!

Rejecting castling is a dubious decision. More solid is 13 ♘h2 ♗d7 14 0-0 ♘a4 15 ♘xa4 ♕xd2 16 ♗xd2 ♗xa4 17 ♖c1 ♗b5 and Black has a very comfortable game.

13...♘a4

After the unlucky 13th move the game is strategically won for Black and the travel-weary b8-knight finally sees some action.

14 e5

This is like trying to put out a fire with petrol! Also after 14 ♘xa4 ♕xa4 15 b3 ♘xe4! Black is much better.

14...♗xf3! 15 exf6 exf6 16 ♗f4 ♗h5!

Of course not 16...♘xc3?? 17 gxf3.

17 ♗xd6
On 17 f3 there would follow 17...f5.
17...♖fd8 18 ♗f4 f5 19 ♘xa4 ♕xa4 20 d6 ♖ab8
After the obvious 20...c4 21 ♕c2! White would have had some respite. But now the black rooks and bishops control all the main lines of the board.
21 ♖b1 ♕xa2 22 ♕c2 ♖b4 23 ♗d2 ♖d4 0-1

Game 57
A.Zaitsev *White* **Gufeld** *Black*
Grozny 1969

1 d4 ♘f6 2 c4 g6 3 ♘c3 ♗g7 4 ♘f3 0-0 5 ♗g5
This plan, with its active deployment of the bishop and retention of a dynamic pawn centre, used to be regularly employed by the 7th World Champion Vasily Smyslov. Before reinforcing the d4 pawn, White moves his bishop to an aggressive position.
5...c5 6 e3
After this placid development Black has a wider choice of possibilities than after 6 d5.

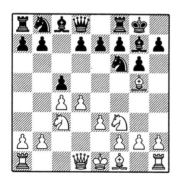

6...♕a5
Despite being very logical, this move, threatening the thrust

...♘f6-e4, is not even considered by the *Encyclopedia*.
The main continuation is 6...d6 7 ♗e2 h6 (also good is 7...cxd4 8 exd4 h6! 9 ♗f4 ♗f5 10 0-0 ♘e4 11 ♘xe4 ♗xe4 12 ♕d2 g5 13 ♗e3 e6!—slightly better for White in Smyslov-Epishin, Rostov on Don 1993; but it seems that instead 8 ♘xd4 is better for White) 8 ♗h4 ♗f5 (in the game Smyslov-Tal, USSR (ch) 1973, there followed 8...g5 9 ♗g3 ♘h5 10 ♕c2?! g4 11 ♘h4 cxd4 12 exd4 ♘c6 13 d5 ♘d4 and Black seizes the initiative, 10 d5 or 10 0-0 was better) 9 0-0 ♘bd7 10 d5 (or 10 ♖c1 ♘e4 11 ♘xe4 ♗xe4 12 ♘d2 g5! with good counterplay for Black) 10...♕b6 11 b3 (after 11 ♘a4 ♕a5 12 ♘d2 ♘b6 13 ♘c3 ♕b4 Black has the better game, Pachman-Smyslov, Amsterdam 1994) 11...g5 12 ♗g3 ♘e4 13 ♘xe4 ♗xe4 with equal chances.
Remarkably, after 6...cxd4 7 exd4 d5 the King's Indian Defence miraculously transforms into one of the variations of the Caro-Kann Defence, Panov Attack, where Black's prospects are not worse. For example, the game Lputian-Gufeld, USSR 1981, proceeded: 8 ♗xf6 ♗xf6 9 ♘xd5 (weaker is 9 cxd5 e6!) 9...♗g7 10 ♘e3 ♕a5+ (much stronger is 10...♘c6!) 11 ♕d2 ♕xd2+ 12 ♔xd2 ♖d8 13 ♗d3?! (correct is 13 ♖d1) 13...♘c6 14 ♘c2 ♗g4 15 d5 ♗xf3 16 gxf3 ♘e5 17 ♗e2 e6 18 ♘e3 exd5 19 cxd5 ♗h6 and Black obtained an advantageous endgame.
7 ♕d2 cxd4 8 exd4 e6!?
With the intention of favourably transferring the game to the track of the Grunfeld Indian Defence by ...d7-d5. But, of course, this does not suit White.
9 ♕f4

The game Smyslov-Gufeld, USSR (ch) Tbilisi 1966/67, proceeded 9 a3 ♘c6 (on 9...d5 there would follow 10 b4 ±) 10 d5! exd5 11 cxd5 ♖e8+ 12 ♗e2 ♘e7 13 ♖d1 d6 14 0-0 and my exchange sacrifice, 14...♘exd5 15 ♘xd5 ♕xd5 16 ♕xd5 ♘xd5 17 ♗b5 ♗e6 18 ♗xe8 ♖xe8 19 ♖fe1 turned out in White's favour.

9...♘h5 10 ♕h4 ♘c6 11 0-0-0?!

The impulsive 11 g4? is countered by 11...♘xd4!. It should be mentioned that it takes a great optimist to castle on the queenside when an enemy knight and queen are training their sights on this part of the board. More solid would be 11 ♗e3, on which I had prepared 11...f5!.

11...f5!

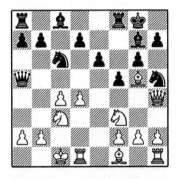

Black secures his kingside, where the enemy forces will turn out to be mere statistics, and begins to develop his own attack against the enemy king.

12 ♗e2 a6 13 ♗d2 b5 14 a3 b4! 15 ♘a2 ♗f6 16 ♘g5

16 ♕h3 would be met by 16...♖b8.

16...♘xd4?!

It was difficult to resist capturing the pawn, especially since it introduces the knight into the attack. However, 16...f4! was much stronger.

17 ♗xh5 ♘b3+ 18 ♔c2

On 18 ♔b1, 18...♕e5 wins.

18...♕a4 19 ♘xb4?

Leading to the loss of a piece. 19 ♔b1 was necessary, on which I had prepared 19...h6!

19...♘xd2+ 20 ♔xd2 h6 21 f4 gxh5 22 ♕xh5 hxg5 23 fxg5 ♗g7 24 g6 ♖e8

The outcome of the game is practically decided. Black just has to put up with a last desperate fling by the white pieces.

25 h4 ♖b8 26 ♕h7+ ♔f8 27 h5 ♖xb4!

Leaving the solitary king to its fate.

28 axb4 ♕xb4+ 29 ♔e3 ♕c5+ 30 ♔d2 ♕f2+ 31 ♔d3 ♗b7 32 c5 ♗e4+ 0-1

Game 58
Ehlvest *White* **Kasparov** *Black*
Horgen 1995

1 d4 ♘f6 2 ♘f3 g6 3 c4 ♗g7 4 ♘c3 0-0 5 ♗g5 c5 6 d5 d6 7 ♘d2 h6 8 ♗h4 a6

Black prepares a pawn offensive on the queenside, but a diversion on the kingside is also possible, e.g. 8...g5 9 ♗g3 ♘h5 10 e3 ♘xg3 11 hxg3 ♗f5 12 e4 ♗h7 13 ♗d3 e6 14 ♘f1 exd5 15 exd5 f5 16 ♘e3 ♕e7 17 ♕c2 ♘d7 18 g4! f4 19 ♗h7+ ♔h8 20 ♗f5 fxe3 21 0-0-0 exf2 22 ♕xf2 ♘e5, reaching a position with chances for both sides, Glek-Wahls, Germany 1995.

9 e4

White can categorically prevent Black's intentions by 9 a4, but this is virtually uncharted territory in view of the rarity of White's mode of development.

9...b5

Now on 10 cxb5 Black can carry on his "demolition work" by 10...e6, although such a sacrificial line cannot easily be evaluated. But one thing is clear—a sharp and dynamic position is reached, totally compatible with the world champion's style of play. The fact that J.Ehlvest agrees with this assessment is proved by his reply.

10 ♗e2 b4 11 ♘a4 ♘h7

Black prepares to bring his second knight to the kingside.

An alternative, 11...♗d7 12 ♖b1 followed by 13 b3, practically forces Black to exchange 13...♗xa4 14 bxa4, after which White can prepare the opening of the b-file (by a2-a3).

12 0-0 ♘d7 13 ♕c2 g5 14 ♗g3 ♘e5 15 ♖ae1 a5

More stubborn is 15...♘g6, saving a tempo and leaving White problems with his knight standing on the edge of the board.

16 ♘f3 ♘g6

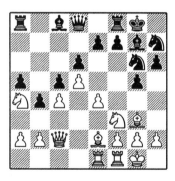

17 e5!?

An interesting pawn sacrifice which has the objective of exploiting the weakened kingside pawn cover. After opening the b1-h7 diagonal White intends 18 ♗d3. But, taking into account that he is playing practically a piece down (the knight on a4 is offside) whereas Black does not suffer from any such inferiority complex, he can hardly count on this proving a success.

17...g4 18 ♘h4 ♘xe5 19 ♘f5 ♗xf5 20 ♕xf5 ♕c8!

The threat of a projected ....f7-f5-f4 forces White into further exchanges.

21 ♕xc8 ♖axc8 22 ♗xe5 dxe5

I would prefer freedom for the bishop by 22...♗xe5, taking into account that White would have to spend several tempi bringing his knight on a4 into play.

23 ♗xg4 f5 24 ♗d1 ♘g5 25 f3 ♘f7

Black transfers his knight to the natural blockading square on d6. After 25...e4 26 h4 ♗d4+ 27 ♔h1 ♘f7? he would have landed in an unpleasant pin by 28 fxe4 fxe4 29 ♗g4 ♖c6 30 ♗e6. Then he would have to retreat by 27...♘h7, but after 28 fxe4 fxe4 29 ♗g4 the knight is not much better than its counterpart on a4.

26 ♗c2 ♘d6 27 b3

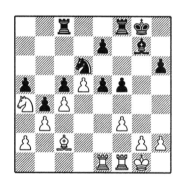

27...e4! 28 g3

Of course the pawn on e4 cannot be taken (28 fxe4 fxe4 29 ♗xe4?? ♗d4+), but 28 ♔f2!? ♗d4+ 29 ♔e2, moving the king closer to the centre of events, deserves attention (Y.Dokhoian).

28...♗d4+ 29 ♔g2 e3 30 f4 ♖fe8 31 ♖e2 ♖b8 32 ♔f3 e6 33 dxe6 ♖xe6 34 ♖g2!

The only way to obtain counter-play is to prepare the move g3-g4.

34...h5 35 ♔e2 ♘f7 36 h3 ♖g6 37 ♖fg1 ♖g7 38 ♗d3 ♖bg8 39 ♘b6

After 28 moves the knight at last leaves his enclosure.

39...h4!?

Not waiting until support arrives by ♔e2-f3. Black himself provokes a crisis by forcing the advance g3-g4.

40 g4 fxg4 41 ♖xg4

After 41 hxg4? h3! 42 ♖h2 ♖xg4 43 ♖xg4 ♖xg4 44 ♔f3 ♖g1 the rook gets behind enemy lines with decisive effect.

41...♖xg4 42 hxg4

The second rook cannot be exchanged since after 42 ♖xg4? ♖xg4 43 hxg4 h3, White could not cope with the separate passed pawns created after 44 ♔f3 h2 45 ♔g2 ♘e4 46 ♘d5 ♘c3 47 ♘xc3 bxc3 etc.

42...h3 43 g5 ♖h8 44 ♘d5 h2 45 ♖h1

Despite the rook's passive position, the pawn pair f4-g5, supported by the invigorated minor pieces, prevents Black making any progress.

45...♔e6 46 ♘c7+ ♔d7 47 ♘d5 ♔e6 48 ♘c7+ ♔d7 ½-½

Game 59
Gulko *White* Gufeld *Black*
Hawaii 1998

Throughout my chess career, like many chessplayers, I have had difficulty against certain players. Among them is Boris Gulko, who always gives me problems.

1 d4 ♘f6 2 c4 g6 3 ♘c3 ♗g7 4 ♘f3 0-0 5 ♗g5 c5 6 d5

Gulko has also given preference to 6 e3 in many games.

6...d6 7 ♘d2

Sorry Boris, but this move is not as good as either 7 e3 or 7 e4. But when a strong player such as Gulko plays a move, you know that he has some interesting ideas.

7...h6

I put the question to the white bishop. What is he doing in my King's Indian territory? 7 ♘d2 will only be good if I play 7...e6 8 e3 exd5 9 cxd5 which results in a Benoni position where the white knight will have an excellent square on c4. But my indication was clearly the King's Indian, not the Benoni.

8 ♗h4 ♕b6!

It is useful ask the opponent a question: "How are you going to defend the b2-pawn?", which at the same time has a bearing on castling.

9 ♖b1

An alternative is 9 ♕c2. Now White's intention is clear, his king will either remain in the centre—which would be very dangerous—or castle kingside.

9...g5

I am not afraid to make this weakening move, because I know that White's king is in more danger if he stays in the centre. In general, this is a good deal for me, because I can exchange off his bishop with my knight.

10 ♗g3 ♘h5 11 e3

It would be adding more water to my mill if White played 11 e4 ♘xg3 12 hxg3 f5 when Black already has a slight advantage..

11...♘xg3 12 hxg3 f5

I think that Black has the better chances because I can punch his position with ...f4. On the other hand 12...♗f5? would have been weak, since after 13 e4 ♗h7 14 g4 White has the advantage.

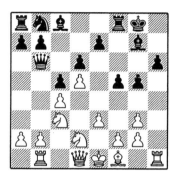

13 f4

I think this is the best reply in this position.

The bluff attack with 13 ♕h5 is not effective—13...♘d7 14 ♗d3 ♘f6 15 ♕g6 ♘g4 ∓.

13...gxf4

Not 13....g4?! 14 ♗d3 ±. The bishops tell me that we need an open position.

14 gxf4 ♘d7?

The knight is heading for the g4-square, but meanwhile 14...e5! suggested itself. How could I miss this move? It is a very strong and logical move which opens up the centre where the white king is detained. Then 15 fxe5 (15 dxe6 ♗xe6 ∓) 15...dxe5 16 e4 ♘a6 or 16...♕g6 leads to sharp play.

15 g4!

I think this is the only move for White to stay on the board.

15...♘f6!?

Of course not 15...fxg4 16 ♕xg4 ♘f6 17 ♕g6 with a clear-cut advantage for White.

16 g5?!

This move enables the knight to hold an active position.

Stronger is 16 gxf5 ♗xf5 17 e4!, forcing Black into a decision. After 17...♘xe4 18 ♘dxe4 ♗xe4 19 ♘xe4 ♖xf4 20 ♗d3 ♖af8 21 ♕d2 ♕d8 22 ♘g3! White covers all the

vulnerable squares whilst retaining his material advantage.

16...hxg5

16...♘g4 also deserves attention: 17 gxh6 ♗f6 and the black king can shelter behind the white h-pawn.

17 fxg5 ♘g4 18 ♕f3

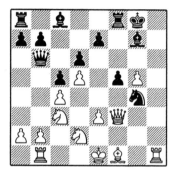

A great philosopher once said that life is a game and that the only game is real life. The same is true of chess—just as in life, there is room for humour. After Gulko played 18 ♕f3, I was feeling a little confused. After all, according to my strict "religious" upbringing in chess, the king in the opening is like a baby and must be protected, indeed cosseted, by castling. But then, a second thought occurred to me: "Perhaps there is a new rule in chess". I wondered to myself. "Is it possible that Gulko moved his rook to b1 and then played his queen to f3 with the profound design of playing history's first short castling on the long side?" As the reader can see from the further course of the game, it would have been better for me if Boris had indeed been struck by the same illusion.

18...♖f7!

An accurate move, which outlines Black's advantage. At first I intended to continue my development with 18...♗d7, but in this case after 19 ♕h3 ♖f7 20 ♘e2 I have to go in for the sacrifice 20...f4 21 ♘xf4 ♖xf4 22 exf4 ♖e8 23 ♗e2! with unclear play.

19 ♕g3

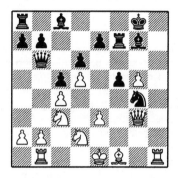

19...e5??

White intends to transfer the knight to f4 in order to carry on his attack and I reacted impulsively to this. The text would have been very strong for me five moves ago. ...e5 was always on my mind, but I chose it at the wrong time and the wrong place. They say it is better late than never—but right now, I suggest it is better never than late for me to play 19...e5. For example, interesting is 19...♘e5!? with the idea of ...♗c8-d7, ...♖a8-e8, ...e7-e6 or ...♗c8-d7, ...a7-a6, ...♕b6-a5, ...b7-b5, on which White would have probably replied 20 ♗e2. But even stronger was 19...e6! 20 ♗e2 ♕d8! (the queen has completed her role on b6 and now proceeds to the other side of the board) 21 ♖h5 ♗e5! (weak is 21...♕f8? 22 ♗xg4 fxg4 23 ♔e2 exd5 24 ♘xd5 ♗f5 25 ♖bh1 or 21...e5 22 e4 f4 23 ♕h4

♘e3 24 ♔f2 and in both cases Black faces difficulties) 22 ♕h3 ♕f8 23 g6 (or 23 ♘f3 ♗xc3+! 24 bxc3 ♕g7 25 ♔d2 ♘f2) 23...♖e7 24 ♘f3 ♗g7 25 ♔d2 ♗d7 26 ♖h1 ♕f6 27 ♘g5 ♘f2 and Black wins.

20 e4! f4?

White stands better, but Black had no grounds for this kind of "activity." He should have reconciled himself to 20...fxe4 21 ♘dxe4.

21 ♕h4 ♘e3 22 ♘f3

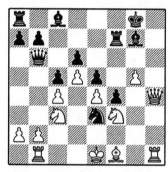

22...♗g4

There was only one way to drag on the struggle (but not save it) 22...♘xf1 23 ♕h7+ ♔f8 24 ♖xf1 ♕b4 (or 24...♕d8 25 ♖g1! a6 26 ♘h4 ♗d7 27 ♘g6+ ♔e8 28 ♕g8+ ♗f8 29 ♘xf8 ♖xf8 30 ♕g6+ and White wins) 25 ♘h4 ♕xc4 26 ♘g6+ ♔e8 27 ♕g8+ ♗f8 28 ♖h1 ♕d3 29 ♘xf8 ♕g3+ (29...♖xf8 30 ♕g6+) 30 ♔d1 ♗g4+ 31 ♔c2 ♕f2+ 32 ♔b3 c4+ 33 ♔a3 ♕c5+ 34 b4 cxb3+ 35 ♔b2 and there are no more reasonable checks.

23 ♕h7+ ♔f8 24 ♘h4 ♘xf1 25 ♘g6+ ♔e8 26 ♕g8+ ♗f8 27 ♖h8 ♕c7 28 ♘xf8 ♖g7 29 ♘e6+ ♖xg8 30 ♖xg8+ 1-0

Fianchetto Variation

First, let me state that although the system based on the fianchetto of the white king's bishop is considered one of the most unpleasant for Black to face, it is not essential to devote specific attention to it. That is to say that, unless Black happens to be a particularly dedicated adherent of the King's Indian, he can sidestep the principal lines at no cost to himself.

The Fianchetto Variation, in which **1 d4 ♘f6 2 c4 g6 3 g3 ♗g7 4 ♗g2 0-0 5 ♘f3 d6 6 0-0** is considered as the main sequence of moves, is one of the most dangerous variations for Black in the King's Indian, but on the other hand it provides him with many potentially thrilling possibilities to plan his forthcoming strategy.

By fianchettoing the bishop, White aims at the queenside, controls the central e4 and d5 squares

and consolidates the position of his king. In addition, the g2 bishop enables him to maintain the pawn tension in the centre, where White can start an offensive—later getting to work on the queenside. Another popular method of play is to close the centre after d4-d5.

Generally speaking, in any variation of the King's Indian where I have a choice where to develop my queen's knight (and this is a fairly major problem!), I prefer deploying it by 6...♘c6! (the exclamation mark is mine!) with a view to ...♘c6-d4. The future of the knight after 7 d5 does not bother Black, since after 7...♘a5 8 ♘bd2 c5 it takes part in counterplay on the queenside. With its logical basis (pressure on the d4 square) the Yugoslav Variation 6...c5 is close to this theme, because after 7 ♘c3 ♘c6 8 d5 ♘a5 a similar position is reached.

The other principal line is to organize an attack on the d4 square by ...e7-e5 after 6...♘bd7. But, in accordance with our theme for the book we will concentrate on the first variation in which Black generates counterplay by attacking the d4 pawn with the knight on c6.

After **6...♘c6 7 ♘c3** the main continuations are 7...♗f5, 7...e5 and 7...a6.

Sometimes 7...♗g4 is played, but in this case it is easier for White to carry out his plans. For example: 8

d5 ♘a5 9 ♘d2 c5 10 h3 ♗d7 11 ♕c2 e5 12 dxe6 ♗xe6 13 b3, and White has a clear plan of exerting pressure in the centre by ♗c1-b2, ♖a1-d1 etc., while the d4 square can be taken under control with e2-e3. White also obtains the advantage after 8 h3 ♗xf3 9 exf3! with d4-d5 to follow.

Controlling the e4 square: 7...♗f5

(1 d4 ♘f6 2 c4 g6 3 g3 ♗g7 4 ♗g2 0-0 5 ♘f3 d6 6 0-0 ♘c6 7 ♘c3)

We shall now look at another way of handling this opening variation for Black—namely 7...♗f5. I was one of the first to play this move—almost a quarter of a century ago against Viktor Korchnoi in a USSR Championship.

Game 60
Korchnoi *White* **Gufeld** *Black*
USSR (ch) Tallinn 1965

1 c4 ♘f6 2 ♘c3 g6 3 d4 ♗g7 4 g3 0-0 5 ♗g2 d6 6 ♘f3 ♘c6 7 0-0 ♗f5

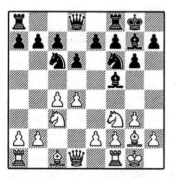

Black takes the e4 square under his control and in some variations occupies it with his knight.
8 ♘h4

Not the best decision. Despite the fact that the bishop is pushed back, the knight's move to the edge of the board turns out to be in Black's favour. But the fact that the three-time USSR Champion played this manoeuvre cannot be considered pure chance. He did not see any particular advantage for White in the theoretical path of those days—8 d5 ♘a5 9 ♘d4 ♗d7 10 b3 c5 11 dxc6 bxc6. In fact, soon after, I managed to show the drawbacks to this plan in my game with G.Barcza, which is looked at below.

Korchnoi did not like the prospect of exchanging the bishop on g2 which could have taken place in the event of 8 ♘e1—8...♕c8 9 e4 ♗h3, though in this position after 10 f4 ♗xg2 11 ♔xg2 e5 12 d5 ♘d4 13 fxe5 dxe5 14 ♗g5 White still maintains some advantage.

However, White can proceed with the development of his pieces without being afraid of the invasion of the knight on e4: 8 b3 ♘e4 9 ♗b2 ♘xc3 10 ♗xc3 ♗e4 11 ♖c1 (in the game Krogius-Gufeld, USSR 1965, was played 11 ♕d2 e5 12 d5 ♘e7 13 ♘e1 ♗xg2 14 ♘xg2 ♕d7 15 e4 f5 16 exf5 gxf5 17 f4 ♘g6 with good play for Black) 11...e5 (11...d5 12 e3 ± also has been played) 12 d5 ♘e7 13 ♗h3 ♗f5 14 ♗xf5 ♘xf5 15 e4 ♘e7 16 c5 and White maintains the initiative. The modern treatment of this variation, instead of 9 ♗b2, recommends 9 ♘d5!? ♗d7 10 ♗b2 f5 11 e3 a6 12 ♖c1 b5 13 ♘d2 ♘g5 14 ♕e2 b4 15 c5 ± Cvitan-Smirin, Tilburg 1993.

8 ♖e1 ♘e4 9 ♘d5!? ♗d7 (or 9...♖e8 10 ♘e3 ♗d7 11 d5 ♘b8 12 ♕c2 ±) is also possible, 10 b3 e6 11 ♘e3 and here, on 11...e5 or 11...f5, White completes the development

of his pieces by 12 &b2 and preserves slightly better chances.

8...&d7

Here I expected the natural 9 e4, on which, after 9...e5, Black sets about controlling the d4 square. For example, the game Csom-Gufeld, Cienfuegos 1984, proceeded: 10 d5 ②d4 11 &e3 (after 11 f4 c6 12 f5 cxd5 13 cxd5 b5 Black develops an initiative on the queenside) 11...c5! (sacrificing the pawn anables Black to "liberate" his bishop with maximum effect) 12 dxc6 bxc6 13 &xd4 exd4 14 ≝xd4 ②d5 15 ≝d3 ②xc3 16 bxc3 ½-½.

All this happened 20 years later, but a long time ago, in 1965, V.Korchnoi made a decision which failed to find any followers. And of course, despite the result, this game had a certain influence on this turn of events.

I think that the reader will be much more interested to get to know about the subsequent events from V.Korchnoi himself, as recorded in his book *Selected Games* (Shakhforum, St Petersburg, 1996).

9 f4?

This is already a serious mistake, after which Black, with an unexpected manoeuvre, seizes the initiative. The correct way was 9 d5 ②a5

10 b3!, leaving White slightly better, perhaps.

9...②a5 10 ≝d3 c5 11 d5?!

Yet another mistake. At the board I did not think my opponent would risk playing 11 e3 because of 11...cxd4 12 exd4 ≝b6 or 12...e5 and Black's tactical ideas look very serious. True, White has enough resources for defence and counterattack. For example: 12...e5 13 fxe5 dxe5 14 &g5! h6 15 &xf6 &xf6 16 ②g6!, and White wins.

11...a6 12 b3 b5 13 &d2 ≝b8

13...b4 looked tempting, but after 14 ②d1 Black would not have been able to extract any advantage from the unprotected rook on a1—the move 14...②xd5 costs the exchange after 15 ≝c1, and the trade of the f6-knight for the d2-bishop (14...②c4) also wasn't in Black's favour.

14 ≝ac1 ≝c7 15 e4 bxc4 16 bxc4 ≝b2 17 ②f3 ≝fb8 18 ≝fe1 &g4!

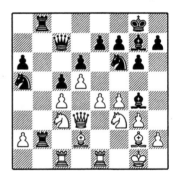

It is easy to assess the present position. Black occupies the only open file and paralyzes White's army because of the need to protect the queenside pawns. Although White's pieces are centralized, it is difficult for them to find a promising plan. White's ace is the uncomfortable position of the knight on a5. After the accurate 19 ♖e2!, to counter the threat of ...♗xf3 followed by ...♘xc4, White, no doubt, would have a chance of neutralizing the opponent's initiative and gradually achieving equality. But White's next is premature and leads to difficult play.

19 e5? ♘e8 20 e6

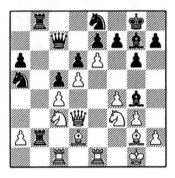

20...f5?

A serious strategical blunder, after which Black's game disintegrates. The correct 20...fxe6! 21 dxe6 ♗xf3 22 ♗xf3 ♘xc4 23 ♕xc4 ♖xd2 24 ♕xa6 ♗d4+ 25 ♔h1 ♗xc3 26 ♖xc3 ♖bb2 would have given Black great chances of victory.

21 ♖e2 ♘f6 22 h3 ♗h5 23 ♗e1 ♖xe2 24 ♕xe2 ♘e8?

More stubborn was 24...♖b4 25 ♘d1 ♖a4 26 ♘e3 ♖a3, but even here, after 27 ♖c3, White retains the advantages of his position—the more pieces exchanged, the more awkward becomes the position of the knight on a5.

25 ♘d1 ♗d4+ 26 ♔h1 ♘f6 27 ♕c2 ♗xf3 28 ♗xf3 ♕b6 29 ♕d3 ♔g7 30 ♘c3 ♕b4

The attempt to create an invincible defensive formation by means of a queen sacrifice fails to a simple refutation.

31 ♖b1 ♗xc3 32 ♖xb4 cxb4 33 ♗xc3 bxc3 34 c5!

With the sacrifice of two pawns White takes away the foothold (the pawn e7!) of the knight f6—which he then wins.

34...dxc5 35 d6 exd6 36 ♕xc3 ♖b1+ 37 ♔g2 ♘b7 38 g4 1-0

Game 61
Barcza *White* **Gufeld** *Black*
Leningrad 1967

1 ♘f3 g6 2 d4 ♘f6 3 g3 ♗g7 4 ♗g2 0-0 5 0-0 d6!

This game was played at a critical moment in a prestigious tournament dedicated to the 50th anniversary of the October Revolution, where I was fighting to gain the grandmaster title. And, needless to say, I chose my favourite King's Indian for such a crucial encounter.

With the present sequence of moves Black had an alternative in 5...d5, with prospects of playing a variation of the Grünfeld Defence.

6 c4 ♘c6 7 ♘c3 ♗f5 8 d5 ♘a5

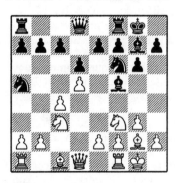

9 ♘d4

White pushes the bishop back. 9 ♘d2 has also been played, in order to gain a tempo by 10 e4 after 9...c5. However, Black has the stronger 9...c6! and the bishop on f5 is in the right place, since it takes the b1 square away from the rook, which can be important, as in the variation 10 b4 ♘xd5 11 cxd5 ♗xc3, even if, after 12 e4, White has compensation for the pawn.

White achieves nothing by 10 e4 ♗g4 11 f3 (weaker is 11 ♕c2 cxd5 12 cxd5 ♖c8 13 ♖e1 b5 and Black already has the initiative, Yusupov-Gulko, Reykjavik 1990) 11...♗d7 and the game is equal.

After ceding the centre by 10 dxc6 bxc6 11 e4 ♗g4 12 ♕c2 ♖b8 (on 12...♖c8 White has 13 b4 ±) 13 a3 c5 Black also obtains good play.

9...♗d7

9...♘e4? 10 ♘xf5 gxf5 11 ♕d3 clearly favours White.

10 b3

The other way to protect the c4 pawn, 10 ♕d3, is examined in the next game.

10...c5 11 dxc6

It is not easy for White to display any activity without this exchange. 11 ♘c2 is met, according to the generally accepted scheme, by 11...a6 12 ♖b1 ♕c7 (premature is 12...b5?! 13 cxb5 axb5 14 b4 and Black ends up in a worse position, Chiburdanidze-Malisauskas, Tallinn (rapid) 1997) 13 ♕d3 ♖ab8 14 ♗d2 b5 with an equal game, Udovcic-Westerinen, Leningrad 1967.

11...bxc6

Also possible is 11...♘xc6 12 e3 ♕a5 13 ♗b2 ♖ac8 14 ♕e2 a6 15 ♖ac1 ♖fe8! 16 ♘xc6 ♗xc6 17 e4 ♘d7 and with projected counterplay by 18...b5, Black's chances are by no means worse, V.Akopian-Poluljahov, Russia 1993.

12 ♗b2 ♖b8 13 ♕d2

Defending himself against the threat of ...♘xc4. 13 ♖b1 could be followed by 13...c5 14 ♘c2 ♕c8 or 14...♘c6 with complex play.

13...c5 14 ♘db5 ♘c6

The knight returns to its "rightful" c6 square (isn't that a triumph for the move 6...♘c6 ?) leaving Black's pieces harmoniously placed and ready for the forthcoming struggle.

15 ♘d5 ♘xd5 16 ♗xg7 ♔xg7 17 ♗xd5 ♘b4!

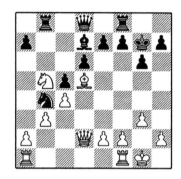

Black takes the opportunity to exchange White's most active piece by a temporary pawn sacrifice.

18 ♘xa7 ♘xd5 19 ♕xd5 ♕c7 20 ♘b5 ♗xb5 21 cxb5 ♖xb5

Despite the material equality, Black's prospects are preferable as he has the possibility of exerting pressure along the semi-open a- and b-files.

22 ♖fc1 ♕b7 23 ♕d2

After an exchange of queens, Black would have to take up a defensive position—nevertheless the drawing tendencies of rook and pawn endgames are well-known.

23...♖a8 24 ♖c3 ♔g8 25 ♖ac1 ♖a3 26 ♖1c2 ♖ba5 27 ♖b2?!

White goes over to passive defence, whereas by playing 27 ♖c4!? he could have reminded Black of the vulnerable points in his position (27...♕a7 28 ♖h4 threatening ♕d2-h6).

27...♕b4 28 ♖cc2 ♕xd2 29 ♖xd2

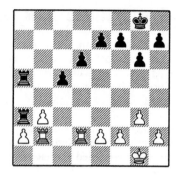

29...f5!

Black develops his initiative. The f-pawn co-operates with the c-pawn in a peculiar tandem and secures control over important central squares.

30 ⌖f1 ⌖f7 31 ⌖e1 ♖a6 32 ⌖d1

Black pins his hopes on the "fire-proof" nature of his position, whereas White should have played 32 f4 restricting Black's possibilities.

32...e5 33 ⌖c1 ⌖e6 34 ♖dc2 ♖6a5 35 ⌖b1 ♖b5 36 ♖c3 d5!

The position reaches its climax.

37 ♖bc2 ⌖d6 38 ⌖b2?

G.Barcza can no longer stand the tiresome siege and gets carried away by a false idea of breaking through with the rooks. He should have remained patient and stood his ground by 38 ♖b2.

38...♖ba5 39 b4?

And a second mistake. But, as we know, it is easier to commit errors in bad positions. It was still not too late to retreat 39 ⌖b1.

39...♖xa2+ 40 ⌖c1 ♖xc2+ 41 ♖xc2 cxb4 42 ⌖b1 b3

Now the rook penetrates to the seventh rank and the game quickly comes to an end.

43 ♖c3 ♖a2 44 ♖xb3 ♖xe2 45 ♖b7 ♖xf2 46 ♖xh7 e4 47 ⌖c1 e3 48 ⌖d1 d4 0-1

Game 62
Leski *White* **Gufeld** *Black*
Los Angeles 1996

1 ♘f3 ♘f6 2 g3 g6 3 ♗g2 ♗g7 4 0-0 0-0 5 c4 d6 6 ♘c3 ♘c6 7 d4 ♗f5

This moment reminded me of my youth. As they say, an old love never dies.

8 d5 ♘a5 9 ♘d4 ♗d7 10 ♕d3 c5 11 ♘c2

After 11 ♘b3, a pawn sacrifice in the spirit of the Benko Gambit is possible: 11...b5!? 12 ♘xa5 ♕xa5 13 ♘xb5 ♗xb5 14 cxb5 a6 15 bxa6 ♖fb8 16 ♗d2 ♕xa6 and the pressure which the major pieces exert along the a- and b-files fully compensates for the sacrificed pawn. Cuellar-Stein, Sousse (izt) 1967.

11...a6 12 b3 b5

This kind of pawn sacrifice is quite natural in such positions and does not require precise calculation. Black has obvious counterplay.

13 ♖b1

A cautious move. If White accepts the pawn sacrifice by 13 cxb5 axb5 14 ♘xb5 then he has to reckon on the manoeuvre 14...♘g4 15 ♘c3 c4! 16 bxc4 when either 16...♘e5 17 ♕d1 ♘exc4, or an immediate

16...♘xc4!?, gives Black active piece play, which fully compensates for the sacrificed pawn.

13...♖b8 14 ♗d2 e6!!

This break closely corresponds with ...b7-b5. White's centre crumbles away and, as in many variations of the King's Indian, it will not be easy for him to exploit the backward d6 pawn.

15 dxe6 ♗xe6 16 ♘e3

An exchange of the c4 pawn also leads to level play: 16 cxb5 axb5 17 b4 ♘c4.

16...♖e8 17 ♖fd1 bxc4

17...♘g4!? 18 ♘xg4 ♗xg4 19 h3 ♗f5 20 e4 ♗e6, with the idea of exploiting the weakening of the d4 square by the knight manoeuvre ...♘a5-c6-d4, also deserves attention.

18 bxc4 ♖xb1 19 ♖xb1 ♘xc4!?

A tactical blow, based on the awkward deployment of the white pieces.

20 ♘xc4 d5 21 ♗g5!

The only move which maintains equality. 21 ♘e3 d4; 21 ♘e5 ♗f5.

21...dxc4 22 ♕xd8 ♖xd8 23 ♘e4

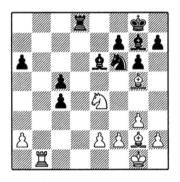

23...c3!

This game shows the value of keeping up to date with the study of chess periodicals. Up to here, M.Leski was following my game with Vaulin (Alushta 1993), which

proceeded 23...♘xe4 24 ♗xd8 ♘c3 25 ♖b8 h5 26 ♗f6+ ♔h7 27 ♗xc3 ♗xc3 28 ♗xe4 and, instead of the "awful" 28...♗f5??, I should have played 28...♗b4 with a reasonable position. After the game A.Vaulin directed my attention to the possibility of the move 23...c3!, mentioned in *Chess Informator 57*. Apparently M.Leski did not know about this and failed to react in the best way.

24 ♘xc3?!

As shown by A.Vaulin, 24 ♘xf6+ ♗xf6 25 ♗xf6 c2 26 ♖f1 ♖d1 27 ♗g5 ♗xa2 or 27...♗c4, with approximately equal chances, was stronger.

24...h6 25 ♗f4 ♘h5 26 ♗c7 ♖d2 27 ♘e4 ½-½

A premature peaceful agreement, since after 27...♖c2 Black's chances are preferable.

Attacking the centre by 7...e5

(1 d4 ♘f6 2 c4 g6 3 g3 ♗g7 4 ♗g2 0-0 5 ♘f3 d6 6 0-0 ♘c6 7 ♘c3)

There are adherents of the King's Indian Defence who like to play it leaving their e-pawn on e7, but I generally prefer to use this pawn to strike at the enemy centre at the first opportunity by **7 ... e5**.

This pawn attack on the d4 square can also be considered as a logical follow-up to the development of the knight on c6.

Game 63
Vaganian *White* **Gufeld** *Black*
Moscow 1972

1 ♘f3 ♘f6 2 g3 g6 3 ♗g2 ♗g7 4 0-0 0-0 5 c4 d6 6 d4 ♘c6 7 ♘c3 e5 8 d5

It would be difficult for White to count on any advantage after 8 dxe5:

(a) 8...dxe5 9 ♗g5 ♗e6 10 ♘d5 ♗xd5 11 ♗xf6 ♕xf6 12 cxd5 ♘e7 13 e4 c6 14 ♕b3 cxd5 15 exd5 ♘f5 16 ♖fe1 ♖ae8 with approximate equality. Thorbergsson-Stein, Reykjavik 1972;

(b) 8...♘xe5 9 ♘xe5 dxe5 10 ♕xd8 ♖xd8 11 ♗g5 ♖d4 12 ♘d5 ♘xd5 13 cxd5 e4 14 ♖fd1 ♗f5 15 ♖xd4 ♗xd4 with equal chances, Adorjan-J.Polgar, Budapest 1993.

8...♘e7

If Black tries to transpose into a position from the Yugoslav Variation by 8...♘a5 9 ♘d2 c5 he must reckon on the possibility of the exchange 10 dxc6 ♘xc6 11 ♘de4 ♘e8 12 ♘b5 ♘d4 13 ♗g5, when White's chances are preferable.

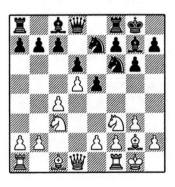

9 c5

This advance is prompted by the pawn structure itself, in which, in Nimzowitsch's terminology, White has a "pawn exchange advantage" on the queenside. The question is: isn't it better to reinforce the centre by 9 e4 first? Nowadays this has become the main continuation for White and the present game may have helped theory to move in that direction.

The tactical justification of the move 9 c5 is 9...dxc5 10 ♘xe5 ♘fxd5 11 ♘xd5 ♗xe5 12 ♗g5 f6 13 ♗xf6!.

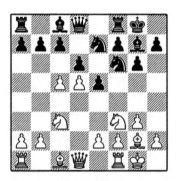

9...e4

With the help of the e-pawn, Black tries to cut off temporarily the bishop on g2 from controlling the d5-pawn.

Black's main reply is 9...♘e8 10 cxd6

(a) 10...cxd6 (after capturing this way the d6 pawn can become an object of an attack) 11 a4 (or 11 ♕b3 h6 12 e4 f5 13 exf5 gxf5 14 ♘d2 ♘g6 15 ♘c4 ♖f7 16 a4 ♗f8 17 ♗d2 ± Vaganian-Stein, USSR (ch) Riga 1970) 11...h6 12 ♘d2 f5 13 ♘c4 g5 14 ♗d2 f4 15 ♘e4 ♘f5 16 e3 ♘f6 17 ♗b4 and White's chances are preferable. Romanishin-Grünberg, Dresden 1988.

(b) 10...♘xd6 11 ♕b3 h6 12 ♖d1 (or 12 ♘d2 ♘ef5 13 e3 h5 14 h4 g5 15 hxg5 ♕xg5 16 ♘f3 ♕g4= Portisch-J.Polgar, Monaco 1994) 12...f5 13 ♗e3 ♗d7 14 ♗c5 b6 15 ♗a3 ♘ec8 16 e4 f4 17 ♘e2 g5 with complex play, Lutz-Gelfand, Munich 1993.

10 cxd6

Later on, 10 ♘g5 was regarded as stronger. Then if 10...dxc5 11 ♘gxe4 ♘exd5 12 ♘xd5 ♘xd5 13 ♗g5 f6 14 ♕xd5 ♕xd5 15 ♘xf6+ ♗xf6 16 ♗xd5+ ♔g7 17 ♗xf6+ ♖xf6 18 ♖ac1 c6 19 ♗g2 b6 20 ♖fd1 and White retains pressure on the centre (P.Nikolić).

10...♕xd6! 11 ♘g5

11 ♗f4 is no good in view of 11...♕b4.

11...♘fxd5!

This is stronger than 11...♘exd5 12 ♘gxe4 ♕e5 13 ♘xf6+ ♗xf6 14 ♗f4 ♕a5 15 ♕a4 ♕xa4 16 ♘xa4 c6 with equality. Furman-Gufeld, Kiev 1963.

12 ♘gxe4 ♕e5 13 ♘xd5?!

13 ♗d2 is better.

13...♘xd5

Black's position is already somewhat preferable.

14 ♕b3

The simplifying exchanging combination 14 ♕xd5 ♕xd5 15 ♘f6+ ♗xf6 16 ♗xd5 c6 would leave Black with a small advantage in the endgame.

14...c6 15 ♖e1 a5! 16 ♘c5?!

A poor decision.

16...♘b4!

Black's pressure on the queenside becomes appreciable, and White finds it difficult to complete his mobilization.

17 a3

On 17 ♘d3 Black has a pleasant choice between the simple 17...♘xd3 18 ♕xd3 ♗e6 and the more spectacular 17...♗e6!.

17...♕xc5 18 axb4 ♗e6!

This intermediate thrust refutes White's plan.

19 bxc5

19 ♕xe6 will not do, in view of 19...♕xb4 when White has two major pieces under attack.

19...♗xb3

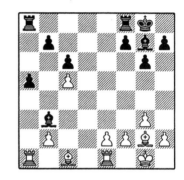

There is material equality on the board and the players have two bishops each—yet here "the advantage of the bishop-pair" lies clearly with Black. The black bishops completely paralyse the entire white army.

20 e4 a4 21 e5

An attempt to block the diagonal of the "Gufeld bishop".

21...♖fe8 22 ♗f4

Nor can the centre be held by 22 f4 f6 23 ♗e4 fxe5 24 f5 gxf5 25 ♗xf5 e4!.

22...♖a5 23 ♖ac1 ♗f8

The stranded white pawns fall prey to the enemy.

24 ♗e3 ♖xe5 25 ♗d2 ♖axc5 26 ♗c3 ♖xe1+ 27 ♖xe1 a3 28 ♗b4 a2 0-1

After 29 ♗xc5 ♗xc5, White cannot prevent the manoeuvre ....♗c5-d4xb2.

Game 64
Kolarov *White* **Gufeld** *Black*
Odessa 1968

**1 d4 ♘f6 2 ♘f3 g6 3 g3 ♗g7 4
♗g2 0-0 5 0-0 d6 6 c4 ♘c6 7 ♘c3
e5 8 d5 ♘e7 9 e4**

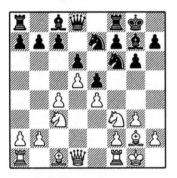

9...♘d7
The merit of this move lies in the
fact that it exerts additional control
over the c5 square, despite the fact
that, when preparing the break
...f7-f5, the bishop on c8 is ob-
structed, which calls for measures to
protect the e6 square.

9...♘e8 10 ♘e1 f5 11 ♘d3 ♘f6
would have transposed back into the
game. But White could have chosen
the more stubborn 10 b4 f5 11 ♘g5
with a promising position. For example, Dautov-Kupreichik, Germany 1993, proceeded: 11...h6 12
♘e6 ♗xe6 13 dxe6 fxe4 (or 13...c6
14 c5 d5 15 exd5 e4 16 d6 ♗xc3 17
♗h6 ± E.Mortensen) 14 b5! a6 15
bxa6 ♖xa6 16 ♖b1 b6 17 ♗e4 ♘f6
18 ♗g2 with the better chances for
White. In the 90s, the theory of this
variation focused on such subtleties
as the knight on f6 finding a place
for itself on g8, after a preliminary
9...♔h8. The young Judit Polgar
used to choose this plan sometimes.
For example, her game with Kasparov (Dos Hermanas 1995)

continued 10 ♘e1 ♘fg8 11 ♘d3 f5
12 f4 exf4 13 ♘xf4 ♘f6 14 exf5
♘xf5 15 ♔h1 ♖e8 16 a4! (if 16
♗d2 then strong is 16...♘d4! with
the idea of ...♗c8-f5) 16...a5 17 ♖a3
♕e7?! 18 ♗d2! and White obtained
an advantage. 17...♗d7!? or
17...♘e3!? deserve attention,
though here too, after 18 ♗xe3
♖xe3 19 ♕d2 ♕e7 20 ♘b5, White
emerges with the better chances.

10 ♘e1
A popular sequel, which is frequently used by present-day cham-
pions. White transfers his knight on
d3, from where it supports the advance c4-c5, and vacates the f3
square for the pawn.

This manoeuvre is less convincing
than in the case of 9...♘h5 10 ♘e1,
where the knight move hinders the
advance ...f7-f5, since the knight on
h5 is left without defence.

10...f5 11 ♘d3 ♘f6
This is stronger and more thematic than the timid 11...h6?! 12 f4
♔h7 13 ♗d2 fxe4 14 ♘xe4 ♘f5 15
♔h1 exf4 16 ♘xf4 ♘e5 17 ♖c1 c5,
Botvinnik-Schmid, Hamburg 1965;
and now 18 dxc6 bxc6 19 ♖e1
leaves the advantage with White.

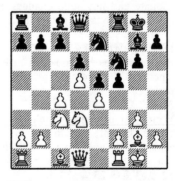

12 f3
A passive move. There is no sense
in White supporting the pawn since,
after its capture, the pieces on their

own can consolidate their grip on the e4 square. The modern continuation is 12 &g5.

12...h6 13 &h1

Black has a strong attack after 13 ©f2 f4! 14 &d2 g5 15 g4 ©g6.

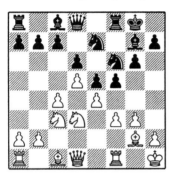

13...g5!

Clearing a path for the queen to the kingside.

Black is not afraid of allowing the opponent's knight control of the e4 square since in return his own knight gains access to an important outpost on d4.

14 exf5 ©xf5 15 ©f2 Ⓦe8 16 ©ce4 Ⓦg6 17 Ⓦd3 &d7

It is clear that Black has done well out of the opening. He controls the d4 square and has good chances of organizing an attack against the enemy king.

18 &d2 ©xe4 19 ©xe4 Ⓡf7

Black doubles his rooks in order to increase the pressure on the f3 square.

20 Ⓡf2 Ⓡaf8 21 Ⓡaf1 ©d4!

White cannot tolerate such an aggressive knight for long, which means that he will have to give up the advantage of two bishops.

22 &e3 &f5 23 &g1 h5!

Beginning a direct assault on the enemy king's fortress.

24 &xd4 exd4 25 Ⓡe2 g4!

Undermining the pawn support of the e4 square, after which Black will attack this crucial strongpoint with all available forces.

26 f4 Ⓡe7 27 Ⓡfe1 Ⓡfe8 28 b4 c6!

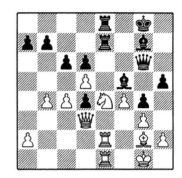

White has managed to withstand the frontal attack on his knight, but after the opening of the c-file Black extends his attacking front.

29 b5 cxd5 30 cxd5 &f8 31 a4 b6 32 &f2 h4 33 &g1 h3 34 &h1 Ⓡc8

Black's pieces suddenly find a way of invading the queenside. Such an outflanking manoeuvre is also frequently encountered in general warfare.

35 Ⓦa3

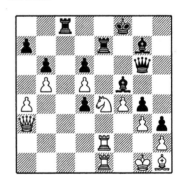

35...d3!

A thematic blow! It opens the diagonal for the dark-squared bishop and lures the queen on to the d3 square, so that the knight will be pinned.

36 ♕xd3 ♖c3 37 ♕d1 ♖c4

Now, with the frontal attack supported by the flank one, the knight will have to retreat.

38 ♘f2 ♖ec7?

A gross mistake. After 38...♗c2! White would incur material losses.

39 ♗e4!

In this way White exchanges his passive bishop for its active counterpart, and the complexion of the battle changes abruptly.

39...♗c3 40 ♗xf5 ♕xf5 41 ♖e8+ ♔f7

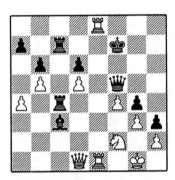

42 ♘e4!

White suddenly creates threats against the black king and Black will need all his resources to save the game. On the other hand, after 42 ♘xg4?! Black could still have played for a win: 42...♕g6! 43 ♖8e6 ♗xe1! 44 ♘h6+ ♔g7! 45 ♖xg6+ ♔xg6 46 g4 ♔xh6 47 ♕xh3+ ♔g7!.

42...♖xe4! 43 ♖1xe4 ♗e5 44 ♕d3 ♖c3

44...♔xe8 is, of course, impossible in view of 45 ♖xe5+.

45 ♖8xe5!

Leading to a drawn queen endgame. Black cannot avoid the perpetual check.

45...dxe5 46 ♕xc3 ♕xe4 47 ♕c7+ ♔g6 48 ♕d6+ ♔f7 49 ♕e6+

♔f8 50 ♕f6+ ♔g8 51 ♕d8+ ♔f7 ½-½

Game 65
Kasparov *White* **Ivanchuk** *Black*
Riga 1995

1 d4 ♘f6 2 c4 g6 3 g3 ♗g7 4 ♗g2 0-0 5 ♘c3 d6 6 ♘f3 ♘c6 7 0-0 e5 8 d5 ♘e7 9 e4 ♘e8 10 ♘e1

As mentioned before, 10 b4 f5 11 ♘g5 deserves attention.

10...f5 11 ♘d3 ♘f6 12 ♗g5

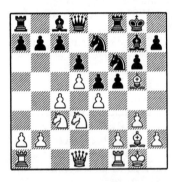

The modern way of consolidating the pawn on e4.

12...h6

After 12...fxe4 13 ♘xe4 the central e4 square falls into White's hands which determines his slight, but enduring, advantage. If 13...♘xe4 14 ♗xe4 ♗h3 then White simply moves the rook 15 ♖e1 ±. In the game Karpov-J.Polgar, Las Palmas 1994, Black played 13...♘f5 14 ♖e1! h6 15 ♘xf6+ ♗xf6 16 ♗d2, but here too White stands a little better.

13 ♗xf6 ♖xf6

13...♗xf6 is considered weaker. For example, the game Karpov-Gelfand, Dos Hermanas 1994, proceeded 14 f4 exf4 15 ♘xf4 ♗e5 16 exf5 ♗xf5 17 ♕d2 c6 18 ♔h1 ♕b6

19 ♖ae1 with advantage to White in view of the weakness of the e6 square.

R.Dautov recommends 17...♕d7!?, not fearing 18 ♘e6 ♗xe6 19 dxe6 ♕xe6 20 ♘d5, in view of the possible exchange sacrifice 20...c6! 21 ♘c7 ♕xc4 22 ♘xa8 ♕d4+! 23 ♕xd4 ♗xd4+ 24 ♔h1 ♖xa8 25 ♖ad1 ♗e5 with sufficient compensation. However, here too, possible is 18 ♖ae1 ±.

14 f4 exf4 15 ♘xf4 ♔h7

It is also useful to look through the game Huzman-Nijboer, Amsterdam 1994: 15...c6 16 ♔h1 ♖f7 17 ♕d2 ♗e5 18 ♘d3 ♗g7 19 ♘f4 ♗e5 20 ♘d3 ♗g7 ½-½. But White could have played the stronger 18 exf5! ±.

16 ♕d3 ♖f8

16...c6!? deserves attention.

17 ♖ae1 ♗e5 18 exf5 ♘xf5

On 18...♗xf5 both 19 ♕e3, or 19 ♗e4 are possible, when future piece exchanges merely increase White's advantage as he has firm control of the e4 square.

19 ♔h1 ♕f6

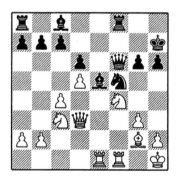

20 c5!

20 g4 suggests itself, with the idea of meeting 20...♘h4 by 21 ♘e6. However Black does not have to move the knight but can play

20...♕h4 21 gxf5 ♗xf4 22 fxg6+ ♔g7.

However, in undermining the foothold of the bishop on e5, White has not forgotten about this idea, which can be carried out after 20...dxc5?—21 g4! ♗xf4 22 ♖xf4.

20...♕g7

It is useful to shift the queen off the same file as the enemy rook—the more so that the indifferent move 20...♗d7?! runs into 21 c6! bxc6 22 dxc6 ♗e8 23 ♘cd5 when after 23...♕f7 24 ♘xc7 ♕xc7 25 ♘e6 ♘xg3+ 26 hxg3 ♖xf1+ 27 ♖xf1 ♕e7 28 ♕b3 White is left with the advantage (R.Dautov).

21 cxd6 cxd6 22 ♘e6 ♗xe6 23 dxe6 ♖ac8

This move allows the knight to invade on d5. In this respect 23...♖ae8 24 ♗d5 ± would have caused fewer problems.

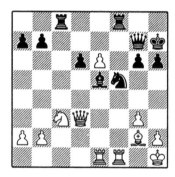

24 ♘d5! ♘e7

One has to reckon with the pawn on e6 (24...♗xb2? 25 e7 ♖fe8 26 ♖xf5! gxf5 27 ♕xf5+ ♔h8 28 ♕xc8 ♖xc8 29 e8=♕+ ♖xe8 30 ♖xe8+ and White wins—R.Dautov). If 24...♖ce8 then possible is 25 ♖c1 ♖xe6? 26 ♖c7.

25 ♘e3

He should not give up the b2-pawn since, after 25 b3, Black would have to reckon with the manoeuvre ♘e3-c4—since if he exchanges knights, the bishop takes firm hold of the d5 square.

25...♗xb2 26 ♖xf8 ♕xf8

V.Ivanchuk sets a subtle trap (26...♖xf8 27 ♕xd6 ±), and the World Champion unexpectedly falls into it.

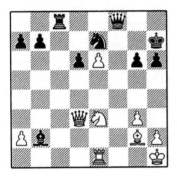

27 ♖f1?!

The simple 27 ♕xd6 would have maintained his advantage, since then 27...♖c1 28 ♖xc1 ♗xc1 29 ♘d5 ♗g5 30 h4 ♗f6 31 ♕c7 does not ease Black's position. Now, however, V.Ivanchuk manages to free himself from his opponent's dangerous clutches.

27...♖c1! 28 ♘d1 ♗f6 29 ♕xd6 ♔g7

The difference between this position and the one considered in the annotations to White's 27th move is that here Black retains an active rook.

30 ♗xb7 ♘f5 31 ♕xf8+ ♔xf8 32 g4 ♘d6 33 ♖xf6+

After 33 ♗d5 ♔e7 34 ♔g2 ♘b5 the knight begins to size up the e6 pawn (the threat is ...♘b5-c7).

33...♔g7 34 ♖f1 ♘xb7 35 ♖f7+ ♔g8 36 ♖xb7 ♖xd1+ 37 ♔g2 ♖e1

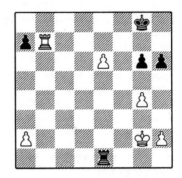

38 ♖xa7

Allowing Black to transpose to a theoretically drawn endgame, whereas after 38 e7! the famous aphorism that "all rook endgames are drawn" would have been confirmed yet again. Let's outline a few directives from an interesting analysis by Rustam Dautov:

(a) 38...♔f7? (this voluntary surrender of the pawn leads to a lost endgame) 39 ♖xa7 ♖e2+ 40 ♔g3 g5 41 a4 ♖b2 42 a5 ♖b3+ 43 ♔f2 ♖b2+ 44 ♔e3 ♖h2 45 a6 ♖a2 46 ♖a8! ♔e7 47 a7 and after 48 ♖h8 White wins.

(b) 38...a6 39 ♔f2 ♖e5 40 ♖b8+ ♔f7 41 e8=♕+ ♖xe8 42 ♖xe8 ♔xe8 43 ♔e3 ♔e7 44 ♔d4 ♔d6 45 a3 and White has a much better pawn endgame.

(c) 38...a5 39 ♔f2 ♖e5 40 ♖b8+ ♔f7 41 e8=♕+ ♖xe8 42 ♖xe8 ♔xe8 43 ♔e3 ♔e7! and in the pawn endgame Black retains drawing chances due to the important resource 44...♔f6 after 44 ♔d4 or 44 a4.

38...♖xe6 39 a4

If 39 h4 possible is 39...h5.

The rook endgame can be viewed as drawn, since, although the black king is cut off along the seventh rank, this is compensated by his counterpart being similarly cut off along the e-file.

39...Ee2+ 40 ♔g3 g5 41 h4

Upon the advance of the a-pawn the following drawing mechanism comes into play: 41 a5 Ee3+ 42 ♔f2 Ee5 43 a6 Ee6 44 Ea8+ ♔g7 45 a7 Ea6 and White faces a deadlock.

41...Ee3+ 42 ♔f2 Ee4 43 ♔f3 Ef4+ 44 ♔g3 h5!

Inventive V.Ivanchuk all over again—even if the neutral 44...♔h8 was also sufficient for a draw.

45 gxh5 Exh4 46 a5 Exh5 47 a6 Eh6

The essence of the position has not changed—only now the white king is cut off along the rank.

48 ♔g4 Ec6 49 ♔xg5 Eb6 50 ♔f5 Ec6 51 ♔e5 Eb6 52 ♔d5 Ef6 53 ♔c4 Ef4+ ½-½

Game 66
Gufeld *White* **Westerinen** *Black*
Jurmala 1978

1 ♘f3 ♘f6 2 c4 g6 3 g3 ♗g7 4 ♗g2 0-0 5 0-0 d6

With this order of moves Black can still confuse matters by 5...c5, so as to retain the possibility of transposing to the Yugoslav Variation, 6...♘c6 after 6 d4, or to remain in the sphere of the English Opening by 6...cxd4 7 ♘xd4 0-0. That's how the game Gufeld-Dvoiris, Sochi 1981, continued. There then followed 8 ♘c3 ♘g4 9 e3 d6 10 b3 ♗d7 11 ♗b2 Eb8? (it was necessary to exchange knights first by 11...♘xd4 12 exd4 Eb8) 12 ♘d5! and White obtained the advantage.

6 d4 ♘c6 7 ♘c3 e5 8 d5 ♘e7 9 e4 ♘d7 10 b4

White chooses a plan involving a queenside pawn assault.

10...a5

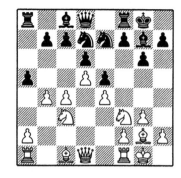

11 bxa5

After this capture White will still have to spend some time developing his bishop, while Black can advance ...f7-f5 in a more favourable situation.

Better is 11 ♗a3 axb4 12 ♗xb4, when the bishop quickly helps with the preparations to advance the c-pawn. Black can combat White's initiative only by energetic counterplay. An attempt to erect "barricades" on the queenside usually fails to stem White's initiative. For example, the game Gufeld-Dvoretsky, Vilnius (zt) 1975, continued: 12...b6 13 a4 ♘c5 14 a5 ♗a6 15 axb6 cxb6 16 ♕e2 ♕c7 17 Ea3 ♗b7 18 ♘b5 ♕d7 19 Efa1 ♗h6 20 h4 Exa3 21 Exa3 f5 22 ♘g5 ♗xg5 23 hxg5 fxe4 24 ♗xc5 bxc5 25 ♗xe4 and White's control of the a-file gave him the advantage.

Stronger is 12...♗h6, after which Black activates the bishop and takes the g5 square under his control. But here too White maintains the initiative. A possible continuation is 13 a4 f5 14 a5 ♔h8 15 ♘d2 ♘g8 16 exf5 (if 16 ♘b3 possible is 16...fxe4 17 ♘xe4 ♘df6 18 ♘c3 Ef7 19 c5 ♗f8) 16...gxf5 17 ♘a4 with the idea of playing c4-c5 and ♘d2-c4 (A.Kharitonov).

11...罝xa5 12 ᗡd2

White carries on preparing the advance c4-c5 by transferring his knight to b3. Introducing the bishop into the preparations by 12 a4 ᗺh8 13 ᗜa3 ᗜh6 14 ᗡd2 f5 15 ᗜb4 罝a6 allows Black to use his queen's rook more actively than in the plan outlined in the previous note. For example, the game Tukmakov-Loginov, USSR 1988, proceeded 16 a5 罝f7 17 ᗡb3 ᗡf6 18 exf5 gxf5 19 c5 ᗡg6 20 罝e1 f4 and Black developed active counterplay.

12...ᗡc5 13 ᗡb3 ᗡxb3 14 ᗞxb3 f5 15 ᗜd2 b6 16 a4

16 f3!?, freeing the knight from protecting the e4 square, also deserves attention. If Black tries to increase the pressure on e4 by transferring his knight to f6 then, after 16...ᗺh8 17 ᗡb5 罝a6 18 a4 ᗡg8 19 a5, White races ahead on the queenside.

16...fxe4! 17 ᗡxe4 罝a6

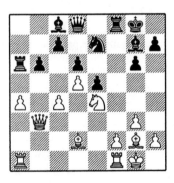

18 c5!

A positional pawn sacrifice, backed up by tactics. White's objective is to destroy his opponent's pawn structure. It becomes clear why nowadays Black frequently resorts to an early prophylactic retreat of the king to h8.

18...bxc5 19 ᗡxc5 dxc5 20 d6+ ᗺh8 21 dxe7 ᗞxe7 22 ᗞc4 罝e6 23 ᗞe4!

From the philosophical point of view, placing a queen in the role of a blockader is an unacceptable luxury: it will be vulnerable to attack from enemy pieces. But in this particular case White must prevent the advance of the e-pawn.

23...ᗜa6 24 罝fc1 罝d8 25 ᗜe3 ᗜd3 26 ᗜxc5! ᗞf7

Black had good reason to avoid an exchange of queens. After 26...ᗜxe4 27 ᗜxe7 罝xe7 28 ᗜxe4 arises an endgame with opposite-coloured bishops, in which the white bishop supports the passed a-pawn.

27 ᗞb7 e4 28 罝a3 ᗜa6 29 ᗞb4 ᗞf5 30 罝e3 ᗜd3 31 a5 罝de8 32 h4

In order to understand the following manoeuvres it is necessary to assess the various pawn "islands". It is not only the quantity of them that is important but the quality. Also significant is the potential weakness of the a1-h8 and a2-g8 diagonals leading to the black king.

32...ᗞd5 33 罝ee1 罝a6 34 ᗜe3 ᗞxa5

A practically forced exchange, since White threatened to deal with the c-pawn anyway. But without queens Black's rear becomes vulnerable.

35 ♕xa5 ♖xa5 36 ♖xc7 ♖a1?!

A doubtful exchange. It was better to try and exchange the more active rook by 36...♖ae5 and 37...♖ee7.

37 ♖xa1 ♗xa1 38 ♗h6!

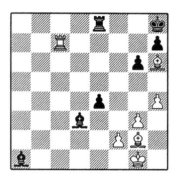

The black king becomes a prisoner in his own domain, since the rook cannot leave the 8th rank.

38...♔g8 39 ♗h3 ♗f6 40 ♗d7 ♖a8 41 ♗e6+ ♔h8 42 ♗d5 ♖d8 43 ♖f7 ♗d4 44 ♔g2 ♗b2 45 g4 ♗d4?

Black misses an opportunity to prevent the opening of the h-file: 45...♗e2! 46 g5 ♗f3+.

46 g5 ♗e5 47 ♖e7 ♗c3 48 ♔g3 ♗d4 49 ♔f4 ♖b8 50 ♗e6 ♖d8 51 h5

The beginning of the end.

51...♗c2

On 51...gxh5, 52 ♗f5 decides.

52 ♖c7 ♗d3 53 hxg6 hxg6 54 ♗f7 ♗b6 55 ♖c1?

White is in a hurry to mate his opponent. 55 ♖b7! was more methodical.

55...♖a8?

Only 55...♖b8! 56 ♖h1 ♗c7+ 57 ♔e3 ♖b1 could have saved Black from the mating attack.

56 ♖h1

With the irresistible threat of ♗h6-f8 mate!

56...♗c7+ 57 ♔e3 ♗b6+ 58 ♔d2 1-0

The Flank Attack 7...a6

(1 d4 ♘f6 2 c4 g6 3 g3 ♗g7 4 ♗g2 0-0 5 ♘f3 d6 6 0-0 ♘c6 7 ♘c3)

The purpose of the follow-up **7...a6**, known in theory as Panno System, is to prepare a pawn attack on the flank by ...b7-b5.

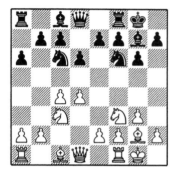

In reply, White employs two main methods of play: (1) he rejects the advance d4-d5, since he endeavours to retain a mobile pawn centre and (2) he closes the pawn centre by d4-d5.

The plans of play without closing the centre

If White chooses the plan without closing the centre, d4-d5, then, in order to occupy the centre by e2-e4 (or to develop by ♗c1-e3), he needs to deprive Black of the possibility of exerting influence on the d4 square with ...♗g4—by playing **8 h3**.

Now, in order to prepare ...b7-b5, the main continuation for Black is 8...♖b8. 8...♗d7, which also occurs in practice, serves the same purpose.

Game 67
G.Kuzmin *White* **Gufeld** *Black*
USSR 1980

1 d4 ♘f6 2 c4 g6 3 g3 ♗g7 4 ♗g2 0-0 5 ♘c3 d6 6 ♘f3 ♘c6 7 h3 a6 8 0-0

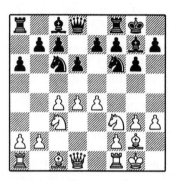

8...♖b8
An important link in Black's plan to prepare ...b7-b5.

With that end in view he also sometimes plays 8...♗d7 9 e4 (or 9 ♗g5 h6 10 ♗e3 ♖b8 11 ♘d5 b5 12 ♘xf6+ exf6 13 cxb5 ♖xb5! 14 ♕d2 g5 with a position offering chances for both sides, Lautier-Shirov, Manila (izt) 1990) 9...e5 10 ♗e3 b5 (or 10...♕c8 11 ♔h2 exd4 12 ♘xd4 ♘e5 13 ♕e2 ± K.Aseev) 11 dxe5 (on 11 d5 a pawn sacrifice is possible: 11...♘d4!? 12 ♘xd4 exd4 13 ♕xd4 ♕c8 14 h4 ♘g4) 11...♘e5 12 ♘xe5 dxe5 13 ♕c2 c6 14 ♖fd1 and White stands somewhat better.

Also possible is 8...e5 and after 9 d5 ♘e7 10 e4 we have a position similar to the main variation, but with the addition of the moves h2-h3 and ...a7-a6. The game Gufeld-Suetin, USSR 1973, proceeded 10...c5 11 dxc6?! bxc6 12 c5 d5 13 ♘xe5 ♘xe4 14 ♘xe4 ♗xe5 15 ♘xd6 ♘f5 16 ♘xc8 ♕xc8 17 ♖b1 a5 18 h4 ♕c7 19 ♕d3 ♖fe8 20 ♗g5 ♘d4 with equal chances. Of

course it is difficult for White to count on obtaining an advantage after giving up the centre. More logical is 11 a4 ♗d7 12 ♘e1 ♘e8 13 ♘d3 f5 14 f4 with a lasting initiative for White. Therefore instead of 10...c5 more reliable is the stereotyped 10...♘e8 or 10...♘d7 followed by ...f7-f5.

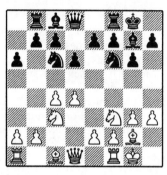

9 ♕c2
A favourite continuation of Gennady Kuzmin in the 80s.

Other players who were fond of exerting pressure on the queenside preferred to develop the rook on the c-file: 9 ♗e3 b5 10 ♘d2 (for the time being 10 cxb5 axb5 11 ♖c1 ♗d7 12 d5 ♘a5= is premature) 10...♗d7 (after 10...♗b7 White closes the centre and the bishop only impedes the development of Black's counterplay: 11 d5! ♘e5 12 b3 c5 13 ♖c1 ♕a5 14 a4 bxa4 15 ♘xa4 e6 16 ♘f3! ♘xf3+ 17 ♗xf3 exd5 18 b4! ± Vyzmanavin-A.Kuzmin, USSR 1987) 11 ♖c1 and the rook is rather effective in exerting pressure along the semi-open c-file: 11...e5 (or 11...♘a5 12 cxb5 axb5 13 b4 ♘c4 14 ♘xc4 bxc4 15 b5 d5 16 a4 ±) 12 dxe5 ♘xe5 13 cxb5 axb5 14 b3 ♖e8 15 ♘de4 and White's position is preferable. Mikhalchshin-Gleizerov, Pavlodar 1987. So perhaps there was some sense in postponing ...b7-b5 until a more appropriate moment and trying 9...e6 10 ♖c1 ♘e7 11 ♕d2 ♘f5, entering uncharted territory.

After the moves 9 ♗g5 h6 10 ♗e3 the thrust 10...b5 presents White with additional opportunities: 11 cxb5 axb5 12 ♕c1 ♔h7 13 d5 ♘a5 (or 13...b4 14 dxc6 bxc3 15 b3! ♘d5 16 ♗d4 ±) 14 b4 ♘c4 15 ♘d4 and White stands better. However, here too, 10...e6 is not bad and, if White impedes ...b7-b5 by 11 ♕c2 ♘e7 12 a4, then after 12...b6 13 ♖ad1 ♗b7 Black can switch to preparing ...d6-d5.

The preliminary 10...♗d7 deserves attention. For example, the game Lautier-Shirov, Manila (izt) 1990, continued 11 ♘d5 b5 12 ♘xf6+ exf6 13 cxb5 ♖xb5! 14 ♕d2 g5 15 d5?! (15 ♖fc1 is more cautious) 15...♘e7 16 ♘d4 ♖xd5! 17 ♗xd5 ♘xd5 and Black gained strong counterplay for the exchange.

The other main continuation, 9 e4, is considered in the following games.

9...♘a5!

This was a new idea for those days, and I often employed it in subsequent games. Black voluntarily moves his knight to the flank in order to attack a concrete object—the pawn on c4.

The pawn assault 9...b5 10 cxb5 axb5 is also possible, and the pawn sacrifice 11 ♘xb5 here is backed up by tactics: 11...♘b4 12 ♕c4 ♘xa2 13 ♘xc7 ♘xc1 14 ♖fxc1 ♖xb2 15 ♖a8 ♗h6 16 e3 ♕d7 and Black defends, G.Kuzmin-Zeshkovsky, USSR 1980. Less promising is to play in the centre: 9...♗d7 10 e4 e5 11 dxe5 ♘xe5 12 ♘xe5 dxe5 13 ♗e3 ♗e6 14 b3 c6 15 ♖ac1 and White's chances are to be preferred, G.Kuzmin-Tukmakov, USSR 1980.

10 ♘d5 b5 11 ♘xf6+ ♗xf6 12 cxb5 axb5 13 ♗h6 ♖e8 14 ♖ac1 c6

Black's pawn structure is quite stable and dynamic. If he manages to deploy his pieces in the formation: ...♕d7, ...♗d7, ...♖fe8, then an advance ...c6-c5 would become rather effective. Therefore White starts to counter this plan.

15 ♘d2!

White takes the c4 square under his control and threatens 16 b4—which also follows after 15...♗xd4.

15...b4 16 e3 ♗a6

More clever is 16...♕b6.

17 ♖fd1

17 ♖fe1 is more accurate.

17...♕b6

It just remains to complete the last link in the chain of the outlined plan—18...♖ec8 and everything will be ready for the advance ...c6-c5. But White is not asleep.

18 h4 ♗e2!

Countering White's initiative. On 18...♖ec8 White had prepared 19 ♗h3! ♖c7 20 h5 so Black manoeuvres his bishop to the kingside.

19 ♖e1 ♗g4

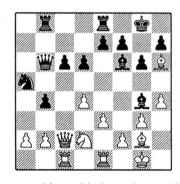

A position with dynamic equality has been reached. White's pressure on the c6-pawn is compensated by the opponent's possibility of counterplay based on ...e7-e5 or ...c6-c5, enlivening his king's bishop. Now 20 ♗c6 ♖bc8 21 d5, with its weakening of the light-squares around the king, would be suicidal.

20 ♕a4

Using the edge of the board to get closer to the c6 pawn. After 20 ♘c4 ♘xc4 21 ♕xc4 ♗d7 Black not only gets rid of his poorly placed knight, but is ready for a counterattack on the centre as well. For example: 22 h5 d5! 23 ♕c2 e5.

20...♖ec8

With the idea of 21...♗e6 and 22...c5.

21 a3! ♗e6 22 axb4

Of course, White did not start the flank attack to sideline his own queen—which would be the case after 22 ♖a1? b3!.

22...♕xb4 23 ♕xb4 ♖xb4 24 ♖a1 ♘b3

24...♖xb2?! is weaker in view of 25 ♘e4.

25 ♘xb3 ♖xb3

25...♗xb3? loses a pawn to 26 ♗xc6.

26 ♖a7 ♖xb2?

Black hurries to reap an endgame harvest. But more effective was 26...c5, bringing the dark-squared bishop into play after 27 dxc5 dxc5 or 27 d5 ♗f5 28 e4 ♗g4.

27 ♖c1 d5

Perhaps Black could seek further activity by the longed-for 27...c5? Alas, no. After 28 d5 ♗f5 29 e4 ♗g4 30 f3 c4 31 ♔h1 ♗d4 32 ♖xe7 he would be a pawn down. But after the text move a position is reached with approximately equal chances.

Therefore... ½-½.

There was a time when the phrase "Efim Geller plays" was a synonym of chess of the highest level. For over forty years he was a leading figure on the world chess stage.

When speaking about Geller's heritage, one should consider his creative contribution to chess, in which the brightest page is his intepretation of the King's Indian Defence. It should be mentioned that Mikhail Botvinnik, who was not lavish with his praise, once said: "Before Geller we did not really understand the essence of the King's Indian Defence". And his successor on the chess throne, Tigran Petrosian, had a high estimation of the power of Geller's King's Indian, which frequently kept even "Iron Tigran" in check. And it is well known how uncompromising Tigran was when playing with White, especially against adherents of the King's Indian. I too have experience of that.

True, when playing this game, Geller, in his mid-50s, had quit playing the King's Indian with Black, preferring only to play against it with White. In the old days he had some problems playing with the knight on d7, but, as a staunchly classical player, he did not dare to move the knight to c6 (in front of the pawn).

Game 68
Geller *White* **Gufeld** *Black*
USSR 1981

1 ♘f3 ♘f6 2 c4 g6 3 ♘c3 ♗g7 4 g3 0-0 5 ♗g2 d6 6 d4 ♘c6 7 0-0 a6 8 h3 ♖b8 9 e4

The idea of this move lies not only in the occupation of the centre, but also in the immediate advance e4-e5.

9...b5

Playing to get ahead in the race. Black has to react energetically, in order not to land in a cramped position.

Of course he could have prevented an advance of the e-pawn by the radical 9...e5, but after 10 ♗e3 exd4 11 ♘xd4 ♗d7 12 ♘xc6 ♗xc6 13 ♕c2, followed by ♖a1-d1, White stands better.

9...♘d7 serves the same purpose, but here too White organizes piece pressure: 10 ♗e3 ♘a5 (if 10...b5 then good is 11 cxb5 axb5 12 ♕c1! e5 13 ♖d1 ±) 11 b3 b5 12 cxb5 axb5 13 ♖c1 (on 13 ♕d2 possible is 13...c5!?) 13...b4 14 ♘d5 e6 15 ♘f4 ± Hübner-J.Polgar, Dortmund 1997.

10 e5

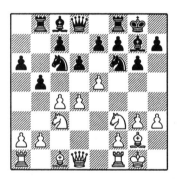

10...♘d7

The *Encyclopedia* considers it possible for Black to transpose into an endgame: 10...dxe5 11 dxe5 ♕xd1 12 ♖xd1 ♘d7 13 e6 fxe6 14 cxb5 axb5

(a) 15 ♗e3 b4 16 ♘a4 ♘ce5 17 ♘d4 ♘b6 18 ♘xb6 ♖xb6 19 ♖ac1 ♖d6 with active counterplay for Black, Nikolić-Zapata, Tunis (izt) 1985;

(b) 15 ♗f4 ♘de5 (also possible is 15...b4 16 ♘a4 ♘b6=) 16 ♘e1 (16 ♘xe5 ♘xe5 17 ♖ac1 c5=) 16...♘b4 17 a3 ♘a6 18 ♖ac1 ♘c4 with equal chances, Vaganian-Sax, Lucerne 1985.

11 e6

As mentioned above, my opponent is a King's Indian specialist who is no less devoted to the opening than I am. So in this case he is playing not only against me but against himself. The last move is a new idea of his. It should be noted that after 11 cxb5 axb5 12 exd6 cxd6, White already has to fight for equality. This occurred in a game in Moscow 1969, where I had Black against yet another brilliant specialist in the King's Indian Defence, Leonid Stein. There followed 13 ♗g5 h6 14 ♗e3 b4 15 ♘d5 ♗b7 16 ♖c1 e6 17 ♘f4 ♘e7, and Black had an excellent game.

11 ♘g5 has often been played, with the threats of 12 ♗xc6 and 12 e6. In reply, Black has two reasonable possibilities: 11...♘xd4 12 ♕xd4 ♘xe5 13 ♕h4 h6 14 ♘ge4 e6! 13 ♕xd8 ♖fxd8 with an unclear position (pointed out by Geller), or 11...dxe5 12 ♗xc6 exd4.

11...fxe6 12 d5 exd5!?

Less successful is 12...♘a5 13 cxb5 exd5 14 ♘d4 ♘f6 15 ♘xd5 axb5 16 ♗d2! with advantage to White, Geller-Chiburdanidze, Moscow 1981.

13 cxd5

Not falling for 13 ♕xd5+? e6 14 ♕xc6? ♗b7, and the queen is trapped.

13...♘a5 14 ♘d4 ♘e5

The position of the knight does not look too secure. However, Black's strategy is aided by a tactical device, 15 f4 c5!.

15 b4

A crucial move, which creates tactical prerequisites for Black along the a1-h8 diagonal. L.Portisch, whose attitude towards the laws of positional play is rather zealous, prefers 15 ♘ce2 ♗d7 16

♘f4 followed by a knight invasion on e6.

15...♘ac4 16 f4

An obvious move, which does not take into account Black's tactical resources. More "tiresome" play would have followed after 16 ♘ce2 ♗d7 17 ♘f4 or 16 ♖b1.

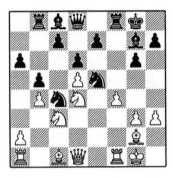

16...c5!

It turns out that the knight doesn't have to retreat and Black can get rid of the backward pawn. However, even after a knight retreat Black has sufficient resources: 16...♘f7 17 ♘c6 ♕e8 18 ♘xb8 ♗f5! 19 ♖f3 ♕b8 and the activity displayed by Black's pieces fully compensates for the exchange, Hübner-Nunn, Johannesburg 1981.

17 dxc6 ♘xc6 18 ♘xc6

18 ♗xc6 would similarly have been answered by 18...♕b6, without check, but with a dangerous pin.

18...♕b6+ 19 ♔h2 ♗xc3 20 ♘xe7+ ♔h8 21 ♘xc8

21 ♘d5 ♕d4 22 ♘xc3 ♕xc3 23 ♖b1 ♗b7 leads to approximate equality.

21...♖bxc8 22 ♖b1 ♖ce8

It is this rook that must occupy the e-file, since on 22...♖fe8 White has 23 f5!. Generally speaking, the position may be evaluated as roughly level.

23 ♖b3 ♗g7 24 ♖d3 a5!

24...♖e7 is well answered by 25 ♖e1!.

25 bxa5 ♕xa5 26 a3 ♖e7 27 ♖d5

Black increases the tension. 27...♘e3 would have led to equality.

27...♖fe8

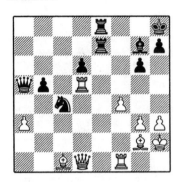

28 f5 ♖e1?!

A typical time-trouble decision. When short of time it is difficult to refrain from such an apparently spectacular invasion of the back rank, especially when it involves a trap.

The straightforward 28...gxf5 is simpler and stronger.

29 ♕d3!

The only move, but quite adequate. Naturally my very experienced opponent did not fall into the trap 29 ♖xe1? ♖xe1 30 ♕c2 ♕b6, and the mating threat is decisive.

29...♘e5

On 29...♖xf1 there would follow 30 ♕xf1! with the double threats of 31 ♕xc4 and 31 f6.

30 ♖xe1!

Now that Black's rooks are split, White can exchange one of them off because of the pin on the knight. Another possibility is 30 ♕xb5 ♕xb5 31 ♖xb5 ♖xf1 32 ♗xf1 ♘f3+ 33 ♔g2 ♘d4, and White's position is preferable.

30...♕xe1 31 ♕xb5 ♖c8

On 31...♖f8, White would happily propose going into an ending with 32 ♕f1!.

32 ♗f4 gxf5 33 ♖xd6

33...♘g6!

Offering yet another pawn, though in return for a maximum activation of his forces after 34 ♕xf5 ♖f8, with sharp play.

34 ♕d5 ♕e7!

Black now makes the only correct queen move: 34...♘xf4?? is of course unplayable owing to 35 ♖d8+. After the text move, the draw is obvious.

35 ♗d2 ♗e5 36 ♖d7 ♕xa3 37 ♖d8+ ♖xd8 38 ♕xd8+ ♕f8 ½-½

Game 69
Arkell *White* **Gufeld** *Black*
Hastings 1994/95

1 d4 ♘f6 2 ♘f3 g6 3 c4 ♗g7 4 g3 0-0 5 ♗g2 d6 6 0-0 ♘c6 7 ♘c3 a6 8 h3 ♖b8 9 e4 b5 10 cxb5

After this premature ceding of the c4 square, White can scarcely count on obtaining an advantage. An immediate 10 e5 is more logical.

10...axb5 11 e5

As in the previous game, White starts forcing play.

However, after the placid 11 ♗e3 b4 12 ♘d5 ♘e4 Black has everything in proper order.

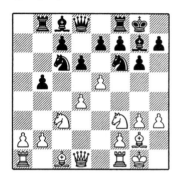

11...♘d7!

This move seemed to be something of a surprise for my opponent, since it is not among those that are considered by chess theory books. Most of these recommend 11...dxe5 12 dxe5 ♕xd1 13 ♖xd1 ♘d7 14 e6, but I didn't want to play with so many pawn islands. Most opening variations are a matter of taste, and I am very confident that if you were to show me somebody's opening repertoire, I'll tell you that person's character.

As regards whether modern opening books keep you informed, I should mention that the move 11...♘d7 had been played by me in the game Stein-Gufeld, Moscow 1969, which went 12 exd6 cxd6 13 ♗g5 h6 14 ♗e3 b4 15 ♘d5 ♗b7 16 ♖c1 e6 17 ♘f4 ♘e7 18 ♗d2 ♘f5 19 ♘e2 ♕b6 20 ♖c4 ♕a6 ½-½.

12 ♘g5

Better than 12 e6 fxe6 13 ♘g5 ♘xd4 14 ♗e3 h6. Now I spent the next thirty minutes remembering what I had prepared thirty years ago, while the spectators were wondering if I had made a mistake in my beloved King's Indian.

12...♗b7!

The idea of sacrificing a piece is in the air, but it is not yet sufficiently well thought out. For instance, after 12...♘xd4 13 ♕xd4 ♘xe5 14 ♕d1, Black does not have enough compensation. And another kind of sacrifice, carried out in the game Nikolić-Nunn, Wijk aan Zee 1982, 12...dxe5 13 ♗xc6 exd4 14 ♘xb5 ♖b6 15 ♘a7 h6 16 ♘f3 ♗a6 17 ♖e1 ♘b8 18 ♗e4 ♕d7 19 b3, did not bring Black complete satisfaction either. Therefore, if one is going to sacrifice, it is better is to do it for the sake of accelerating the development of one's pieces.

13 e6 ♘xd4

A positional sacrifice. Compensation: a very strong centre.

14 ♗xb7

Perhaps it was better to keep the bishops on.

14...♖xb7 15 exd7

If 15 exf7+ ♔h8 16 ♗e3 e5 17 ♗xd4 ♕xg5 and if 15 ♘xf7 ♕e8 with good compensation.

15...♕xd7 16 a4

The position is complicated and it is not possible to calculate all variations. So I relied on intuition to make brillant moves. Here intuition and experience says that Black has enough compensation.

16...bxa4 17 ♖xa4 c5 18 ♘f3

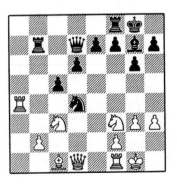

18...e5!

The knight on d4 is like a bomber, escorted by two fighter planes on c5 and e5. 18...♕xh3?! 19 ♘xd4 cxd4 20 ♖xd4! ♗xd4 21 ♕xd4 would leave White with a comfortable advantage, because in the middlegame two pieces are stronger than two pawns.

19 h4 h6

19...♕c6 (K.Arkell) 20 ♘xd4 cxd4 21 ♘e2 d3 22 ♘c3 e4 and the centre pawns are driving forward like a locomotive picking up steam.

20 ♘xd4 cxd4 21 ♘e2

The alternative 21 ♘d5 ♕b5 22 ♘b4 ♖c8 is hardly better for White.

21...f5 22 b4 f4!

Psychologically, it may have been better for me to retain more of my initiative by 22...d3 23 ♘c3 e4. Now, however, Black has possible problems with his weak 6th rank.

23 ♘xf4!

The merit of an extra piece lies not only in its physical value, but in the possibility of returning it for certain dividends. Anyway, 23 gxf4 d3 24 ♘g3 exf4 25 ♘e4 f3 is clearly in Black's favour.

23...exf4 24 ♗xf4 d5! 25 ♕b3 ♖c8?!

25...♕b5! maintains a positional advantage, for example, if 26 ♖c1

♖c8 or 26 ♖e1 ♕c4. Also interesting is 25...d3 with the idea of 26...♖xf4!.

26 ♖a6 ♔h7 27 ♖d6 ♕f7

After 27...♕b5? 28 ♖xd5 ♕xb4 29 ♕xb4 ♖xb4 30 ♖d7, I might even lose the game.

28 ♕xd5 ♕xd5 29 ♖xd5 ♖c4!

Erroneous is 29...♖xb4? 30 ♖d7 ♖b5 31 ♖e1! and Black already has to deal with two rooks.

30 ♗d2

Weaker is 30 ♗d6?! ♖d7 31 ♖c5 ♖xb4.

30...♖c2 31 ♖d1 ♖e7 32 ♗e1 ♖b2 33 ♔f1 ♔g8 34 ♖d6 ♔f7 35 ♗d2 ♗e5 36 ♖c6 ♖e6 37 ♖c5

White achieves nothing by an exchange of rooks: 37 ♖xe6 ♔xe6 38 ♗xh6 ♖xb4.

37...♗g7 38 ♔g2 h5 39 b5 ♗e5

More accurate is 39...♗f6, with the idea of ...♖e6-b6. Yet it still won't be too late to play it on the next move. But, alas, Black is running out of time.

40 ♖d5

At this moment the flag on the Black's clock dropped.

1-0

After 40...♗f6 a draw would have been a fair result.

The plans of play with the closing of the centre

It is no accident that the position after 1 d4 ♘f6 2 c4 g6 3 g3 ♗g7 4 ♗g2 0-0 5 ♘f3 d6 6 ♘c3 ♘c6 has been called the 'modern' line. It is modern in both a direct and an indirect sense, since it reflects the contemporary tendencies in opening play. The idea of this line is revealed after the natural 7 d5 ♘a5 8 ♘d2 (practically forced) 8...c5 9 0-0

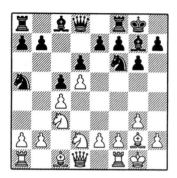

Here the main lines of play are associated with 9...a6, 9...e6 and 9...e5.

Game 70
Gufeld *White* **Rashkovsky** *Black*
Kirovobad 1973

1 ♘f3 ♘f6 2 g3 g6 3 ♗g2 ♗g7 4 0-0 0-0 5 c4 d6 6 ♘c3 ♘c6 7 d4

The irony of fate: the King's Indian is my favourite opening with Black, and now I find myself playing against it with White. And as for the bishop on g7—I felt some inner voice saying to me, "This bishop will be your enemy..." But fortunately my adherence to the move 1 e2-e4 has, for the most part, helped me to avoid the need to fight against my beloved piece. Things like this happen sometimes, as when, for tactical reasons, I choose to begin a game with the Réti Opening.

Nevertheless, an invitation to play against yourself is a well known psychological trick and Naum Rashkovsky no doubt enjoyed confronting me with my favourite opening.

In one of his more recent interviews David Bronstein said: "I have lost a lot of my King's Indian games when playing White, because I did not want to reveal how to win against my defence". However I am inclined to consider David's rejoinder as a joke. Nobody likes to lose a game—especially when playing White.

7...a6 8 d5

It is not my habit to avoid principled continuations in the opening.

8...♘a5 9 ♘d2 c5

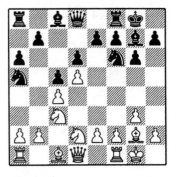

This position can also arise by transposition of moves via the Yugoslav Variation.

10 ♕c2

It is necessary to defend the knight on c3 before developing the dark-squared bishop. Moreover, on the c2 square, the queen prepares the bishop development on b2 from where it can counteract the ambitions of the g7-bishop along the long diagonal. Later on, as the variation developed, White began to play 10 ♖b1 (preparing for Black's counterplay ....b7-b5 with a possible opening of the b-file), when, after 10...♖b8 11 b3 b5 12 ♗b2, there arise some particular nuances. For example, after the reply 12...♗d7, 13 ♕c2 can again be played, after which 13...e6?! is no good. (see the annotation to the 13th move).

10...♖b8 11 b3 b5 12 ♗b2 e6

Lately 12...♗h6 has been more often played, provoking 13 f4 when after 13...bxc4 14 bxc4 e5 the rook

b8 and dark-squared bishop, in tandem, become very active—and the idea of an exchange sacrifice on b2, very real. This theme is examined below in the game Yusupov-Kindermann.

13 ♖ab1

For the time being, nothing concrete is obtained from releasing the pawn tension by 13 dxe6 fxe6 14 axb5 axb5. Therefore it is useful to transfer the rook to a more promising position where it defends the bishop in case of an opening of the b-file.

13 e4 bxc4 14 bxc4 deserves attention, since after 14...♘d7 15 ♖ab1 ♗d4 16 ♘e2 White exchanges off the dark-squared bishops.

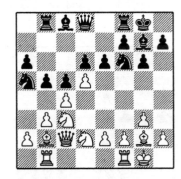

13...exd5

The main drawback of Black's position is the offside position of the a5-knight, which can be exploited as a tactical motif. For example, after the natural development 13...♗d7?, the pawn on d6 is left unprotected for a moment, which allows an exchanging combination, typical for such formations: 14 dxe6 fxe6 15 cxb5 axb5 16 ♘ce4 ♘xe4 17 ♗xg7 ♔xg7 18 ♘xe4 ♗c6 19 ♕c3+ ♔g8 20 ♘xd6 and White wins a pawn.

After the exchange on d5, a couple of minor pieces from each side will be exchanged off, when White's space advantage limits his opponent's counterplay.

Matters are not changed after 13...bxc4 14 bxc4 exd5 15 ♘xd5! ♘xd5 16 ♗xd5 ♗b7 17 ♗xg7 ♔xg7 18 ♕c3+ when Black is playing practically without his a5-knight. Instead of capturing on d5, 14...♘d7!? is worth considering, although in fact, here too, after 15 e4 White's chances are to be preferred.

In the game Spassky-Ivkov, Santa Monica 1966, Black preferred to retain the pawn tension: 13...♖e8 14 e4 ♗d7 15 ♖fe1 ♗h6, but after 16 dxe6 ♗xe6 17 ♘d5 White's position still turned out to be better.

14 ♘xd5 ♘xd5 15 cxd5 ♖b7 16 ♗xg7 ♔xg7 17 e4 ♖e8 18 f4 ♖be7 19 ♖be1

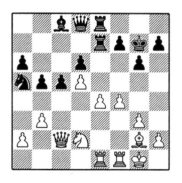

White has a space advantage and chances to realize it.

19...♕b6 would be followed by 20 h4 c4+ 21 ♔h2.

19...f6 20 h3 ♘b7 21 ♘f3 ♕c7 22 g4

The signal for an attack on the king.

22...♘d8 23 g5 fxg5 24 ♘xg5 h6

After 24...♘f7 White breaks through the centre by 25 ♕c3+ ♔g8

26 ♘xf7 ♖xf7 27 e5 and obtains a clear-cut advantage.

25 ♘f3 ♘f7 26 ♕c3+ ♔h7 27 ♕f6!

The queen is activated at once. The e4-pawn is untouchable (27...♖xe4? 28 ♖xe4 ♖xe4 29 ♘h4) and at the same time e4-e5 is threatened. Black has to take active measures.

27...c4 28 bxc4 bxc4 29 ♕d4!

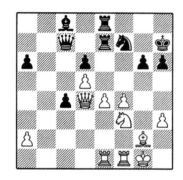

The c-pawn is cut off from its base and it is time to follow the advice of the great José Raúl Capablanca who attached great importance to centralizing the queen.

On the other hand, 29 e5? fails to 29...dxe5 30 fxe5 ♘xe5 31 ♖xe5 ♖xe5 32 d6 ♕c5+ 33 ♔h2 ♖f5 and White faces a deadlock.

29...c3 30 ♖e3 c2 31 ♖c3 ♕b8 32 ♘e1!

From here the knight not only attacks the pawn, but also can be manoeuvred to a better position.

32...♕b2 33 ♘xc2

More accurate is 33 ♘d3! ♕xa2 34 ♖c1, capturing the pawn with the rook and, together with the knight, supporting an advance of the e-pawn.

33...♕xa2 34 ♘b4

34 ♕f6!? ♕b2 35 ♖f3, tieing the rook on e7 to the protection of the knight, deserves attention.

34...♕b2 35 ♘c6?

This move is far too optimistic! White misses Black's tactical resource. 35 ♘d3 was necessary.

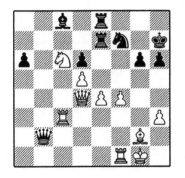

35...♖xe4! 36 ♗xe4 ♖xe4 37 ♕xe4

37 ♕f6 does not work due to 37...♘h8!.

37...♕xc3 38 ♕f3 ♕f6 39 ♔h2 h5 40 ♕e3 ♗d7

White's broken pawn structure offers Black some compensation for the exchange.

Here 40...h4!? certainly deserved attention.

41 ♘d4! ♘h6 42 ♖a1!

The reason for the retreat of the knight was to allow White to bring the rook to this square. White is not after the e6 square but a rook invasion—which will decide the game.

42...♘f5 43 ♘xf5

This exchange is made possible by the fact that 43...♕xa1? loses to 44 ♕e7+.

43...♕xf5 44 ♖xa6 ♕xd5 45 ♖a7 ♕f7 46 h4!

Since Black is practically in *zugzwang* it is useful to improve the position of the h-pawn.

46...♕g7 47 ♖b7 ♔h8 48 ♔g3

Not 48 ♕a7? ♕e7! when Black's pieces spring to life.

48...♕f7

Black should not have ceded the long diagonal: 48...♔g8 would have been better.

49 ♕d4+ ♔g8 50 ♕xd6 ♕e6 51 ♕xe6+ ♗xe6 52 ♔f2

After exchanging off the queens the game passes on to the technical stage where the king hastens to set up a joint operation with the rook.

52...♗f7 53 ♔e3 ♔g7 54 ♖b6 ♗d5 55 ♔d4 ♗a2 56 ♔e5 ♗c4 57 ♖b7+ ♔h6 58 ♔f6

The king heads for g5.

58...♗d5 59 ♖b8 ♔h7 60 ♔g5 1-0

Game 71
Yusupov *White* **Kindermann** *Black*
Baden-Baden 1992

1 d4 ♘f6 2 c4 g6 3 ♘f3 ♗g7 4 g3 0-0 5 ♗g2 d6 6 0-0 ♘c6 7 ♘c3 a6 8 d5 ♘a5 9 ♘d2 c5 10 ♕c2

Against Kindermann, in the German Bundesliga 1998, Yusupov chose 10 ♖b1. This "mysterious rook move" (in the terminology of A.Nimzowitsch) is made in anticipation of the opening of the b-file after 10...♖b8 11 b3 b5 12 ♗b2.

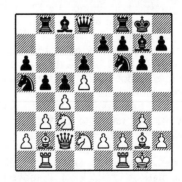

This position is worthy of more detailed consideration.

Black has a few logical continuations, but in each of them he comes across certain difficulties.

The aforementioned game continued 12...e5 13 dxe6! (this is stronger than 13 ♕c2 ♗f5 14 ♘ce4 ♘xe4 15 ♗xe4 ♗d7 16 ♗c3 b4 17 ♗b2 f5 18 ♗g2 ♘b7 19 f4 e4 with equal chances, V.Akopian-Shirov, Groningen (m/1) 1997) 13...fxe6 14 ♘de4! bxc4 15 ♘xd6 cxb3 16 axb3 ♖xb3 17 ♘a4 ♕c7? (necessary was 17...c4!) 18 ♖c1 with advantage to White.

The plan of attacking the c4 pawn has also been played: 12...bxc4 13 bxc4 ♗h6 (after the stereotyped 13...e6 14 ♗a1! White exercises control over the b-file, since 14...♖b4 15 a3 ♖xb1 16 ♕xb1 exd5 17 ♘xd5 ♗f5 18 ♕b2 ♘h5 19 ♕c1 ♘f6 20 ♗c3! does not help, and Black faces problems with the knight on a5, Vaganian-Van der Wiel, Biel (izt) 1985) 14 ♗a1 ♗f5! 15 e4 ♗g4 16 f3 ♗e3+ 17 ♔h1 ♗d7 18 h3! (parrying ...♘f6-g4, after f3-f4) 18...♗xd2 19 ♕xd2 ♘xc4 20 ♕e2 ♘a3 21 ♖bd1!? and, owing to the weakness of the a1-h8 diagonal, White has sufficient compensation for the sacrificed pawn, Matlak-Kulczewski, corr 1990. In this respect, an immediate 12...♗h6 is also possible when 13 ♗a1 loses a pawn after 13... ♗xd2 14 ♕xd2 bxc4 15 bxc4 (15 ♘e4 ∓) 15...♘xc4 16 ♕f4 ♖xb1 17 ♖xb1—though White undoubtedly has sufficient compensation for it.

One final point. On 12...♗d7 White can return to 13 ♕c2, after which 13...e6?! is no good in view of 14 dxe6 fxe6 15 cxb5 axb5 16 ♘ce4 ±, which is examined in the annotations to Black's 13th move in the game Gufeld-Rashkovsky, Kirovobad 1973.

10...♖b8 11 b3 b5 12 ♗b2 ♗h6 13 f4

Black threatened to win the c4 pawn by an exchange on d2. After the exchange 13 cxb5 axb5 14 e4 ♗a6 the activity of the black bishops would increase. But now follows a standard break in the centre.

13...bxc4 14 bxc4 e5 15 dxe6

It is impossible to keep the rooks under lock and key: 15 ♖ae1 exf4 16 gxf4 ♘h5 17 e3 The game Osnos-Suetin, Tbilisi 1967, proceeded 17...♗g7! 18 ♘d1 ♗f5 19 ♗e4 ♗xb2 20 ♘xb2 and here, as noted by G.Kasparov, Black could have retained equality by sacrificing the exchange.

In the event of 15 ♖ab1 the same manoeuvre is possible 15...exf4 16 gxf4 ♘h5!? 17 e3 ♗f5 or 16...♖e8 exerting pressure along the e-file.

15...♗xe6 16 ♘d5

Hoping, after 16...♗g7 17 ♗c3!, to get down to business on the b-file.

16...♖xb2!

There was time when this sacrifice of the exchange brought confusion to supporters of this variation, but nowadays it is considered almost standard.

Other attempts are 16...♗xd5 17 cxd5 ♘g4 18 ♘b3 f5! 19 h3 ♘f6 20 ♘d2 and here, in the game Stohl-Kindermann, Dortmund 1991, instead of 20...♘h5? 21 ♔h2, which proved to be in White's favour, as shown by S.Kindermann, 20...♖e8 21 ♗f3 ♗g7 22 ♗c3 ♖e3! would maintain equality.

17 ♕xb2 ♗g7 18 ♕c1

On 18 ♕c2 possible is 18...♘xd5 19 cxd5 ♗xa1 20 ♖xa1 ♕f6 with approximately level chances, but after the text manoeuvre White would recapture 20 ♕xa1, making it impossible for Black to move his queen to f6 when, after e2-e4, White gains an advantage.

If the queen instead moves to the side, 18 ♕a3, Black can win a pawn: 18...♘xc4 19 ♘xc4 ♘xd5 20 ♖ac1 ♘b4 21 ♔h1 d5 22 ♘e5 (or 22 ♘b2 ♕d6= Hübner-Nunn, Wijk aan Zee 1982) 22...♗xe5 (22...♕d6 is not bad either) 23 fxe5 ♕b6 24 ♕b2 ♕a7! with sufficient compensation for the sacrificed exchange. Cosma-Nevednichy, Bucharest 1994.

18...♗xd5 19 cxd5

After 19 ♗xd5 ♘xd5 20 cxd5 the g7 bishop becomes active. In the game Stohl-Babula, Czech Republic 1996, after 20...♗d4+ 21 ♔h1 ♕a8 22 e4, according to I.Stohl, Black could play 22...♗xa1! 23 ♕xa1 f5 24 ♕c3 fxe4 25 ♕xa5 ♕xd5 and the mobile centre pawns fully compensate for the sacrificed knight.

But it seems Black need not be in any hurry to win back the exchange: 20...♕e7! 21 ♖b1 ♕xe2, retaining more active pieces, was played in Stohl-Kindermann, Germany 1997.

19...♘g4 20 ♖b1 ♗d4+ 21 ♔h1 ♘e3

After 21...♘f2+ 22 ♖xf2 ♗xf2 23 ♘f3! c4 24 e4 White threatens to break through in the centre, Marin-Istratescu, Bucuresti 1995.

22 ♕a3

22 ♖e1 would be met by the same reply as in the game.

22...♖e8

After winning back the exchange by 22...♘xf1 23 ♗xf1 ♖e8 24 e4 the position is simplified—but Black is again handicapped by the out-of-play knight on a5.

23 ♕d3 ♕a8!

A rare case when a queen displays great activity from the corner of the board. If 24 ♖f3?! then follows 24...♘xg2 25 ♔xg2 ♕xd5.

24 ♗f3 ♘xf1 25 ♘xf1

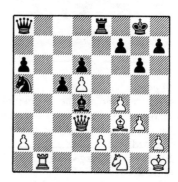

25...♕a7

The presence of opposite-coloured bishops is a drawing factor only in the endgame. With major pieces still on the board a bishop, having no rival, can be a dynamic attacking force. Black should have exchanged off his opponent's only active piece, as in Alonso-de la Paz, Cuba 1994, 25...♖b8! 26 ♖xb8+ ♕xb8 and now it turns out that after 27 ♕xa6 ♕b1 28 ♔g2 c4! the passed pawn is very dangerous, as confirmed by the game continuation 27 e3 ♗f6! 28 ♕xa6 ♕b1 29 ♔g1 c4!.

26 ♘d2 ♖e3 27 ♕c2 f5?

Black leaves the knight on a5 without attention for a moment and the initiative finally passes over to White. It was necessary to parry the threat ♕c2-a4 by 27...♖a3 or 27...♕d7 and, though White stands more actively, the outcome of the struggle is not yet clear.

28 ♕a4 ♕c7

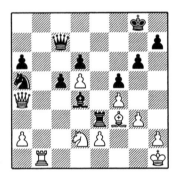

29 g4!

After this break the vulnerable position of the black king becomes clear. The opening of the g-file is threatened.

29...fxg4 30 ♗xg4 ♔g7 31 ♘f3 ♗f6 32 ♗e6

32 ♘g5 ♗xg5 33 fxg5 ♕e7 facilitates Black's defence.

32...c4 33 f5! ♖xe2

The advance of the c-pawn is less dangerous than the exposed position of his king, as demonstrated by an analysis of Arthur Yusupov: 33...c3 34 fxg6 c2 (or 34...hxg6 35 ♖g1 c2 36 ♕e8 with a mating attack) 35

♖c1 ♖xe2 36 gxh7 and the king is laid bare.

34 ♖g1 ♖f2?

Black overlooks the crisis on the g6 square. But 34...♕d8! 35 fxg6 h6 would merely drag out the resistance.

35 ♕e8! 1-0

Game 72
Blátny *White* **Gufeld** *Black*
Los Angeles 1997

1 ♘f3 g6 2 c4 ♗g7 3 ♘c3 d6 4 d4 ♘f6 5 g3 0-0 6 ♗g2 ♘c6 7 d5 ♘a5 8 ♘d2 c5 9 ♕c2

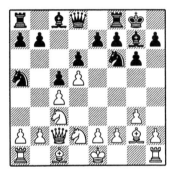

After 9 0-0 is reached by transposition of moves a position from the Yugoslav Variation (6...c5 7 ♘c3 ♘c6 8 d5 ♘a5 9 ♘d2 c5), which is examined below. P.Blátny hopes to exploit the tempo saved by not castling, to develop an initiative on the queenside. However, with the position bearing a closed character, it does not matter too much.

9...e5 10 a3 b6 11 b4 ♘b7 12 ♘b3

Until now Blátny has travelled along the beaten track, but here, instead of 12 ♖b1 or 12 ♗b2, he prefers to increase the pressure on the c5 square (in some cases it is possible to exchange on this square with a subsequent seizure of the b-file).

The logic of this manoeuvre shows itself after the exchange 12...cxb4?! 13 axb4 ♗d7 14 c5—and the knight does its business.

12...♘d7

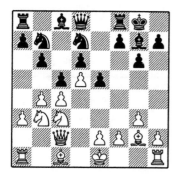

This retreat, a theoretical novelty, is in full accord with Black's claim on the c5 square as well as with the main objective of his counterplay. Previously Black used to prepare ...f7-f5 by 12...♘e8 or 12...♘g4.

13 e4 f5 14 exf5 gxf5 15 0-0 e4!?

Offering additional possibilities for the knight on d7. Now it can reach the coveted square e5. From the e8 square (with the same sequence of moves) it could only reach f6, which is not bad either.

16 ♗b2 ♘e5 17 ♘e2 ♗d7

The bishop has no objections to moving to a4 and White is practically forced to close the queen's flank.

18 b5 ♕f6 19 ♗c3

White repels the threat of 19...♘f3+.

On 19 ♖ab1 I had prepared 19...a6!, liquidating all White's hopes on the queenside in connection with the advance a3-a4-a5.

19...♘d8 20 ♘d2 ♕h6!

20...♘df7?! could be met by 21 f4, restricting the possibilities of the knight. But now this thrust would have weakened the e3 square.

21 ♘f4 ♘df7 22 f3!

A well-timed undermining of the pawn centre.

22...♖ae8?!

Black parries 23 fxe4? in view of 23...♘g4, but it is a waste of time anyway. Moving the second knight to e5 at once would be more energetic: 22...exf3 23 ♘xf3 ♘xf3+ 24 ♗xf3 ♘e5, maintaining the initiative. But now White gets a break.

23 ♖ae1 exf3 24 ♘xf3 ♘xf3+ 25 ♗xf3 ♘e5 26 ♗h5! ♘g6 27 ♖xe8

27 ♗xg7 ♕xg7 28 ♘e6 ♗xe6 29 dxe6 ♕f6 30 ♗f3 f4 leads to an unclear position.

27...♖xe8 28 ♗d2 ♗d4+ 29 ♔h1

29...♗e3!

In fighting for the weak e3 square, Black is ready to exchange off his active bishop (my beloved piece!). If Black prefers to get out of the pin by 29...♕g7, then after 30 ♘e6! ♗xe6 31 dxe6 ♖xe6 32 ♕xf5 he has to cede the initiative to White.

30 ♗xe3 ♖xe3 31 ♕c1!

The queen replaces the bishop.

31...♖e5 32 ♗f3

White could have won a pawn by 32 ♘xg6 ♕xc1 33 ♖xc1 hxg6 34 ♗xg6 ♔g7, but the fact that Black controls the e-file is more than sufficient compensation.

32...♘xf4 33 gxf4 ♖e7 34 ♖g1+ ♔g7 35 ♖e1

White even manages to deprive Black of the e-file, but this is only temporary.

35...♕f6 36 ♕e3 ♔f8 37 ♗h5 ♖e7 38 ♕xe7+ ♕xe7 39 ♖xe7 ♔xe7 40 ♔g2 ½-½

Yugoslav Variation 6...c5

(1 d4 ♘f6 2 c4 g6 3 ♘f3 ♗g7 4 g3 0-0 5 ♗g2 d6 6 0-0)

In the system with the fianchetto of the bishop, attacking the centre by **6...c5** can be recommended along with 6...♘c6. The sequence of moves where ...c5 precedes the knight development ...♘b8-c6, characterizes the Yugoslav Variation.

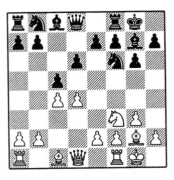

Black has left his e7-pawn at home for the moment and strikes at the centre from the other side, trying to increase the range of his King's Indian bishop. Now, if White tries to maintain the tension in the centre with 7 ♘c3, Black will increase the pressure on d4 with 7...♘c6. Since White can hardly count on struggling for the advantage in a symmetrical position after the exchange 8 dxc5 dxc5, his hopes can only lie with the closing of the centre by 8 d5—with 8...♘a5 9 ♘d2 to follow. As a matter of fact this transposes to

a position arising from the move order 6...♘c6 7 d5 ♘a5 8 ♘fd2 c5 9 ♘c3.

If White closes the centre with 7 d5, then Black can switch to a very sharp position from the Benko Gambit by means of 7...b5!?. On the other hand 7...e6?! 8 dxe6 ♗xe6 9 ♘g5 ♗xc4 10 ♗xb7 ♘bd7 11 ♘a3! is not so clear. One may, of course, continue the battle on the lines of the Benoni System, with ...♘b8-a6, ...b7-b6, ...♗c8-b7 and ...♘a6-c7. Many leading Yugoslav chessplayers are fond of this kind of set-up. Finally, White has the possibility of exchanging in the centre with 7 dxc5 dxc5.

Game 73
Vukić *White* **Gufeld** *Black*
Yugoslavia-USSR, Tuzla 1979

1 d4 ♘f6 2 c4 g6 3 ♘f3 ♗g7 4 g3 0-0 5 ♗g2 d6 6 0-0 c5 7 ♘c3
The main continuation, after which White is asking the opponent to make up his mind what he wants to do with his centre.

Another plan. 7 b3, frequently adopted by Romanishin, also deserves attention. Then 7...♘c6 (also possible is 7...cxd4 8 ♘d4 ♘c6, since accepting the pawn sacrifice by 9 ♘xc6 bxc6 10 ♗xc6 ♗h3! favours Black) 8 ♗b2 cxd4 9 ♘xd4 ♗d7 10 ♘c3 ♘xd4 11 ♕xd4 ♗c6 12 ♘d5 ♗xd5 13 ♗xd5! ♘e8 (in the game Romanishin-Gufeld, Tbilisi 1988, my subconscious desire to keep my beloved piece just led to more problems after 13...♕a5?! 14 ♗c3 ♕c7 15 ♖ac1±) 14 ♕d2 ♗xb2 15 ♕xb2 ♖b8 16 ♖fd1 ♕b6 17 ♗f3 ♘f6 and, though White retains some initiative, Black's position is stable enough, Romanishin-Rashkovsky, Lvov 1981.

7...♘c6

Apart from this obvious move, the pawn sacrifice line 7...cxd4 8 ♘xd4 ♘c6!? is interesting, e.g. 9 ♘xc6 bxc6 10 ♗xc6 ♖b8 11 ♗g2 ♕a5 12 ♘b5 (on 12 ♕c2 possible is 12...♗e6 13 b3 d5) 12...♗b7 (12...♗e6!? also deserves attention) 13 ♗xb7 ♖xb7 14 ♗d2 ♕a6 15 ♗c3 ♖c8 with active piece play.

8 d5

A principled advance where the knight is pushed to the edge of the board. After 8 dxc5 dxc5 a symmetrical position arises in which, if he defends accurately, Black will maintain equality.

8...♘a5 9 ♘d2 e5

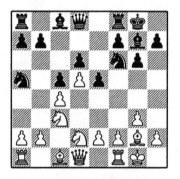

With this closed formation, Black places his priorities in the centre and on the kingside. At the same time he is ready to hold the line of defence on the queenside, where the knight on a5, together with the closed character of the position, does not play a much of a role.

Another plan of play, involving a counterattack in the centre and on the queenside, is based on undermining the pawn chain by ...e7-e6 and ...b7-b5. Usually this starts with the move 9...a6, a mode of play examined in the game Gufeld-Rashkovsky.

Sometimes Black varies the order of moves and is in no hurry to reveal his intentions. In this respect interesting is 9...♖b8 10 ♕c2 e6!? 11 ♖b1 (if 11 dxe6 then good is 11...♗xe6! 12 b3 d5 and Black's chances are already preferable) 11...exd5 12 cxd5 ♖e8 13 e4 ♗d7 and Black, who maintains pressure on the centre, is ready to counter on the queenside with ...b7-b5, Balogh-Istratescu, Krynica (zt) 1998.

10 e4

There are different opinions about this move. Efim Geller used to play it regularly, reckoning that he would have the advantage after any ...f7-f5 advance since in the main area of battle he is effectively a piece up—the knight on a5 being "offside".

On the other hand, Mark Taimanov thinks that there is no reason to make it easier for an opponent to exploit a resource, especially a main one. He recommends 10 a3 b6 (10...♕c7 11 b4! cxb4 12 axb4 ♘xc4 13 ♘b5 ♕b6 14 ♘xc4 ♕xb5 15 ♘xd6 ♕xb4 16 ♗a3 ♕g4 17 ♘b5, with a clear-cut advantage for White, is no good) 11 b4 ♘b7 12 ♗b2 (or 12 ♖b1) 12...♘g4 (if 12...♘e8 then White builds the same barricade) 13 h3 ♘h6 14 e3! f5 15 f4 with complex play.

White can also ignore the knight on a5 and carry on with his development by 10 b3, controlling the centre by the e3 and a4 pawns, along the lines of the previous variation. This plan is considered below in the game Beliavsky-Kasparov, Linares 1994.

10...♘g4

The principal method of preparing ....f7-f5. Black is not deterred by having his knight pushed back to h6. But also possible is 10...♘e8. For example, the game Smejkal-

Hübner, Leningrad (izt) 1973, proceeded 11 b3 a6 12 ♗b2 ♖b8! (this is more clever than 12...♗d7 and fully corresponds with my conception that in such positions the queen's bishop may take part in the struggle from its initial position) 13 ♕c2 f5 14 exf5 gxf5 15 ♖ae1 b5 16 ♘d1 ♖b7! 17 f4 e4 18 ♗xg7 ♖xg7 and Black's chances are preferable —he is ready to play on both flanks by ...h7-h5 and ...b5-b4, whereas White is forced to adopt wait and see tactics. Taimanov assesses 11 a3 b6 12 b4 ♘b7 as more promising, since at least it exercises a firm grip on the queenside.

11 h3

E.Geller, in his book *King's Indian Defence* (1980), recommends 11 b3 f5 12 exf5 gxf5, but now, in reply to 13 h3, the knight may retreat to its "motherland" position by 13...♘f6 and after 14 ♗b2 a6 15 ♕c2 ♖b8 Black prepares ...b7-b5 in a more favourable situation than with the knight on h6.

11...♘h6 12 b3 f5

Queenside play is also possible: 12...a6 13 ♗b2 ♖b8 followed by ...b7-b5.

13 exf5 gxf5 14 ♗b2 ♗d7

M.Gurevich recommends 14...b6 15 f4 ♘f7 16 fxe5 ♘xe5 with equal chances.

15 ♕c2

White's plan is to provoke a crisis on the e5 square by posting the queen's rook on e1, the c3 knight on e2 and advancing f2-f4. Since an exchange on f4 is not in Black's favour, due to the creation of a chronic weakness on f5, he should be ready to reply ...e5-e4.

15...a6

Organising a counter-plan by 15...b6 16 ♘e2 ♕c7 17 f4 ♖ae8

looks more logical, although after 18 ♖ae1 White's chances remain preferable, Vaganian-Spassky, Tilburg 1983.

16 ♖ae1 ♕g5!

16...b5 also deserved attention, but Black prefers an active queen.

17 ♘e2

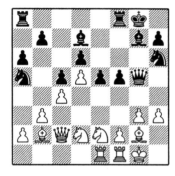

17...♖ae8?

A mechanical move after which the position turns out in White's favour. Apart from the knight on a5, the black pieces are all deployed actively. He now has to prepare himself for the advance f2-f4 by a preliminary 17...♕g6, intending 18 f4 e4, after which Black would have reasonable play.

18 ♗c3 b6 19 f4 exf4?

He shouldn't have given up the e5 square. 19...♕g6 was necessary.

20 ♘f3!

I overlooked this intermediate move. Now after 20...♕g6 21 ♘xf4, 21...♕xg3 is no good because of the loss of the queen after 22 ♘h5. So the queen has to retreat to her original square, which enables White to take the initiative.

20...♕d8 21 ♗xg7

The right order of moves. After 21 ♘xf4?! ♗xc3 22 ♕xc3 ♕f6, the Black pieces spring to life.

21...♔xg7 22 ♘xf4 ♔g8 23 ♘h5!

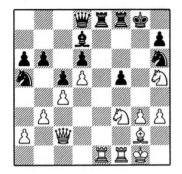

Preventing 23...♕f6. Black's position has become very difficult.

23...♖xe1 24 ♖xe1 ♖e8

After 24...♗e8 25 ♘f4 ♗f7 26 ♕c3! Black stands badly, because of the out-of-play knight on a5.

25 ♕c3 ♖xe1+ 26 ♕xe1

Depriving Black of all chances of lively play—possible after 26 ♘e1 ♕e7.

26...♔f8 27 ♕c3 ♕e7 28 h4 ♘g8 29 ♘g5 h6 30 ♘f4 ♕e8 31 ♘ge6+ ♗xe6

31...♔e7 32 ♕e3! does not save Black either.

32 dxe6 ♘c6 33 ♗xc6 ♕xc6 34 ♘g6+ ♔e8 35 ♕h8 1-0

Game 74
Beliavsky *White* **Kasparov** *Black*
Linares 1994

1 d4 ♘f6 2 c4 g6 3 g3 c5 4 ♘f3 ♗g7 5 ♗g2 0-0 6 0-0 d6 7 ♘c3 ♘c6 8 d5 ♘a5 9 ♘d2 e5 10 b3

When looking at how to play this position, the first idea that suggests itself is—do not pay any attention to the out-of-play knight on a5, just try to exploit your greater number of forces in other parts of the board. However, this is not as easy as it might seem.

10...♗d7

On 10...♘e8 (with idea of 11 ♗b2 f5 threatening ...e5-e4) White usually plays 11 e4 f5 12 exf5 gxf5 13 ♗b2.

11 ♗b2 ♘g4 12 h3 ♘h6 13 e3

White chooses a plan involving the blockade of the f5-pawn. More often played is 13 e4 f5 14 exf5 gxf5 15 ♕c2 with f2-f4 to follow.

13...f5 14 f4 a6 15 ♕c2 b5 16 ♘d1

White strives to provoke a crisis on the e5 square by the manoeuvre ♘d1-f2-d3 Also possible is 16 ♖ae1, but in this case Black's queenside pawns come into play: 16...b4 17 ♘d1 ♘b7 and afterwards ...a6-a5-a4.

16...♖b8

17 ♗c3!

A useful move, removing the bishop from the rook's "x-ray", since, after exchanges on c4, White has to reckon with the threat of an exchange sacrifice on b2. For the present, 17 fxe5 dxe5, which vacates an important blockading square on d6 for one of the black knights, is premature.

17...Xe8

In the event of 17...b4 18 &b2, White has to reckon with an opening of the a-file after a2-a3.

18 Xb1

This "mysterious rook move" prepares for any opening of the b-file (after an exchange on c4), which allows White to carry out the manoeuvre ♘d1-f2 in a more favourable situation.

18...♘f7

One of Black's ongoing problems in this variation is bringing into play his knights, which are presently confined to camp. For the time being their paths cross on the d8 square.

19 ♘f2 exf4

In such positions one has to keep an eye constantly on the a5-knight. An exchange on c4, 19...bxc4 20 bxc4 Xxb1 21 Xxb1 exf4 22 exf4 Xe3 23 &xg7 &xg7 24 ♘f1, would jeopardize the knight.

20 exf4 Xe3 21 &xg7 &xg7 22 Xfe1!

The knight is uncomfortably placed on a5 because of the danger of a check by the queen on c3. For this reason one the rook must be removed from e3.

22...Xxe1+

He can no longer hold out on e3, since after 22...We7 there follows 23 ♘f3 with the threat of 24 Xxe3 Wxe3 25 Xe1. And 22...Xxg3 is no good because of 23 ♘f1 winning the exchange.

23 Xxe1 Wf6

It is important to occupy the long diagonal, since otherwise after 23...bxc4? White will control it himself by 24 Wc3+ &g8 25 bxc4. But now this exchange is threatened.

24 cxb5

The queen cannot be shifted by an advance of the g-pawn, 24 g4 bxc4 25 g5, due to the intermediate manoeuvre 25...Wd4 26 ♘f3 cxb3.

24...axb5 25 b4 cxb4

Apparently 25...♘b7 was also possible, but he could not resist the chance to vacate the c5 square for the knight.

26 Wc7 Wd8 27 Wxd8 Xxd8 28 ♘d3 Xc8 29 ♘xb4 &f6 30 &f2 ♘d8 31 &f1

An attempt to strengthen his position by 31 g4 is best ignored by Black, who can carry on with 31...Xc3 (31...fxg4? is no good in view of 32 ♘e4+ &g7 33 ♘xd6 Xc7 34 hxg4 with advantage to White) 32 g5+ &f7 33 &f1 ♘db7 etc.

31...♘db7 32 Xe3 h6 33 Xe1

A silent peaceful offer.

33...g5 34 Xe3 Xc7 35 Xe1 Xc8 36 Xe3 Xc7 37 h4 g4 38 Xe1 Xc3 39 Xe3 Xc1 40 Xe1 Xc3 41 Xe3 ½-½

Game 75
Pigusov *White* **Gufeld** *Black*
Nikolaev 1981

1 d4 ♘f6 2 ♘f3 g6 3 c4 &g7 4 g3 0-0 5 &g2 d6 6 0-0 c5 7 dxc5
The idea of this exchange in the Yugoslav Variation stems from

Miguel Najdorf. White counts on being able to exploit his extra tempo in a symmetrical position. However, it is not easy to do this since Black has no real weaknesses.

7...dxc5

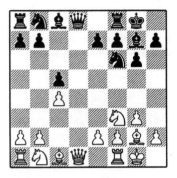

8 ♕xd8

Najdorf usually preferred 8 ♘e5, preventing the development of the knight on c6. For example, the game Najdorf-Boleslavsky, Zurich (ct) 1953, proceeded 8...♕c7 9 ♘d3 ♘c6 10 ♘c3 ♗f5 11 ♗f4 ♕a5 12 ♗d2 ♗xd3 13 exd3 ♕c7 14 ♗e3 and the advantage of the two bishops in an open position favoured White. In my game with Whiteley, Hastings 1989, I improved Black's play: 9...♗e6!? 10 ♕b3 ♘c6 11 ♘xc5 ♗g4 12 ♕xb7 ♕xb7 13 ♘xb7 ♘d4 14 ♘c3 ♘xe2+ 15 ♘xe2 ♗xe2 16 ♖e1 ♗xc4 17 ♖xe7 ♘d5 18 ♖d7 ♘b6 19 ♖d1 ♗e2, in fact, though Black has clear-cut activity for the pawn, I still had a lot of work to do in order to get a draw. Subsequently it was found that 8...♘fd7, exchanging off the active knight, was stronger: 9 ♘xd7 ♘xd7 10 ♘c3 ♘e5. In the game Szabolcsi-Nagy, Szolnok 1988, after 11 ♕b3, Black sacrificed his queen by 11...♕d4 12 ♗d5 e6 13 ♗e3 exd5 14 ♗xd4 dxc4 15 ♕b5

cxd4 16 ♘d5 ♗e6 17 ♘c7 ♗d7 18 ♕xb7 ♖ab8 19 ♕a7 ♖xb2 20 ♘d5 ♗h3 21 ♖fe1 d3 and developed a strong attack.

The main continuation is 8 ♘c3.

8...♖xd8 9 ♘e5

Without queens Najdorf's idea does not seem so effective. But even after 9 ♗e3 Black does not face any specific problems. Besides 9...♘fd7 10 0-0 ♘c6, possible is the sharper 9...♘c6 10 ♗xc5 ♗e6 11 ♘d2 ♘d7 12 ♗a3 ♗xc3! (weaker is 12...♘b6, which is met by 13 ♗xc6! bxc6 14 ♗xe7 ♖e8 15 ♗xc5 ♘xc4 16 0-0-0± Geller-Bertok, USSR-Yugoslavia 1959) 13 bxc3 ♘de5 with equal chances.

9...♘e8

Black quickly transfers the knight to d6, at the same time activating the bishop on g7. 9...♘fd7 looks somewhat artificial but it works after the automatic 10 ♘d3, on which, in the game Bronstein-A.Kuzmin, Moscow 1982, Black without prejudice replied 10...♘c6! and, after 11 ♗xc6 bxc6 12 ♘d2 ♘b6 13 a4 ♖d4, obtained excellent play. But, at any rate, after the simple 10 ♘xd7 ♘xd7 11 ♖d1 White's position is better.

10 ♘d3

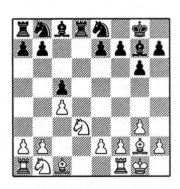

10...♘a6!

As an alternative, it would be interesting for the reader to familiarise himself with the game Vaganian-Kasparov, USSR 1981, which proceeded 10...♘d6 11 ♘xc5 ♘c6! 12 ♘a3 ♖b8! 13 ♘a4 (13 ♖e1!? deserves attention, on which G.Kasparov recommends 13...♘a5 or 13...b6) 13...♗e6 14 ♗f4 ♖bc8 15 ♖ac1 ♘d4 16 ♖fe1 b5! (weaker is 16...♗xc4?! 17 ♘xc4 ♖xc4 18 ♘c3 ±) 17 ♗xd6! ♖xd6 18 ♘b5 ♘xb5 19 cxb5 ♖xc1 20 ♖xc1 ♖d2 21 ♗f3 ♗xb2 ½-½.

My decision to protect the pawn saves Black from carrying on such a high-tension struggle—a style of play which, however, is second nature to Kasparov.

11 ♘c3 ♘d6

It is clear that, even it meant winning a pawn, I couldn't bring myself to play 11...♗xc3?! 12 bxc3 ♘d6 13 ♗f4!, because then the bishop-pair would cut through Black's most important lines of communication.

12 ♘d5 ♔f8! 13 ♘e3

The knight is forced to retreat, suggesting that White's plan has not been a success. Now the black pieces will be more active in the symmetrical pawn position: whereas Black can exchange off White's "long-range gun", White cannot do the same.

13...♖b8

The best way to develop the second bishop.

14 ♗d2 b6 15 ♖ab1 ♗b7 16 ♗xb7 ♖xb7

Black already stands better. His active minor pieces coordinate much better than their tangled counterparts. However, tournament considerations came into play here and peaceful negotiations were concluded.

½-½

Game 76
Adorjan *White* **Gufeld** *Black*
Hastings 1986/87

1 c4 g6 2 ♘f3 ♗g7 3 d4 ♘f6 4 g3 0-0 5 ♗g2 d6 6 0-0 c5 7 ♘c3 ♘c6 8 dxc5

Adorjan turns down the principled 8 d5 ♘a5, hoping to bring the King's Indian fan down to earth with the symmetrical variation.

8...dxc5

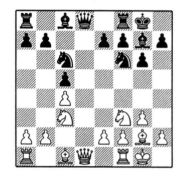

9 ♗f4

White chooses a plan with piece pressure on the opponent's queenside and, if the opportunity arises, intends ♘f3-e5.

In symmetrical positions the advantage of the first move always has specific importance. This is seen especially after 9 ♗e3. Black can maintain the symmetry as far as 9...♗e6, but on 10 ♗xc5 already bad is 10...♗xc4? 11 ♘d4! ♘xd4 12 ♗xd4 and problems arise with the b7-pawn: although, it is true that, by playing 10...♕a5! 11 ♗a3 ♗xc4, Black holds the position. 10 ♕a4 is considered to be stronger, but here too the symmetry 10...♕a5?! 11 ♕xa5 ♘xa5 12 ♗xc5 ♘xc4 is rather risky: 13 ♘g5!? ♘d7 14 ♘xe6 fxe6 15 ♗xe7 and White obtains the better chances (A.Mikhalchishin). Therefore on 10

♕a4 more decisive is 10...♘d4! 11 ♖ad1 (or 11 ♗xd4 cxd4 12 ♘b5 ♘d7 13 ♘fxd4 ♘b6!= I.Almasi) 11...♗d7 12 ♕a3 ♘c2 13 ♕xc5 b6 14 ♕g5 h6 15 ♕f4 g5 16 ♕e5 ♖c8 and Black maintains equality, K.Grigorian-Kasparov, USSR 1981

But it is simpler to deviate from the symmetry—9...♕a5 and now 10 ♘d5 e6 11 ♗d2 ♕d8 12 ♘c3 ♘d4 or 10 ♗d2 ♗f5 11 ♗d2 ♕d8 12 ♘h4 ♗g4 13 h3 ♗d7 14 ♗c3 e5 gives Black equal chances.

9...♘h5

In those days it was considered useful to drive away the bishop from its active position.

Indeed, after the active 9...♘d4, good is 10 ♗e5! ♘c6 11 ♕xd8 ♖xd8 12 ♗c7 ♖f8 (or 12...♖d7 13 ♗f4 ♘d4 14 ♖fd1±) 13 ♘e5 ♘d4 14 ♘d3 ♘d7 15 ♖fd1 ♖e8 16 ♖ac1 a6 17 e3 ♘e6 18 ♘d5 and White's position is preferable, Ribli-Gligorić, Linares 1981.

On 9...♗e6 Black has to reckon on 10 ♘e5! Now the mass exchanges 10...♘xe5 11 ♗xe5 ♘d7 12 ♗xg7 ♔xg7 13 ♗b7 ♖b8 14 ♗d5 ♗xd5 15 ♕xd5 ♖xb2 16 ♖fd1 lead to a clear-cut advantage for White.

But later it was concluded that after 10...♘a5 11 ♕c2 (insufficient is 11 ♕a4 ♘d7 12 ♘xd7 ♗xd7 13 ♕c2 ♘c6 14 ♖ad1 ♘d4=) 11...♘h5 12 ♖ad1 ♕e8 13 ♘d5 ♘xf4 14 gxf4 ♖c8 the position is double-edged, Tukmakov-Spraggett, Berne 1995

10 ♗e3 ♘d4

It is difficult to resist the temptation to gain a foothold for the knight on this central square. Also played is 10...♕a5 and after 11 ♕c1 the thrust 11...♘d4 12 ♖e1 ♗e6 gains in strength. However, stronger is 11 ♘d2! (with the idea of transferring the knight to b3) 11...♖d8 12 ♘d5

♕a6 (12...♗xb2? 13 ♘b3 ♕a6 14 ♘xe7+! with advantage to White, Bareev-Kovalev, Moscow (ol) 1994) 13 ♘b3 ♕a6 14 ♕c1 ♗xd5 15 cxd5 and now 15...♘d4 leads by force to a favourable endgame for White: 16 ♘xc5 ♘xe2+ 17 ♔h1 ♘xc1 18 ♘xa6 ♘d3 19 ♘c5 and White has a real advantage with his two bishops (E.Bareev).

11 ♘d2

White avoids exchanges, which are possible after 11 ♕d2 ♗g4 12 ♖ad1 ♗xf3 13 ♗xf3 ♘xf3+ 14 exf3 ♕xd2 15 ♖xd2 ♗xc3 16 bxc3 b6 17 ♖d7 ♖e8, with a level endgame.

But somewhat stronger is 11 ♕c1 ♕a5 (or 11...♗g4 12 ♖d1 ±) 12 ♖e1 ♗e6 13 ♗d2 ♕d8 14 b3, although White's advantage is only symbolic—he intends to exchange off the dark-squared bishops.

11...♖b8

Black is anxious to solve the problem of his light-squared bishop, since on the straightforward 11...♗f5 he has to reckon with 12 h3. With the text move he prepares a pawn sacrifice, placing his hopes on the power of his "special" bishop, which is left without a counterpart.

12 ♘b3

12...b6! 13 ♗xd4

Now the g7-bishop will become master of the long diagonal.

13...cxd4 14 ♘b5 ♗b7 15 ♘5xd4

After 15 ♗xb7 ♖xb7 the capture of the pawn by 16 ♘5xd4? is impossible due to the pin by 16...♖d7.

15...♗xg2 16 ♔xg2 ♖c8!

Black has sufficient compensation for the pawn and therefore a peaceful settlement was agreed. Now 17 ♖c1 does not protect the pawn on c4 because of 17...♖xc4! 18 ♖xc4 ♕d5+. And on 17 ♕d3 I had prepared 17...♕d7!, intending to meet 18 ♖fd1 with 18...♕a4 or even 18...♕g4.

½-½

Four Pawns Attack

For a long time the sharp Four Pawns variation 1 d4 ♘f6 2 c4 g6 3 ♘c3 ♗g7 4 e4 d6 5 f4 did not have a good reputation.

It seems that the view expressed by the witty grandmaster Savielly Tartakover: "Not death in the centre, but death to the centre," was mainly addressed to this variation.

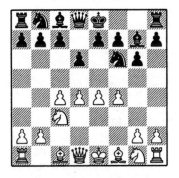

This aggressive line was first encountered more than a hundred years ago in the historic game Englisch-Tarrasch, Hamburg 1885. Nevertheless, despite its advanced age, the Four Pawns Attack—which at times leads to extremely wild positions—is one of the less well-investigated systems of the King's Indian Defence.

Here White declares his intentions unequivocally. He occupies the centre from very beginning of the game, in order to gain an advantage in space. However, Black can

sometimes successfully provoke a clash in the centre, exploiting his advantage in development. Nevertheless the system remains quite flexible. Practice has shown that the most effective counterplay for Black lies in an immediate strike against the powerful enemy centre by means of ...c7-c5 or ...e7-e5. One of the most popular ways of development in this variation is 5...c5 6 d5 0-0 7 ♘f3, after which a fundamental position of the Four Pawns Attack is reached (or, by transposition of moves from the Modern Benoni: 1 d4 ♘f6 2 c4 c5 3 d5 d6 4 ♘c3 g6 5 e4 ♗g7 6 f4 0-0 7 ♘f3). White retains his pawn centre and forces Black to spend time and energy challenging it: 7...e6 8 ♗e2 exd5 9 exd5 (9 cxd5 is a Modern-Benoni).

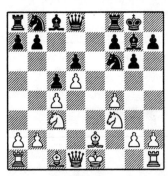

In this sharp position the main continuations for Black are 9...♗f5, 9...♘h5, 9...♖e8 and 9...a6. At the present moment, the pawn sacrifice 9...b5 is premature, since after 10

cxb5 a6 11 a4 Black fails to obtain full compensation for it.

A no less principled struggle arises in the variation 5...c5 6 dxc5, where the position assumes a semi-open character.

Game 77
Nei *White* **Gufeld** *Black*
USSR (ch) Leningrad 1963

1 d4 ♘f6 2 c4 g6 3 ♘c3 ♗g7 4 e4 d6 5 f4 0-0 6 ♘f3 c5 7 d5

The most principled continuation. The alternative is 7 dxc5.

7...e6 8 ♗e2 exd5 9 cxd5

A typical modern chameleon variation. This position occurs in the Modern Benoni System (1 d4 ♘f6 2 c4 c5 3 d5 e6 4 ♘c3 exd5 5 cxd5 d6 6 e4 g6 7 f4 ♗g7 8 ♘f3 0-0 9 ♗e2).

But the capture 9 exd5 is recorded by theory under the King's Indian Defence.

9...b5

The main continuations here are 9...♖e8 and 9...♗g4, but this pawn sacrifice, based on the instability of White's pawn centre, has a logical basis. Black threatens to push away the knight on c3 and therefore forces White to react quickly.

10 e5

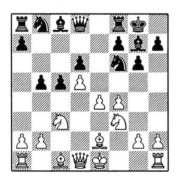

The straightforward 10 ♗xb5 would be met by 10...♘xe4 11

♘xe4 ♕a5+ 12 ♔f2 (12 ♘c3? ♗xc3+ 13 bxc3 ♕xb5 is weaker) 12...♕xb5 13 ♘xd6 ♕a6 with good play for Black.

10...dxe5

White's pawn couple, d5/e5, is not only a power, but a weakness as well. From this point of view 10...♘fd7 11 ♗xb5 dxe5 looks less logical: 12 0-0 ♕b6 13 a4 exf4 14 ♗xf4 a6 15 a5 ♕b7 16 ♗xd7 ♘xd7 17 ♕d2 ♘f6 18 ♗e5!, and White controls the situation in the centre, Lautier-Rogers, Erevan (ol) 1996.

11 fxe5 ♘g4 12 ♗g5

After 12 ♗f4 ♘d7 13 e6 fxe6, the bishop comes under fire and White is practically forced to give up his pawn centre after 14 dxe6 ♖xf4 15 ♕d5 ♔h8 16 ♕xa8 ♘b6 17 ♕xa7 ♗xe6 18 0-0 ♘e3 19 ♖f2 b4, but the win of the exchange is some consolation for him. The black pieces are very active, as was proved in the game, Keres-Spassky, Riga 1965, 20 ♘b5 ♖f7 21 ♕a5 ♕b8 22 ♖e1 ♗d5= and also Goldin-Suetin, Russia 1995, 20 ♘d1 ♘c2 21 ♖c1 ♘d4=.

12...♕b6 13 0-0

White played the opening quite quickly, so it can be assumed that he had prepared himself for this position with home analysis.

13...c4+

If 13...♘xe5 14 ♘xe5 ♗xe5 15 ♗e7 ♘d7 16 d6 ♗b7 17 ♘d5, with the better chances for White, Gorelov-Vasyukov, Moscow 1981

14 ♔h1 ♘xe5

This immediate capture is best, otherwise after 14...♘d7 the pawn will have to be reckoned with: 15 e6 fxe6 16 dxe6 ♘df6 17 e7 ♖e8 18 ♕d4 ♗d7 when, in the game, Kaidanov-Gleizerov, USSR 1986, White could have obtained a better endgame by 19 ♕xb6 axb6 20 ♘d4.

Of course not 14...♘f2+? 15 ♖xf2 ♕xf2 16 ♘e4 with an irresistible attack.

15 ♗e7

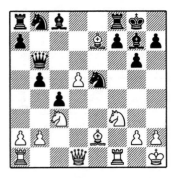

The whole point of the variation White has chosen probably depends on this move. Indeed, if Black were forced to play 15...♖e8, he would have a very difficult game. For example: 16 d6 ♗b7 17 ♘d5 ♗xd5 18 ♕xd5 ♘bd7 19 ♘xe5 ♘xe5 20 a4!.

15...♘bd7 16 d6

White decides not to take the exchange yet. After 16 ♗xf8 ♔xf8 Black has, in my view, sufficient compensation for the small material deficit.

16...♗b7 17 ♘d5 ♗xd5

I spent a long time on this move, being very reluctant to part with my strong bishop. But I did not like 17...♕c5 because of a continuation such as 18 ♘xe5 ♘xe5 19 d7!? (19 ♘f6+ ♗xf6 20 ♗xf6 ♖ad8 21 ♗e7 ♖fe8 with a fine game) 19...♕xd5 20 ♕xd5 ♗xd5 21 ♗xf8 ♔xf8 22 ♖ad1 ♘d3 23 ♗xd3 ♗e6 24 ♗e4 ♖d8 25 ♖d2, and it is not clear if Black can win (whereas I had evaluated my position as better at the outset).

18 ♕xd5 ♘g4 19 a4

Probably the best move.

19...♘f2+ 20 ♖xf2

Although there is no smothered mate after 20 ♔g1, the threat of discovered check is unpleasant enough.

20...♕xf2 21 ♗xf8 ♖xf8 22 ♕xb5 ♕xe2 23 ♕xd7 ♕xb2 24 ♖e1

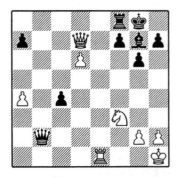

The position is quite fascinating. The impression is that the c-pawn should decide the outcome of the struggle, but an immediate advance achieves nothing: 24...c3? 25 ♕xa7 c2 26 ♕c5 ♗h6 27 ♘g5!

Black intends to realize his advantage with a preconceived plan. Since White's counterplay depends on the d-pawn, it is necessary for the black pieces to control its queening square. For this, the bishop should be placed on f6 and the queen on the d-file, and at the first opportunity the a-pawn must be removed from attack.

24...♗c3!

Before carrying out my scheme it is useful to eject the rook from the open file.

25 ♖f1 ♕e2 26 ♖g1 a5 27 ♕c7 ♕d3 28 d7 ♗f6 29 ♖e1 ♔g7!

This move is directed against the threat of 30 ♖e8. If 29...c3 is played at once, then, after 30 ♖e8, Black cannot play 30...♕f1+ 31 ♘g1 ♗d4 because of 32 ♖xf8+ ♔g7 33 ♖xf7+!.

30 h3 c3 31 ♖e8 c2 32 ♕c5 ♖g8
This is the whole idea of the manoeuvre starting with 29...♔g7.

33 ♕c8
In time trouble, White opts for this natural move and gives Black the chance to conclude the struggle in spectacular fashion. Even so, after the better 33 ♖c8 ♖d8! his position would still be difficult.

33...♕f1+ 34 ♔h2
After 34 ♘g1 c1=♕ 35 ♖xg8+ ♔h6 36 ♕f8+ ♔g5 the king escapes the checks.

34...♗e5+! 35 ♖xe5
Or 35 ♘xe5 ♕f4+ 36 g3 ♕d2+ 37 ♔g1 c1=♕+.

35...c1=♕ 36 ♕xg8+ ♔xg8 37 d8=♕+ ♔g7 38 ♕d4 ♕cc4 39 ♕xc4 ♕xc4 40 ♖xa5 ♕c7+ 0-1

Game 78
Bagaturov *White* **Shirov** *Black*
USSR 1989

1 d4 ♘f6 2 c4 g6 3 ♘c3 ♗g7 4 e4 d6 5 f4 0-0 6 ♘f3 c5 7 d5 e6 8 ♗e2 exd5 9 exd5

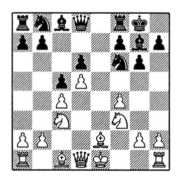

9...a6
With the present pawn structure, Black also has other ways of obtaining a reasonable game:
(a) 9...♗f5 10 0-0 ♖e8 11 ♗d3 ♕d7 12 ♕c2 (or 12 h3 ♘a6 13 a3

♘c7 14 g4 ♗xg4! 15 hxg4 ♕xg4+ 16 ♔h2 ♕h5+ 17 ♔g2 ♕g4+ 18 ♔h2 b5! and Black's attack fully compensates for the sacrificed piece, Conquest-Mestel, Hastings 1986) 12...♘a6 13 a3 ♘c7 14 ♗xf5 gxf5 15 ♗d2 b5 16 cxb5 ♘cxd5 17 ♘h4 ♘xc3 18 ♗xc3 ♖e4 with chances for both sides (A.Vaiser).
(b) 9...♘h5 10 0-0 ♗xc3 11 bxc3 f5 12 ♘g5 ♗g7 13 ♗f3 ♘d7 14 ♖e1 ♘f6 15 ♖b1 ♖e8 16 ♖xe8+ ♕xe8 17 ♖b2 ♗d7 18 ♖xb7 ♖b8 19 ♖xb8 ♕xb8 and the game is equal, Forintos-Gligorić, Ljubljana 1969; 12 ♗e3!? may be better.

10 0-0
After 10 a4 Black can switch to the theme 10...♘h5.

10...b5!
A typical pawn sacrifice to take the initiative. Black opens the b-file and vacates squares for the deployment of his pieces.

11 cxb5 axb5 12 ♗xb5 ♘a6 13 ♖e1 ♘c7 14 ♗c4
On 14 ♗c6, Black exchanges off the bishop after 14...♖b8 and 15...♗b7.

14...♖b8 15 a3!?
White intends to transfer his rook, via a2, to e2.

15...♖e8 16 ♖a2 ♖xe1+ 17 ♕xe1
White fails to save a tempo (to defend the d5 pawn) by the retreat 17 ♘xe1 ♘d7 18 ♘a4 ♘a8! when, after posting the knight on b6, Black activates all his pieces to the maximum.

17...♗b7 18 ♕d1 ♘d7 19 ♘a4 ♘f6 20 ♘c3 ♘d7 21 ♘a4 ♕e8?!
Black's has achieved an obvious moral success: White is happy to draw.

But Shirov declines the draw in not the best way. He should have selected the manoeuvre 21...♘a8! with a transfer of the knight to b6.

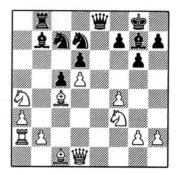

22 b3!
White follows the outlined plan. After 22 ♕d3 A.Shirov showed a nice variation 22...♘xd5!! 23 ♗xd5 ♗d4+! 24 ♘xd4 ♕e1+ 25 ♕f1 ♕xf1+ 26 ♔xf1 ♗xd5 27 ♘c6 (27 ♘c3 ♗xa2 28 ♘c6 ♖b6 29 ♘e7+ ♔f8 30 ♘c8 ♖c6 31 ♘a7 ♖a6 loses) 27...♗xc6 28 ♘c3 d5 and Black gains the advantage.
22...♕e4 23 ♖e2 ♕f5 24 ♖e7

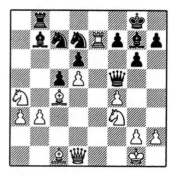

24...♘xd5!?
This interesting sacrifice allows Shirov to unravel the position. On 25 ♖xd7 he had prepared 35...♕xd7 26 ♗xd5 ♗xd5 27 ♕xd5 ♕e6! and Black's chances are not worse.
25 ♗d3 ♘xe7 26 ♗xf5 ♘xf5 27 ♗b2 ♘f6!
It is important to keep the dark-squared bishop.
28 ♘b6 h5 29 ♘c4 ♗a8!

29...d5 is premature in view of 30 ♘a5 ♗a8 31 ♗e5 ♖b5 32 b4! cxb4 33 ♕a4 ♖c5 34 ♘b3 ♖c8 35 axb4 with advantage to White (A.Shirov).
30 ♘g5 d5 31 ♘e5 d4! 32 ♕e2?
After 32 ♘exf7 ♗d5 33 ♘e5 White would have maintained a promising position. But now Black's initiative cannot be contained.
32...♗d5 33 ♕a6?! ♖xb3 34 ♕c8+ ♗f8 35 ♕d8 ♖xb2 36 ♕xf6 ♗e7 37 ♕a6 ♖xg2+ 38 ♔f1 ♘e3+ 39 ♔e1 ♘c2+ 40 ♔d1 ♘e3+ 41 ♔e1 c4 0-1

Game 79
Lanka *White* **Gufeld** *Black*
Jurmala 1977

1 d4 ♘f6 2 c4 c5 3 d5 d6 4 ♘c3 g6 5 e4 ♗g7 6 f4 0-0 7 ♗d3
7 ♘f3 e6 is encountered more often. We shall look at this system in greater detail in the following game.
7...e6

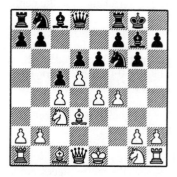

8 dxe6
An original choice. As a rule, the continuation 7 ♗d3 (in contrast to 7 ♗e2) is linked to the development of the king's knight on the e2 square. For example, 8 ♘ge2 exd5 9 exd5 ♗g4 (9...♘h5!? 10 0-0 f5 is also interesting) 10 0-0 ♘bd7 11

♕c2 ♘h5 12 h3 ♕h4! with fine play for Black.

8...♗xe6

A small surprise. 8...fxe6 9 ♘ge2 is considered by the *Encyclopedia* as the main line, in which Black creates a "small centre" d6/e6. Its drawback, a backward pawn-pair, is compensated by the opportunity for him to exercise control over the d4-square. Here are some examples from contemporary practice:

(a) 9...♘c6 10 0-0 a6 (the immediate 10...♘d4 11 ♘xd4 cxd4 12 ♘e2 ♕b6= is also possible) 11 ♘g3 ♖b8 12 a4 ♘d4 13 ♗e3 ♗d7 with a comfortable game for Black. McMahon-Gufeld, London 1995;

(b) 9...e5 10 f5 (or 10 0-0 exf4 11 ♗xf4 ♘h5=) 10...gxf5 11 exf5 d5 12 cxd5 e4 13 ♗c2 c4 14 0-0 ♘a6 15 ♘g3 ♘b4 16 ♗g5 and Black runs into difficulties, Peev-Bologan, Moldova 1997.

9 f5

White cannot delay, or Black obtains counter-chances in the centre.

9...♗d7

An attempt to get rid of the backward d6-pawn after 9...♗d7 10 ♘ge2 gxf5 11 exf5 d5 12 cxd5 ♘xd5 13 0-0 ♘b4 (parrying the threat 14 ♘xd5 ♕xd5 15 f6) 14 ♗e4 enables White to exercise control with his pieces in the centre.

10 ♘f3 ♘c6

10...gxf5?! is weaker in view of 11 0-0! fxe4 12 ♘xe4 ♘xe4 13 ♗xe4 and the white pieces are very active. Besides the text move, 10...♗c6 is possible, followed by ...♘b8-d7.

11 0-0 ♘g4

Black strives to occupy the e5-square with a piece (the weakness of the backward d6 pawn, as in many variations of the King's Indian is not of great importance),

because after 11...♘e5 12 ♘xe5 dxe5 13 ♗e3 ♕e7 14 ♘d5 the position favours White—since if the knight on d5 is exchanged, it will be replaced by a passed pawn.

In the game, Lein-Polugaevsky, Sochi 1976, play continued 11...♖e8 12 ♗g5 h6 13 ♗f4 gxf5 14 exf5 ♘e5 15 ♕d2 ♔h7 16 ♖ae1 ♗c6!? 17 ♘xe5 dxe5 18 ♗xe5 ♕d7! and, though Black has some compensation for the pawn, White's chances are preferable.

12 ♘d5

On 12 ♗g5 would follow 12...f6 13 ♗f4 ♘ce5 with complex play.

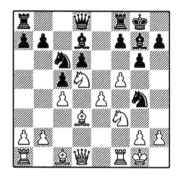

12...♘b4!

The symmetrical position of the black knights creates an artistic impression.

It is essential to swap off the strong centralised knight. The exchange of the other knight by 12...♘d4 13 h3 ♘xf3+ 14 ♕xf3 ♘e5 15 ♕g3 is to White's advantage.

13 ♔h1

Or 13 h3 ♘e5 14 ♘xe5 ♗xe5 15 ♗f4, and now not 15...♕h4 16 ♕d2 ♘xd5 17 exd5 with advantage to White, but 15...♘xd5!? 16 exd5 ♕f6 with double-edged chances.

13...♘xd5 14 exd5 ♖e8

After this move we may conclude that the opening stage has turned out in Black's favour. However 14...♕e8?! 15 ♗f4 ♘e3 16 ♕d2 ♘xf1 17 ♖xf1 leads to an unclear position.

15 ♗g5 ♕a5!

This is the best square for the queen. The attempt to win a pawn works out badly: 15...♕b6 16 ♕d2 (16 ♘d2!? ♘e3 17 ♕f3 ♘xf1 18 ♖xf1 is also interesting) 16...♕xb2 17 ♕xb2 ♗xb2 18 ♖ab1 ♗g7 19 ♖xb7 ♗c8 20 ♖c7 and White has an obvious advantage. 15...♗f6 16 ♕d2 ♗xg5 17 ♘xg5 ♘e3 is also dubious in view of 18 ♘xf7!?.

16 ♕c1

If 16 ♗d2, then 16...♕b6 is good.

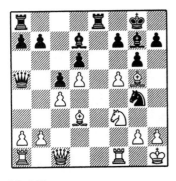

16...b5!

At the earliest opportunity, Black undermines the centre and opens up play on the queenside.

17 ♕f4

White's threats on the kingside look very dangerous; nevertheless, as the game shows, it was worth thinking about 17 b3, trying to neutralise Black's counterplay.

17...bxc4 18 ♕xd6

On the retreat of the bishop, 18 ♗c2, both 18...♖e2 and 18...♘e3 are strong.

18...♗b5

After 18...cxd3? 19 ♕xd7, White has serious threats.

19 fxg6

The correct reply to 19 a4 is 19...cxd3 20 axb5 ♕xb5, maintaining some advantage; but not 19...♗a6? 20 fxg6 fxg6 21 ♗xg6!.

19...fxg6 20 ♗xg6! hxg6!

The acceptance of the sacrifice is the best decision. The exchange of queens leads to an unclear position: 20...♕b6 21 ♕xb6 axb6 22 ♗xe8 ♖xe8.

21 ♕xg6

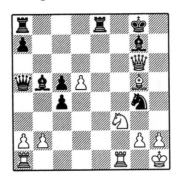

21...♕a6!

Only with this, far from obvious, move may White's attack be parried and the material advantage retained. It is necessary to control the d3 square!

22 d6 c3 23 ♖ae1

The point of the move 21...♕a6! is revealed: in the variation 23 ♗h6 ♘xh6 24 ♘g5 ♗d3! Black wins; or 23 ♘h4 ♘e5.

23...♕xa2! 24 ♗e7

On 24 ♗h6 I had prepared the crushing defensive manoeuvre 24...♕f7! and after 25 ♕g4 ♗xf1 Black wins.

24...♗xf1 25 ♖xf1

Again 25 ♘g5 is refuted by 25...♗d3!.

25...♕c4 26 ♖e1 ♘f2+ 27 ♔g1 ♕f7

27...♕g4! 28 ♘g5 ♘h3+ is even more accurate, concluding the struggle immediately.

28 ♕c2

The exchange of queens leads to disaster: 28 ♕xf7+ ♔xf7 29 ♔xf2 cxb2.

28...♘h3+ 29 ♔h1 cxb2 30 ♘h4 ♘f2+ 31 ♔g1 ♗d4 32 ♘f5 ♘d3+ 33 ♔h1 ♕xf5 0-1

Game 80
Pribyl *White* **Gufeld** *Black*
Budapest 1970

1 c4 g6 2 ♘c3 ♗g7 3 d4 ♘f6 4 e4 0-0 5 f4 c5 6 d5 b5

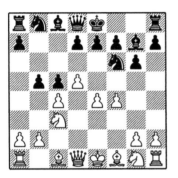

Of course, it would be somewhat risky to assert that the move ...b7-b5 is a novelty in this position. When I showed this game to Lajos Portisch, he exclaimed: "I will cheer up my brother that he's got followers!" True, he added that Ferenc plays 6...d6 7 ♗e2 first, and only then 7...b5.

In the opening, besides seizing the centre with pawns, no less a role—and perhaps a greater one—is played by the rapid deployment of forces. I will reveal a little professional secret: when I cannot evaluate an opening position precisely, I count the pieces developed both by myself and my opponent. In the present case Black's pieces are better developed, so I decided to proceed with active operations.

7 e5

It is difficult to resist such a tempting continuation. But it is not good to begin a pawn offensive before completing one's development. 7 cxb5 would be wiser, on which I had intended to continue 7...a6, temporarily managing without the move ...d7-d6.

7...♘e8 8 ♘xb5

White's reason for playing 7 e5 was to avoid having to spoil his pawn chain here by 8 cxb5.

8...d6 9 ♘f3 ♘d7!

Attacking the centre by means of 9...♗g4 seemed less convincing to me in view of 10 ♗e2.

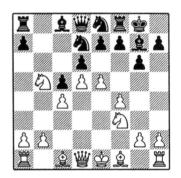

10 e6?

Perhaps already a serious mistake. White should play 10 exd6. Possibly Pribyl did not like the position after 10...a6 11 ♘c3 ♘xd6. In reply to 11 ♘c7 Black would play 11...♖b8 12 ♘xe8 ♖xe8 with a strong initiative.

10...fxe6 11 ♘g5 ♘df6 12 dxe6 ♗b7 13 ♗d3 d5

Of course there was no sense in calculating variations which win the pawn back. Black's whole strategy is directed towards a speedy development of his forces rather than materialistic considerations.

14 0-0 ♕b6 15 ♕e2 dxc4 16 ♗xc4 a6 17 ♘c3 ♘d6 18 ♗e3 ♘xc4 19 ♕xc4 ♕xb2

Despite the apparent simplicity (mate is threatened on g2), this move demanded accurate calculation.

20 ♗f2!

20 ♘f3? ♘g4 and 20 ♘e2 ♗d5 21 ♕d3 c4 etc. are weaker.

20...♕b4

20...♘g4 21 ♖ab1 ♕xc3 22 ♕xc3 ♗xc3 23 ♖xb7 ♘xf2 24 ♔xf2 ♖xf4+ 25 ♔e2 ♖xf1 26 ♔xf1 is not as good, as White can defend successfully. Black refrained from the tempting 20... ♘h5 in view of 21 ♖ab1 ♕xc3 22 ♕xc3 ♗xc3 23 ♖xb7 ♘xf4 24 g3! and there is nothing decisive.

21 ♕xc5

White's position is hopeless after 21 ♕xb4 cxb4.

21...♕xf4

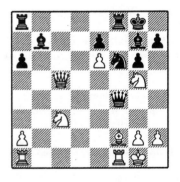

22 ♗g3

It was necessary to weigh up the consequences of the move 22 ♕xe7, on which I had prepared 22...♘g4! (22...♗xg2 23 ♔xg2 ♕xg5+ 24 ♗g3 is inferior) 23 g3 ♕d4!. This is the whole point.

Now on 24 ♗xd4 there follows 24...♗xd4+ 25 ♖f2 ♗xf2+ 26 ♔f1 ♗c5+, and Black wins. But if the queen is not taken, there is no defence against 24...♖xf2, for example: 24 ♖ad1 ♖xf2 25 ♖xd4

♖g2+ 26 ♔h1 ♖xh2+ 27 ♔g1 ♖h1 mate.

22...♘d7!

Now everything is decided by this effective move. Its difficulty is purely psychological: all the time Black was looking for a mating attack, then suddenly the position demanded positional play.

23 ♗xf4

My opponent could have up more stubborn resistance by 23 ♖xf4 ♘xc5 24 ♖c4.

23...♘xc5 24 ♗d2 ♖fd8 25 ♗e3

Material loss is also inevitable in the event of 25 ♗e1 (25 ♖ad1 ♖xd2) 25...♘d3 26 ♗d2 ♘b4.

25...♗xc3 26 ♗xc5

26 ♖ac1? ♘a4 is bad.

26...♖d2 27 ♘f3 ♗xf3 28 gxf3 ♗xa1 29 ♖xa1 ♖e2 30 ♗xe7 ♖xe6 31 ♗c5 ♖c8 32 ♗f2 ♖c2 33 a4 ♖ee2 34 ♗g3 ♖a2 0-1

Game 81
Zilberberg *White* **Gufeld** *Black*
Los Angeles 1987

1 d4 ♘f6 2 c4 g6 3 ♘c3 ♗g7 4 e4 d6 5 f4 0-0 6 ♘f3 c5 7 d5 b5

The pawn sacrifice, on the lines of the Benko Gambit, is no less well-grounded in this position. Black loses no time in undermining his opponent's pawn bastions, quickly mobilizes his queenside pieces and organizes pressure along the semi-opened a- and b-files. These factors are quite sufficient compensation for the pawn.

8 cxb5 a6 9 bxa6

Not the best reaction, since now it becomes easier for Black to carry out his plans. The main continuation is 9 a4

9...♕a5 10 ♗d2

After 10 ♕d2 ♗xa6 Black is not afraid to push the e-pawn: 11 e5

♘fd7 12 e6 fxe6 13 ♘g5 ♗xf1 14 ♖xf1 e5 and sacrificing the exchange is insufficient (A.Shirov).

10...♗xa6 11 ♗xa6 ♕xa6!? 12 ♕e2

12...♘fd7!
Strange as it might seem, this move has escaped the attention of theorists, who only examine the game Karasev-Vasyukov, USSR 1974, 12...♘bd7 13 ♕xa6 ♖xa6 14 0-0 ♖b8, when Black has some compensation for the pawn.

The knight retreat, in my opinion, is stronger, not only because it activates the bishop on g7, but also because it allows Black to deploy his knights in a more harmonious way —which is a perennial concern in the King's Indian.

13 ♕xa6 ♘xa6 14 ♔e2 ♘b6 15 b3

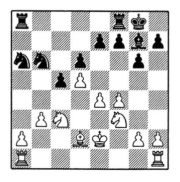

15...f5!
Revealing the weakness of the d5-pawn, since on 16 e5 would follow 16...♘b4. Now the white centre collapses like a house of cards.

16 ♘g5 fxe4 17 ♘e6
Convinced that 17 ♘gxe4 ♘b4 leads to the loss of a pawn, White decides to eliminate Black's dark-squared bishop.

17...♗xc3 18 ♗xc3 ♖f5
This roundabout rook manoeuvre leads not only to the win of the d5 pawn, but also to an invasion of the opponent's camp.

19 g4 ♖xd5 20 f5
A naive attempt to trap the rook (20...gxf5 21 ♘f4), but Black ignores this trick.

20...♖d3 21 ♖ac1 ♘d5 22 ♗a1 ♘ab4
The triumph of the black cavalry! Now White's queenside is defenceless.

23 a4 ♖xb3 24 fxg6 ♖xa4 25 gxh7+ ♔xh7 26 ♖hd1 ♘a2 27 ♖c2 ♘ac3+ 0-1

Game 82
Lautier *White* **Shirov** *Black*
Belgrade 1997

1 d4 ♘f6 2 c4 g6 3 ♘c3 ♗g7 4 e4 d6 5 f4 0-0 6 ♘f3 c5 7 d5 b5 8 cxb5 a6 9 a4
The main continuation.

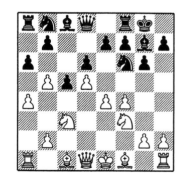

9...axb5

It would be more logical to carry on with an undermining of the white centre by 9...e6 10 dxe6 (if 10 Be2 then possible is 10...axb5 11 Bxb5 exd5 12 e5 dxe5 13 fxe5 when A.Vaiser recommends 13...Ng4!? 14 Qxd5 Qxd5 15 Nxd5 Nxe5 with approximately level chances) 10...Bxe6 11 Be2 axb5 12 Bxb5 d5! (this is more energetic then 12...Na6, played in the game Gorelov-Gufeld, USSR 1981—after 13 0-0 Nb4 14 Kh1 Qb6 15 Qe2 d5 16 exd5 Nfxd5 17 Ne5 Black failed to rid himself of his problems) 13 exd5 Nxd5 14 Nxd5 Bxd5 15 0-0 Nc6 and Black's posiiton was not worse.

Black achieves nothing of consequence with the pin 9...Qa5 10 Bd2 Qb4 11 Bd3 c4 12 Bc2 Qc5 13 Qe2 axb5 14 Be3 (14 Nxb5? is no good in view of 14...Nxe4!∓, but worth special attention is 14 e5 dxe5 15 fxe5 Nfd7 16 Be3 Qb4 17 Bd4 bxa4 18 0-0 Nc5 19 e6! when White achieved an advantage, Glek-Yanvariov, USSR 1989; obviously he shouldn't have ceded the centre—14...Ng4!?) 14...Qb4 15 0-0 bxa4 16 e5 White is in firm possession of the initiative, Glek-Sorin, Odessa 1989.

10 Bxb5 Ba6 11 Bd2

After 11 Rb1 Bxb5 12 axb5 Nbd7 13 0-0 Nb6 14 Qe2 Qc8 15 Kh1 e6 16 dxe6 Qxe6 Black has sufficient compensation for the pawn, Vaiser-Garcia Martinez, Bayamo 1985.

11...Bxb5 12 axb5 Rxa1 13 Qxa1 Qb6 14 0-0 Nbd7

Weaker is 14...Ne8 15 Qe1 Nc7 16 Qh4 Nxb5 17 Nxb5 Qxb5 18 Qxe7 ±, Nogueiras-Sax, Graz, 1984.

15 Qe1!

A multi-purpose move. White prepares a pawn advance and at the same time intends to transfer his queen to the king's flank.

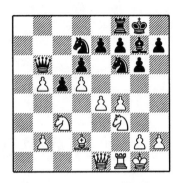

15...Qb7

This move allows an attack on the king after 16 Qh4, but J.Lautier preferred to break in the centre. It could be opposed by the manoeuvre 15...Qd7 16 Qh4 Qg4 The game Rausis-Lanka, Germany 1998, proceeded: 17 Qxg4 Nxg4 18 h3 Nf6 19 Ra1 Rb8 20 Ra7 Kf8 21 Kf1 Ne8 22 Be1 Nc8 23 Rd7 Nb6 24 Ra7 Nc8 25 Rd7 Nb6 ½-½.

16 e5

White has two tempting continuations, out of which J.Lautier chose the pawn sacrifice. But after the game the French grandmaster changed his mind and suggested the attack by 16 Qh4! as better, with the possible follow-up: 16...e6 17 dxe6 fxe6 18 Ng5 Re8 19 e5 dxe5 20 Nce4. But the real value of this idea can only be assessed by practical trials.

16...Nxd5

After 16...dxe5 17 fxe5 Nxd5 18 e6 N7b6 19 exf7+ Rxf7 20 Qxe6 the position assumes a more open character with White having an enduring initiative.

17 e6 N7b6

18 exf7+

Tempting was 18 f5 gxf5 19 ♘g5 (or 19 ♘h4 ♗d4+ 20 ♔h1 fxe6 21 ♕xe6+ ♔h8 22 ♖xf5 ♘f6 and Black defends himself) 19...f6! 20 ♘xh7 ♔xh7 21 ♕h4+ ♔g8 22 ♖f3 ♕c8 and White has a choice between 23 ♖g3 ♕xe6 24 ♖xg7+ ♔xg7 25 ♕h6+ ♔f7 26 ♕h5 and 23 ♖h3 ♕xe6 24 ♕h7+ ♔f7 25 ♕h5 (J.Lautier).

18...♖xf7 19 ♘g5 ♗d4+

It is useful to activate the bishop with tempo.

20 ♔h1 ♖f5?!

He shouldn't have allowed the queen to e6, After 20...♖f6 21 ♕e4 ♕a8 22 f5, the initiative, of course, is still with White, but there is nothing clearly substantial.

21 ♕e6+ ♔h8

If 21...♔g7 then Black has to reckon on 22 ♕e4 with the threat of ♘g5-e6.

22 ♘f7+ ♔g7 23 ♘d8 ♕a8 24 ♘c6 ♕g8?

An unsuccessful exchange of queens, after which the "planned" b-file passed pawn unexpectedly shows its teeth.

The transfer of the queen to f8 looks more active, but it is not profitable to do this at once: 24...♕f8? 25 ♘xd5 ♘xd5 26 g4! and Black loses a piece, but after the preliminary 24...♗c3 this move is already possible.

25 ♕xg8+ ♔xg8 26 ♘xd5 ♘xd5 27 b6 ♘xb6 28 ♘xe7+ ♔f7 29 ♘xf5 gxf5 30 ♗c3 ♔e6

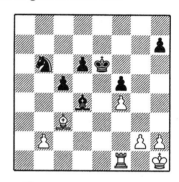

31 ♖e1+?!

The play transposes to the endgame, in which an extra exchange should bring White victory. But pushing the king to the centre goes against the laws of endgame play—especially since, in this particular case, Black is presently "a king up" ... Of course 31 ♗xd4 cxd4 32 ♔g1 was necessary.

31...♔d5 32 g4?!

Such sharp play is unjustified, since Black will stop the passed pawn. Also here 32 ♗xd4 was possible.

32...fxg4 33 f5 ♘d7 34 ♖e7

An alternative is 34 ♔g2 ♘f6 35 ♖e6 ♘h5! (35...♘e4 36 ♖xe4 is no good) 36 ♖h6 ♘f4+ and Black manages to hold the position. (J.Lautier).

34...♘f6 35 ♔g2 h5!? 36 ♔g3 ♘e4+! 37 ♖xe4

After 37 ♔f4?! ♘xc3 38 bxc3 ♗xc3 39 ♔g5 c4 Black runs no risk of losing.

37...♔xe4 38 f6 ♗xf6

In the event of 38...♗e3? 39 ♔h4 Black loses his kingside pawns without any compensation.

39 ♗xf6 d5!

40 ♔h4?!

Now the d-pawn will cost a bishop. Victory is achieved after 40 b3! d4 as was revealed later by thorough analysis. We will cite just the main variations, shown by J.Lautier.

(a) 41 ♗e7 d3 42 ♗g5 ♔d4! 43 ♗d2 ♔e4 44 ♔h4 ♔f3 45 ♗c1 ♔e2 46 ♔xh5 d2 47 ♗xd2 ♔xd2 48 ♔xg4 ♔c3 49 h4 ♔xb3 50 h5 c4 51 h6 c3 52 h7 c2 53 h8=♕ c1=♕;

(b) 41 ♔f2 ♔d3 42 ♗e7 h4! 43 ♔e1 g3! 44 h3 (or 44 hxg3 hxg3 45 ♗xc5 g2 46 ♔f2 ♔c3 47 b4 d3=) 44...g2! 45 ♔f2 ♔c2 46 ♗xc5 d3 47 ♗e3 ♔xb3 48 ♔xg2 ♔c2 49 ♔f3 d2 50 ♗xd2 ♔xd2 51 ♔g4 ♔e3 52 ♔xh4 ♔f4=.

40...d4! 41 ♔xh5 ♔f3 42 ♔g5

On 42 b3 sufficient for a draw is 42...g3.

42...d3 43 ♗c3 c4! 44 ♔f5 ♔e2 45 ♔xg4 ½-½

Game 83
Topalov *White* **Kasparov** *Black*
Linares 1994

1 c4 g6 2 e4 ♗g7 3 d4 d6 4 ♘c3 ♘f6 5 f4 0-0 6 ♘f3 c5 7 dxc5

White strives for a semi-open position, reckoning that he will get ahead in development after Black's standard manoeuvre to recover the pawn, ...♕d8-a5xc5.

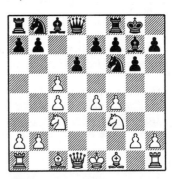

7...♕a5

Apparently 7...dxc5 8 ♕xd8 ♖xd8 9 e5 ♘e8 followed by ...♘c6 is also possible.

8 ♗d3

The capture 8 cxd6?! ♘xe4 9 dxe7 ♖e8 is too risky to be recommended, since White is clearly behind in development.

8...♕xc5 9 ♕e2 ♗g4

More often 9...♘c6 is played first.

10 ♗e3 ♕a5

The most frequently seen retreat of the queen. After 10...♕h5 11 0-0 ♘c6 12 h3 Black is practically forced to concede to his opponent the advantage of two bishops, 12...♗xf3 13 ♖xf3, although after 13...♘d7 he has quite good practical chances.

11 0-0 ♘c6

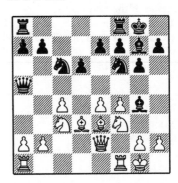

The most typical position for this variation.

12 ♖ac1

12 h3 involves a loss of time. After 12...♗xf3 13 ♖xf3 ♘d7, Black seizes the initiative due to the threats of ...♘d7-c5 and ...♗g7xc3.

12...♘d7

A typical transfer of the knight by ...♘f6-d7-c5, which enables Black to introduce the g7-bishop into play and at the same time attack the one on d3.

13 ♕f2

On 13 ♕d2 possible is 13...♗xf3 14 ♖xf3 ♘c5 or 14...♗d4.

13...♗xf3 14 gxf3

14 ♕xf3 ♗xc3 15 ♖xc3 ♕xa2 involves the loss of a pawn, although White has compensation in a possible attack on the kingside.

14...♘c5

This is more accurate than 14...♖fc8 15 ♖fd1 ♘c5 16 ♗b1 (16 ♗f1!? also deserves attention) 16...♘a4 17 ♘xa4 ♕xa4 18 b3 ♕a5= Shaked-Xie Jun, Wijk aan Zee 1998.

15 ♗b1 ♘a4!

Black exchanges off an important knight, and extends the sphere of activity of his pieces on the queenside.

16 ♘xa4 ♕xa4 17 b3 ♕a3 18 c5

After opening the position it is easier for White to exploit the advantage of the two bishops.

18...dxc5 19 ♗xc5 ♕xc5! 20 ♖xc5 ♗d4 21 ♖d1 ♗xf2+ 22 ♔xf2 ♖fd8 23 ♖cd5 e6 24 ♖xd8+ ♖xd8 25 ♖xd8+ ♘xd8

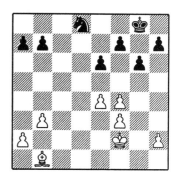

A small wrangle has ended with an approximately level endgame.

26 ♔e3 ♔f8 27 f5?!

This attempt to rid himself of the doubled pawns leads to ceding the d4 square to the knight, which is to Black's advantage.

27...e5! 28 f4 f6 29 fxe5 fxe5 30 fxg6 hxg6 31 h4 ♔g7

Stronger is 31...♔e7! ∓.

32 ♔d3!

The king heads for d5.

32...♔f6

Sergei Makarichev showed the consequences of going for the h4 pawn: 32...♔h6 33 ♔c4 ♔h5 34 ♔d5 ♘c6 35 b4! a6 36 a3 ♔xh4 37 ♗d3 g5 38 ♔d6 g4 39 ♗e2 ♘d4! and White is forced to give up the bishop, which, however, is enough for a draw, since a mass elimination of pawns takes place.

33 ♔c4 ♔e6 34 ♔c5 b6+! 35 ♔b5 ♔d6 36 b4 ♔c7 37 a4 ♘e6 38 ♗a2 ♘d4+ 39 ♔a6 ♔b8 40 ♗f7 ♘f3 41 ♗xg6 ♘xh4 42 ♗f7 ♘f3 43 a5 bxa5 44 bxa5 ½-½

Index of Variations

Index of Games